STILL LIFE WITH RHETORIC

STILL LIFE WITH RHETORIC

A New Materialist Approach for Visual Rhetorics

LAURIE E. GRIES

UTAH STATE UNIVERSITY PRESS
Logan

© 2015 by the University Press of Colorado

Published by Utah State University Press
An imprint of University Press of Colorado
5589 Arapahoe Avenue, Suite 206C
Boulder, Colorado 80303

 The University Press of Colorado is a proud member of
The Association of American University Presses.

The University Press of Colorado is a cooperative publishing enterprise supported, in part, by Adams State University, Colorado State University, Fort Lewis College, Metropolitan State University of Denver, Regis University, University of Colorado, University of Northern Colorado, Utah State University, and Western State Colorado University.

The paper used in this publication meets the minimum requirements of the American National Standard for Information Sciences—Permanence of Paper for Printed Library Materials. ANSI Z39.48-1992

ISBN: 978-0-87421-977-7 (paperback)
ISBN: 978-0-87421-978-4 (ebook)

Library of Congress Cataloging-in-Publication Data
Gries, Laurie E.
  Still life with rhetoric : a new materialist approach for visual rhetorics / Laurie E. Gries.
    pages cm
  Includes bibliographical references.
  ISBN 978-0-87421-977-7 (pbk.) — ISBN 978-0-87421-978-4 (ebook)
1. Visual communication. 2. Rhetoric. I. Title.
  P93.5.G75 2015
  302.2'2—dc23

                    2014007897

Portions of this work appeared in earlier versions in "Iconographic Tracking: A Digital Research Method for Visual Rhetorics and Circulation Studies," *Computers and Composition* 30 (4) (December 2013):332–348.
    Portions of Chapter 3 appeared in earlier forms in "Agential Matters: Tumbleweed, Women-pens, Citizen-hope, and Rhetorical Actancy," in *Ecology, Writing Theory, and New Media: Writing Ecology*, ed. Sidney Dobrin (New York: Routledge, 2011). Republished with permission of Routledge; permission conveyed through Copyright Clearance Center, Inc.
    IMAGE CREDITS. Top, left to right: Jobs © Oliver Wolfson; Abide © Zach Burns; Yes We Scan © René Walter; Dope © Jeff Rankin (CC BY-SA 3.0); Hope © Patrick St. John. Bottom, left to right: Joke © James Lillis; Nope © United Unknown; Brains © Jared Moraitis; Hope © Mario Piperni, NoDerivs 2.0 Generic (CC BY-ND 2.0); Chenge: © Kinsey L.

Rhetoric has material force beyond the goals, intentions, and motivations of its producers, and it is our responsibility as rhetoricians not to just acknowledge that, but try to understand it.

—Carole Blair, "Contemporary U.S. Memorial Sites"

CONTENTS

ILLUSTRATIONS

PREFACE

I was twenty years old when I first read *Still Life with Woodpecker* by Tom Robbins and became fascinated with people's interactions with everyday objects. It was not until I read *Skinny Legs and All* with its focus on the travels of a spoon, a can of beans, a painted stick, a conch shell, and a dirty sock, however, that I became fascinated with *animated* objects. Since, then, I have had a strange attachment to objects, personifying them beyond rational explanation and attributing much of my own mood to their relations with me. Such regard has manifested in an intense fascination with material artifacts—most particularly the design, feel, and placement of contemporary objects in interior spaces but also the construction and function of artifacts in past cultures. One of my favorite pastimes, in fact, is to peruse the shelves of antique stores. I tend to spend a lot of time in each store, picking up objects, wondering where and how they have traveled, whom they have encountered, and what lives they have led. It is no surprise, then, that my first full-length book project focuses on the rhetorical life of things. I am particularly curious about the relations we develop with things and the active roles they play in (re)arranging collective life as they weave in and out of various relationships. The purpose of this book is to establish a unique approach for studying this relationality and collective activity, especially as I feel rhetorical study has not fully attended to rhetoric's intense materiality, temporality, and consequentiality.

The exigence for developing this particular approach emerged, in part, from an earlier study of material rhetoric published in my 2009 article "Practicing Methods in Ancient Cultural Rhetorics." That project began with my curiosity about how we can accurately and ethically recover nonverbal ancient rhetorical practices on their own terms if we do not have a society's own "terms" to begin with. In an effort to address this methodological dilemma, I turned to the ancient burial practices of Moche elite rulers, evidence of which exists in an archeological reconstruction of ancient tombs first built on the northern coast of Peru between 100 and 800 CE. As a research method, I performed genre and rhetorical analyses of these ritual practices to discover what rhetorical purpose they might have served. I ultimately determined that while we could see these practices were indeed rhetorical, we simply lacked enough evidence to accurately determine what consequences emerged from these artifacts in use at the time of production. I thus ended up arguing that even though we can identify specific rhetorical actions within pre-Columbian traditions, we must practice self-restraint in assigning meaning to these rhetorical acts.

That research prompted me to think more deeply about consequentiality, temporality, and materiality in relation to rhetoric. I specifically began to wonder how we could ethically recover rhetorical practices without a firm understanding of the consequences those practices have at the time of their initial production; while such consequences cannot always be recovered, material artifacts do "live" on beyond their initial moments of production and delivery. And during circulation, material artifacts generate traceable consequences in their wake, which contribute to their ongoing rhetoricity. Rhetoric, I came to believe, is a process that unfolds and materializes with time and space. We can thus learn a lot about rhetoric, I imagined, by focusing on the material consequences that unfold during futurity—those spans of time beyond the initial moment of production and delivery. *Still Life with Rhetoric* attempts to develop a new materialist research approach to account for this dynamic, materialist, and consequentialist sense of rhetoric.

When I first began working on this project in 2007, I had never heard of new materialism. Instead, I was heavily drawn to Bruno Latour's work with actor-network theory because I appreciated its disposition toward nonhuman things and I knew its research practices of tracing and following would be useful for studying circulation. I also found myself turning to the work of Gilles Deleuze and Felix Guattari to help deepen my understanding of becoming, process, and change. It was not until a couple of years later that I discovered that many other scholars both beyond and within the field of rhetoric and composition were being influenced by these thinkers too and thus thinking in similar, parallel ways. Jane Bennett and Bill Brown, for instance, were beginning to generate thing theories while Jenny Edbauer Rice and Byron Hawk were writing about circulation and vitalism. In reading such scholarship, I began to develop the theoretical assumptions articulated herein without really knowing what I might call them. It is only within the last few years as the the term *new materialism* has gained recognition as a shared inquiry across several fields of study that I realized I have been working on a new materialist approach to rhetorical study all along.

Since this discovery, I have worked hard to weave in much contemporary new materialist scholarship to help develop my own version of a new materialist rhetorical approach. In the following pages, therefore, you will find that I act as a bricoleur to forge, synthesize, and appropriate a broad range of theories, philosophies, and research practices to (a) articulate the guiding assumptions of the new materialist approach herein and (b) introduce a new research method to help recover the rhetorical life of things. Readers will find that Gilles Deleuze's and Felix Guattari's work with the virtual and actual (as well as assemblages), Bruno Latour's work with actor-network theory, Jane Bennett's work with vital materialism, Karen Barad's work with agential realism, and Annemarie Mol's work with empirical philosophy are particularly influential. Yet, this approach is just as directly informed by studies of circulation mentioned below as well as contemporary studies of rhetoric and writing, such as Kevin Porter's and Louise Wetherbee Phelps's philosophical work on discourse and time, Jenny Edbauer Rice's work with rhetorical ecologies, Paul Prior et al.'s and Clay Spinuzzi's work with activity theory, Collin Brooke's work with new media rhetorics, and Byron Hawk's work with vitalism. In synthesizing, appropriating, and adding to such scholarship, the new materialist rhetorical approach offered herein can be considered a remix of what Phelps calls "productive theories"—theories that, whether intended to or not, afford the production of new practices, inquires, ideas, and so forth (Rodrigue 2013). Because I hope this book will be used in research methods courses as well as visual rhetoric courses at graduate and advanced undergraduate levels, I have tried to be as transparent as possible about the productive theories I draw on to inform this methodological project. I especially want readers to see how, at its heart, this book is an enactment of heuretics, Greg Ulmer's term for using theory to invent new forms and practices (Ulmer 2003, 4).

A WORD ABOUT THIS BOOK'S STRUCTURE

In further commitment to transparency, *Still Life with Rhetoric* moves in three parts from theory to method to practice—a movement that is felt in tone, structure, and content. As Eileen Schell (2012) writes, "With our desire to bring materiality to rhetoric, composition, and literacy studies must come the responsibility of deploying materiality with an awareness of what it means to purport to do material analysis and to lay claim to what historical and theoretical traditions we are drawing upon" (138). The first part of this book thus necessarily takes on a theoretical perspective, as its purpose is to articulate the methodological principles that undergird the new materialist rhetorical approach offered herein. I purposively move slowly in this section for readers who may not be familiar with the thought style on which I am drawing. This first three of these principles—becoming, transformation, and consequentiality—particularly relate to the spatiotemporal matters I believe are useful for thinking intuitively about and studying things in a dynamic, consequentialist sense. The last three principles—vitality, agency, and virality—articulate an ecological disposition toward things that acknowledges their vital, transformative, and often contagious characteristics. These principles, in short, are what this particular new materialist rhetorical approach is made of—the stuff that makes this approach distinct from others, even as its guiding assumptions overlap with other approaches such as actor-network theory (ANT) and activity theory. As is made explicitly visible in a conceptual diagram in the conclusion of this book, an articulation of these principles thus helps distinguish a new materialist approach from other approaches (see figure 9.17).

These principles ought be useful for rhetorical studies at large; therefore, I have tried to discuss them in a broad way so they can resonate with scholars interested in studying a variety of things. Such open-endedness is important; while this approach is certainly useful for visual rhetoric (as evident in the book's title), it is not particular to visual rhetoric. The theories of becoming, agency, vitality, transformation, consequentiality, and virality can be useful for thinking about how a wide range of things flow, transform, and produce material consequences in the world. Yet, for the sake of developing coherence across this book, in part 1, I use visual things as examples to help readers better understand the theories and philosophies driving the new materialist rhetorical approach herein. I also devote part 2 of this book to articulating how these principles can especially help develop new research methods for visual rhetoric. Chapter 4 articulates how these principles act as accountabilities that push scholars to study visual things in an intransitive, vital, and collective sense. I specifically discuss how the research actions of following, tracing, embracing uncertainty, and describing can help discover how visual things act as vital actants that are constantly changing, circulating, and triggering all kinds of collective actions. While such descriptions are useful in a general sense, they do not offer a specific method constituted by concrete research strategies for studying the rhetorical life of visual things. Chapter 5 thus introduces the method of iconographic tracking to elucidate how this particular method can be put to work. Part 2 is thus descriptive in a methodological sense, as its purpose is to forward a new method for doing visual rhetorical research.

Moving toward practice, part 3 offers research findings from a four-part case study that employs iconographic tracking to account for the complex rhetorical life of Obama Hope—a single multiple image that became widely recognized in the Obama works of Shepard Fairey. Readers interested only in the rhetorical life of Obama Hope might thus choose to go straight to chapters 6, 7, 8, and 9. While the chapters in part 1 are obviously theoretical, the case study is just as obviously descriptive in that I try, as Bruno Latour (2005b) suggests, to embrace thick description, refrain from over explanation, and write in a way that is as faithful to Obama Hope's experience as possible. At the end of each of these chapters, I elucidate what Obama Hope teaches us about the way things move, transform, effect change, and become rhetorical, thus modeling how scholars can generate new insights from such research findings. However, in order to stay focused on the book's methodological aims, I simply present enough empirical evidence and insights for readers to realize the potential of new materialism and iconographic tracking for visual rhetoric and rhetorical studies at large. (My plan in a subsequent book-length project is to fully develop this case study into a rhetorical biography of Obama Hope.) In a practical sense, then, in addition to disclosing Obama Hope's intense and distributed rhetorical ecology, part 3 intends to demonstrate the affordances of the new materialist theories and methods offered herein.

A WORD ABOUT THIS BOOK'S INTENT

In introducing this new materialist rhetorical approach, *Still Life with Rhetoric* could be conceived in a broad sense as contributing to object-oriented studies that are proliferating across the humanities, sciences, social sciences, and arts. On the whole, object-oriented studies are interested in ontologies of nonhuman objects and the contributions they make to collective life. With Marilyn Cooper's keynote and many subsequent sessions focused on the rhetoric of things, the scholarship presented at the 2013 Western States Rhetoric and Literacy conference shows that rhetorical study at large is poised to make strong contributions to object-oriented studies. Yet I would argue that with its long-term investment in exploring how a broad range of visual things—posters, comics, cartoons, film, video games, advertisements, and so forth—acquire power to shape society, visual rhetoric is particularly poised to make strong contributions. While visual rhetoric has done remarkable work illuminating how visual things make arguments, construct ways of seeing, and influence subjectivity, there are other contributions to collective life that visual things make, other actions that visual things do, that need to be more fully acknowledged. The method of iconographic tracking described herein is generative in this sense in that it offers a way to track the multiplicity of rhetorical contributions a single image makes during its lifetime.

As will become evident in parts 2 and 3 of this book, this approach does not eliminate the practice of interpreting signs that constitute a picture in the concrete sense nor does it totally eliminate attending to representation. In relation to visual rhetoric, it simply enacts what W.J.T. Mitchell (2005) calls a dislocation in which, rather than construing them as subalterns who have no voice other than the one assigned to them by us (46), visual things are recognized and studied as co-constituting reality and having a rhetorical life of their own. This dislocation requires entering into a different relationship with visual things—a humble relation in which visual things are recognized as important actants, intimately involved in multiple kinds of collective action, that may want "equal rights with language, not to be turned into language" (Mitchell 2005, 47). Visual things are complex individuals (much like we are) who play multiple, active roles in shaping collective existence. Things, such as the Obama Hope image, deserve to be studied as the complex and full-fledged rhetorical actors they become as they circulate with time and space. They deserve to be taken seriously as dynamic actors who transform not only themselves but also those lives whom they encounter. *Still Life with Rhetoric* can be conceived, then, as contributing to object-oriented studies by articulating a new materialist approach that moves beyond studying the still life of rhetoric toward confronting rhetoric's dynamic and consequential potentials (hence the double entendre in the book's title). This approach is best enacted when we embrace an intuitive mindset to account for the spatiotemporal complexities of rhetorical becoming and an ecological mindset to recognize a thing's vitality. With its concerted focus on visual rhetorics, *Still Life with Rhetoric* aims to elucidate how such perspectives can help cultivate such dislocation.

Still Life with Rhetoric could also be conceived as participating in a growing area of research called *mobility studies*—a transdisciplinary approach to studying how things (ideas, texts, images, people, capital, artifacts, etc.) move within and across and influence public culture. Like other work in this emergent field, my methodological project addresses a host of transdisciplinary concerns—sociological concerns about collective formation, spatial-temporal concerns about scale and flow, new materialist concerns about matter and agency, and cultural concerns about images, representation, and subjectivity—"all the while inflecting each with a relational ontology of the co-constitution of subjects, spaces and meanings" (Sheller 2011). However, this book mainly addresses rhetorical concerns; as such, it intends to most directly contribute to an area within rhetorical study we might think of as *circulation studies*—an interdisciplinary approach to studying rhetoric and writing in motion.

Circulation studies, if we can call it that, has been emerging as a shared inquiry in the field of rhetorical study for some time. In addition to Edbauer, scholars such as Maureen Goggin, Vicki Tolar Burton, Kristen Seas, John Trimbur, Jim Ridolfo, Dànielle DeVoss, Byron Hawk, Sid Dobrin, and Rebecca Dingo have written about circulation to inform their studies of history, theory, writing, and transnational feminism. In communication, in addition to Cara Finnegan, Robert Hariman, and John Lucaites, scholars such as Lester Olson have done archival research to investigate the circulation of photographs, motifs, and other pictorial representations and generate theories about how visual things contribute to public life. Catherine Chaput has also advocated for developing a rhetorical circulation model to account for rhetorics's affective and dynamic dimensions. And more recently, as evident in a forum published in a 2012 issue of *Rhetoric and Public Affairs*, communication scholars interested in public address are focusing their efforts on circulation, insisting, as Mary E. Stuckey (2012) notes, that circulation "impinges on every aspect of theory and criticism" (609) and thus can serve as "a strong organizing principle" for rhetorical study (610).

Such circulation studies are important for rhetorical study as they have helped scholars (a) draw attention to rhetoric's dynamic movement and fluidity; (b) reconfigure theories of rhetoric and publics to account for discourse's dynamic, distributed, and emergent aspects; (c) rethink composing strategies for writing in a digital age; and (d) revamp pedagogy to account for writing's full production cycle. Scholars such as Mary Queen have also pointed toward new methodologies for studying the flow of rhetoric, writing, and digital representations. Yet while such work is underway, more theories and methods need to be developed to help explain not only how images circulate within a distributed network of collective activities but also how new media images become rhetorical in a viral, digital economy. *Still Life with Rhetoric* should be considered as taking up this challenge as it develops new materialist perspectives for disclosing not only how things, especially images, flow but also how they become rhetorical with time and space.

By articulating the new materialist rhetorical approach herein, *Still Life with Rhetoric* also aligns with Amy Propen (2012) in advocating for a new shared tradition of inquiry to be taken up in visual rhetorics (or what Propen has suggested we think of as "visual-material rhetorics") that moves beyond thinking of visual things merely in the representational sense and toward studying them in consequentialist sense. As Carole Blair (1999) has noted, too often we are so busy thinking about and investigating things in terms of symbolization that we neglect to explore their consequentiality. Such a tradition of inquiry can only develop if we make transparent the theories and philosophies that underlie, motivate, and guide our research practices *and* articulate how to actually study the rhetorical life of things in terms of method. In order for a shared tradition of inquiry to develop, such methods especially must be published in order for other scholars to replicate and extend this work (L'Eplattenier 2009; Phelps 2010). Scholars, then, need to not only describe the theories and philosophies that guide their approaches but also to articulate in print how to go about putting those theories into action. Clay Spinuzzi's (2003) book *Tracing Genres through Organizations* is constructive in this regard, as its sole focus is introducing the methodology of genre tracing and modeling it at work in four interrelated case studies. Such transparency about method helps readers see how to employ a novel research approach for their own scholarly purposes. This book attempts to be constructive in similar ways by discussing research matters on a theoretical, methodological, and practical level. My hope here is that readers will begin to imagine how they might take up this new materialist approach for their own work, wherever their research journeys might take them.

ACKNOWLEDGMENTS

A broad collective of people and things has influenced my thinking, research, and writing over the last seven years and made this book possible. I am deeply grateful to Collin Brooke, without whose guidance, patience, and intellectual energy this project would not have come to fruition. Collin was instrumental in introducing me to many of the theories and philosophies that undergird this book project and helping me develop the method of iconographic tracking. I also deeply appreciate Louise Wetherbee Phelps for believing in the value of this project since its inception and helping me negotiate the complexities of not only theory and method but also publication. To a great extent, I see this project as building on the work Phelps did with contextualism and process in the late 1980s; her philosophies on time, discourse, and method ground this project and were, thus, integral to its invention and development.

I am also grateful to a number of people who have offered me feedback on the ideas and writing herein over the years. Eileen Schell, Lois Agnew, Iswari Pandey, Bradford Vivian, and Anne Demo played a valuable role in early stages of this project, while scholars such as Derek Mueller, Nathaniel Rivers, Paul Nathaniel, Casey Boyle, Scot Barnett, Jeff Rice, and Sid Dobrin helped me develop ideas for articles that have been adapted, revised, and folded back into this project. I am also grateful for those who offered emotional support in addition to helping me think through ideas, sometimes at odd hours and in odd places: my cohort at Syracuse University—Zosha Stuckey, Tanya Rodrigue, Trisha Serviss, and Laura Davies; my long-time mentor Heather Bruce; and my contemporary colleagues here at the University of Florida—Jodi Schorb, Raul Sanchez, and Brandy Kershner, among others. Of course, I am also grateful to my family, and especially my husband Jono, whose patience, love, and thoughtfulness will be forever appreciated.

In terms of institutional support that made this project possible, I am grateful to the University of Florida, and the College of Liberal Arts in particular, for awarding me two Humanities Scholarship Enhancement Grants to support to my research and writing. I also received a number of travel grants to present ideas from this book at national and international conferences, grants that would not have been possible without the support of my chairs, Pamela Gilbert and Kenneth Kidd. I am further grateful to the Herskovits Library of African Studies and curator David Easterbrook for making my archival research so easy and productive. I also cannot thank Michael Spooner and the Utah State University Press enough for making this publication possible. From the first time I spoke to Michael about this project, he has been hyperpresent, efficient, and supportive. I am grateful to him not only his feedback and advice but also for putting me in touch with a number of excellent reviewers, all of whom helped co-create the published text you are reading here. In terms of co-creation, I also cannot express gratitude enough to Karli Fish at USUP for doing such a wonderful job with the index as well as the entire team at the University Press of Colorado, especially Laura Furney for her editing expertise, Daniel Pratt for designing the book cover and handling other production matters, and Kelly Lenkevich for helping with copy editing.

I am also so appreciative of the many photographers, artists, and other people who contributed to my qualitative research and gave me permissions to reprint their work in this book. Working under contemporary understandings of Fair Use, in some respects, I felt free to reprint their artwork since it is being used for educational purposes such as commentary and criticism. However, I made concerted efforts to get permissions for every JPEG printed in this book. This book includes 89 JPEGs depicting diverse visual things: posters, stickers, sculptures, AR objects, maps, political cartoons, paintings, parodies, murals, dresses, signs, pumpkins, and so forth. While in a few cases I had to pay licensing fees to nonprofit news agencies such as the Associated Press and professional photographers, most professionals and amateurs alike granted me permissions with no fees. While I am especially grateful to Shepard Fairey, Ray Noland, and Yosi Sergant, I am also grateful to everyone for sharing their work, and I hope my own scholarship has done justice to their art and accelerates its circulation and rhetorical transformation.

Last but not least, in the true spirit of new materialism, I am grateful for those nonhuman things that have helped me develop this project. This list, of course, could never be complete. But I am particularly grateful for my two dogs, Hokis and Irwin, who offered me valuable distractions during different parts of the composing process and unconditional love when I needed a lift. I'm thankful for my multiple Apple computers—I literally typed the letters off the keys of the first laptop when working on early stages of this project; my yoga mat, the St. Augustine beaches, and the Oregon trails for providing spaces where I could turn off my mind so that ideas could flow more freely; other scholars', journalists', artists', cartoonist's, and designers' ideas that have been reproduced, remixed, and extended in this book; and of course, the Obama Hope image itself. When I first began tracing this image, I had no idea its life would take off and become as rhetorically complex as it has. I have been fortunate to enjoy the unpredictable nature of life in this regard. For it is only via my empirical research tracing Obama Hope's unforeseeable circulation that I have been able to understand and develop the theories and methods herein.

STILL LIFE WITH RHETORIC

1

CURRENT MATTERS

An Introduction

Pictures want equal rights with language, not to be turned into language. They want neither to be leveled into a "history of images" nor elevated into a "history of art," but to be seen as complex individuals occupying multiple subject positions and identities.

—W.J.T. Mitchell, *What Do Pictures Want?*

April 27, 2006, is an important date for visual rhetoric. On this date, Hollywood actor George Clooney, Senator Sam Brownback, and then-Senator Barack Obama were holding a press conference at Washington's National Press Club. Clooney had just returned from a trip to Darfur and was publicly demanding that the US government act more quickly to stop the ongoing genocide. On the sidelines a photographer for the Associated Press (AP) sat, intending to capture photos of Clooney in an important political performance. Little did the photographer know, when he turned his camera toward Obama, that he would capture one of the most iconic images to surface in recent US history.

The photograph taken by Mannie Garcia is now familiar to those of us who closely followed the 2008 US presidential election, have paid attention to US popular culture over the last few years, or have simply passed the image captured in the photo on the street one day while walking to work. For the image in Garcia's photograph transformed into the now-iconic Obama Hope image designed by street artist Shepard Fairey (see Figures 1.1 and 1.2). The Obama Hope image in its "Faireyized" version (henceforth referred to as simply Obama Hope) entered into circulation in late January 2008 in an effort to help then-Senator Obama become the 44th US president. Today, digital manifestations and remixes of this image can be found on more than two million websites while numerous physical renditions can be found tattooed on

DOI: 10.7330/9780874219784.c001

human bodies, plastered to urban walls, and waving at protests across the globe. As it has circulated both within and beyond US borders, this image has played a plethora of rhetorical roles ranging from political actor to advertising agent to social critic to international activist. Today, its materialization in Fairey's *Hope* poster is also widely recognized as a cultural icon and national symbol. *New Yorker* art critic Peter Schjeldahl (2009) has gone so far, in fact, as to deem Fairey's *Hope* poster the most efficacious political illustration since *Uncle Sam Wants You*.

How has this particular image come to lead such an extraordinary rhetorical life? How did it go from materializing in one among hundreds of photographs taken at a press conference in April of 2006 to a cultural icon, national symbol, and powerful rhetorical actant in just a few short years? When asked how the Obama Hope image gained the wide recognition needed to become a cultural icon, Fairey himself said the image simply "went viral." Made popular with the boom of the Internet in the mid-to-late 1990s, "going viral" is a common means of explaining how ideas, trends, objects, videos, and so forth spread quickly, uncontrollably, and unpredictably into, through, and across human populations. Such explanation is linked to a ubiquity of tropes and concepts related to epidemiology that has become part of the US American social imaginary in the twenty-first century. As Chad Lavin and Chris Russill (2010, 67) have argued, this imaginary has manifested in response to an anxiety constituted, in part, by a destabilized sense of space and time produced by an unprecedented emergence of global economic and communicative networks. Deeply entrenched, this epidemiological imaginary can be thought of as "the logic of the viral," which helps makes sense of not only the spread of diseases but also the spread of culture in a networked social landscape (Seas 2012, 6). According to this logic, a thing is commonly said to be viral when it is perceived as being socially contagious due to its capacity to garner mass attention and spread via word of mouth and media. In common parlance, then, we say something like a video has gone viral based on the sheer speed at which the video has attracted a wide viewing, often, but not always, because it has circulated widely across media, been remixed, and inspired imitative spinoffs.

In an attempt to explain how something such as Obama Hope can go viral, Fairey explained in a Terry Gross (2009) interview on *Fresh Air* that a viral phenomenon is made possible by first creating an image that is highly desired and admired, and second, by ensuring that a broad audience has access to that image so it can be redistributed. The Internet makes viral campaigns especially possible as images and messages can reach audiences dispersed across the world in a matter of seconds. With

Figure 1.1. Photograph of Barack Obama, Mannie Garcia, 2006. Permissions from the Associated Press.

Figure 1.2. Obama Hope, *Shepard Fairey, 2008. Courtesy of Shepard Fairey-ObeyGiant.com.*

the recent emergence of YouTube, Facebook, Twitter, and other social-media sites, the capacity for an image and message to circulate widely has only been amplified. Thus, as an explanation of how the Obama Hope image has become a cultural icon, "it went viral" might seem like an easy-enough-to-understand answer. This answer, however, offers little theoretical and practical understanding of *how* images actually circulate, transform, and replicate in both physical spaces and cyberspace. In an increasingly participatory culture in which a variety of groups produce and distribute media for their collective interests (Jenkins, Ford, and Green 2013, 2), such an answer particularly elides the logics, structures, practices, collectives, and platforms that enable images to circulate and transform widely. This answer also offers little understanding of *how* things become rhetorical as they circulate and transform with time and space and contribute to collective life. From a new materialist perspective, things become rhetorically meaningful via the consequentiality they spark in the world. By accepting Fairey's explanation of how Obama Hope has become a cultural icon, then, we miss the opportunity to learn *how* an image such as Obama Hope becomes an important rhetorical actor as it materializes and actually effects change in our daily realities. Or in simpler terms, by accepting the explanation of "it went viral," we miss learning how Obama Hope has made and continues to make (rhetorical) history.

In one sense, this book is an attempt to get at these *how* inquiries. Chapters 6–9 present a four-part case study that makes visible how, since 2006, Obama Hope has influenced cultural, political, and economic materialities and thus, in Bruno Latour's (2005a) terms, "reassembled the social." However, while this book may begin with a focus on the Obama Hope image and spend much time throughout discussing its rhetorical life, throughout most of the chapters, Obama Hope ironically acts as a representative anecdote in that the theories and methods included herein have been constructed around the Obama Hope phenomenon.[1] In addition, alongside other images such as the Mona Lisa and the Raised Fist, Obama Hope acts as an example to help accomplish the book's ulterior purpose. As Brian Massumi (2002) draws on Giorgio Agamben to note, the example is an "odd beast" (17). The example is one singularity among others, yet, simultaneously, the example "stands for each of them and serves for all." As a singularity, the example is neither general nor particular. It belongs to itself and simultaneously extends to everything else with which it might be connected (17–18). As both a representative anecdote and an "odd beast" in this book, then, while the Obama Hope image tells its own unique rhetorical story, the image also exemplifies what we can learn by taking a new materialist approach to studying the *futurity* of visual rhetoric. For another important purpose of this book is to articulate what a new materialist approach to visual rhetoric might entail and how it might contribute to rhetorical and circulation studies at large.

NEW MATERIALISM

First coined as a term in the latter half of the 1990s and independently of one another by Rosi Braidotti and Manuel De Landa, new materialism or neomaterialism is an emergent interdisciplinary theory informed by contemporary scholarship emanating from the intersections of science studies, feminist studies, and political theory.[2] From a definitional standpoint, new materialism is difficult to pin down. In one sense, new materialism is not new at all in that new materialists build on the work of scholars such as Spinoza, Bergson, Deleuze, and Guattari and can thus simply be thought of as an extension of a longstanding monist tradition (Dolphijn and der Tuin 2012, 94–95). Furthermore, new materialism is not a unified shared inquiry, especially since it is being taken up across multiple fields such as political science, women's studies, social science, history, and, as of late, rhetorical studies. Nonetheless, new materialism can be thought of as part of a nonhuman turn[3] taking place across several disciplines as scholars challenge the modernist paradigm (heavily influenced by Descartes and Kant) that perpetuates dualist kinds of thinking, which many scholars find reductive and unproductive. As Latour (1993) explains in *We Have Never Been Modern*, modernity tries to divide the world into separate, opposing spheres with humans/subject/culture on one side and things/objects/nature on the other. New materialists reject such dualism, arguing that any bifurcation of humans and things, culture and nature, object and subject fails to acknowledge the ontological hybridity that constitutes reality. In order to make sense of the complex material realities we face in the twenty-first century, then, new materialists focus on what Donna Haraway (2003) has called "natu-recultures," or what Latour (1993) calls "collectives," to acknowledge the significant, active role nonhuman things play in collective existence alongside a host of other entities.

New materialism, in part, is an ontological project in that it challenges scholars to rethink our underlying beliefs about existence and particularly our attitudes toward and our relationships with matter. In a broad sense, new materialists conceive of matter as vital, transformative, and morphogenetic; in this sense, as Tianen and Parikka (2010) have argued, matter is both "self-differing and affective-affected." New materialism is also a philosophical project as it works to develop new concepts that can help develop new insights about collective matters. In any tradition of inquiry, a common discourse is needed so scholars can communicate and build on each other's knowledge. As such, new materialists are developing a lexicon filled with neologisms such as *intra-action*[4] and new concepts such as body multiple[5] that push us to think otherwise about matters we tend to take for granted. Yet new materialism is also a methodological project. Like all parties involved in the nonhuman turn, new materialists critique linguistic and social constructivisms and "the overconfidence about human power that was inadvertently embedded in the postmodernisms of the 1980s and 90s" (Bennett 2012). Karen Barad (2007), perhaps, states this problem best: "Language has been granted too much power. The linguistic turn, the semiotic turn, the interpretive turn, the cultural turn: it seems that at every turn lately every 'thing'— even materiality—is turned into a matter of language or some other form of cultural representation" (132). As such, new materialists are developing new modes of analysis that give "material factors their due in shaping society and circumscribing human prospects" (Coole and Frost 2010, 2–3), modes that often offer a broader and messier perspective than representational approaches typically offer.

New materialism is motivated to a great extent by an emergence of complex phenomena such as climate change, genetically modified foods, and ewaste, all of which are constituted by a complex, dynamic assemblage of intermingling and historically produced discursive, material, natural, social, technological, *and* political actants—an entanglement that Andrew Pickering (1995) might call a "mangle." But new materialists recognize that mangles are not specific to such recent phenomena of pressing concern. As Susan Hekman (2010) notes so succinctly, "Mangles are everywhere. They construct the world we inhabit in all of its complexity" (126). Such complexity cannot be investigated via methodologies that give too much weight to language's ability to account for reality, agency, and ontology. Nor can such complexity be "understood in the modern metaphysics that distributes Nature and Society into pure ontological zones . . . and allows us to disavow our responsibility for the consequences of our sociotechnical activity" (Herndl 2012). For new materialists, then, new kinds of empirical investigations that foreground distributed relations and attend to the nonlinear processes of materialization are needed to make sense of our contemporary existence. In a manifesto-like tone, Diana Coole and Samantha Frost (2010) claim that, in fact, "foregrounding material factors and reconfiguring our very understanding of matter are prerequisites for any plausible account of coexistence and its conditions in the twenty-first century" (2).

Across the humanities, new materialist approaches such as Jane Bennett's work with vital materialism and Barad's and Hekman's feminist work with agential realism and social ontology, respectively, are emerging to help give material factors their due. While each mode of inquiry is distinct, all consider reality to be collectively, materially, *and* semiotically constructed via a variety of actants that have equal ontological footing. New materialists thus acknowledge the vital and transformative characteristics of matter—characteristics typically reserved for humans alone. In this agential sense, new materialists embrace what Levi Bryant (2011) refers to as "parity reasoning"—a form of reasoning that, in refusing to grant one sort of agency control of development, emphasizes distributed causality (201). Thus, while discourse clearly plays a role in many phenomena, parity reasoning forces new materialist scholars to extend their analysis to a variety of different causal factors in any given phenomenon (202). Here, then, agency becomes a distributed enactment of entangled things intra-acting within phenomena

(Barad 2007, 235). In addition, such new materialist scholarship insists on investigating "materialization as a complex, pluralistic, relatively open process" (Coole and Frost 2010, 7). As such, the notion of becoming that is found in process philosophies undergirds many new materialists' sense of time and space. Such materialization will be explained in more detail in chapter 2 in order to help readers better understand the theories driving the new materialist notions offered herein. Important to simply note here is that because matter is conceived of as a productive, dynamic, and resilient force that shapes reality, new materialists take things—stuff, if you will—seriously. New materialists specifically wonder, "What happens when the 'propensities, affordances, and affectivities of nonhumans' are included in the action of assembling our collective common world?" (Herndl 2012).

Still Life with Rhetoric argues that such inquiry is productive for rhetorical and circulation studies at large, but it is especially important for visual rhetoric. Instrumentalist frameworks of rhetoric often focus on human agents producing and delivering persuasive discourse in a situated context to an immediate audience (at the very least in the imagined sense). Rhetoric, in this framework, is conceived as not only the faculty one has to create and deliver a persuasive object of some sort but also as the object itself, whether it is delivered in the form of a speech, a text, or a picture. In such latter cases, rhetoric is thought about in the transitive sense (Brooke 2009, 176). Much like everyday products, rhetoric is an already-produced and already-delivered object. Hence, in visual rhetoric, much scholarship is synchronic in that it focuses on the still life of rhetoric and works to identify how an already-materialized image makes communication and persuasion possible in a limited snapshot of time. As Obama Hope's rhetorical life makes visible, however, rhetoric is not as still as we may think. Rhetoric prevails beyond its initial moment of production; once unleashed in whatever form it takes, rhetoric transforms and transcends across genres, media, and forms as it circulates and intra-acts with other human and nonhuman entities. Rhetoric also moves in nonlinear, inconsistent, and often unpredictable ways within and across multiple networks of associations. In addition, as rhetoric becomes part of various collectives, a multiplicity of often unforeseeable affective and rhetorical consequences materialize that, in turn, spark other consequences. As such, rhetoric, especially in a digitally mediated environment, is more like an unfolding event—a distributed, material process of becomings in which divergent consequences are actualized with time and space. In this intransitive sense, rhetoric is everything but still. Many studies of visual rhetoric simply do not acknowledge that once rhetoric is initially distributed, there is still much life with rhetoric and thus neglect to account for this dynamic eventfulness.

In light of this neglect, this book argues that more work ought be done to empirically disclose how things such as Obama Hope and its various materializations become rhetorical in diverse ways as they flow, transform, and alter multiple realities. We need, in other words, to turn our scholarly gaze toward futurity—the time spans beyond a thing's initial production and delivery—and create risky accounts of how rhetoric unfolds as things enter into complex associations and catalyze change. Only with an eye toward futurity can rhetoricians, working in a digitally networked culture, actually account for how things circulate, take on a life of their own, and help constitute and reconstitute collective existence.

WORKING DEFINITIONS

Before I move forward any further, I ought to probably pause here to define a few key terms that ground this methodological project. Just as I conceive of rhetoric in distinct ways that may differ sharply from how others think of it, I must also make transparent how I think in particular ways about life, visuals, images, pictures, and things in relation to rhetoric. Throughout the book, I use the word *life* to refer to things' complex and intense vitality. I specifically employ *life* in an effort to challenge our anthropocentric notions of rhetorical agency—a position to be further discussed in chapter 3—and acknowledge the active contributions things make to collective existence. Christopher Pinney (2005) argues that using *life* in reference to nonhuman things runs the risk of perpetuating a "human besotted vision of reality" (259). When I use *life* to in relation to things, he might argue, I actually fail to move beyond anthropocentric notions of materiality. However, while such risk is noted with concern, moving beyond anthropocentric accounts of materiality is impossible, as we can never get outside human consciousness even if we can acknowledge that things exists on their own accord. What we can do, however, as I articulate in chapter 5, is create less asymmetrical accounts of rhetorical activity in our scholarship, recognize the intimacy we share with nonhuman things, and acknowledge the vital force things exert in reality. As such, I follow W.J.T. Mitchell's (2005) lead and embrace the term *life* anyway to acknowledge the vitality of things that we too often deem far too inert.

In terms of visual rhetoric, I attempt to consistently use the words *visuals*, *images*, and *pictures* in distinct ways throughout this book. While these terms are often used interchangeably, I believe it is important to acknowledge their distinction and make more concerted efforts to establish consistency across our scholarship so as not to confuse our readers. In a general sense, I consider a visual to be "that which we think we see" whether *that* is interpreted as an alphabetic letter or a cloud or a political poster. Anne Marie Seward Barry (1997) explains that "that which we perceive" is never reality; it is always a mental configuration that emerges as an end result of a complex perceptual process that begins with a detection of light in the eye and proceeds as different parts of the brain interpret electrical signals that *represent the environment*" (37). Barry actually calls such mental configuration an "image," but as a visual rhetorician writing about a specific image in this book, I find it useful to save *image* for a more specific immaterial thing that actualizes in various concrete forms and think of visuals in the broader sense as *that which we see*. In this book, then, I use the term *visual* as an adjective only so as not to create confusion and instead speak of images and pictures as nouns, and, more specifically, two distinct kinds of visual things.

Let me explain this distinction in more detail by drawing heavily on the work of W.J.T. Mitchell. In "Visual Literacy or Literary Visualcy?" Mitchell (2009) explains that the distinction between images and pictures could be understood in the phrase "you can hang a picture but you can't hang an image" (16). According to this line of thinking, a picture is an image that "appears in a material support," which includes photographs, posters, digital reproductions, murals, or other material things. (16). An image, on the other hand, can be conceived of as "an immaterial entity, a ghostly, fantasmatic appearance that comes to light or comes to life (which may be the same thing) in [such] material support" (18). An image, then, in simpler terms, is that which appears in a picture and survives a picture's destruction, as it is able to transcend media (16). In this sense, an image, while highly abstract, can be evoked in word as long as recognition takes place (17). It is recognized because it resembles something familiar to us, whether that thing is a physical entity that a materialized image (picture) depicts or something, mental or physical, that is entirely different yet has some familiar attribute.

Mitchell offers the example of the clone to clarify the image/picture distinction. But for this book's purposes, take a look at the collage in Figure 1.3 consisting of six pictures, in all of which the Obama Hope image has materialized. In some pictures, Obama Hope materializes in similar, even seemingly exact, ways as it did in Fairey's *Hope* poster and is thus easily recognizable if you are familiar with Fairey's work. Yet in other pictures, such as Matt Sesow's painting *Rhetoric* in the upper right-hand

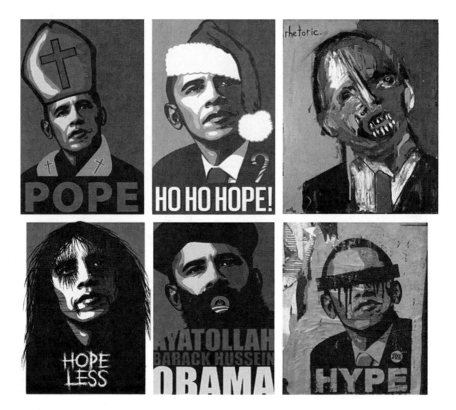

Figure 1.3. Collage of Obama Hope remixes.[6] *Pictures courtesy of Filippo Marongiu (top left), Matt Cornell (top middle), Matt Sesow (upper left), Klutch (lower left), Shahab Siavash (lower center), and Pablo Perez (lower right).*

corner and Klutch's *Hopeless* in the bottom-left corner, Obama Hope is barely recognizable. One must be intensely familiar with the specific colors, style, arrangement, and content of Obama Hope to recognize its presence. Nonetheless, as is evident here, the Obama Hope image haunts and transcends all these pictures. When I speak of visual things in this book, then, I am referring to both an image and the various material supports in which an image comes to life.[7] And, more specifically, when I speak of Obama Hope, I am referring to the image that first actualized in Garcia's photograph but more typically is associated with Fairey's red, white, and blue stylized rendition of Obama's portrait that materializes in a wide range of different pictures and on a wide range of things, sometimes in relation to a word such as *hope* and other times not.

Also important to note here is that both image and picture are real things in that both stimulate actual material consequences. To understand an immaterial thing, it might be useful to think of an image as being virtual (Vivian 2007). As will be discussed in more detail in chapter 2, virtual entities cannot be physically touched like an actual thing such as a painting or poster. Yet virtual entities do not just exist and circulate in cyberspace either. As Gilles Deleuze (1994) helps us understand, the virtual is "the characteristic state of ideas; it is on the basis of reality that existence is produced, in accordance with a time and space that is immanent in the Idea (211). The virtual, it might be easiest to understand, is a potential thing that, via the process of materialization, or in Deleuze's term "actualization," becomes a material force. As will be made evident by a four-part case study of Obama Hope, virtual things spark material consequences in all kinds of ways. In this book, for instance, the Obama *Hope* image comes to life both in a variety of pictures and in the words I use to describe its circulation, transformation, and consequentiality. Thus, even as I have never encountered the physicality of the image itself, Obama Hope is an active actant in that it has, among other things, deepened my understanding of rhetoric and shaped my thoughts and actions in all kinds of intense ways for the last four-plus years. While an image is virtual, immaterial, then, it is also a real thing that sparks traceable consequences in the world.

Now, in relation to *thing*, as readers might have already gathered, I specifically employ this term throughout the book to draw attention to the materiality of visual artifacts, which become rhetorical with time and space as they spark a diverse range of consequences. By *rhetorical*, I refer to something's ability to induce change in thought, feeling, and action; organize and maintain collective formation; exert power, etc.; as it enters into relation with other things (human or nonhuman). I resist the notion that something is rhetorical just because it has been intentionally created to persuade and has been delivered to a particular audience with that intended goal in mind. Instead, my understanding of rhetoric is that all things have potential to *become* rhetorical as they crystallize, circulate, enter into relations, and generate material consequences, whether those consequences unfold in conceptual or physical realms. Rhetoric here, then, is conceived of as a virtual-actual event that unfolds with time and space as things—whether they be images, pictures, books, movies, rocks, trees, or animals—enter into material relations with humans, technologies, and other entities. In one sense, as part 1 of this book elucidates, rhetoric, as a disturbed event, comes into existence from signs-in-use, from discourse conceived in its broadest sense. However, I worry that speaking about images and pictures in terms of discourse places too much emphasis on signification and too little emphasis on materiality, transformation, and consequentiality.

In addition, while I do focus on visual things produced by humans in this book, I do not believe that rhetoric is the specific domain of human language.[8] This sentiment is much aligned with Wayne Booth's (1974) thoughts about rhetoric as articulated in a footnote in *Modern Dogma and the Rhetoric of Assent*:

> There is a sense in which even the lowest animals can be said to intend meanings or to influence the rest of the world rhetorically; I would not even resist defining the universe as essentially rhetorical: it is created, as Whitehead says, in processes of interchange among its parts. Each least particle—whatever that turns out to be—just like each gross beast and 'dead' star, could be defined as a steadily changing 'field of influences,' receiving, processing, and transmitting 'information.' (126).

While Booth suggested in this same footnote that such perspective of rhetoric "takes us nowhere" and turns "rhetorical influence" into a "foggy metaphor," I argue the contrary. From a new materialist perspective, thinking about things' rhetorical influence takes us everywhere, and while we are hesitant to follow this path in the name of human exceptionalism, new materialism, with its focus on relationality and post-humanism, can help us forge this difficult yet promising path. As Scot Barnett (2010) has drawn on Graham Harman to argue, we can study "rhetoric as both a human art *and* an ontological condition potentially operable alongside human beings in the world's vast and inexhaustible carpentry of things" (my emphasis).[9] When writing about images and pictures in this book, then, I most often use things, rather than discourse,[10] in order to help reimagine the traditional boundaries of rhetorical study. I specifically draw on Bennett's vital materialist understanding of things and Latour's definition of thing to emphasize the way rhetoric emerges from the material relations and activities that unfold as a diverse ecology of nonhuman and human things assemble and intra-act in various collectives.

As I will discuss in more detail in chapter 3, things acquire power to shape reality as they become entangled in complex relations with humans and other nonhuman entities. Too often, we miss the opportunity to acknowledge the force of things because we assume they are inert tools used by human agents whom we typically credit with full-blown agency. Yet, if we study a thing with a new materialist sensibility, we can recognize its *thing-power*—the power things acquire when working alongside other entities to produce change, even as they all have different degrees of power (Bennett 2010). One major kind of change that is important for this book is the ability to reassemble collective existence. As Latour (2005a) explains, *thing* as defined in the English dictionary originally designated a type of assembly. Still in such use in many Nordic and Saxon nations, *thing* has meant an issue that brings people together even as it may divide them in the process (13). Things such as Obama Hope often provoke and engage in assemblage because they attract entities that are aligned with and want to work toward similar goals, but things also induce and participate in assemblage because of divisive matters. In addition, no matter the reasons for assemblage, assemblages are always in flux as participating entities move in and out of assemblage. In thinking about visual things, then, we are not only reminded of rhetoric's ability to induce cooperation, as Kenneth Burke emphasizes, but also to induce assemblage (and reassemblage). In this sense, things such as the Obama Hope image become rhetorical, in part, as a consequence of their emergent ability to mobilize various entities into relation, help materialize change, and thus reassemble collective existence.

In addition, thinking about images as visual things cultivates attention to what Latour calls "matters of concern." As Latour (2005b) explains in *Reassembling the Social*, "To be 'treated like things'. . . is not to be 'reduced' to mere matters of fact, but allowed to live a life as multifarious as that of matters of concern" (255). As matters of fact, things are considered to be transparent, obvious, discrete objects easily taken for granted. They are not complicated, as Latour (2004) draws on Ludwik Fleck to explain: "They are never simultaneously *made* through a complex history and new, real, and *interesting* participants in the universe" (159). As matters of concern, things are more elusive and provocative; they are dynamic, complex entanglements that often change right before our very eyes as they experience new associations. In this sense, things are more like phenomena. As such, they cannot be easily identified nor understood as they are mediating, assembling, and gathering many more folds that could be detected if considered to be already delivered (Latour 2004, 173). However, as matters of concern, *things* force us to acknowledge that the things with which we are so closely enmeshed may be what Timothy Morton (2012) has identified as "strange strangers" (17), but they nonetheless acquire mediational potential to shape all kinds of matters—political, emotional, psychological, relational, familial, and so forth—via their dynamic relations with human and nonhuman entities. We may not be certain as to how this mediation occurs, but that is precisely the point. In wondering how visual things become rhetorical, we are encouraged to seek out the dynamic, consequential, unfolding, and mediated activities that enable visual rhetoric to manifest and impact reality. Rather than be certain that this thing is rhetorical in this way and this time and space, then, this new materialist rhetorical approach seeks to empirically discover how an image becomes rhetorical in divergent ways as it circulates with time, enters into new associations, transforms, and generates a multiplicity of consequences—a process I call *rhetorical transformation.*

THE FUTURITY OF RHETORIC

In order to account for rhetorical transformation, this new materialist rhetorical approach turns the scholarly gaze mostly toward futurity. By *futurity*, I am referring to the strands of time beyond the initial moment of production and delivery when rhetorical consequences unfold, often unpredictably, as things circulate and transform across space, form, genre, and function. In terms of research, a new materialist rhetorical approach advocates for conducting empirical investigations to make transparent what happens not only to an image but also to the people and other entities an image encounters when they all enter into complex relations. A new materialist rhetorical approach recognizes that this "happening" occurs before and while an image is being produced. However, in order to account for a thing's complex rhetorical life, this approach is most interested in what happens after the image is initially produced and distributed. To account for this unfolding eventfulness, methods such as iconographic tracking can take a new materialist rhetorical approach and attend to seven distinct yet co-implicating material processes: composition, production, distribution, circulation, transformation, collectivity, and consequentiality. Such scholarly attention can help disclose how an image undergoes recomposition, reproduction, redistribution, and reassemblage, which intensify the circulation, transformation, and consequentiality of not only that image but also its derivatives. As will become clearer in part 2, when conducting iconographic tracking, these processes are not taken up in a linear, chronological fashion. Yet, in order to generate complex, ontological accounts of an image's distributed rhetorical becomings, all these processes are attended to throughout the research process.

Developing such an empirical and dynamic understanding about rhetoric demands turning to models of communication and rhetoric and developing new approaches that can help recover rhetoric's dynamic materiality, movement, and consequentiality. As Jenny Edbauer Rice (2005) notes in "Unframing Models of Public Distribution," oversimplified models of communication and the rhetorical situation model do not capture how rhetoric unfolds in public life. Publics are created and maintained by circulating discourses that unite strangers in a real or abstract sense (Warner 2002). Models that present communication in triangulated terms of *sender, receiver,* and *text* cannot account for the dynamic movement of discourse nor the divergent networked activity that takes place to make possible public communication. The rhetorical situation model is meant to complicate such communication models by emphasizing and exploring the contextual dimensions of rhetoric (Edbauer Rice 2005, 6). However, this model tends to position rhetoric as emanating from or being produced within a rather static scene constituted of entities perceived as already formed, stable, and discrete (Biesecker 1989; Edbauer Rice 2005; Krause 1996; Phelps 1988). In reality, the discrete elements typically accounted for in the rhetorical situation—audience, rhetor, exigence, constraints, text—operate in, as Louise Wetherbee Phelps (1988) puts it, a "flux" (60), or as Edbauer Rice (2005) puts it, a "wider sphere of active, historical, and lived processes" (8).

Rhetoric is also an emergent process distributed across a complex web of physical, social, psychological, spatial, and temporal dimensions (Edbauer Rice 2005, 12–13; Syverson 1999, 23)—a contingent process that becomes ever more complicated in a viral economy made possible by the Internet and other digital technologies. Writing in 1996, Steve Krause argued that components of the Internet such as listserves and newsgroups "facilitate and encourage situations in which multiple rhetors and audiences participate, dramatically problematizing the origins of discourse and the definitions of 'rhetor' and 'audience' presumed of classical and modern rhetorical situations." With the proliferation of the World Wide Web, social networking sites, blogs, electronic news and information sources, digital file hosting services, and so forth that make possible a viral economy, this problem is only exacerbated as the circulatory range, consequentiality, and thus force of rhetoric intensifies with each new encounter. As Edbauer Rice (2005) puts it rather bluntly, "(Neo)Bitzerian models cannot account for the amalgamations and transformations—the viral spread—of this rhetoric within its wider ecology" (19). With a tendency to focus on the predictable effects of rhetoric, such models especially cannot account for the unforeseeable material consequentiality that unfolds as things such as the Obama Hope image go viral and become rhetorical beyond a creator's own anticipation and imagination. We thus need, as Amy Propen (2012) has also recently argued, new models that can better account for the material and spatial dimensions of rhetorical things.

Edbauer Rice's rhetorical ecology model is useful in this regard as it has potential to account for the distributed emergence and ongoing circulation of rhetoric. This model also has potential to account for the transituationality and the divergent transformations rhetoric experiences within a viral economy. However, generating such models is not enough to account for how rhetoric unfolds in a highly networked, digital culture. We also need, as Edbauer Rice (2005) herself argues, to continue working hard to develop and deploy new concepts (or recuperate and/or appropriate older ones) in order to theorize how rhetoric materializes, moves, transforms, replicates and, especially, how publics, or I would prefer *collectives*, materialize in relation to such distributed rhetorical activity. These new concepts are especially necessary in the case of visual rhetoric, which, as I discuss in subsequent chapters, has potential to spark contagious desires that consciously and unconsciously draw people into collective activity. While scholars such as Tony Sampson (2012) have drawn on Tarde's work to produce theories of virality that help explain how such social contagion occurs in a networked culture, visual rhetoricians can do their part by producing theories about how images contribute in unique ways to such contagious phenomena. Such theories can only develop from empirical research that can "testify" to such rhetorical contagion (see also Edbauer Rice 2005). Thus, in addition to embracing a rhetorical ecological model, we must develop new research methods that can empirically account for the distributed, contingent, and contagious process of visual rhetoric. *Still Life with Rhetoric* attempts to be useful in this regard by turning to the futurity of rhetoric and articulating how we can account for the circulation, transformation, and consequentiality of things in both theory *and* practice.

AN ARGUMENT FOR CIRCULATION

While scholars such as Cara Finnegan, Lester Olson, Robert Hariman and John Lucaites have studied circulation in relation to visual rhetoric, not all scholars applaud this move. In their forward to the 6.2 issue of *Enculturation*, for example, Kevin Deluca and Joe Wilferth argue that circulation, as a concept for making sense of visual things, is "dependent on habits of analysis indebted to print, calling for the studious gaze of the academic and reinstantiating the print perspective" (para. 13). As evidence, they point out that when Cara Finnegan (2003) tries to account for the rhetorical circulation of FSA photographs in her book *Picturing Poverty*, she tends to "skew photographs into objects palpable for a print gaze" (para. 13) and read them within a limited context. Such turn to circulation and contexts is an act of a taming, in Roland Barthes's terms, that "enables us to turn our eyes away from the madness, excess, and ecstasy of the singular photograph (para. 6). Because such taming "inevitably eclipses the intractable immanence of images" (para. 6), DeLuca and Wilferth argue that such an approach rarely captures an image's rhetorical force nor acknowledges its ontological status. Thus, while they praise Finnegan for attempting to do something different with photographs by attending to circulation, they advocate for letting go of "the mindset and methods of print" (para. 11), studying image as a dynamic event, and adopting a more image-oriented approach that can capture an image's complex ontology and emergent character.

As is evident in my commitment throughout this book to attend to rhetoric's dynamic eventfulness, I greatly appreciate and even take up DeLuca and Wilferth's productive challenge. Images, like music, often flow in and across a wide and diverse range of physical and digital ecosystems once they are distributed in networked pathways (Hawk 2011, 171). As images become part of new associations and transform in genre, medium, and form at seemingly simultaneous rates, divergent materializations arise with time and space. Furthermore, as an image and its various renditions intra-act with human and nonhuman entities, a multiplicity of diverse, and often unpredictable, affective and rhetorical consequences materialize. In a viral economy, as already noted, the rhetorical force, circulatory range, and dynamic transformation of images only intensify. Especially as visual things such as Obama Hope spread across networked environments, images do experience, as Derrida (2002) puts it, "an absolute arrival." DeLuca and Wilferth's call for studying image as event is thus a necessary move if scholars want to recover rhetoric's dynamic, distributed, and contingent qualities and unpredictable contributions to collective life.

Studying an image's eventfulness is also necessary for addressing the complexities of visual production, distribution, and circulation brought on by a viral economy. As is evident in recent debates about two controversial congressional bills, SOPA (Stop Online Piracy Act) and PIPA (Protect Intellectual Property Act), as well as in recent debates about fair use in relation to Obama Hope, our current digital landscape is characterized by "drastic changes in delivery," rising debates over intellectual property, and an increasingly complex politics of publication and distribution (DeVoss and Porter 2006, 201). Consequently, scholars must interrogate the ethical dynamics of production and delivery brought on by the Internet, especially in relation to the economies of textual and image production (DeVoss and Porter 2006, 194). Scholars also must better account for *how* different kinds of collective actions influence viral circulation on the web. While authors and artists can attempt to account for rhetorical velocity by anticipating the third-party recomposition of their own work (Ridolfo and DeVoss 2009), they can never fully control where or how the things they produce will circulate. Things, especially in a digital age, simply, or rather complexly, flow. We need methods that can explain how new media practices enable things to experience reproduction and redistribution and thus circulate widely at viral speeds. We especially must better account for how digital technologies, participatory media platforms, and various actor networks contribute to the circulation and transformation of things in both digital and physical realms. In both theory and practice, then, studying the dynamic eventfulness of visual rhetoric is useful as it helps address the economic and methodological complexities brought on by a digital age.

Unlike DeLuca and Wilferth's work, however, *Still Life with Rhetoric* does not advocate for moving away from circulation if we want to account for a single image's complex and distributed ontology. Circulation, as a way of making sense of rhetoric, is not intrinsically linked to the habits of reading and contextualizing that DeLuca and Wilferth take issue with, nor is it inherently a transcendent category that automatically leads scholars to "corral images, interpret images, or give us their meaning" (para. 13). As I touch upon in the following chapter, these methodological habits of meaning making are deeply embedded in rhetorical study due to contemporary influences of semiotics (Goggin 2004), cultural materialism (Trimbur 2000), and rhetorico-hermeneutics (Sanchez 2006). They are also heavily informed by a longstanding tradition of representationalism that has gotten transposed onto studies of visual rhetoric (Vivian 2007). A representational framework presumes that visual artifacts can be conceived of and studied as visual language with potential to both refer to and distort that which is being described. Working under such presumption—as DeLuca and Wilferth themselves note—scholars tend to "reduce images to representations of the real" and confine them to regimes of representation (para. 15)—a reduction and confinement that eclipses their ontological complexity.

In addition, as they manifest in photographs, posters, and so forth, images appear before us like buildings and books—as stable things that have already been built and delivered. As such, we not only have a habit of studying images much like we read books (DeLuca and Wilferth 2009, para.13), but we also tend to treat them as language-like symbols that lack power unless scholars intervene with their own explanations of intention, meaning, and significance (Marback 2008). Rather than give images their due by fully acknowledging the distinct ways each image uniquely experiences rhetorical transformation and contributes to collective life, scholars thus tend to put images into limited contexts to help make rhetorical sense of that agential and dynamic event that so often eludes us. As a consequence of such transcendent and synchronic research habits, we often "narrow and limit the [image's] projection" (Marback 2008, 64) and do sometimes end up, as Wilferth and DeLuca claim, "eras[ing] the event in favor of interpretation" (para. 8). The heart of the problem DeLuca and Wilferth seem to be concerned with, then, has less to do with circulation in and of itself than with habits of method that constrain our ability to adequately account for rhetorical transformation and circulation in a viral age. While I share this methodological concern, I think we must be careful about unnecessarily marrying circulation to such representational and synchronic habits of study.

Circulation, as defined herein, refers to spatiotemporal flows, which unfold and fluctuate as things enter into diverse associations and materialize in abstract and concrete forms. From a new materialist perspective operating in conjunction with a rhetorical ecology model, things must be studied as divergent, unfolding becomings in order to account for their unique, distributed rhetorical ontology. Circulation is at the heart of this process, especially for new media images. Not only are the intuitions and feelings that drive an image's rhetorical productions and subsequent activities always in flux (Rice 2011, 12), but, especially in an age of viral media, once they are produced and distributed in a networked pathway, and enter into both physical arenas and cyberspaces, images rapidly undergo change in terms of location, form, media, genre, and function. In addition, as metaculture erupts from an actualized image's encounters with humans and other entities, images are often catapulted back into flow in divergent directions and generate even more configurations, which themselves often spur more circulation, transformation, and consequentiality. Thus, if we want to begin to understand how visual things spread and become rhetorical with time and space, we cannot help but acknowledge an image's ephemerality and mobility[11] and attend to an image's decentralized transformation and circulation.

In addition, methodologically speaking, by helping us tune in to rhetoric's flux and flow, circulation has proven productive for pushing scholars to *trace* and *follow* things' dynamic movement. In her work with RAWA, for instance, Mary Queen (2008) models how we can trace the transformations of continually evolving, yet materially bound, rhetorical actions through the "links embedded within multiple fields of circulation" (476). By tracing an iconic photograph's history of official, vernacular, and commercial appropriations and following how it is reproduced, highlighted, altered, and/or parodied, Robert Hariman and John Louis Lucaites (2007) also model how attention to circulation helps account for the role of photographic icons in public culture (29). While I would agree with DeLuca and Wilferth (2009) that, in the latter case, Hariman and Lucaites do undercut the rhetorical force of images by reading them within a liberal-democratic context, such scholarship, alongside Queen and others, models how tracing the constant transformation of things can be a productive research strategy for acknowledging rhetoric's dynamic dimensions. Such a strategy is especially useful for visual rhetoric in that it helps make visible how the complex, distinct rhetorical life of a single multiple image unfolds. As I discuss in chapters 4 and 5, when we follow the circulation of an image's transformation and trace its collective activities via digital research, for example, we can begin to disclose how images such as Obama Hope become part of overlapping assemblages and participate in divergent rhetorical activities. Such collective activity often strays far beyond its imagined function and can only be tapped into by following a particular image in and out of assemblage and tracing its lively encounters. Thus, in terms of method, circulation is also important as it helps cultivate the habitus of following an image in flow and tracing its rhetorical activities to help disclose how visual things co-constitute collective life.

With this respect for circulation, then, *Still Life with Rhetoric* aims to show that if we think intuitively and ecologically about rhetoric and commit to creating symmetrical accounts of rhetorical activity, studies of circulation actually do have potential to disclose how rhetoric unfolds as a complex, distributed event. This is not to say that studies of circulation alone can help account for the complex ontology of a single image or any other thing in an "age of contagion" (Sampson 2012, 3). We must also attend to the ways things are composed, produced, distributed, and transformed as well as the ways they induce assemblage, spark collective action, and catalyze change that registers on affective and rhetorical dimensions. Also, such work does demand taming our representational and synchronic habits of reading, as DeLuca and Wilferth (2009) seem to suggest. Yet, more precisely, such work demands supplementing these ways of meaning making with other approaches than can follow a single thing's dynamic movement and trace its distributed materiality and consequentiality. Rather than move away from circulation in visual rhetoric, then, what if we hyperfocus on an image's constant flow and transformation and try to account for a single multiple image's[12] distributed rhetorical becomings? This is the central inquiry that drives *Still Life with Rhetoric*.

Notes

1. See Kenneth Burke's (1969) *Grammar of Motives* for how representative anecdotes are "something around which an analytic vocabulary is constructed" (59).

2. See Dolphijn and der Tuin's (2012) "The Transversality of New Materialism" in *New Materialism: Interviews and Cartographies.*

3. The "nonhuman turn" was the theme in 2012 for the annual conference put on by the Center for 21st Century Studies at the University of Wisconsin-Milwaukee. According to the program, new materialism, as it is taken up in feminism, philosophy, and Marxism, is working alongside various different intellectual and theoretical developments such as actor-network theory, affect theory, animal studies, assemblage theory, new brain sciences, new media theory, varieties of speculative realism, and systems theory.

4. Invented by Karen Barad (2007), *intra-action* is a neologism that recognizes that the boundaries and properties of all involved entities become determinate with time and space and within phenomena. This concept is also discussed in detail in chapter 3.

5. *Body multiple* is Annemarie Mol's (2002) term for designating the ontological multiplicity of an object. This concept is discussed in chapter 2.

6. Filippo Marongiu's *Pope* Obamicon, Matt Cornell's *Hobama* Obamicon, Matt Sesow's Painting *Rhetoric*, Klutch's *Hopeless* Obamicon, Shahab Siavash's *Ayatollah Obama* Obamicon, and Pablo Perez's Photograph *Obama Hype* have all been reprinted courtesy of the artists.

7. In writing this book, I struggled when drawing on others' work to talk about images and pictures because authors often define *image, visual,* and *picture* differently than I do. In order to not confuse my readers, I try to adhere to the way authors define and deploy *image, picture,* and *visual* when recounting their ideas. Yet, whenever I am presenting my ideas, I stick to the definitions offered in this introduction.

8. I want to thank Collin Brooke (2015) for turning me on to this quote from Wayne Booth (1974). See Collin's article, "Bruno Latour's Posthuman Rhetoric of Assent" (forthcoming in *The Object of Rhetoric: Assembling and Disassembling Bruno Latour,* edited by Nathaniel Rivers and Paul Lynch).

9. For other rhetorical scholars pursuing similar observations about rhetoric, see, among others, Nathaniel Rivers's (2014) "Tracing the Missing Masses: Vibrancy, Symmetry and Public Rhetoric Pedagogy" as well as Alex Reid's (2012) video in *Internations,* "What is Object Oriented Rhetoric," and Barnett's and Boyle's (2015) forthcoming edited collection *Rhetorical Ontologies: Rhetoric through Everyday Things.*

10. In subsequent chapters, I attempt to respect the way other scholars use terms such as *discourse* and *object* by using their exact terms when describing another scholar's own perspective about visual rhetoric.

11. As Mary Queen (2008) reminds us, electronic texts "change not only because they are ephemeral—forming and dissolving simultaneously—but also because they are mobile: they circulate, and, in the process of circulation, they encounter and are transformed by other forces" (475).

12. As I draw on Aarie Mol's (2002) scholarship to articulate, a single multiple image is one that is able to materialize in divergent actualizations yet simultaneously maintain a recognizable whole. See chapter 2 for more on single multiple images.

PART I

A New Materialist Rhetorical Approach in Theory

2

SPATIOTEMPORAL MATTERS[1]

If some of us have professed something like a dynamic, relativistic view of structure, or at least have been quick to repudiate a static one, few if any composition professionals have really believed it enough to act on it.
—Louise Wetherbee Phelps, "The Dance of Discourse"

Typical perceptions of matter view material things as inert, whole objects with analyzable compositional elements that distinguish them from other solid entities. When we study objects such as books, or photographs, or other things from such a perspective, we tend to stand over or in front of the object, gaze at it from a distanced perspective, and attempt to identify its fixed internal properties in order to determine its possible rhetorical meanings. The object is studied as a static entity before us in terms of both its essence and its location in the world. Writing back in 1988, Louise Wetherbee Phelps explained that the field of rhetoric and composition likes to think it moved away from such static perspectives of discourse during the process movement as scholars turned to the composing process and situated writing practice as a productive event of "making" texts. Ironically, however, "texts became even more quintessentially objects—inanimate, static, self-contained, and rigidly organized—by comparison with the vital, creative, temporal, subjective, fluid, open-ended features of composing" (Phelps 1988, 135). Therefore, and I believe this still holds true today, while we think of composing as a process, we still think of composed matter as static, stable things that circulate in the world as fixed entities. Such a perspective reinforces a static model of discourse structure in which we "view meaning as an object contained in the text, accessible to an 'objective' description, capable of spatialization and thus open to simultaneous comprehension of all its parts" (139). As a consequence of this static model, we often refrain from accounting for the constant yet often-unpredictable change and movement that discourse experiences.

Within rhetorical study, this methodological dilemma is troublesome for visual things such as Obama Hope, largely due to transmission models

DOI: 10.7330/9780874219784.c002

of delivery. In our everyday understanding of delivery, we speak about objects being delivered in a specific context (Brooke 2009, 170). More particularly, we think of someone transmitting some thing to someone else in a precise moment and a specific place. A mail carrier delivers books to our doorstep. We deliver conference papers to a room full (we hope) of colleagues (Brooke 2009, 170). Such perspectives entrap us into thinking about delivery in terms of a fixed thing, a knowable author, a knowable audience, and an identifiable immediate situation. Such transitive thinking about delivery also perpetuates the notion that intended audiences are passive, albeit interpretive, receptors of delivered things. In a viral economy, in which both intended and unintended audiences play such an interactive role in remixing, appropriating, and spreading images, we know that "delivery" is not something so direct or controlled. We also know that digital things are rarely stable in and of themselves. *Wikipedia* is one clear example. With no stable, discrete object existing in the form of a deliverable physical product, *Wikipedia* is an instance of active performance in which information is constantly being revised and updated (Brooke 2009). Yet, if we take a long view, we can also see that images such as Obama Hope are often in flux in terms of form, medium, genre, and activity. As such, it would behoove us to think about visual things as *circulating*, not some *thing* to be circulated. In this intransitive model, performance, or enactment, constitutes reality as visual things are not only constantly taking place (Brooke 2009, 192) but are also on the move and undergoing (and producing) change.

Suffice it to say, even as we may intellectually know this to be true, it is still difficult to imagine and study the dynamic flow of visual matter typically categorized as still (photograph, poster, painting, etc.). At any given moment an image draws our attention in some actualized form, it appears, much like a building, "desperately static," which makes it difficult to "grasp as movement, as flight, as a series of transformations" (Latour and Yaneva 2008, 80). And even if we do conceive of visual matter as continuous flow, as pure event, events by their very nature resist capture. An event, after all, is "an absolute arrival: it surprises and resists analysis after the fact" (Derrida 2002, 20).

> At the birth of a child, the primal figure of the absolute *arrivant* . . . you can analyze the causalities, the genealogical, genetic, or symbolic premises, and all the wedding preparations you like. Supposing this analysis could ever be exhausted, you will never get rid of the element of chance, this place of the taking-place, there will still be someone who speaks, someone irreplaceable, an absolute initiative, another origin of the world. Even if it must dissolve in analysis or return to ash, it is an absolute spark." (Derrida 2002, 20)

This spark—this event—can never be fully captured in our analyses and interpretations because an event is a process of *inexplicable* becoming. Simultaneously, an event is insuppressible; that which we identify as event is always unfolding into an unknown future. Conceived here as morphogenesis—"instances of evolving and ever-changing forms" (Borić 2010, 64)—an event is thus also a process of *unpredictable* becoming. Even though we can try to encapsulate something we identify as event, we can never quite catch up with this dynamic unfolding phenomenon.[2]

In visual rhetoric, this difficulty is exacerbated by the lack of theoretical perspectives and research methods that enable us to study an image as event—as a dynamic network of distributed, unfolding, and unforeseeable becomings.[3] Jenny Edbauer Rice's (2005) work with *rhetorical ecologies*, as discussed in chapter 1, is useful in this regard in that it draws our attention to the fluidity and circulation of rhetoric as it is embedded in the "ongoing social flux" that constitutes society (9). As Edbauer Rice explains, "networked life" is constituted by flows of historical and cultural forces, energies, rhetorics, moods, experiences that emerge in spaces of contact between humans and their organic and inorganic surroundings. Rhetoric is a distributed act that emerges from between these affective encounters and interactions, not among individual discrete elements (author, text, audience) in any given rhetorical situation. In this theoretical sense, rhetoric is a "process of distributed emergence and . . . an ongoing circulation process" whose circulatory range is affected by the social flux of forces, energies, encounters, and so forth (13). The notion of rhetorical ecologies is productive for visual rhetoric, then, because it challenges us to imagine how images emerge and flow within a network (or field) of forces, affects, and associations.

The concept of *rhetorical transformation* discussed in the next two chapters is intended to be productive in similar regards. By rhetorical transformation, I am referring to the process in which things become rhetorical in divergent, unpredictable ways as they circulate, transform, and catalyze change. A new materialist approach to visual rhetoric is especially interested in how images acquire *thing-power*—that "curious ability . . . to animate, to act, to produce effects dramatic and subtle" (Bennett 2010, 6). This ability—which we might also think of as a thing's "rhetorical can-do-ness," to borrow Sharon Crowley's (2006, 55) phrase—does not derive solely from an actualized image's rhetorical design, nor is it a static affair, especially when it comes to images that experience viral circulation. Rather, as images materialize in different versions and enter into divergent associations, they become rhetorically diverse as they work alongside other entities, human and nonhuman, abstract and concrete, to alter collective life. Such alteration includes, as many rhetorical scholars have noted, establishing a particular way of seeing or gaze (DeLuca and Demo 2000; Fleckenstein, Hum, and Calendrillo 2007), producing a multiplicity of visual realities (Vivian 2007) and negotiating civic identities (Hariman and Lucaites 2007). Yet, visual things also become rhetorical when they reassemble collective life as they draw people and other things into relations to achieve a variety of nuanced purposes. As a concept, rhetorical transformation acknowledges that such rhetorical becoming is a spatiotemporal, distributed process that intensifies with each new actualization and with each new encounter.

Rhetorical transformation, as a process, is unique to singular images (and other things[4]) and can only be disclosed by tracing their distinct, albeit divergent, rhetorical lives. This process can seem quite simple, short-lived, and/or inconsequential if an image does not spread and/or transform widely or leave many traces of rhetorical activity. However, in regards to an image such as the Mona Lisa that first materialized between 1503 and 1506 or the Raised Fist (also referred to as the Clenched Fist) that can be traced back even further,[5] this process can be quite complicated; some images have been circulating across the globe and transforming in terms of genre, media, form, and function for hundreds of years. With a new media image such as Obama Hope, which took on a plethora of rhetorical roles in countries as disparate as the United States, Turkey, and England within just a few months of entering into circulation, rhetorical transformation can also be quite convoluted. Research methods such as iconographic tracking can help recover the rhetorical transformation of images with such complex, convoluted lives, but how are we to understand this distributed process on a theoretical level? This chapter attempts to address this question by discussing intuitive ways for thinking about rhetoric.

To think intuitively in a general sense is to perceive reality as change, as mobility. As Henri Bergson (2007) suggests, immobility is only an abstract moment, "a snapshot taken by our mind of a mobility" (22). While intelligence is concerned with the static and makes of change only an accident, intuition sees everything as mobility, as change (22). According to Bergson, intuition is also bound to duration, which can be thought of as growth, evolution, "an interrupted continuity of unforeseeable novelty" (22). As I discuss below, timescapes of networked society complicate such evolutionary notions of duration. However, in order to understand rhetorical transformation, it is still useful to think of reality as constituted by an entangled web of creations, or becomings, each moving toward something new. It is also useful to think in terms of flow and, in working like Gilles Deleuze and Felix Guattari's artisan, follow the flow of matter. As Deleuze and Guattari (1987) explain in *A Thousand Plateaus*, "To follow the flow matter is to itinerate, to ambulate. It is intuition in action" (409). Thinking intuitively about things such as Obama Hope, then, entails perceiving and tracing images as they undergo divergent change and flow—as pure event. To foster this intuition, a new materialist rhetorical approach adopts nonmodern perspectives of time and space and works hard to acknowledge an image's unfolding transformations, differenciations, and virtual-actual constitutions.

Thinking intuitively about rhetoric also entails acknowledging the divergent consequences that unfold as a visual thing circulates, enters into diverse associations, and, in the case of an image such as Obama Hope, transcends media. According to a new materialist rhetorical approach, a thing's rhetorical meaning is constituted by the consequences that emerge in its various material encounters, affects, and intra-actions. Meaning is not something, then, that can be fleshed out from an actualized image, nor is it ever stable, as an image is constantly transforming change and rearranging space. Before landing on this page, for instance, Obama Hope was already wildly consequential as it had, among other things, affected unconscious desires, spurred people to organize for political change, inspired vehement critique, and raised ongoing debates about copyright and fair use. These consequences will only continue to propagate as this image lives on beyond this moment. Already new consequences, and thus meanings, are forming as I type this chapter and new people and entities encounter the actualized image in their own time and space. Tomorrow, even more consequences will materialize. We can only be open to tracing such multifaceted meanings by thinking intuitively about rhetoric, especially in an age of viral circulation. Thus, in essence, thinking intuitively is an exercise in attending to the futurity of things; it helps form the habitus of method necessary for attending to the open-ended rhetorical becomings that so often remain invisible in much of our scholarship.

TIME, SPACE AND BECOMING

In the remainder of this chapter, I explicate some of the theories and philosophies about time, space, and meaning that undergird the kind of intuitive thinking for which I have been advocating. Conceptions of time and space influence not only how we produce rhetoric, but also how we comprehend, theorize, and study it. The conceptions of time and space grounding any approach, in fact, *create the conditions* for its praxis. Consider, for instance, the difference between clock time, the timescape of many Euro-American industrialized societies, versus ICT time, the timescape of late twentieth- to early twentieth-century network societies. In timescapes of many industrialized, capitalist societies, time is perceived as durational and linear—a succession of instant moments in which events unfold into an irreversible future. Time is also decontextualized from matter, as well as from the rhythms and seasons of the earth, and divisible into uniform, quantifiable units of clock time. In addition, time is conceived of as neutral, something that objects and persons move through, and abstract, without the capacity to affect actual change in the world. Time, especially in capitalistic industrialized societies, becomes something humans think they can control; future outcomes are, as Barbara Adam (2004) puts it, "amenable to human regulation" (141). In temporal perspectives characterized by clock time, the future is, thus, often conceived as being somewhat predictable.[6]

In timescapes of network society, or ICT time, perceptions of time compression, as many scholars have noted, have manifested through high-speed, electronic, communication technologies. Especially with the emergence of the Internet, the passage of time is distorted, as information—conceived as flow—converges toward simultaneity with no past or future (Castells 1996). Duration (conceived here in relation to time), in other words, is eradicated in this timescape in favor of an eternal present. Space (extension) is also eliminated, as communication technologies seem to create the conditions to be everywhere at once and nowhere in particular; "No-where and now-where have become interchangeable" (Adam 2004, 146). As Adam (2007) explains, this sense of instantaneity, and simultaneity especially, shapes our perception of the future: "With instantaneity (which means processes without a gap between cause and effect in the linear chain of events) there can be no interception, no intervening action. With simultaneity (which means action that is happening at the same time and is dispersed across space) there can be no certainty over effects. That is to say, when there is no durational gap for establishing difference and change, when there is no discernible sequence, and when the speeds involved operate outside the capacity of the conscious mind, then the control achieved over clock time processes is rendered inoperable" (xi). In simpler terms, in the "real instant," "no one has control" (Virilio 1993, 18); the future is utterly unpredictable.

In actuality, ICT time is bound to clock time in our daily operations, so it's not as if one version of time is more right/true than another. Plus, as Tiziana Terranova (2004) points out, time and space are not completely annihilated when it comes to Internet communication, which heavily influences perceptions of ICT time. Rather, on the Internet, which is itself a network of networks, a complex mangle of "layered and overlapping topologies" unfolds in a single communication space (53). In this sense, while we may think that new media communication unfolds in an instantaneous and simultaneous fashion, if we could freeze frame the Internet, we might see that each message on the Internet is experiencing its own movement in which it is carving out space in various dimensions and at differing temporal intensities (53). Nonetheless, the point I want to emphasize here is that in the timescape of ICT time, time and space are perceived differently from clock time, and such differing *matters*. Our conceptions of time and space influence how we orient ourselves, how we attune to other things, how we communicate, and, especially, how we understand rhetoric to happen.

With its inherent beliefs in linearity and predictability, clock time, for instance, is embedded in speaker, dyad models of communication and transitive models of delivery that still undergird much rhetorical thinking. From the perspective of clock time, we can compose a message, deliver it, and expect the future to unfold in a somewhat predictable manner even if we cannot fully guarantee it. From the perspective of ICT time, on the other hand, our messages seem much more everywhere at once and nowhere in particular. This is especially the case in network culture in which information spills from network to network both on the Internet and outernet[7] and messages do not flow from a sender to a receiver but spread, mix, mutate, converge, diverge, and interact in a complex multiplicity of communication channels (Terranova 2004, 1–2). As such, and as implied in Ridolfo and DeVoss's (2009) notion of rhetorical velocity, we have no idea where things are going to end up because they seem to just keep moving and transforming. This helps explain why from the perspective of ICT time, it feels intuitive to conceive of rhetoric as a distributed emergence, an ongoing circulation, and an ever-changing enactment.

Such articulated notions of ICT time heavily influence the new materialist rhetorical approach discussed herein. However, it is also just as influenced by process philosophies, particularly the notion of becoming.[8] Becoming, in the sense I am referring to it here, is a virtual-actual process in which any given thing, better thought of as a multiplicity, "changes in nature as it expands its connections" through its *constant*[9] production with time and of space (Deleuze and Guattari 1987, 8). Rhetoricians have long been interested in the ontology of becoming.

Nathan Crick (2010), in fact, insists that "the connection between rhetoric and the ontology of becoming . . . is present at the very origins
of rhetoric" (22). Most typically in rhetorical study, this concern has
to do with the identity formation, subjectivity, and civic development
of human beings as well as the health of democracy. We might interpret, for instance, the purpose of progymnasmata in ancient Greece as
teaching pupils how to become rhetorical and develop public virtue—a
notion emphasized by David Fleming (2003), who argues that rhetoric's
ongoing educational function is to help students become rhetorically
self-conscious and flexible civic actors. We might also read the sophist
rhetorician Protagoras as being committed to the ontology of becoming, as he believed that "all things are in motion" and that "the verb 'to
be' must be totally abolished."[10] This recognition of flux, Crick (2010)
argues, is evident in John Dewey's own belief that the power of discourse
lies in its ability to move the individual self (and thus a democratic public) toward unknown possibilities. From a new materialist perspective
that believes in a democracy of things (i.e., all things have equal ontological footing), however, human subjects are not the only ones who experience rhetorical becoming. Rhetoric is a distributed event that unfolds
with time in and across networks of complex, dynamic relations. At the
heart of this process is rhetorical transformation—a virtual-actual process of becoming in which rhetoric unfolds in unpredictable, divergent,
and inconsistent ways. Nonhuman things, such as images,[11] also experience rhetorical becoming(s) in that their potential to alter reality and
reassemble collective life is constantly materializing via their multiple
and distributed encounters.

A BRIEF VIGNETTE ABOUT RHETORICAL TRANSFORMATION

In this book, Obama Hope acts as the quintessential example of how
contemporary new media images experience rhetorical transformation; few, if any, other images in recent history have experienced such
an intense eventfulness with such long-reaching and divergent rhetorical consequences. In countries such as Australia, Mexico, and Germany
over the last few months of 2013 alone, for instance, Obama Hope,
respectively, became part of the prohemp movement, rallies against
US deportation policies, and protests against the US National Security
Agency. Obama Hope has also recently surfaced in posters to critique
Obama's military use of drones, in political cartoons to satirize Obama's
decision to seek congressional approval for Syria military action, and
in Obamicons[12] to commemorate Nelson Mandela's life-long fight for

freedom and equality. As it attracts people across the globe into relation with it for diverse purposes and becomes rhetorical in such unexpected ways, Obama Hope proves that nearly eight years after it first entered into circulation, its thing-power is still quite intense. But if ever there was an image with *long-standing* thing-power, it is Mona Lisa.[13] It is thus worth pausing here to note how a single image's rhetorical transformation can span multiple centuries before moving on to explain how such transformation happens on a theoretical level.

As most people are aware, part of Mona Lisa's lure is the lack of certainty over who is depicted in the image that comes to life in Leonardo da Vinci's now-iconic painting. Mona Lisa's identity has been debated for centuries, but many art historians now believe that da Vinci's painting was originally commissioned in the early 1500s by the husband of Lisa del Gherardini, who wanted to hang a portrait of his Italian wife in their new home to celebrate the birth of their new child. However, whether or not this story is true, Mona Lisa never experienced this intended life as a portrait. Instead, da Vinci instead took the painting to the court of Francois I, the French King at the time, who eventually purchased it and entered it into the royal collection. After residing in several royal palaces, and even Napoleon's own bedroom for a short time, in the late 1700s, the *Mona Lisa* eventually found its permanent home as a work of art at the Louvre, where it still resides today. Interestingly, in its painted, framed version, the *Mona Lisa* has actually not traveled much since it landed in the Louvre. In fact, while today the *Mona Lisa* is, according to many, the most famous and widely recognized and parodied painting in the world, it sat largely unnoticed in the Louvre for almost half a century. But as an image with an ability to transcend media and genre in abstract, physical, and digital forms, Mona Lisa has since circulated broadly and acquired much thing-power through a wide variety of rhetorical encounters.

Some of Mona Lisa's most notorious transformations began occurring in the nineteenth century when Mona Lisa enticed British and French writers to write about it as both an object of mystery and a femme fatale. When it was stolen from the Louvre in 1911, it also gained a lot of rhetorical notoriety as its disappearance sparked a two-year-long investigation, followed closely by the press, and it became a source of French national pride. Mona Lisa's popularity, Donald Sassoon (2001) notes, did not die after the painting was recovered; instead it "continued to thrive on the oxygen of publicity" (196). More particularly, the image's mass circulation and transformation cultivated a celebritism, which was "kept alive" by both the avant-garde who began to deride it and popular-fiction writers who deployed it as a "hook on which to hang stories" (196). With modern advances that led to mass travel, advertising, and the rise of popular culture during the second half of the twentieth century, Mona Lisa's rhetorical transformation only escalated as the painting attracted hordes of tourists, artists, historians, and writers who were mesmerized by its aesthetic style and haunting smile. Some were so taken by its thing-power that they even went so far to write Mona Lisa letters and love songs.

Like Obama Hope, as Mona Lisa experienced distributed circulation and materialized in a diverse array of media and forms, it took on a variety of rhetorical roles, many with transnational consequences. As early as 1919, for instance, Mona Lisa worked to protest against the museumification of art when surrealist artist Marcel Duchamp produced a version of her with a moustache and a goatee. Later, in the 1960s and 1970s, it became a diplomat, as the *Mona Lisa* was loaned to the United States in an attempt to improve Franco-American relations, and the image made a stunning appearance in John F. Kennedy's speech at the painting's unveiling at the National Gallery of Art. In the late twentieth century, especially as technologies afforded digital play, Mona Lisa also became a popular enactment of parody, as contemporary artists, comedians, and everyday citizens across the world began to produce various remixes of it. It also began to surface in advertisements, selling everything from condoms and vacuum cleaners to chocolate and IUDs, and it popped up in songs by Cole Porter, Nat King Cole, and more recently, will.i.am. Today, many of these advertisements and remixes can be found on billboards across the United States. Yet also, thanks to the work of Banksy and other graffiti artists, Mona Lisa is showing up on urban walls around the world making arguments about women's bodies, arms trade, and public space.

Unsurprisingly, perhaps, new technologies and artistic practices are only diversifying Mona Lisa's transformation. In one of its most interesting recent manifestations, Mona Lisa has become a call for a post-national iconography as the image is "Frenchised" by Amir Baradaran, an artist who created an augmented reality (AR) object[14] in which the image in da Vinci's painting comes to life to don a tricolor hijab (see Figure 2.1). Yet even more relevant to this research project are the digital remixes of Mona Lisa that have been produced in the style of Obama Hope, many of which have been generated by new software designed specifically for creating such designs (see Figure 2.2).[15] Such instances, of course, are only a fraction of the rhetorical functions Mona Lisa has taken on throughout its life, but in just these few examples, we can see

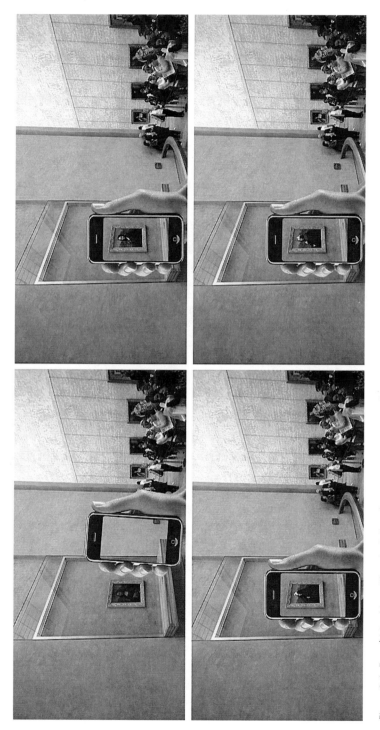

Figure 2.1. Frenchising Mona Lisa, Amir Baradaran, 2011. Courtesy of Baradaran.

Figure 2.2. Mona Lisa *Remix, Filippo Marongiu, 2012. Courtesy of Marongiu.*

just how complex and unpredictable a rhetorical life Mona Lisa has come to lead. If we take the long view, we can also see how distributed Mona Lisa's life has been, as it has materialized in a diverse array of forms, genres, and media and has become embroiled in various activities. Such an unpredictable and distributed affair is impossible to grasp theoretically from a modern perspective, in which matter is typically conceived as bounded, stable entities—marked by solidity—and movement is thought to obey fundamental and invariable laws of motion and is thus deemed somewhat predictable and controllable. Adopting nonmodern perspectives of matter and thinking intuitively about an image's virtual-actual constitution, however, can be helpful in grasping the distributed process of rhetorical transformation. Such a perspective is especially productive when trying to track the rhetorical life of images such as Obama Hope, which may not have experienced as much transformation as Mona Lisa has over the long haul, but whose speed of circulation and frequency of transformation over the short haul have certainly been more intense.

VIRTUAL-ACTUAL IMAGES

When we adopt nonmodern perspectives, matter's dynamic dimensions and nonlinear movement come to light. As Latour (1993) explains, "We do not fall upon someone or something, we do not land on an essence, but on a process, on a movement, a passage" (129). From a new materialist perspective, we also land on becoming, the opening up of events into an unknown future. From this perspective, materiality itself is perceived as a fluctuating flow of matter and energy, events and forces, in which all things are "relatively composed" (Bennett 2010, 349). This flow, or movement, especially on the Internet, does not take place in homogenous space; it does not entail the linear passage of a fixed entity from point A to point B. Rather, movement is nonlinear and entails the production of space and time. In this spatiotemporal sense,[16] circulating things such as Obama Hope and Mona Lisa experience a virtuality of duration—"the qualitative change that every movement brings not only to that which moves, but also to the space that it moves in and to the whole into which that space necessarily opens up" (Terranova 2004, 51). From such perspective, becoming cannot help but take place. Things do not just move inconsequentiality and unchanged through space and time; they are both impacted by and impact that which they encounter. Despite their stable appearance at a given moment, then, things—especially those that experience viral circulation—constantly exist in a dynamic state of flux and are always generative of change, time, and space.

In reference to images, but certainly not particularly so, this dynamic becoming and consequentiality is dependent on a thing's relation to other things—a point I will more fully develop in chapter 3. Yet, an image's dynamic becoming and consequentiality are also dependent on its virtual-actual constitution and its variability—its ability to exist in "different, potentially infinite versions" (Manovich 2001, 36). While *actual*, here, pertains to an image's concrete, physical manifestation, *virtual* refers to an image's undeterminable unique potential[17] that is immaterial yet not inconsequential. The virtual, to further explain, is productive or generative; it is, as Steven Shaviro (2007) explains so clearly, like a field of unexpended energies, or a reservoir of untapped potentialities, that makes the actual capable of coming into existence. This does not mean that an image prefigures or predetermines its actualized version, that is, a picture, or photograph, or painting. Instead, an image should be understood as a creative force that affords each materialized version the opportunity to appear or manifest as something new, "something that has never existed in the universe in quite that way before" (Shaviro 2007). In this sense, we might think of an image such as Obama Hope or

Mona Lisa as the impetus for creation, or "the real of genuine production, innovation, and creativity" (Grosz 1999, 27).

Such creation does not just manifest in a single instance of an image's
materialization, nor in a predictable one. Rather, as we have seen with
both Obama Hope and Mona Lisa, a complex, distributed web of surprising actualizations often manifests, which, in turn, sparks a network
of other creative consequences. If a virtual image can be understood in
terms of creative potential, then, actualization can be best understood
as the constant yet unpredictable creation of an image into something
new. In Deleuzean terms, I understand this process to be one of "differenciation"[18] in which a creative process of divergent variation takes
place. This process of materialization, to reiterate, is not preordained or
determined by a virtual image. Although virtual potentials are an ever-
present dimension of any given entity that contribute to how an image
is dramatized in space, actualization is a divergent process dependent on
a diverse array of influential external factors, or exterior relations. Such
relations involve a wide ecology of human interventions but also nonhuman things such as external light, which influences an actualized entity's color, and technologies that shape its production and distribution,
just to name a few. Because a virtual image has potential to enter into a
wide range of exterior relations at seemingly simultaneous moments, its
actualizations are divergent and multiple, especially in a viral economy.
divergent and multiple. The actual, we must keep in mind, then, is not
a singular entity, as is evident in the collage of Obama Hope remixes
depicted in Chapter 1 (see Figure 1.3); it is a multiplicity, constituted by
heterogeneous materializations with virtual-actual dimensions.

During the process of actualization, which the Obama Hope case
study will help make clear, divergent paths of development constantly
unfold in different series, directions, and spatial configurations as well
as different time frames, tempos, and patterns. Actualization is, in other
words, a mode of constant (but not continuous) individuation in which
multiple varieties materialize with time and space. Some of the varieties, or versions, in which images actualize are quantitative. For instance,
when images such as Obama Hope manifest in a specific mosaic or
Mona Lisa materializes in a painting, they become actual, objective, and
extensive in that their actualized selves can be easily identified as differing in degree, represented in space, and counted by the human eye or a
machine (Tampio 2010) (see Figure 2.3). We can see and feel how their
actualized versions are bending space. Others, which Deleuze calls "qualitative," are not so easily identifiable, as they are subjective and intensive
and cannot be easily defined, counted, and quantified (Tampio 2010).

Figure 2.3. Obama Hope LEGO Construction, Hope of Obama, *Freelance LEGO® Artist Mariann Asanuma, 2009. Photograph Courtesy of Asanuma.*

For instance, when I speak about the Obama Hope image, a mental picture may come to mind as an actualized form in my imagination. However, that picture is not necessarily objective in the sense that it can be measured, nor is it the exact same one that likely materializes in your brain, especially when so many remixes of an image have been produced that we begin to lose sight of its original instantiation. Because of such quantitative and qualitative actualizations, we must understand that, as Annemarie Mol (2002) puts it, "reality is distributed" (96). Thus, rather than thinking of images such as Obama Hope or Mona Lisa as singular, it might be more useful to think of them as "single multiple," meaning both one and many (Mol 2002, 142).[19]

SINGLE MULTIPLE IMAGES

In *The Body Multiple: Ontology in Medical Practice*, Mol uses the example of atherosclerosis to explain how this single disease is a multiplicity in both senses described above. As her ethnography of this disease conducted in a Dutch university hospital makes evident, atherosclerosis does have some sense of coherence in that via a range of coordinations, or tasks such as making images, performing case studies, and so forth, it does form and maintain some sense of identifiable whole. Yet, without being totally fragmented so that it cannot go under a single name, it concurrently has multiple versions, depending on factors such as what person is discussing it, in what moment and place it is being discussed or treated, and what apparatus is engaging with it. While some of these versions are easy to locate in print materials or x-rays, others are subjective and cannot always be ascertained even as they have a consequential presence. Some patients, for instance, who have in mind and are affected by their own conception of atherosclerosis, are not always able to totally access and define their understanding of it. While singular, then, in that it has an actual body, this disease is also multiple, many. As such, from the perspective of what Mol calls "empirical philosophy," we can think of atherosclerosis as a body multiple—a multiplicity constituted by heterogeneous versions that emerge with their own spatiotemporal configurations yet hang together to give the disease a sense of wholeness.

Images such as Obama Hope are also body multiples. As a virtual entity that first actualized in Mannie Garcia's photograph and then in Shepard Fairey's Obama Works,[20] Obama Hope has since manifested in many different versions in a variety of media, locations, and genres. Like Mona Lisa, it has also transformed many times over in terms of form and/or function, depending on what associations it enters into. As chapter 8 will make especially clear, such multiplication began early on in Obama Hope's life. During the first year of its life, for example, Obama Hope surfaced not only in stickers, posters, and murals, but it was also remixed in advertisements, made into a cake decorations, cross-stitched onto canvases, constructed out of Post-It notes and thumbtacks, tattooed onto human bodies, and carved onto pumpkins (see Figure 2.4). Such actualizations surfaced not only in cities stretching across the United States but also in places as far away as London, Turkey, and Australia. By early 2009, for instance, it had showed up in Istanbul to sell banking services as well as digital parodies in prowhite forums to poke fun of Obama. (So many parodies of the Obama *Hope* poster have surfaced since then, in fact, that the Obama *Hope* poster might just give the *Mona Lisa* a run for its money for being the most widely parodied picture of all time.)

Such viral spreading and transformation of an image is often, in part, a consequence of its imitation suggestibility—its ability to tap into the tendency for increasingly connected populations to pass on and imitate

Figure 2.4. Barack O'Lantern, *2008. Photography Courtesy of Mark Johnson.*

the suggestions and behaviors of others (Sampson 2012, 5). As Tarde
has helped us understand, repetition and imitation constitute the fabric
of social reality. As people become influenced by the "shove and buzz"
of the crowd, they often get caught up in a complex network of desire
events that translate biological desires into social desires and drive imitative thoughts, opinions, and behaviors (qtd. in Sampson, 43). When
we turn to futurity, such imitative encounters at work in relation to a
particular image or thing become obvious. In the case of Obama Hope,
for instance, as more people recognized that actualizations of Obama
Hope could actually spread desires for progress, hope, and change
(which appropriated biological needs for a better quality of life), they
began repeating and imitating this social invention of desire to achieve
goals similar to Fairey's and the Obama campaign's. People also began
adapting Obama Hope for other goals that often ran counter to its pro-
Obama purposes. Yet, as Tarde puts it, "There is nothing more imitative
than fighting against one's natural inclination to follow the current . . .,
or than pretending to go against it" (qtd. in Sampson, xvii). By becoming a rhetorical adversary and appropriating Obama Hope's style, content, or arrangement for alternative justifications, "one simply becomes
more and more associated in the assemblage of imitation" (Sampson,
190) and more and more co-responsible for a visual thing's viral

transformation and circulation. Thus, no matter whether Obama Hope was circulating and transforming in support of Obama, to sell random services, or to critique Obama, it experienced viral contagion as a countless multiplicity of actualized versions of Obama Hope materialized.

Despite such divergent actualizations, however, images such as Obama Hope maintain some sense of wholeness, allowing us to recognize their presence in various actualizations and account for their complex rhetorical life. This sense of wholeness is evident when you type *Obama Hope* into Google Images. Sure, a few random pictures of Obama show up in the gallery, but for the most part, Obama Hope materializes in a variety of pictures, most often in digital reproductions of Fairey's *Hope* poster but also in political cartoons, remixed Obamicons, and a variety of crafts. Such is also the case when you type in *Raised Fist*. Many pictures of the band Raised Fist appear in the gallery, but you also find traces of the rhetorical activity of the image working to fight for justice in the Occupy movement, advertising cultural events, protesting in various strikes, and advocating for white pride, among a constellation of other enactments. In such instances, the Raised Fist is rarely repeated exactly in form. Variations exist in color, style, composition, and relation to other images within a picture as well as medium. Yet as an image that transcends media, the Raised Fist haunts and materializes in all these various actualizations, as does Obama Hope in relation to its particular manifestations. Such repetition and reproduction across media and pictures helps stabilize these images' identities even as it must be acknowledged that they actually are always in flux in terms of form, location, and function.

CHRONOTOPIC LAMINATION

While such processes of stabilization are interesting, the new materialist rhetorical approach is more interested in accounting for a single multiple image's flux, especially its rhetorical transformation. This approach, especially when studying new media images, demands adopting not only an intuitive, nonmodern perspective that sees things as undergoing constant change but also a nonlinear spatiotemporal perspective. Rather than thinking of transformation in terms of chronology (extending through space in sequential moments of time), then, transformation is understood as unfolding in divergent, nonlinear spatial configurations at different temporal intensities—a perspective that is characteristic of ICT time described earlier. To ground this point, we might think of this spatiotemporal process in terms of chronotopes.

Chronotope, as a concept, recognizes the relativity of time and space. As defined by Mikhail Bakhtin (1981), a chronotope refers to the intrinsic connectedness of temporal and spatial relationships artistically expressed in literature (84–85). However, as I understand them, chronotopes can also be thought of as distinct yet interlaminating spatiotemporal configurations that unfold during any given activity. Consider, as an example, an investigation conducted by a collective of sleuths composed of journalists, art collectors, and computer programmers, among others, intra-acting with a variety of digital technologies to solve what would come to be called by those involved as the Obama Hope Photo Mystery. Important to know is that when Fairey was first asked which source photo he used for his Obama *Hope* poster, Fairey said he could not recall where he found the photo. Unsatisfied with not knowing what photo Fairey used as a reference, Obama Hope became the subject of an intense investigation to find the original source of the *Hope* poster, which by that time had become quite famous. Such collective activity, as I detail in chapter 7, entailed an interlaminated network of private investigations, enacted by different configurations of people, technologies, and institutions, that took place in different locations and for different periods of time. As such private investigations unfolded, Obama Hope transformed in different ways as many different players began messing with its original instantiation in Mannie Garcia's photograph to see if it matched up with Fairey's stylized version in Obama *Hope* (see Figure 2.5). Such rhetorical transformation that unfolded as a spatiotemporal process—or what Prior and Shipka (2003) might draw on Bahktin to call "chronotopic lamination"—did not unfold in regular, predictable patterns. Nor could many of the private investigations have been foreseen, as some activity in the collective investigation fed off the other private investigations while other investigations took place simultaneously unbeknownst to others in the collective. Because each event in this collective investigation had its own individual time and carved out is own distinct space, the chronotopic layers of activity constituting this collective investigation unfolded in a relative, aperiodic, and indeterminate fashion.

From a new materialist perspective, this chronotopic understanding of time is key to conceiving of and studying how a single multiple image becomes rhetorical over its lifetime as it materializes in different versions, each with their own spatiotemporal configuration. Time here is understood as being discontinuous in the sense that while, say, an image is conceived as a spatiotemporally distended event and thus experiences virtual duration, the process of materialization, or actualization, is not durational for the entire life span of that visual thing. Instead, a

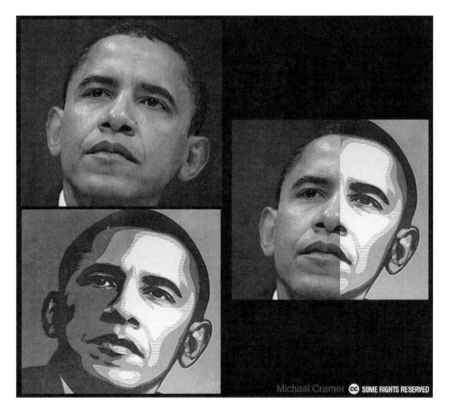

Figure 2.5. Photoshop Manipulation of Obama Hope, *Mike Cramer, 2009. (CC BY-SA 2.0).*

multiplicity of various spatiotemporal configurations unfolds with varying intensities, each of which constitutes an image's eventfulness. An image, one could say, is a distributed event constituted by many micro-events. This point is especially important to understand for a theory of visual rhetoric founded on the notion of becoming. Typically, we might think of becoming as one continuous process that exists into eternity. However, the rhetorical transformation of an image unfolds at differing speeds and in different spatial configurations, depending on what kinds of actualizations it emerges in, on whether these actualizations manifest in physical or cyberspace, and any number of structures of networks, coded infrastructures, and institutional, economic, political, or personal factors that may shape their design, production, distribution, circulation, and maintenance.[21]

At any given time, for instance, the Obama Hope image may be concurrently actualizing on the streets of Santa Fe in a pro-Obama mural that takes five hours for artists to create; in a mosaic created out of credit cards that takes three days to complete; or in a digital remix composed in Photoshop by investigators in the Obama Hope Photo Mystery case over the span of forty-five minutes. While the mural may stay in tact for only two months before it is painted over by people with dissenting political views, the mosaic may be preserved in a craft museum or personal home and live for one hundred years. The digital remix, on the other hand, may remain uploaded on some of the investigators' blogs, where it remains visible for five years but then disappears when an investigator decides to take down their entire blog or the site becomes inaccessible for a number of reasons. Such chronotopic activity and differenciation does not happen in a neat, easily mappable, linear fashion. This nonlinear spatio-temporal configuration is especially the case in a participatory, networked culture in which Internet and digital technologies (ie. codes, algorithms, protocols, etc.) are so involved in a thing's circulation. The new materialist rhetorical approach herein thus relinquishes chronological concepts of time that make possible and create desires for neat narrative accounts of rhetorical transformation. Instead, this approach embraces the immediacy and nonlinearity that ICT time and chronotopic understandings of time demand and acknowledges how transformation actually unfolds in seemingly simultaneous and divergent ways.

While a new materialist rhetorical approach is concerned with how images experience a constant state of divergent transformations, it also recognizes that as images actualize in different versions via their relations, they become rhetorically consequential, or meaningful, in divergent ways. These consequences are multitudinous in and of themselves, begin to take on lives of their own, and stimulate more rhetorical activity. In this sense, images often spark an explosion of rhetorical activities that unfold in divergent spatiotemporal configurations across the globe and accelerate their own circulation. As I articulate in the following section, we often miss the opportunity to study such distributed activity and widespread consequentiality because, in an effort to locate the meaning of a visual text, we are too busy going back to events that happened before an image's initial production and delivery. A new materialist rhetorical approach turns to futurity to locate meaning in the unbridled multiplicity of a single multiple image's material encounters and consequences. Making a philosophical move toward meaning consequentialism and a methodological move toward disclosure can be particularly productive in this regard.

TIME, SPACE, AND MEANING

Meaning has long been thought to be recoverable from the still life of rhetoric by an astute reader capable of decoding and interpreting the compositional elements that reside within an already delivered text, picture, or other material artifact. Much work with visual rhetoric tries to decode various signs within pictures and identify how the associations between verbal and nonverbal signs generate meaning via their interaction. Such scholarship is grounded in the pervasive assumption that even though pictures have no intrinsic meaning, pictures embody meaning, or representational content, that can be fleshed out in semantic terms (Vivian 2007, 476). Such a notion pushes scholars to discover how persuasive influence is made possible with the use of purposeful, decipherable appeals that are actually foreign to the things themselves (476). In treating pictures and other visual things as texts and/or arguments, the power and meaning that pictures are presumed to embody can be interpreted and made clear, especially if read within specific contexts.

This representational approach to visual rhetoric has been influenced by semiotics, especially as developed by Charles Peirce, which focuses on signification within context. Whereas Saussure's structuralism pushed investigations of signs to unlock how language is constituted by a system of signs, Peirce's semiotics, especially with its focus on icon, index, and symbol, demonstrated that signs do not have definite or stable meanings. From this perspective, our job as scholars is to interpret and determine how signs-in-use function not only as a tool for communication but also to make meaning as a mediator between subject, reality, and community (Hum 1996). While Peirce's body of work on signs has yet to be fully taken advantage of in rhetorical study, his work especially influenced, among others, I. A. Richards, who made the influential argument that meanings are derived from immediate context and past experiences of use. Richards, more specifically, worked to debunk the "proper meaning superstition," which holds that a word or sign has only one meaning, independent of context. He argued that all discourse has a multiplicity of meanings since the meaning of signs shifts from context to context and is derived from a text as a result of interaction among writer, text, *and* reader. Scholars can thus identify possible meanings of a text by using past experiences to make associations and interpreting signs at work within that text in their immediate context. Such semiotic and rhetorical theories have become the foundation of visual rhetoric today as much scholarship works hard to interpret how the production of visual rhetoric within a specific context influences human thoughts and behaviors.

Yet while semiotics and its influence on new rhetoric must certainly be credited for popularizing representational approaches to visual rhetoric, cultural studies has also played a significant role. The influence of cultural studies has not only helped expand the range of "texts" considered for rhetorical observation but also boosted poststructuralist modes of rhetorical investigation (Berlin 1996). As Barbara Stafford (1998) has argued, the poststructuralist move toward decoding language pushes scholars to treat all "artifacts, behavior and culture as if they were layered pages in a book demanding sustained decoding" (6). This tendency to decode encourages scholars to investigate practically everything but especially visual things as "texts" that need to be "analyzed, critiqued, and demystified by the expert readings of specialist critics" (Trimbur 2000, 197). This perspective is especially evident in a rhetorico-hermeneutic disposition that has come to govern much visual rhetorical study—a disposition, based in strong, suspicious social constructionism, that positions visual phenomena as vehicles of meaning, instruments of power, projections of ideology, or technologies of domination (Mitchell 2005). In all these cases, visual things are presumed to "'make or negotiate meaning' *a priori*"—a presumption which again "assigns representational, or immaterial, significance to an image's material, non-linguistic dimensions" (Vivian 2007, 475–76). Thus, in much study of visual rhetorics, researchers look to the compositional elements and strategies within a visual object to locate and interpret the hidden meaning and ideologies represented therein. It is no surprise, then, that questions commonly asked are: What rhetorical power is made possible via the interplay of signs within the visual? How is meaning created by rhetorical choices the designer has made? And how does this power and meaning shape the way we come to be, know, see, and construct our world?

As Carole Blair (1999) argues, rhetoric has mostly been studied in such terms of symbolicity (and signification) because we have yet to come up with a model for accounting for some of its "most fundamental—arguably definitive—characteristics: its capacity for consequence and partisanship" (20). Consequence is rarely taken up as a central focus of rhetorical study because we hardly pay attention to futurity and what happens once rhetoric has been produced and initially distributed. And when consequence is taken up, we typically attend to the ways a rhetorical text accomplished its intended goals, thus perpetuating the notion that the rhetor's goals are the only measurable effect legitimate for rhetorical study (21). As such, we have yet to fully acknowledge that rhetoric has consequences that often exceed its intentional goals. Thus, just as we have yet to fully acknowledge rhetoric's dynamic qualities, we have yet to attend fully to its consequentialist ones. The problem with underemphasizing consequence in studies of visual rhetoric is that we evade not only an image's "ponderous, awesome materiality" (qtd. in Blair, 22) but also its complex distributed, rhetorical ontology and thus, as DeLuca and Wilferth (2009) put it so provocatively, its "madness, excess, and ecstasy" (para. 6).

Blair claims that in order to broaden our studies of rhetoric beyond effect (or goal fulfillment) to the actual consequences that emerge from material action, we must ask not what a text or artifact means but rather we ought be asking what a text does and what happens as a result of its existence—an argument echoed in DeLuca's and Wilferth's argument for letting go of the mindset and methods of print that undergird our interpretive, domesticating tendencies in visual rhetoric. While I agree with focusing on a visual thing's *doing* in practice, there is a way to theoretically reconfigure the meaning of visual things to account for consequences so that we do not have to altogether quit searching for meaning, as these scholars suggest. This reconfiguration can be described as making a shift from *meaning apriorism* to *meaning consequentialism.* In *Meaning, Language, and Time,* Kevin Porter (2006) describes this shift as a philosophical one toward discourse, but I think it can also be an important methodological shift for visual rhetoric. As such, I want to briefly elucidate how a shift from meaning apriorism to meaning consequentialism might help us rethink how we look for meaning in studies of visual matter. As will become clear, this shift is especially important for disclosing how things become rhetorical with time and space.

DISCLOSING CONSEQUENTIALITY

Meaning apriorism can be understood as the assumption that the meaning of a thing is always to be found in or grounded by something temporally or logically prior to that thing or to any interpretation of it. In this assumption, meaning is "marked by *retrogressivity:* The movement of meaning is a movement backwards in time" (Porter 2006, 44). Working under this assumption, when we search for rhetorical meaning in studies of visual rhetoric, we investigate what happened before an actualized image has entered into association with other entities, including ourselves—the rhetorical situation in which it was produced, the compositional design strategies, and so forth. In opposition to meaning apriorism is meaning consequentialism—the assumption that the meaning of a thing is constituted by the consequences it propagates (12). From this latter perspective, meaning is not contained within a picture, nor can it be traced back to something that happened prior to its trigger of consequentiality. Therefore, in terms of visual rhetoric, analysis of a picture's composition in relation to its original audience, genre, context, and so forth, is rendered insufficient in determining rhetorical meaning. Instead, meaning is believed to be temporally and spatially distended (54). As an image materializes in various renditions, different outcomes arise as a consequence of that single multiple image's actualizations and intra-actions in various collectives. Meaning can thus rather be ascertained by tracing the often inconsistent and unpredictable consequences that propagate after an image emerges as a particular material version. Looking back is necessary, but working under the assumption of meaning consequentialism, scholars would largely work to disclose or bring to light the material consequences that propagate after an image has already been produced, begun to circulate, and entered into various associations.

Disclosure is a term I use to give name to a methodological strategy that can help account for the material consequences that emerge in a distributed reality. Disclosure in this context is not to be confused with Susan Hekman's use of the term in *The Material of Knowledge* (Hekman 2010). There, Hekman argues that since reality can be brought to light, or disclosed, from different perspectives, it is useful to compare the material consequences of such disclosures and make arguments about certain advantages of some over others rather than declare one to be more right, truthful, or objective. While I agree with such a suggestion, here I deploy disclosure as a means to shed light on not only a single image's divergent actualizations but also on the divergent meanings that propagate as material consequences of a single multiple image's varied relations. Within such multiplicity of consequences, human interpretations are considered important consequences. Yet consequences "extend beyond human cognition and into the material world" (Porter 2006, 53). As became clear in both the brief vignette about Mona Lisa and the Obama Hope Photo Mystery, visual things acquire thing-power as they enter into all kinds of material relations; as such, they have potential to spark all kinds of material consequences and reconfigure collective space in various dimensions. Meaning consequentialism pushes us to see that a single multiple image's meaning—its consequentiality—is thus as distributed as its virtual-actual constitution.

When we work to disclose a single multiple image's material consequences, we can see how things become rhetorically meaningful in ways just as inconsistent and unpredictable as the formation of the things themselves. During rhetorical transformation, meaning splinters. As an

Figure 2.6. Remix of Pepper Spray Cop, Mary Madigan, 2011. (CC BY 2.0).

image actualizes in various versions, each of which experiences its own spatiotemporal configuration, divergent consequences materialize that also endure[22] for different periods of time. The time (and space) in which each consequence unfolds is dependent on a number of affective, psychological, physical, historical, political, cultural, semiotic, and biological dimensions. In some cases, as will likely be the case in the battle over copyright and fair use in which Obama Hope has become embroiled, it might take generations for some actual changes to come about even if visual things are intently and continuously working for specific persuasive purposes.[23] In other instances, especially with the immediacy made possible by digital technologies, visible change occurs within hours or days after an image actualizes in cyberspace. Consider, for example, the case of the image that has now become known as the Pepper Spray Cop. This image first materialized in Louise Macabitas's photograph depicting Lieutenant John Pike pepper spraying students at an Occupy protest in November 2011 at UC Davis. Within two days after Macabitas's photograph was posted to Reddit, the photograph itself began to circulate broadly, showing up on various new sites and blogs where it stimulated discussions about everything from police brutality to the dangers of pepper spray to the role of the cell phone in gathering news and inciting activism. However, especially as anger and disbelief about the incident spread, remixes of Pepper Spray Cop (see Figure 2.6) also began to circulate on Facebook and other social media sites, where this single multiple image often sparked heated discussions across the blogosphere. The consequentiality, the meaning, of Pepper Spray Cop is thus inconsistent and aperiodic. Just as it can be said that images have their own unique life spans, we can think of differing consequences having their own life spans as well.

Due to such inconsistencies—and especially because we cannot presume the stability of an image's meaning just as we cannot presume its stability of form—it becomes difficult to account for single multiple image's distributed meaning. An image, much like an utterance, "has as many meanings at it has consequences" and "cannot be exhausted of meanings until it no longer generates consequences" (Porter 2006, 53). Things that propagate the fewest and most consistent consequences have the most stable meanings (56), making them easier to keep track of. But often, things have a multiplicity of meanings that simply go unnoticed by scholars because case studies are typically bound by certain contextual elements—place, time period, function, and so forth—and scholars are often most concerned with not only their intended effects but also the cognitive changes they spark, such as persuasion and interpretation. Obama Hope, for example, has become known as an important political actor in the 2008 presidential election because most of its consequences that have gained attention are related to galvanizing support for Obama. Yet this image has sparked numerous other traceable consequences as it has become a touchstone for debates about copyright; a poster child for new media literacy campaigns; an international activist; a social invention that sparks imitative behavior; and so forth. As such divergent consequences proliferate and Obama Hope's meaning becomes much less stable, the question becomes, how do we keep up with such propagating material consequences?

This methodological enterprise is especially difficult because a single multiple image's rhetorical meaning is unforeseeable. Once an image actualizes in divergent ways, consequences manifest beyond what Porter (2006) calls the "event horizon of meaning," which can be thought of, in relation to visual rhetoric, as the boundary between an actualized image and its consequences. According to theories of the event horizon, keep in mind, the future does not actually exist; it is "but a name for the infinity of nothingness that lies beyond the limit of the present" (260). Thus, we always exist in the present, and we always "fall through" an event horizon into an uncertain future (260). The event horizon, then, "marks the boundary of the eventfulness of the present"; what occurs beyond this mark cannot be predetermined. Accordingly, the meanings that exist beyond an event are also indeterminate. Even if we make accurate predictions about the future of an image's meanings, we cannot "*see* past the event horizon of meaning" (261). Thus, we cannot know what consequences will arise "because there is nothing beyond the event horizon to be seen or known" (261). In other words, it is only in tracing a single multiple image's transformations that unfold with time and space that we can discover what divergent consequences emerge and thus know for certain what rhetorical meanings have materialized.

Working from meaning consequentialism, the new materialist rhetorical approach herein looks to futurity and works hard to empirically account for the unforeseeable rhetorical meanings that emerge after a visual thing's initial production and distribution. This is not to say that a single multiple image's consequences cannot and should not to be identified before its initial composition and production. Ideas, feelings, and affects—what Phelps (1985) has called "precursors to writing"—are all important consequences that often emerge before the initial composing process begins. Even as such consequences to the body get played out in chronotopic laminations, cannot be easily traced, and thus are often ignored, they contribute to the entire process of rhetorical transformation and thus ought to be accounted for. When possible, then, a researcher should try to recover the designer's/creator's own explanations of their feelings and even intentions and realizations to account for a fuller range of consequences. However, we still know little about rhetoric's consequentiality, specifically how a divergent range of meanings unfolds during the life span of an image's distributed reality. In taking a new materialist approach to visual rhetoric, then, investigation mainly focuses on the divergent rhetorical meanings that arise as images flow and transform unpredictably beyond the initial moment of production and delivery.

CONCLUSION

During this investigation, as the next chapter makes clear, thinking ecologically about rhetoric is as important to the new materialist rhetorical approach herein as is thinking intuitively. While intuitive thinking, as I have suggested in this chapter, helps draw attention to a visual thing's dynamic, unfolding dimensions, thinking ecologically helps disclose how visual things come to matter via their complex, emergent relations. As you will find, a new materialist perspective holds that things exist independently from our conception of them. Things are out there circulating, influencing actions, and bending space in divergent ways that cannot be fully captured by our perceptions and studies. To put it simply, things are vital assemblages that both have lives of their own and influence the lives of others. Yet, even though things have a reality and co-constitute reality (and are not fixed nor stable), when we come into association with them, our perceptions intervene as do other involved entities in a particular association, influencing the co-constitution of that thing. In Bergson's (2007) terms, as discussed in this chapter, we take a snapshot of a thing's or event's mobility, and in Barad's (2007) terms to be discussed in the following chapter, we make an agential cut with which we separate ourselves ontologically from the thing or event as we make judgments about its rhetorical existence. In this sense, the things we study are complex paradoxes. They both exist in their own right and come into being when we encounter them. As discussed in this chapter, single multiple images are also coming into being, stimulating material consequences in divergent ways and continuing to transform as they are engaging in multiple assemblages at seemingly simultaneous moments. Because their reality and consequentiality is distributed, this ontological paradox is thus even more complex. How do we account for such a distributed ontology and consequentiality to help explain the ways a single, multiple image becomes rhetorical as it reassembles collective space? This is the question I continue to explore from an ecological perspective in the following chapter.

Notes

1. Parts of this chapter have been adapted for my chapter "On Rhetorical Becoming" in *Rhetorical Ontologies: Rhetoric through Everyday Things*, edited by Casey Boyle and Scot Barnett and forthcoming with the University of Alabama Press.
2. An event under study is always influenced by a scholar's own actions (Barad 2007; Law 2005). As we intra-act with the things we study, our own subjectivities and actions as well as the phenomena under study are impacted. In this book, for instance, Obama Hope acts as a representative anecdote and an example for the ways in which images become rhetorical with time and space. As such, its rhetorical function here contributes to its circulation and consequentiality.
3. I use the phrase *networks of becomings* to emphasize that an image does not unfold in a single-threaded, sequential, continuous manner but rather along divergent and seemingly simultaneous spatiotemporal channels.
4. Because this book is focused on visual rhetoric, I use images as examples to discuss rhetorical transformation from a new materialist and intuitive perspective. However, I believe we can just as easily think about a certain concept, story, or figure.
5. The Raised Fist has dates back to ancient Assyrian stele and pre-Columbian earthenware, making it a fascinating object of study for rhetorical biographies (see chapter 10).
6. This perspective is dependent on linear reductionism that derives from teleological approaches to knowledge as well as philosophical and scientific frameworks, espe-

cially mechanism and scientific determinism—all of which have infiltrated indus- trialized ways of knowing (see Barry Brummett's [1976] "Some Implications of 'Process' or 'Intersubjectivity': Postmodern Rhetoric").

7. In *Network Culture*, Terranova (2004) defines the outernet as "the network of social, cultural and economic relationships which criss-crosses and exceeds the Internet— surrounds and connects the latter to larger flows of labor, culture and power" (75).

8. According to Castells (2009), in network society's construction of time and space (ICT time), "being cancels becoming" (35). However, I would argue that this dia- lectical understanding of time and space is unproductive. If we track the rhetorical transformation of something such as Obama Hope, we can see how something can be emerging in seemingly simultaneous events yet also experiencing transforma- tion over the *longue durée*. Annemarie Mol's (2002) notion of the body multiple, discussed later in this chapter, helps explain how a single thing can experience both simultaneous eventfulness and divergent becoming.

9. *Multiplicity* here refers to the state of things in which no totality or unity exists, only multidimensional relationality. *Constant* refers to the fact that "now" is not a static moment in time but rather is a "now" always undergoing a process of trans- formation.

10. These quotes are taken from Socrates's account of Protagoras's philosophy in Plato's *Theatetus*.

11. Images, of course, are not the only nonhuman things to experience rhetorical transformation. Concepts, artifacts, ideas, and so forth also become rhetorical with time and space as they are taken up in diverse ways by various actors. See Steven Mailloux's (2006) "Places in Time: The Inns and Outhouses of Rhetoric."

12. Obamicons are digitally born posters produced in the Obama Hope style via an array of digital technologies. For more on Obamicons, see chapter 9.

13. To be clear, when I refer to Mona Lisa, I am referring to the icon of the woman who first appeared in da Vinci's painting, the *Mona Lisa*, but who like other images transcends media and materializes in diverse material supports. To differentiate the image from da Vinci's painting, I do not italicize the image's name as I do when I am referring to da Vinci's painting.

14. To see Badaran's AR Object, go to http://amirbaradaran.com/ab_futarism_mona lisa.php. While it is beyond the scope of this book to explore AR technologies, such projects complicate rhetorical transformation as they multiply the layers of pictures one is looking at within a given place and moment. In doing so, AR objects appear to change relations between viewers, visual things, and environment; generate new visual, sonic, tactile, or textual associations; and complicate our understanding of how images move in a world of, as John Tinnell (2014) puts it, "post-desk-top circulation" (11).

15. Numerous software programs as well as apps have been created specifically for generating pictures in the Obama Hope style. See chapter 8 for more on digital technologies specifically designed to create Obamicons.

16. Here, I draw on Jeff Rice's (2011) work with Henri Lefebvre (1991) to empha- size that "'spaces are produced' as a variety of forces come into contact with one another on an everyday basis" (11). These forces include institutional, economic, and political factors that construct a network or set of networks, yet also "non- instrumental or non-structural modes of communicative organization: feeling, sensation, and intuition" (12). Yet, I also draw on Steven Shaviro's (2009) work in *Without Criteria*, who, in commenting on Whitehead's "reformed subjectivist principle," reminds us that "time is not given in advance; it needs to be effectively produced, or constructed, in the course of subjective experience. . . . Time is pro- duced in and through experience; and experience, in turn, is implicitly temporal"

(77). Such subjective experience is not limited to human entities but is extended to all entities, which, according to Whitehead, are subjects (77).

17. Here, I diverge from Deleuze's monist perspective of the virtual, which suggests that discrete entities emerge from a single virtual substance. My thinking about the virtual is thus more in line with what Levi Bryant calls a "virtual proper being," which is a dimension of every individual thing that acts as a generative mechanism. See Bryant's (2011) *The Democracy of Objects*.

18. In *Difference and Repetition*, Deleuze (1994) makes distinctions between differentiation and differenciation. While differentiation entails the "determination of the virtual content of an Idea," differenciation refers to the "actualisation of that virtuality in species and distinguished parts" (207).

19. I want to thank Doug Walls for turning me onto Mol's work at the Computers and Writing Conference in May of 2012.

20. The "Obama Works" is a phrase used in the official complaint that Fairey and his lawyers filed against the AP Press (See vs. AP [2009] titled "Complaint for Declaratory Judgment and Injunctive Relief"). It refers to Fairey's "series of works designed to capture the optimism and inspiration created by Obama's candidacy . . . through which Fairey hoped to compel further support for Obama" (3).

21. By structures of network, I am drawing on Nahon's and Hemsley's (2013) work in *Going Viral* to refer to both "the rules, practices, and arrangements through which the behavior of people is regulated in networks" and "the typology of interconnected nodes," as discussed by Castells (2009), that influence social networks (81–82). By computer infrastructures, I am referring to the coding, algorithms, digital protocols, etc. that influence how images and pictures, among other things, circulate on the web. This includes coded infrastructures, which, as discussed by Kitchen and Dodge (2014) in *Code/Space: Software and Everyday Life*, includes computing networks, broadcast entertainment networks, cellular networks, etc. that are productive of space and influential in our everyday life. See also David Beer's (2013) *Popular Culture and New Media: The Politics of Circulation*.

22. Such inconsistency has led anthropologist and visual culture scholar Christopher Pinney (2005) to "treat images as unpredictable 'compressed performances' caught up in recursive trajectories of repetition and pastiche whose dense complexity makes them resistant to any particular moment" (266).

23. A consequence can also be affective, resulting in a brief change of bodily experience that may last for only an instant. See chapter 3 in this book for more on rhetoric and affect.

3

AGENTIAL MATTERS[1]

Ecology shows us that all beings are connected. The ecological thought
is the thinking of interconnectedness. The ecological thought doesn't
just occur "in the mind." It's a practice and a process of becoming fully
aware of how human beings are connected with other beings.
— Timothy Morton, *The Ecological Thought*

Ecology is predicated on the belief that biological and social worlds
are jointly composed of dynamic networks of organisms and environments that have different spatiotemporal configurations and are inter-
dependent, diverse, and responsive to feedback. In the simplest terms,
to consider something from an ecological perspective is to recognize
its vital implication in networked systems of relations. In less simple
terms, thinking ecologically acknowledges the dynamic complexity of
these networked systems, the interrelated, laminated layers of activities that constitute them, and the mutual transformation that occurs
among intertwined elements. In relation to rhetoric and writing, thinking ecologically has resulted in much productive scholarship. Among
some of its most provocative uses, an ecological perspective has helped
introduce new models for writing (Cooper 1986); develop new research
approaches for composition (Dobrin and Weisser 2001; Syverson 1999)
and genre studies (Spinuzzi 2003) ; craft new conceptions (Phelps 1988)
and histories of rhetoric and composition (Hawk 2007); and revise
rhetorical theory by challenging our notions of the rhetorical canons
(Brooke 2009; Prior et al. 2007), the rhetorical situation (Edbauer Rice
2005), and rhetorical agency (Cooper 1986; Herndl and Licona 2007;
Miller 2007). The study of visual rhetoric, however, has yet to take full
advantage of ecological thinking, especially the kind of relational thinking undergirding much work in new materialism that has the potential
to give images "their due."

To give things their due in rhetorical study, in the simplest terms,
means acknowledging the multiplicity of active and diverse rhetorical contributions things make to collective life. As images actualize in

DOI: 10.7330/9780874219784.c003

various versions and enter into divergent associations, they become a material force that generates ripples of collective change. Such alteration of bodies and space is dependent on the compositional design of visual things; certainly the rhetorical strategies and semiotic resources at work within an actualized image influence its ability to generate collective action. However, when trying to account for how a single multiple image becomes rhetorical with time and space as it reassembles collective life, we must be carefully about giving too much credit to a visual things' interior dimensions or interior relations. Such undermining, in Graham Harman's (2011) terms, fails to recognize that in addition to a visual thing's compositional design, a thing's external relations are just as important in creating the conditions necessary for manipulating reality. Agency—an act of intervention—is not some capacity that any single image has and carries with it just as it is not some capacity that any single person has. Agency is a doing, an enactment generated by a variety of components intra-acting within a particular phenomenon (Barad 235). In addition to acknowledging an actualized image's interior relations (design, content, arrangement, etc.), then, simultaneously zooming in on a single multiple image's emergent, exterior relations helps discover how something becomes rhetorical with time and space as it participates in a distributed dance of agency with other entities.

This new materialist perspective, I believe, maps nicely onto the ecological sensibility toward agency that has emerged in recent years in rhetorical study but has yet to be fully considered in visual rhetoric. Especially evident in contemporary rhetorical theory is the growing awareness that agency is both multidimensional and dispersed among author, audience, technologies, and environment. Karilyn Kohrs Campbell (2005), for instance, argues that agency is "communal, social, cooperative, and participatory and, simultaneously constituted and constrained by the material and symbolic elements of context and culture" (3). For Carl G. Herndl and Adela C. Licona (2007), agency "arises from the intersection of material, (con)textual, and ideological conditions and practices (14) while John Louis Lucaites and Celeste Michelle Condit posit agency as being "bound in relationship, rather than the solitary product of some sort of determinism" (Lucaites and Condit 1999, 612). Carolyn Miller (2007) even goes so far to define agency as "the kinetic energy of rhetorical performance," which does not exist prior to or as a result of that performance but rather is a property of the performance itself (137). Similarly, the new materialist perspectives of vitality, agency, and actancy presented in this chapter try to make clear how rhetoric emerges from a dynamic assemblage of entities, each with its own historicity and propensity for efficacy, each involved in ongoing intra-actional enactments. As I explain in more detail below, as an image such as Obama Hope enters into a distributed dance of agency within and across dynamic assemblages of people and other things, it not only experiences but produces rhetorical transformation. It is only via the divergent *intra-actions*[2] between human and nonhuman entities in an unfolding network of assemblages, I argue, that an image emerges as a generative, distributed, material force in the world.

As rhetoricians, of course, we have long acknowledged that rhetoric matters. Visual rhetoric scholars, especially, push hard to argue that visual things make active contributions to civic life. But I am not convinced that our rhetorical theories and research methods work hard enough to make visible *how* visual things, in all of their complexity, actually matter to collective life. For reasons previously discussed, representational and synchronic approaches to visual rhetoric especially fall short of providing convincing accounts that visual things shape reality in the ways scholars argue they do. Studies limited by context, time, function, influence, or scale especially cannot fully account for a single image's rhetorical complexity. I would also argue that the relation between visual rhetoric and affective contagion has not been adequately explored to account for how visual things move other bodies to imitate feelings, thoughts, and actions. As a consequence, we are left with a belief that visual things play an important role in constructing our world and little empirical evidence to demonstrate how that actually happens. We need theories and empirical methods that better account for an image's intense, unfolding, and distributed materialization in order to make visible how they become consequential in divergent ways. As Hariman and Lucaites (2007) model for us in *No Caption Needed*, visual rhetoric scholars can do a better job of making visible how visual things actually contribute to public life.

Thinking ecologically about visual matter from a new materialist perspective is useful in this regard as it pushes us to disclose the messy lives of those visual things with which we are intensely interconnected and via which collective life is co-constructed. In this chapter, I specifically articulate how not only assemblage theories but also recent developments in vital materialism,[3] distributed cognition, agential realism,[4] contagion theory, and actor-network theory can help disclose how rhetorical agency, or actancy, unfolds via an image's divergent intra-actions within and across phenomena. Using an affirmative method, I specifically advocate for adopting a new materialist sensibility toward images that recognizes their distributed *vitality*—their tendency to endure across various forms and catalyze change as each of their manifestations intra-acts with humans and other nonhuman entities.

VITALITY, MATERIALITY, AND LIFE

Read almost any account today about the *Mona Lisa* and you will find allusions to its vitality whether writers are referring to Mona Lisa's enigmatic smile or its remarkable power to attract tourists, art historians, and most recently archaeologists determined to dig up the ancient remains of Lisa Gherardini del Giocondo. The same is true in the case of Obama Hope. Many note that during the 2008 election season, it began to take on a life of its own when it materialized in Fairey's *Hope* poster. But many, as I discuss in chapter 8, also accuse the image of luring millions of naïve voters to fall for Obama's rhetoric and vote him into presidential history. Such discourse pushes us to explore why it is that many of us consider visual things to be alive, as if visual things have a power of their own not only to move but also to influence human thought and action.

Such thoughts about vitality, of course, are nothing new. As W.J.T. Mitchell (2005) discusses in *What Do Pictures Want?* things such as totems, fetishes, and idols have long been considered to be animated things that desire, demand, and even require things of us—food, money, blood, respect, and so forth (194). We might also think about various superstitions that accuse images of seducing people to act in various, even bizarre, ways. In ancient Scotland, as just one of many examples, people believed that they could cause injury to or even the deaths of people they disliked by making images in clay or wax of those people and then baptizing the actualized images in a ceremony during which the people depicted in the images would be able to feel whatever was being done to the images (Napier 2008, 88). In such conceptions, an "image possesses a kind of vital, living character that makes it capable of feeling what is done to it" Mitchell (2005, 127). As Mitchell insists, an image "is not merely a transparent medium for communicating a message but something like an animated, living thing . . ." (127).

In the past, many scholars have attributed such beliefs about vitality to the irrational, bewitched, and/or naive minds of uncivilized savages, non-Westerners, and/or premoderns. With the rise of new scientific and technical possibilities and the epidemiological social imaginary, such beliefs are also evident, however. One has only to consider, Mitchell notes, how pictures of Dolly, the cloned sheep, and the World Trade Center arouse certain feelings and behaviors or how viruses that infect not only bodies but also electronic networks and power grids evoke much contemporary anxiety. One also has only to consider how viral metaphors in reference to memes, YouTube videos, and GIFs have infiltrated popular discourse. In this climate, Mitchell is right when he says the slogan of our times is not "things fall apart" but rather "things come alive" (172). He is also right when he agrees with Latour in saying *we have never been modern.* "We are stuck with our magical, premodern attitudes toward objects, especially pictures," and "our task is not to overcome these attitudes but to understand them" (Mitchell 2005, 30).

Mitchell argues that such contemporary attitudes toward things are rooted in romanticism. During this era, the mysterious life force of physical things became a lively concern as biology came to the forefront of intellectual matters, mechanistic understandings of the world were challenged, and the totem and fossil (images of nature that expressed new understandings between human and nonhuman things) took on cultural and scientific force.[5] We need to be careful of conflating vitalism with romanticism, however. As Catherine Packham (2012) has elucidated, romanticist concerns with vitalism were present in not only scientific and philosophical writings but also in literary, political, and cultural domains well before romanticism. Therefore, romanticist occupations with vitalism ought to be understood as a "step-change from writing and thinking of an earlier period" (208). Second, if we understand vitalism to be a set of philosophies and theories concerned with the simple, yet impossibly complex, inquiry "What is life?" then vitalism has been taken up differently across many different cultures, epistemes, periods, and schools of thought. As Byron Hawk (2007) has noted, while each explores this question within its own discourse and logics, "they are all trying to come to grips with what drives self-organization and development in the world" (4–5). Within the modern episteme alone, answers to this question have been quite diverse. Some who adhere to what Hawk calls "oppositional vitalism" have attributed life to something outside of and operating on the world. This something might be an external substance, a god, a universal vegetative force, or, for those who draw on theories of energy, a balance of magnetic and electrical forces that exert influence over organic processes (137). Others adhering to investigative vitalism have attributed life to something in the world, some kind of evolutionary and physico-chemical process. Still others attribute life to a complex ecology of material, biological, historical, social, linguistic, and technological processes, the combination of which produces emergence. Life from this latter perspective is indicative of a complex vitalism that arose in the twentieth century with the influence of quantum mechanics. From this perspective, life is situated in a complex, dynamic network of processes as opposed to some transcendent force or simply physico-chemical or biological processes (5).

The new materialist perspective offered herein is perhaps most in line with this latter kind of vitalism, as it is heavily influenced by assemblage theories, vital materialism, and agential realism—all of which push us to conceive of materiality in a relational, emergent, and contingent sense. To be explicit, this materialist perspective does not divorce life from materiality in that it does not buy into bifurcations that attribute lively activity to organic matter and inert passivity to inorganic matter. Instead all matter is thought to be constituted by a "contingent materialization—a process within which more or less enduring . . . assemblages sediment and congeal" (Coole and Frost 2010, 29). Life, in this sense then, is understood to be a generative, dynamic, and unpredictable affair driven not only by the process of differenciation as described in chapter 2 but also by a process of assemblage and reassemblage. As I briefly describe below, this process constantly takes place as a multiplicity of entangled entities within and across assemblages intra-act and catalyze change to collective space. In this conception of life and materiality, an actualized image is just one of countless vital assemblages[6] involved in the ongoing mattering of the world. Yet, like all other matter, it is an active and lively mediator that not only experiences but also produces rhetorical transformation.

(RE)ASSEMBLING COLLECTIVE LIFE

To be clear, assemblages, as conceived of here,[7] are composed of heterogeneous entities, both assemblage and entities of which are results of historical, natural, cultural, technological, biological, material, and semiotic processes. Assemblages exist on a single scale within a network of overlapping assemblages and have different spatiotemporal configurations so that while actualized versions of Obama Hope themselves may be considered visual-material assemblages constituted by intermingling components, they also become part of other assemblages in which they are co-involved with other entities. The entities or components that constitute assemblages have their own characteristics[8] and dynamics, have potential to enact change, and are separable from an assemblage in which they participate. Thanks to some of these components working to stabilize or maintain an assemblage in terms of space, time, semiotics, and/or rhetorics (a process called *territorialization*), assemblages can acquire a stable identity, which helps explain how, in Mol's terms, body multiples can be fragmented yet simultaneously maintain a sense of whole and be easily recognized. Yet assemblages are also composed of relations of exteriority, meaning that some of the components that constitute one assemblage, even ones that help stabilize it (such as the outlines of Obama's upper body in the case of Obama Hope), may detach from it and become part of a different assemblage in which they experience different intra-actions.[9] As such, while appearing stable—even concrete—assemblages such as Obama Hope are constantly in flux as they are always simultaneously undergoing a process of destabilization or dissipation (deterritorialization).

Furthermore, assemblages are actors in their own right. While assemblages are constituted by entities or components that in and of themselves influence outcome, assemblages themselves are also "living, throbbing confederations" (Bennett 2010, 33) that produce consequentiality. Consequentiality, as discussed in Chapter 2, does not result from some kind of linear causality or mechanized process. Rather, consequentiality emerges in nonlinear and unpredictable ways as the various components' own active, vital contributions get played out in complex ways as they respond to the other components within an assemblage. Consequentiality is also dependent on an assemblage's entanglements with other assemblages beyond it that are capable of influencing it. When Obama Hope first materialized in Fairey's poster and began to circulate, for instance, many people began responding to its design on various blogs. Some, of course, felt inspired by the design, yet others were moved to express dismay at what they perceived to be socialist propaganda. Entire heated discussions on various blogs even arose that took place for days on end. In this sense, as an assemblage in and of itself (constituted by various components such as lines, color, etc.) participating in other assemblages (of people, digital technologies, words, etc.), the Obama Hope image is vital in that its actions on the blog are vibrant, energetic, lively, and productive. As a phenomenon abuzz with vital materiality, it thus ought to be acknowledged as "a creative not-quite-human force capable of producing the new" (Bennett 2010, 18).

For visual things, especially ones that experience viral circulation and transformation, such a tendency to spark change goes far beyond communication and persuasion. Visual things are mediators, able to transform, modify, and rearrange collective space as they co-influence the assemblages of which they are and become a part. While I discuss other ways below, such assemblage often takes place as a consequence of a visual thing's ability to translate biological desires into social desires and produce affective encounters. Drawing on Sampson's explications of Tarde's social-epidemiological diagram, social inventions such as Obama

Hope exert an indirect mesmeric and magnetic force that attracts various entities into relation and induces imitative encounters. Such assemblage often takes place as a consequence of "an imitative-suggestibility passed on in the collective nonconscious" so that the biological desires appropriated, articulated, and transmitted by image-inventions such as Obama Hope "become etched onto the body and the porous self" (Sampson 2012, 36; Thrift 2008, 237). Such etching often goes on unacknowledged because affect "passes unconsciously through the skin into the vicerality of human experience, guiding automative [imitative] behavior before it moves *upstream* to the conscious reflective mind and dream of volition" (Sampson 140). As such, people may appear to be hypnotized and behaving unconsciously in certain ways without learning, practicing, thinking critically—a blind devotion and obedience of which we will see Obama supporters being accused. Yet, it is more likely that people (and perhaps other organic beings) often assemble because they are susceptible to affective contagions that trigger "the felt reality of relation" (qtd. in Sampson 93). This unconscious perception recognizes how the "individual body" is "always-already plugged into a collectivity" (Massumi 2002, 129) and moves people and other things to imitate the behaviors, feelings, and opinions of others with which they are in relation—an imitation that arises from conscious and unconscious actions working in concert with one another (Sampson 93). Visual things such as Obama Hope especially have the potential to simultaneously trigger such unconscious perceptions, unconscious and conscious imitative behaviors, and deliberate collective activity.

INCORPOREAL TRANSFORMATION

While such affective consequentiality of visual things is difficult to empirically disclose, it is perhaps most evident in the traces of evidence left behind by those who experience what Deleuze and Guattari (1987) call incorporeal transformation. Incorporeal transformation occurs when an entity experiences a transformation in identity, sense of purpose, position in society, or relations even as its body may not undergo significant change on the outside that can easily be detected. One commonly stated example is the transformation that a defendant being charged with murder experiences when a judge or jury passes down a guilty verdict. The verdict, in that instant, actually transforms the person into a criminal. While perhaps no significant change happens within the body that can be observed, the defendant's identity, social standing, and relationality to others are altered. As is evident in many testimonies and actions, a number of those who became involved with Obama Hope over the last few years experienced such incorporeal transformation. Tayyib Smith, for instance, is one of many people across the country who volunteered to distribute Obama *Hope* posters during the primary season of 2008. Smith, copublisher of *215 Magazine* and co-owner of Little Giant Creative Agency, is not by any means an inactive character; he has been labeled by Garron Gibbs (2013) as "one of the most influential figures in Philadelphia." However, Smith discussed how transformed he felt during his intra-actions with Obama *Hope*: "In '08, I had the opportunity to volunteer my resources to the Obama campaign by way of the Shepard Fairey poster initiative; our office was the central point of distribution for all of PA; it gave me an eye opening perspective how someone like myself who traditionally would be excluded from [such] an active role [in] politics could use my skill set to be an agent of change, forming, or re-forecasting public opinion" (qtd. in Ruffin 2010). This transformation was not momentary for Smith; due to this experience, he became "open to exploring future opportunities to put ideas into action in pursuit of civic good" (qtd. in Ruffin 2010).

As such transformation happens on an individual level for many who come into relations with visual things such as Obama Hope, the transformative feeling often becomes infectious, leading to reassemblage of collective life. In this sense, Obama Hope functions as constitutive rhetoric in that it calls not only a collective identity (White 2010, 37) but also collective action into existence (Sloane 2001, 617). Such transformation is especially evident with the Obama art movement. As is evident in the work of artists such as Michael Murphy and Ray Noland, art for Obama began popping up across the country prior to the birth of Obama Hope. However, many artists who encountered Obama Hope and witnessed its ability to spread and spark change clearly were inspired to become politically active, create their own art for Obama, and join forces with others to catalyze change. Not only do artists testify to such transformation, but their new, often imitative behaviors provide evidence of how such transformation helped mobilize the Obama art movement. Toward the end of the campaign in 2008, for instance, Obama Hope was transformed into a seven thousand-square-foot installation of land art in rural Pennsylvania (see Figure 3.1). Jim Lennox, the artist responsible for this installation, was moved to complete this project, which took over sixty hours to create, when the media began reporting that Obama might not win Pennsylvania, especially because he lacked support in rural settings. Lennox had first seen Obama Hope while walking past the Obama campaign office in Wilkes-Barre but then began seeing it "all over the

Figure 3.1. Field of Hope, *Jim Lennox, 2008. Photograph courtesy of Lennox.*

Internet." Lennox chose to rework the Obama Hope poster over other choices because he felt it was the most inspiring picture he had encountered all election season. His land installation was surely intended to show support for Obama, but Lennox (pers. comm.) claims his main purpose was to "to show that when a person has an inspiration, and that person creates a plan to execute that inspiration, follows with the work required to complete the project, transformation happens. That's how things change." For all those who didn't believe in change, he wanted— like Fairey, Noland, and others—to use art to lift consciousness and express the belief that "we can do better."

Margaret Coble (2009), an artist from New Orleans, is another who wanted to support Obama's campaign, but like many other others she did not have the financial means to do so. So to do her part, she created a *Believe* stencil design and sold it as prints and on t-shirts, generating a total of $600 from the sales of her own work. With the help of Yosi Sergant, Coble also created bike-spoke cards from this design, which were mailed to Portland, Oregon, where they could soon be seen spinning around town working to garner votes for Obama (see Figure 3.2).

Figure 3.2. Believe *Bike Spokes, Art by Margaret Coble, 2008. Photograph Courtesy of Yosi Sergant.*

As she explains, "I was originally inspired by the Shepard Fairey's now iconic 'Hope' and 'Progress' posters of Obama, which spread like wildfire throughout the underground street-art community and then eventually hit mainstream pop culture and were embraced by the campaign itself. I felt like this was the most important election of my adult life, so I wanted to do my part as an artist—however small—to help his campaign." Artists Rafael Lopez (pers. comm.), one of the nine Artists for Obama who was hired to design art for the official Obama campaign (see chapter 6), also explains that Obama Hope became a cultural icon that inspired him to produce his own Obama art. By invoking so many artists such as himself to work for change, Lopez claims Obama Hope helped galvanize an entire grassroots movement committed to political activism.

Chapter 9 discloses how Obama Hope's transformative and constitutive power in the movement is undeniable, as hundreds of craftspeople and artists took up Obama Hope for their own creative efforts to get on the rhetorical bandwagon during the election. Because visual things such as Obama Hope helped transform people's lives and catalyze the emergence of novel assemblages in such ways, from a new materialist perspective the visual things we so often deem to lack vitality acquire much more power than we may acknowledge. Although in any given phenomenon, different entities have different types and degrees of power, visual things, in their various encounters, often become active, creative, and dynamic forces that co-constitute collective change. Such attitudes toward life and visual things admittedly reek of monism and anthropomorphism, but from a vital materialist perspective, a touch of monism and anthropomorphism is healthy for cultivating an ecological sensibility toward visual things so that their distributed ontology and rhetorical contributions to collective life can be disclosed in all of their complexity.

As both John Dewey and Bruno Latour among others have insisted, publics emerge in response to problems or matters of concern. At any given moment, a multiplicity of entities are assembling and disassembling in various configurations as they respond to particular pressing issues. As evident in the Obama Hope Photo Mystery discussed briefly in chapter 2, oftentimes visual matter is construed as the problem itself, a matter of concern that induces a diverse assemblage of entities to gather around it to address problems and find solutions. At other times, visual matter is part of a public (or many distributed ones at once) that emerges in response to a problem sometimes related to it and other times not as much. For example, Obama Hope began working in all kinds of assemblages, or collectives, to address issues of fair use and remix after it became embroiled in a copyright infringement case in 2009. Yet, in other unforeseeable cases, Obama Hope worked for causes that had little to do with itself, such as when it began to work for environmental justice in places as far away as Indonesia and France. From a new materialist perspective, our job as visual rhetoric scholars is to account for an image's distributed, emergent materializations in a nonteleological fashion and disclose the complexity of predictable *and* unpredictable ways its actualized versions contribute to collective life. Then and only then can we begin to "transform the divide between speaking subjects and mute objects into a set of differential tendencies and variable capacities" and recognize visual matter's thing-power (Bennett 2010 108). Then and only then can we also begin to finally give visual things the recognition they deserve in (re)assembling collective space and contributing to (rhetorical) history.

DISTRIBUTED COGNITION, AGENCY, AND INTRA-ACTION

Such recognition of visual matter's vitality, of course, is totally dependent on how we think about and account for rhetorical agency. Recent developments in distributed cognition are useful in this regard in that they complicate our notions of intentionality and force us to reconsider the linear causality we normally attribute only to human volition and action. As Marilyn Cooper (2011) discusses, "We experience ourselves as causal agents," and influenced by classical physics, we commonly believe that "causation is a linear process in which an agent's action prescribes a certain result" (437). From this perspective, agency derives from a human's capacity to create prior intentions and perform conscious actions that result in predictable, intended effects. Contemporary work in distributed cognition, however, pushes us to understand that agency is not as linked to human intentionality as we may think. As Andy Clark (2008) argues, for instance, the biological brain is no longer considered solely responsible for our rhetorical choices and acts. The brain is simply one part of "a spatially and temporally extended process, involving lots of extra-neural operations, whose *joint action* [my emphasis]" creates any given outcome (12–13). As a distributed process, cognition may be dispersed across various, heterogeneous components of an assemblage or assemblages as well as space and time. Essentially, cognitive science today makes it clear that our brains, bodily components, and actions cooperate with other entities within or across assemblages to enact change. Agency, in this sense, is a property neither of humans or things; it is not something, in other words, that humans or nonhumans have or even acquire. Agency is an act of change that arises from an entanglement of human and nonhuman entities and other environmental factors, each of which is but a phenomenon of ongoing historicity.

Distributed cognition challenges us not so much to divorce human beings from agency altogether as to recognize that agency does not always stem from a human being's *prior* intentionality. Prior intention refers to "premeditated or deliberate action where presumably the intention to act is formed in advance of an action itself" (Malafouris 2008, 29). Prior intention is not the *only* intentional state that shapes action. Unpremeditated action emerging from our relations with other entities within an assemblage also unfolds, giving rise to consequences. Drawing on Searle's work with "intention-in-action," Lambros Malafouris (2008), for instance, identifies what we can think of as an *extended intentional state* that we might envision taking place in "morphogenetic space." During this state, objects and material structures "project towards" us just as much as we project toward them (33). As a concrete example, Malafouris asks us to imagine the interactions that unfold at a potter's wheel. The clay, wheel, and water are physical resources fully integrated into the action of making pots. Each of these material elements is not just used by the potter nor does this use follow the command of the brain. Instead, each of these elements triggers the intentions of the potter to shape a pot in specific ways. As water interacts with clay, for instance, the hands of the potter constantly respond to the clay, to which the clay responds, to which the hands respond, and so forth. As such, the activity of pottery is a "dynamic coupling of mind and matter that looks like a dance of agency"; this dance, in which material entities and humans project toward each other, can be construed as an *extended intentional state* (33). From this perspective of distributed cognition, then, agency is not derived *solely* from a human's prior intentions and ability to make those intentions come true by bringing together form and matter. Instead, agency is understood as a distributed, emergent affair that actualizes as a consequence of the configurations, affordances, and constraints of all involved entities.

While all matter (human and nonhuman) actively contributes to change when involved in a complex network of activities within a dynamic assemblage, this is not to say that in any given phenomenon, all entities equally contribute in degrees and types of influence (as iterated before) nor that human beings must always be involved in every enactment of agency. However, such a distributed notion of agency is important for recognizing that via their associations with various entities, visual things become capable of coproducing all kinds of actions—authorizing, permitting, affording, persuading, protesting, attracting, luring, inducing. Such agential contributions are difficult to pin down within any given phenomenon for a variety of reasons I want to spend the remainder of this section unpacking. First, visual things often move beings to action via persuasion (change via ethical, logical, and emotional appeals), identification (change via consubstantiality), propaganda (change via coercion), fragmented argumentation (change via unstated propositions, indirect and incomplete claims, visual refutation, and implied alternatives),[10] and affect (change through energy transfer and sense appeals).[11] Such processes are rarely discretely at work, making it difficult to account for how any single thing specifically induces change within a particular phenomenon. Second, in relation to affect, visual things tend to, in Barthes's terms, advene.[12] Bennett (2010) draws on David Panagia to succinctly explain that *to advene* means to intervene in perception—to jut or intrude into "the regime of the sensible" (262). This intervention "strikes without designating" (262); as such, this intervention can be sensed but not known and is thus not easily captured in words. Affect is also, as previously discussed, difficult to trace as it often moves a body in ways that an outside observer as well as the person it

impacts are unaware. Therefore, while people's imitations and partici-
pations in collective activities may be hypervisible, such actions' initial
affective prompting is hard to pinpoint.

Third, any given phenomenon is constituted by an entanglement of
dynamic assemblages constituted themselves of intermingling entities —
materials, beliefs, words, historical forces, practices, and so forth—each
of which acquires its own "thing-power" and contributes in its own right
to agency. Such entities are so entangled within assemblages and phenomena that their separation is all but impossible. In addition, when any
phenomenon comes under investigation, we (our bodies, dispositions,
location, practices, etc.) are always implicated in it. As Karen Barad
(2007) puts it, we are not exterior to any phenomenon under study; "*We
are a part of that nature that we seek to understand*" (27). The various material entities (i.e., "tools") and other entities in our research assemblage
are also not passive, innocent bystanders. In light of such entanglement,
the degree to which a visual thing contributes to agency is a difficult, if
not entirely impossible, enterprise to decipher.

To complicate matters even more, the visual things we study are
not determinate things that embody specific, fixed characteristics and
properties that we can interpret and decode without influencing them.
The physical boundaries we like to imagine existing between any particular thing and ourselves do not ontologically or even visually exist
(Barad 2007, 156). Rather, in our intra-actions with them, the visual
things under study *only* become temporarily determinate when we
take a snapshot of their mobility and make an "agential cut," marking
them (objects), as well as the other things we engage with to perform
research,[13] off from us (subjects). In actuality, the visual things we intra-
act with are both phenomena in their ongoing materialization and part
of an ongoing reconfiguring of the world (23). Such processes are not
frozen when we conduct our research. The research methods we deploy,
the digital technologies we use to trace the visual thing, our familiarity
with the political discourses that are already mapped onto it, the new
materialist perspective from which we choose to think about it—all
these factors and entities (as well as unmentioned others) influence
not only the constitution of the visual thing itself but also the dance of
agency within a given phenomenon. Furthermore, and especially in the
case of a single multiple image such as Obama Hope, a visual thing is
also involved in a multiplicity of other phenomena taking place often at
simultaneous times and viral rates. Agency, in this sense, is a dynamic,
distributed dance that cannot be turned on and off like a water fountain. Accounting for a visual thing's contributions to rhetorical agency is

made even more difficult, then, as both thing and agency are always in excess of what we can capture in our studies.

TUMBLEWEED AND MUTUAL TRANSFORMATION

Despite such difficulties, from a new materialist perspective we must try our best to account for the ongoing spatiotemporality of consequentiality that unfolds as an image materializes and intra-acts with a multitude of entities in distributed acts of agency. During such investigation, our job is to disclose how single multiple images become powerful forces that co-construct collective life as they experience *and* stimulate transformation. As is signified in the term *intra-action* itself, when visual things come into a relation in various assemblages, they and the other entities with which they are entangled are *mutually* transformed. When accounting for the enduring vitality of visual things, then, we ought to pay attention not only to how things undergo constant change as they circulate with time and space but also to how they cogenerate change via their material encounters.

The vital force I always like to visualize to help me make sense of this distributed process of agency and coevolving mutual transformations is, oddly perhaps, tumbleweed. Having lived in the Rocky Mountain West for over fifteen years, I have had many encounters with tumbleweeds and have always been amazed by their movement and capacity for change. When I lived on eighty acres outside Santa Fe, for example, tumbleweeds would roll through my property, pausing by a barbed wire fence on the side of my house—sometimes for hours, sometimes for days—before moving on. The tumbleweeds varied in size; some came in the shape of basketballs, some much bigger, the size of giant beach balls. At rest and with time, tumbleweeds often visibly transformed as other plant particles collected in the tumbleweeds' branches. Sometimes other debris such as blowing plastic bags, even, would get caught in their reaches, becoming part of the tumbleweeds' transforming assemblage. This may sound kind of strange, but I often felt sorry for the tumbleweeds caught there on the fence, blowing in the strong New Mexican winds. At times, I even walked out and "freed" tumbleweeds, helping them reenter circulation. This action, I now realize, was based on a belief that tumbleweeds desire to keep moving; their "job" is always to be on the road, in flow. Tumbleweeds acquire new, significant meaning, in other words, during circulation.

After learning a little bit about tumbleweed, I now realize that my beliefs were not too far off. Tumbleweed is the aboveground part of a plant that, once mature and dry, breaks off in the wind and begins to circulate. Tumbleweed is often conceived of as dead matter. Yet, it is not a stable or inert entity. Tumbleweeds are transformed by various elements—the wind that pushes them along the ground, animals that forage on them, other plants that gather in their branches. Through these relations, tumbleweeds change not only in shape but also in action. They also splinter, with each broken-off part continuing a life of its own. In addition, as they circulate, tumbleweeds also transform their environment and thus take on new functions. As diaspore, tumbleweeds scatter seeds both when they tumble and when they are at rest in wet locations, giving rise to other plants in that particular species of tumbleweed. They also transform the soil by contributing to erosion. When tumbleweeds rest, they soak up water, and when they move, they transform the surface of the soil, making the soil vulnerable to subsequent wind damage and topsoil loss. As they soak up water, tumbleweeds thwart the growth of other surrounding plants even as they may simultaneously act as food for animals that sometimes forage on them. In multiple ways, then, just as tumbleweeds are transformed through intra-actions, tumbleweeds transform other elements they encounter.

Humans too are affected by their engagement with tumbleweeds. For certain, our landscapes are changed, but so too are our actions. In addition to sparking a complex ecology of beliefs, desires, and so forth, tumbleweeds move people to behave in all kinds of ways. While some attract scores of people to gather round them, such as is the case with the town-center Christmas trees made out of tumbleweed in Chandler, Arizona, others inspire people to write poetry or music lyrics. Still others, like me, are simply deeply affected and drawn to pick them up and influence their future journeys. What I find particularly interesting is how tumbleweed acquires power as it experiences iconic circulation. When I see tumbleweed in a movie, for instance, I feel nostalgic for the Rockies—such a strong yearning for the West emerges, in fact, that I often ache to get back home. And even now, as I am writing, tumbleweed has found itself on the page, influencing my understanding of how rhetoric matters. In this regard, tumbleweeds still impact me even though it has been over five years now since I have actually encountered one in person. Can we really say under such circumstances that tumbleweeds are "dead," inert, passive? New materialism challenges us to consider otherwise—to recognize that while perceived as dead matter, tumbleweeds acquire a viable force to effect change as they circulate and undergo and produce change. In this sense, from a new materialist perspective, tumbleweed, like all things, is better thought of as a vital force that generates—through its intra-actions with other entities—mutual transformation.

Images such as Obama Hope can be conceived of in a similar manner. That is, from a new materialist perspective we can think of an image as a vital force that, once unleashed, acquires thing-power through its various material encounters. As a virtual entity, an image circulates as it transcends media, materializes in different material versions (which themselves splinter and experience lives of their own), and thus intra-acts with human and nonhuman, concrete and abstract, entities. As it circulates, an image also moves in nonlinear, inconsistent, and often unpredictable ways within and across multiple networks of assemblages. And via these intra-actions, an image reassembles collective space in often surprising ways as different actualized versions and consequences emerge that far exceed deliberate acts of communication. Like a tumbleweed, in other words, an image faces an unforeseeable future as it circulates throughout and across various ecosystems and experiences rhetorical transformation as it induces various kinds of change.

ACTANCY AND SYMMETRY

Understood from a new materialist perspective, rhetorical agency as a concept can signify how such matter participates in a dynamic dance of intra-actions capable of generating mutual transformation. Yet, playing off Latour, *rhetorical actancy* might better describe such distributed relations and intra-activity. In *Pandora's Hope*, Latour (1999), like Malafouris, Bennett, and others, advocates for understanding nonhumans as full-fledged actors in collectives that neither have mastery over us nor are mastered by us (176). Instead, humans are transformed by the relations they enter into with nonhumans just as nonhumans are transformed as they enter into relations with humans. As evidence, Latour asks us to think about the relations between a citizen and a gun, an exercise that would be particularly poignant considering the recent proliferation of smart guns on the current market. But for our purposes, think about the following relation between a young girl and an Obama Hope poster (see Figure 3.3). The young female citizen with the poster in hand is not the same as a young girl without the poster, just as the poster in a girl's hand is not the same as the poster sitting dusty in a storage space. Both girl and poster are transformed through their material engagement and/or relationship. Latour wants us to realize that a third social actor emerges from such relation (179). This hybrid actor, which he calls the *actant*, reminds us that it is nonsensical to claim one actor has willpower

Figure 3.3. Three for Barack Obama, *Tony Fischer, 2008. Photograph Courtesy of Fischer, (CC BY 2.0).*

over the other and that rhetorical action (in this case, perhaps, protest) can be attributed to one (typically human) actor. As such, claims such as "girl rallies with poster" are rendered inaccurate. Instead, by thinking of *actant*, we acknowledge that, in fact, "girl-poster" rallies. As Latour states, "Action is simply not a property of humans *but of an association of actants* . . . in the process of exchanging competencies, offering one another new possibilities, new goals, new functions" (182). *Rhetorical actancy*, then, is a powerful supplement to rhetorical agency because it reminds us that rhetoric always emerges from the relations and activities of mutually transforming entities within assemblages.

Rhetorical actancy also helps cultivate a fluid sense of collective life so integral to a new materialist rhetorical approach. From a Latourian perspective, reality[14] is fluid, as entities (themselves always assemblages) are always assembling and reassembling as they are drawn into activities, or enactments of agency, to address divergent matters of concern. Such activities, which leave traces of evidence we can (in part) observe and track, are never constituted by a human, or any other, actor working alone. Rather they are constituted by human, nonhuman, material,

conceptual, semiotic, and technological entities, all of which are moving and making each other do things in and across assemblages to inno-
vate, solve problems, respond to stimuli, and so forth. As Latour (2005b)
notes, "'Making do' is not the same thing as 'causing' or 'doing'" (217).
Rather, it is best to think of it as "triggering into action" (217). The real
power of rhetorical actancy as a concept, then, is its insistence that collective life is constituted by a multiplicity of circulating entities that are
mutually influencing each other and bending space as a consequence
of their divergent activities. Considering such fluidity, a researcher's job
can't help but be "to follow the flow" (237) to see how various actants
such as Obama Hope are both being triggered and triggering various
other actors into action as they circulate and engage in divergent acts
of agency.

To account for this distributed sense of actancy, as I discuss in the
following chapter, we need to develop new methodological habits of following and tracing. However, analytical leveling is also needed in our
studies to identify how the entanglement of human and nonhuman entities mediates rhetorical action. In Latour's terms, we can think of this
leveling as *symmetry*, which attempts to conflate the dichotomy between
human and nonhuman and subject and object. Too often, the force of
things is dismissed because we create false dualities between subject and
object. We assume, in other words, that things are inert tools or objects
used by human subjects to whom we typically credit full-blown agency.
As Jean Baudrillard (1999) writes, "It is the subject that makes history,
it's the subject that totalizes he world," whereas the object is "shamed,
obscene, passive" (111). This duality occurs especially because when we
make agential cuts, we tend to deem the nonhuman things with which
we come into intra-action to be intermediaries rather than mediators.
While intermediaries enter into diverse relations without necessarily
transforming them, mediators transform, distort, modify, and so forth
(Latour 2005b, 39). The point with symmetry is not to demonstrate the
"equal" ability of human and nonhuman entities to effect change. Nor is
the point "to extend subjectivity to things, to treat humans like objects,
to take machines for social actors (76). Rather, the objective is to avoid
imposing "a priori some spurious *asymmetry* among human intentional
action and a material world of causal relations" (76). Without deny-
ing that differences exist between humans and nonhumans, then, symmetrical accounts avoid situating humans at the ontological center of
research and writing. By acknowledging distributed agency and mutual
transformation, researchers ought try to account for the complex network of actants that intra-act in any given rhetorical encounter.

Figure 3.4. Tension, Michael Murphy, 2008.

INTRA-ACTING ACTANTS

Consider once again the Obama art movement as an example of actants intra-acting with other things to catalyze change. During 2008, as the movement began to take visible shape, the Obama Hope image began to circulate so widely and transform in such unexpected ways that a number of websites specifically devoted to documenting Obama art emerged, which ultimately themselves became important actants in the election. *The Obama Art Report* blog[15] administered by Ken Hashimoto was one such site. On the blog, you could find all sorts of examples of Obama art produced throughout the election campaign by Obama supporters, ranging from street artist and graphic designer Ray Noland to sculptor Michael Murphy to pop artist Robert Indiana (see Figure 3.4). You could also find reports of various art auctions and fundraisers as well as gallery shows featuring Obama art. The Obama Hope image, in all its various transformations, especially received much attention. In one post, for instance, an eBay auction of a Barack Obama portrait designed in the Obama Hope style but crafted out of eight thousand LEGOs was announced. In other posts, reports of fraudulent reproductions of the Obama *Change* posters were reported, and in still others, readers were told when and where they could purchase the latest of Fairey's Obama Works and where and when the latest sighting of the Obama Hope image was made.

In an interview with Marisa Nakosone (*Examiner.com*, October 30, 2008), Hashimoto explained that this blog, which started halfway through the primaries in 2008, began as a simple site with simple intentions yet snowballed into a major vehicle for circulating Obama art. In her article, Nakosone went so far as to claim, in fact, that *The Obama Art Report* blog had become "a leading resource for documenting the largely guerilla, and street-influenced art inspired by the 2008 Presidential election." As a result, Hashimoto's entire life was transformed. Working as wine buyer at Whole Foods and as a restaurant server in Oakland, he had always been a big fan of Fairey and others, such as David Choe. Yet during the election, he noticed how their and other artists' Obama art began to proliferate. He also noticed how people on Flickr were documenting sightings of such work; smaller "do-it-yourself" artists were putting up their art on sites such as Esty; eBay was emerging as marketplace for Obama art; and large companies such as Upper Playground were helping to distribute Obama art to raise funds for Obama. By late May, Hashimoto realized "how historically artistic this campaign was quickly becoming" (Nakosone, *Examiner.com*, October 30, 2008). Hashimoto had intended to set up a site to both document this historical artistic phenomenon and alert others as to where they could purchase the art for good prices. Over time, he also began interviewing artists, including Fairey, people started following the blog, and he became a leading expert on Obama art. The blog, as a surprise to even himself, simply took off and became an important actant in the Obama art movement.

As such intra-actions between the Obama Hope image, other art, and various people and technologies materialized, political agency emerged on the grassroots scene in ways that Fairey could never have imagined upon the initial production of his designs. Making visible how political agency emerged via these encounters illustrates the impossibility of pinpointing who or what was responsible for the movement's impact. To whom or what, after all, would we attribute the political agency that emerged during the Obama art movement—Fairey, the Obama Hope image, the artists, the materials and technologies used to construct the artwork, the blogs, the Internet, George Bush, Obama himself? Certainly we can recognize the human agent's role in responding to the Obama Hope image and other cultural, social, and political forces and ultimately making a choice to participate in the Obama art movement. As documented here, humans made deliberate choices in transforming, producing, and distributing a diverse range of Obama Hope renditions. Yet, if we were to attribute the political agency that emerged during the 2008 presidential election to human citizens alone, we would fail to acknowledge (a) the complexity of intra-actions that took place between humans, the Obama Hope image, and other nonhuman entities within the phenomenon of the Obama art movement and (b) the significant and divergent ways these intra-actions worked to catalyze change. We would fail to produce, in other words, a detailed and authentic account of how rhetoric emerged and unfolded during the Obama art movement. Rhetoric is a distributed event that emerges between intra-acting agents with different degrees of power; it is influenced not only by flows of historical and cultural forces, energies, discourses, moods, and experiences but also by the affordances of different technologies, indexicalities, and emergent relations. As such, a distinct responsible agent in the Obama art movement becomes nearly impossible to pinpoint.

What does become clear when we zoom in on the networks of activities that constitute this movement, however, is how, through the intra-actions of various actors with differing degrees of power mediate change (the Obama Hope image, digital technologies, art materials, craftspeople, artists, every day citizens, etc.), a dynamic assemblage of hybrid actors emerged on the grassroots scene that catalyzed change during the 2008 presidential election. As will become clear in the four-part case study that follows, the Obama Hope image intra-acted with various technologies, artistic materials, "canvases," and people in a diverse range of environments to manifest hope and catalyze change. Yet each emergent actant helped produce new actants that then began to circulate and engage in new collective activities, which generated even more rhetorical actancy. Rhetorical agency, historically linked with human potential, cannot capture this rhetorical becoming in which both humans and our material counterparts are mutually transforming and transformed. We need a concept such as rhetorical actancy to acknowledge the distributed, relational, dynamic, and temporal phenomena that agency actually entails.

To help generate such symmetrical accounts in visual rhetorics, we might develop research methods that, in operating from a new materialist disposition, disclose how, via their distributed relations, visual things acquire the material force to shape collective life. Case studies can be particularly useful in this regard, as they rely on a diverse range of research strategies and descriptive accounts to shed light on a particular phenomenon or a network of interrelated phenomena. To achieve ontological leveling, we can make visual things such as the Obama

Hope image the main characters in our case studies and follow them as they emerge in distinct ways via different relations and undergo rhetorical transformation as they cogenerate a multiplicity of consequential impacts. Such studies would mainly focus on futurity then—the strands of time beyond the initial moment of production and delivery when material consequences unfold, often unpredictably, as images transcend media, circulate, and materialize in wildly unpredictable ways. Such research, to be clear, would also focus on the mutual transformations that emerge as the single multiple image we are following intra-acts with various entities. It must be kept in mind, after all, that while circulating images constantly undergo transformation, they also transform collective space as they trigger multiple other entities into action. Symmetrical accounts in visual rhetoric, thus, would also mainly focus on a visual thing's complex exterior relations to highlight the divergent ways visual things become rhetorical and vital with time and space as they induce all kinds of collective change.

CONCLUSION

In this chapter, I have tried to demonstrate how thinking ecologically about visual matter can elucidate the ways visual things become vital, powerful forces as they intra-act with various entities in and across assemblages. As Timothy Morton (2012) helps us understand, thinking ecologically is always a challenging and complicated business. It demands a radical openness to the life forms, or vital things, we find ourselves connected with, "generating care and concern for beings, no matter how uncertain we are of their identity, no matter how afraid we are of their existence" (19). Ecological thought also necessitates thinking big, joining dots, and "think[ing] through the mesh of life forms as far out and in as it can" (18). The more we tune into the interconnectedness of things to see the big picture, the more messy and strange things become. Also, the more we come to realize how entangled we are, the more open and ambiguous everything becomes (17). Such uncertainty, ambiguity, and messiness can be troubling to some. However, a new materialist rhetorical approach, as the following chapter will make clear, embraces such conditions of ecological thought to help account for the distributed ontology and rhetorical transformation of a single multiple image. From a new materialist perspective, it is only via an examination of its messy interconnectedness that we can become more fully aware of how a single multiple image, in all of its complexity, comes to rhetorically matter.

Notes

1. Parts of this chapter have been published in (Gries 2011) "Agential Matters: Tumbleweed, Women-pens, Citizens-hope, and Rhetorical Actancy" in *Ecology, Writing Theory, and New Media: Writing Ecology*, edited by Sid Dobrin.

2. In *Meeting the Universe Halfway*, Barad (2007) argues that a crucial perceptual shift occurs when we think in terms of intra-action versus interaction. Interaction "presumes the prior existence of independent entities" (815). Intra-action, on the other hand, recognizes that the boundaries and properties of the "components" or relata become determinate with time and space and within phenomena. Such relata, in other words, do not preexist relations; they do not lead an independent, self-contained existence. Rather, individuals emerge through and as part of specific phenomena in which they are intra-acting with a mangle of other entities. See also pages 139–40.

3. *Vital materialism*, as described in *Vibrant Matter*, is Jane Bennett's (2010) name for a philosophical and political project that works to "paint a positive ontology of vibrant matter"; "dissipate onto-theological binaries" such as life/matter, human/animal, organic/inorganic; forward a style of analysis "that can better account for the contributions of nonhuman actants"; and cultivate an ecological sensibility toward all matter (x).

4. Agential realism is an epistemological-ontological-ethical framework developed by Karen Barad (2007) in *Meeting the Universe Halfway* that attempts to deepen understandings of the role that human and nonhuman, material and discursive, and natural and cultural factors play in scientific and other social-material practices (26).

5. Mitchell (2005) challenges us to think of the totem as a romanticist longing for an intimate relation with nature and the fossil as a recognition of extinction and thus the inevitable defeat of the desire for reunification with nature (185). As the composite of the romantic image, these figures brought a new order of temporality that both informed natural history and imbued the poetic imagery of the romantic era. Such structure of feeling not only undergirded critiques of modernity in the works of scholars such as Marx, Nietzsche, and Freud, but today it also haunts much contemporary cultural and literary history and critical theory. As such, Mitchell argues, not only have we never been modern, we have also "always been Romantic" (187).

6. In this chapter, I sometimes refer to a visual thing as an *assemblage*, but I also refer to it as an *entity*. As I try to explain, visual things are themselves assemblages constituted by a multiplicity of material and enunciative components or entities. Yet, simultaneously, visual things are part of larger assemblages in which they are but one of many diverse components or entities. All entities are actually assemblages from my perspective, but to avoid confusion, I refer to visual things as entities when I am referring to them as intra-acting within a larger assemblage.

7. This explanation is based on my understandings of theories developed by Deleuze and Guattari, Manuel De Landa, Jane Bennett, Tony Sampson, and Bruno Latour, and so forth. This explanation is admittedly stripped of its complexity for simplicity's sake. For a deeper understanding of assemblage, see the work of previously mentioned scholars cited in the bibliography.

8. Entities may be constructed of any number of things: materials, ideas, words, images, affects, feelings, moods, institutions, and so forth.

9. Manuel De Landa (2006) in *A New Philosophy of Society* makes this claim on page 10, but he speaks of interactions rather than intra-actions, which I take from Karen Barad (2007).

10. See Delicath and DeLuca's (2003) "Image Events, the Public Sphere, and Argumentative Practice: The Case of Radical Environmental Groups" for more on fragmented argumentation of image events.

11. For more on affect, see Teresa Brennan's (2004) *The Transmission of Affect*. Also, see Cory Holding's (2007) review essay "Affecting Rhetoric" that was published in *College Composition and Communication*.

12. While Barthes himself refuses to acknowledge that photographs themselves are animated, in *Camera Lucida* Barthes (1982) uses such description to discuss how a photograph animates him (20).

13. For more on agential cuts, see Barad's (2007) *Meeting the Universe Halfway*.

14. Latour often refers to reality as "the collective." While I agree that we can refer to the common world as the *collective*, and hence often use the term as an adjective before *life*, I also deploy the term to signify assemblages that congeal on various spatiotemporal dimensions and leave evidence of rhetorical activity. I discuss such collectives in the remaining chapters of this book.

15. The *Obama Art Report* blog is unfortunately no longer accessible.

PART II

A New Materialist Rhetorical Approach in Practice

4

NEW MATERIALIST
RESEARCH STRATEGIES[1]

*If researchers wish to understand a world (or an activity in the world)
that is complex and messy, "then we're going to have to teach ourselves
to think, to practice, to relate, and to know in new ways" (2), in ways
that are complex and messy.*
                —Fleckenstein et al., "The Importance of Harmony"

At its core, *Still Life with Rhetoric* is interested in cultivating a new materialist habitus of method for rhetorical study, particularly visual rhetorics.
In a methodological sense, a habitus of method can be understood as a
set of dispositions embodied in a shared tradition of inquiry that influences a community of scholars to conduct research in certain ways. A
habitus of method, of course, is not governed by preestablished rules
that scholars can simply pick up and begin to use in a systematic fashion. Generally though, as Louise Wetherbee Phelps (2003; 2011) has
noted,[2] a body of scholars is accountable to and for similar objects of
study, a set of philosophical principles, and/or a body of theoretical
perspectives, which constitute their research dispositions. Thus far in
this book, I have tried to articulate some of the theories and philosophies particular to a new materialist rhetorical approach articulated
herein. The cross-disciplinary agenda of new materialism attempts to
complicate our notions of self in relation to the material world—to help
us see ourselves as one form of matter intra-acting with and transforming alongside other matter. One hope with new materialism is to break
down destructive binaries that continue to position humans over nonhuman matter. Rather than focus primarily on representation and signification, new materialism is also concerned with "affect, force, and movement as it travels in all directions" (Dolphijn and der Tuin 2012, 113).
New materialism thus works hard to create symmetrical accounts that
explain the dynamic movement of matter and the vital contributions it
makes to collective life. Visual rhetoric, I argue, can do its part by disclosing in theory and practice how visual things circulate and acquire power

DOI: 10.7330/9780874219784.c004

to co-constitute collective life as they enter into divergent associations, undergo change, and spark a wide range of consequences.

The theories and philosophies related to time, space, meaning, vitality, agency, and virality articulated in chapters 2 and 3 are intended to help in this regard by articulating how thinking intuitively and ecologically about visual rhetoric can help draw out visual matter's dynamic and vital dimensions. From these chapters, we can extract six principles indicative of the *thought style* particular to the new materialist rhetorical approach herein.

PRINCIPLE OF BECOMING

Becoming is an opening up of events into an unknown future. Reality is change, an open process of mattering and assemblage. From such perspectives, a new materialist rhetorical approach recognizes that things constantly exist in a dynamic state of flux and are productive of change, time, and space.

PRINCIPLE OF TRANSFORMATION

Rhetorical transformation is virtual-actual process of becoming in which rhetoric unfolds in unpredictable, divergent, and inconsistent ways. To account for a thing's distributed ontology, a new materialist rhetorical approach tries to disclose the rhetorical transformations that things experience as they materialize in differing spatiotemporal configurations.

PRINCIPLE OF CONSEQUENTIALITY

The meaning of matter is constituted by the consequences that emerge with time and space via its relations with other entities. These consequences emerge before, during, and after a thing's initial physical production and delivery. Turning to futurity, a new materialist rhetorical approach focuses most attention on the consequences that emerge once matter is initially produced, has been perceived as relatively stable, and enters into circulation.

PRINCIPLE OF VITALITY

Things have lives of their own and exert material force as they move in and out of various assemblages and trigger diverse kinds of change. A new materialist rhetorical approach tries to account for a thing's distributed, emergent materializations in a nonteleological fashion and discloses the complexity of unsurprising and unpredictable ways it impacts collective life.

PRINCIPLE OF AGENCY

Agency, better thought of as actancy, is a distributed, dynamic dance enacted by diverse entities intra-acting within and across assemblages. To cultivate a fluid sense of collective life and to explore how rhetoric emerges from the distributed relations and activities of mutually transforming entities, a new materialist rhetorical approach discloses a thing's emergent and unfolding exterior relations.

PRINCIPLE OF VIRALITY

Virality—the tendency of things to spread quickly and widely—is a consequence of a thing's design, production, distribution, circulation, transformation, collectivity, and consequentiality. Things are especially contagious when they propagate affective desires that induce unconscious collective identifications and unconscious imitative feelings, thoughts, and behaviors.

Thought styles, as Ludwik Fleck (1979) has argued, are representative in that they indicate a historical-cultural conditioning that manifests when individuals are exposed to the exchange of scholarly ideas from a particular thought collective or closely related thought collectives.[3] Thought styles are also productive and rhetorical in that they are both the means by which research communities develop knowledge and the means by which they make that knowledge persuasive (Phelps 2003) Yet, and perhaps most important, thought styles are also constraints on what researchers "can think, say and do" (Phelps 2003). As such, principles like the ones described above can be conceived of as accountabilities in that they hold scholars responsible for doing and writing about research in ways that do not betray a methodology's guiding assumptions or various commitments.

In a general sense, the principles above challenge us to study things in an intransitive, diachronic sense—as vital actants that are constantly changing, circulating, and triggering all kinds of collective actions via their multiple, divergent relations. Rather than study visual things such as Obama Hope as visual texts that can be read, decoded, and interpreted *within* specific contexts, then, the challenge is to investigate how such vital actants are actually *productive of* space (and time) as they materialize, flow, and intra-act with a variety of entities in and across various assemblages. By space, I am referring to spatiotemporal events constructed out of interrelations that occur on multiple qualitative and quantitative dimensions—geographical, biological, digital, conceptual, affective, cultural, material, semiotic. Single multiple images become rhetorical as they produce and participate in events that are distributed, divergent, and unpredictable. Such eventfulness is never entirely capturable, even as traces of activity generated by various assemblages leave evidence that can be mapped out in a nonlinear fashion. Nonetheless, in order to empirically account for the complex, distributed process of rhetorical transformation, new materialist research practices try to account for how visual things move, transform, intra-act, and produce a wide range of collective actions. While thinking intuitively and ecologically about visual matters can help, we need actual research strategies that put such thinking into productive practice.

While the next chapter offers a specific method I call *iconographic tracking* for putting the principles above into research action, in this chapter I discuss how the research actions of following, tracing, embracing uncertainty, and describing can help empirically account for rhetorical transformation. This is not to say, as will become clear throughout the remainder of this book, that reading, analysis, and interpretation are unimportant or even absent from the research process (as if this were possible anyway). A new materialist rhetorical approach simply privileges following, tracing, embracing uncertainty, and describing in order to construct the empirical evidence needed to learn how single multiple things become rhetorical as they reassemble collective life. As Latour (2005b) explains, to create empirical evidence means to research and write in a way that is as "faithful to experience" as possible (240). It means confronting things as mediators and, through our studies, listening to them when they say, "We are beings out there that gather and assemble the collective just as extensively as what you have called so far the social, limiting yourselves to only one standardized version of the assemblages; if you want to follow the actors themselves, you have to follow us as well" (240). It means, as Raul Sanchez (2012) notes in "Outside the Text," engaging in a kind of "neo-empiricism" that can better account for how visual things are produced, distributed, taken up, reproduced, and redistributed in contemporary networks of activities (237). The strategies of following, tracing, embracing uncertainty, and describing are especially useful in conducting such neoempiricist research in that they help account for an image's diachronic movement, complex relationality, and distributed materialization and impact.

These strategies, as will become apparent to readers familiar with Latour's work, are heavily inspired by actor-network theory in that they mimic Latour's (2005a) "quest for composition" in order to construct more realistic accounts of how visual things actually contribute to collective life (41). Yet while actor-network theory aims to account for the rhizomatic topology of societies and natures (Latour 1996), the research actions described below aim to account for the rhetorical transformation that images experience with time and space so that the complex, unfolding rhetorical life of a single image can be disclosed. The research strategies of following, tracing, embracing uncertainty, and describing, as I describe them below, are also imbued with and constrained by the new materialist principles above. My hope in articulating these principle-driven research actions is for scholars to begin visualizing how they might employ this new materialist rhetorical approach for their own research needs. This approach is particularly useful, I believe, in that it privileges new strategies for conducting and writing about visual rhetoric research.

FOLLOWING

In light of the principles of vitality, agency, and virality, a new materialist rhetorical approach is accountable for disclosing how circulating things reassemble collective life via a multiplicity of associations. When it comes to a single multiple image that experiences a distributed reality, it is important to not only keep track of how a single image undergoes transformation in terms of form, medium, and genre but also to make transparent how it plays a significant role in generating, sustaining, and influencing the continual assemblage and reassemblage of collective existence. If scholars can keep track of a single multiple image's divergent transformations and produce a thick, descriptive account of its diverse collective activities, such empirical inquiry does not necessitate scholars' *heavily* imposing their own interpretations as to how an actualized version of an image communicates or makes identification possible. Instead, at least as much as possible, scholars can seek out a visual thing's divergent connections and discover what various actors in divergent collectives reveal about actors' own dynamic intra-actions with the actualized images under study. As I discuss in the following chapter, qualitative strategies that give empirical access to people that come into intra-action with the image under study are particularly useful in that that people often try to give voice to their affective responses and disclose their own experiences and relations with that image.

Following, to be specific, is a research strategy that can help discover how collectives are held together by the interactions of various actants—human and nonhuman, material and semiotic, individual and institutional. This research strategy is deployed not so much to explain how collectives both assemble and disassemble but rather to track how a single image transforms across form, genre, media, and function as it actualizes in divergent versions. Such transformation cannot be determined by a scholar *a priori* but rather must be discovered by following images-in-action within and across various assemblages. As with the case of other actants, following images entails trying "to catch up with their often wild innovations in order to learn from them what the collective existence has become in their hands" (Latour 2005b, 12). Following an actant is very useful in trying to discover why a certain technological system or invention fails to materialize, as is modeled by Latour in *Aramis or the Love of Technology*. Yet it can also help account for how an image-invention comes into existence and becomes an important "civic-actant" in collective life. This latter purpose, I believe, is especially useful for visual rhetoric scholars who wonder how something such as Obama Hope becomes rhetorical and vital in a viral economy within and across cultures.

As a research strategy, following an actant is often a challenging enterprise. In some cases, researchers find that in following an image, they discover assemblages, or what I prefer to call *collectives*, that have already been titled by others who identify these collectives' unique spatiotemporal configurations. Many of these collectives, of course, are dynamic and have unfixed borders, yet, whether loosely or tightly connected, they do leave traces of activity that can be empirically investigated and used to identify their unique spatiotemporal configurations.[4] For instance, as I discussed in chapter 2, during my research with Obama Hope I discovered a small collective of human and nonhuman actors engaged in a sleuthing activity, which some members referred to as the Obama Hope Photo Mystery. This collective began to congeal when people in different locations and careers became interested in finding the reference for Fairey's Obama *Hope* poster. To find the reference, photojournalists, bloggers, and computer programmers intra-acted with various nonhuman and human entities such as Photoshop, Tineye, newspaper editors, and so forth for roughly two weeks in early 2009. Because such coordinated efforts were recorded in detail via blogs and e-mail, I could easily follow this image as it participated in this collective activity. In other cases, however, researchers will have to work harder to follow actants as they participate in a more distributed network of activities, even if those assemblages have already been identified as organized entities by others. For instance, my research following Obama Hope also lead me to discover the Obama art movement discussed in chapter 3—a network of interrelated and often overlapping microcollectives that emerged in individual cities and online spaces to raise support for Obama during the 2008 election season. Because such collective activity took place in chronotopic laminations over nine months in such divergent spaces, following Obama Hope in and out of assemblages within this movement (which we might think of as a loose assemblage) in an attempt to recover its collective activities is difficult.

Because some things such as the Obama Hope image are what Yrjö Engeström (2007) might call "runaway objects," following single multiple images in and out of such collectives is an especially challenging enterprise. Runaway objects, to be clear, are those things with the "potential to escalate and expand up to a global scale of influence" (47). Generally, they are things that may begin as insignificant innovations but that become larger than any of the distinct activity systems oriented toward them (47). As they become embedded in different activities that take on their own unique spatiotemporal configurations, they become what Mol (2002) calls "body multiples" that can no longer be closely bounded. Not only do they exceed their original material insubstantiation, they also become multiperspectival, multidimensional, and polycontextual (Spinuzzi 2011, 453). As such, runaway objects or body multiples are "poorly under anyone's control and have far-reaching and unexpected side effects" (Engeström 2007, 47). Due to the Internet, the World Wide Web, and digital technologies that easily afford reproduction, appropriation, and viral circulation, this "out-of-controllness" and far-reaching, unforeseeable consequentiality is especially the case for single multiple images such as Obama Hope. As will become clear in part 3, such images often take on "lives of their own and resist goal-rational attempts at control and prediction" (Engeström 2006, 194). Due to such wild abandon, "keeping up" with a single multiple image to learn how it contributes to collective life is difficult at best.

To keep up with a runaway object or a body multiple such as a viral image, scholars must relinquish their own control to a certain extent and be flexible enough to follow the thing under study wherever it takes them. This research process—as will be discussed further below—entails being comfortable with the uncertainty created by not knowing not only where exactly research will lead but also what consequences might unfold. This research process also entails being comfortable with the uncertainty created by what we might call *a concern for boundaries.* All research necessitates bounding in order to create a reasonable "site" of analysis. One way to bound a study of runaway objects or body multiples is by location, as Mol (2002) does in studying atherosclerosis with the site of a single Dutch hospital or as Edbauer Rice (2005) does is in tracking the Keep Austin Weird sticker in Austin, Texas. Another way to constrain a study is by organizational activity as Clay Spinuzzi (2003) suggests and models for us in describing how to bound a fictional study of grant writing. Still other ways to bound are by function, such as would be the case if I limited my case study to how the Obama Hope image became an important political actor during the 2008 election. One could even limit a case study by genre; I could have limited my study to the Obama Hope role in political campaign materials. However, if one is interested in discovering the complex rhetorical life of a thing and the multiple ways it contributes to collective life, the limitations of such boundaries must be fully considered; a case study bound by narrow conceptions of space, time, activity, function, and genre often delimit a thing's rhetorical becomings in ways the fail to acknowledge its complex, unfolding ontology.

A new materialist rhetorical approach acknowledges that, more often than not, when it comes down to it, the boundaries of case studies intent on discovering how a thing reassembles collective life throughout its lifetime are governed by limitations such as funding, time, resources, and so forth. Yet the methods and artifacts with which one engages to perform research also place boundaries on one's case study. Case studies that rely on digital research are especially limited by filter bubbles[5] produced by search engines such as Google and Facebook and various coded infrastructures that constrain research findings beyond a researcher's awareness. Research, of course, is also always rhetorical. Case studies are bound not only by the theories and philosophies that undergird a scholar's methodology but also and especially by a scholar's choice of which evidence to present in a descriptive account of a thing's rhetorical life. As Cheryl Glenn (1995) reminds us, mapping never reflects "a neutral reality. In choosing what to show and how to represent it, . . . maps 'do' something: they subtly shape our perceptions of a rhetoric englobed" (291). Therefore, as with any approach, setting boundaries when taking a new materialist rhetorical approach is always a logistical and politically motivated act.

In line with the principle of agency, this is not to say that the boundary of a case study is not impacted by the very thing under study. A new materialist rhetorical approach, in fact, tries to let the thing under study and its collective encounters guide the bounding process as much as possible. As Kristie S. Fleckenstein, et al. argue, ecologically sound research begins by drawing mutable circles around the feedback pathways constituting the phenomenon under study (Fleckenstein et al. 2008, 397). For instance, they draw on Gregory Bateson to explain that in order to understand how a blind man walks, "the scope of a study must include the pathways forming the ecosystem of blind-person-walking-on-the-street-with-cane: communication among the man, the street, and the cane" (397). Choosing which feedback pathways of an organism-in-its-environment to include in one's research circle is extremely difficult when dealing with a runaway object or single multiple image such as Obama Hope for reasons I have already touched upon. However, drawing on Spinuzzi's (2011) work with runaway objects,[6] we can make certain research moves that allow us to appropriately bound a case study of a single multiple image's rhetorical life:

- Provisionally bound a case by dwelling in data long enough to identify a particular image that transcends media, genre, and form.
- Identify divergent collectives of which actualized versions of that image have become a part.
- Identify various rhetorical activities actualized images that begin to participate within and across collectives.
- Rebound a case study by identifying trends in an image's different rhetorical activities, noting key actors involved in those collective activities.
- Describe common rhetorical roles that images begin to play within collectives as a collaborative attempt to achieve certain image-related outcomes.

Such research can become quite messy, but as long as a researcher remains flexible (and patient) enough to follow a thing as it flows among and across various collectives, such complexity of rhetorical becoming can be disclosed. This flexibility simply requires growing comfortable with leaving "the actors free to deploy the full incommensurability of their own world-making activities" (Latour 2005b, 24). In the case of visual rhetorics, this means that if we follow a single multiple image long enough, its numerous transformations will lead us to a multiplicity of divergent collectives whose rhetorical activities we can trace. In this sense, the image *shows us* where to draw the boundaries of our case studies.

TRACING

All of this will become clearer in the following chapter as I model what a new materialist rhetorical approach might look like in the method of iconographic tracking. Yet for now realize that collectives that come to be studied are not preordained when taking a new materialist rhetorical approach; they appear to researchers only when the researchers have followed a thing's transformations long enough for traces of collective engagement to become evident through empirical investigation. To conduct such tracing, scholars must turn their attention to a thing's exterior relations so they can disclose the process whereby an image circulates, materializes in different versions, intra-acts with other concrete and abstract entities, and triggers changes that leave evidence in its wake. While a thing's interior relations are certainly considered as it undergoes transformation, a single multiple image constantly in flux demands tracing a relatively composed thing's "nomad existence," if you will. According to Deleuze and Guattari (1986), nomads occupy what they call "smooth space," which we can think of as an "open space throughout which thing-flows are distributed" and undergo deformations, transformations, and continuous variations (18–20). Smooth spaces, Deleuze and Guattari further explain, are "wedded to a very particular type of multiplicity: nonmetric, acentered, rhizomatic multiplicities which occupy space without 'counting' it and can 'only be explored by legwork'" (34). Such indefinite smooth space, whose essential feature is its "polyvocity of directions," cannot be conceived as unfolding in a linear fashion nor can it be visually demarcated from a distant, bird's-eye perspective from the outset of research (53). To see how "nomads" occupy smooth space, a researcher can only trace a nomad's activities via the lingering evidence that becomes obvious during empirical investigation. The focus of research here, then, is not so much on the internal properties of the nomad or thing but rather on the multiple, external traces of activity paths it leaves behind as it enters into various associations.

One methodological challenge with this research strategy arises because some collectives that orient themselves toward a thing, as with the Obama Hope Photo Mystery, often burst on the scene only to quickly fade away. As such, the visible connections a thing establishes in various collectives are often short lived, making its traces of activity only momentarily visible. "If no trace is produced," as Latour (2005b) explains succinctly in talking about things in the plural, "they offer no information to the observer and will have no visible effect on other agents. They remain silent and are no longer actors: they remain, literally unaccountable" (79). Thus, often a researcher must seek out collective activities when this "momentary visibility" is enhanced enough to generate a strong account (80). For visual rhetoric scholars, social, political, and environmental campaigns are events rich with traces of collective activity in which things we might typically deem to be passive clearly become visible, vital, and contagious. Scholars such as Lester Olson (2004) show it's possible to trace an image's collective activity in historical campaigns. However, in an era when social media in the form of Twitter, Facebook, blogs, and websites function to organize community actions, raise funds, and make communication between various political actors easy and immediate, tracing a thing's contemporary campaign activities becomes especially productive and yields much insight into how it becomes rhetorical via diverse collective actions. As will become apparent in the Obama Hope case study, this was especially the case during the 2008 and 2012 elections as Obama, his campaign team members, and various constituents took advantage of social media for diverse reasons. While much of this activity went unrecorded and can no longer be accessed, an enormous number of collective activities involving Obama Hope are still traceable on the Internet. We simply need methods such as iconographic tracking that can recover such activities.

Strikes, protests, and political movements are also events in which the activity of things becomes highly visible and thus traceable. Interestingly, it was during the social upheaval of the late 1960s when public protests were so prominent in the United States that scholars at the 1970 Wingspread Conference and the National Conference on Rhetoric felt the need to advocate for expanded conceptions of rhetoric to account for visual and other material artifacts' influence on beliefs, actions, attitudes, and so forth (Olson 2004, 2). During such times, things typically thought of as intermediaries or passive vehicles become full-blown mediators whose encounters with human beings in various associations overtly function to create actual change. It is no wonder, then, that as things such as protest art, political posters, and so forth became highly visible in the 1960s, their impact upon their surroundings caught the attention of scholars and thus prompted more attention to visual rhetoric. Today, we see a similar phenomenon happening in image events, "staged acts of protest designed for media dissemination" (Delicath and DeLuca 2003, 315) produced by groups such as Greenpeace, WTO protesters, the Guerilla Girls, and so forth. Image events in movements such as the Arab Spring, in which things such as smart phones become active participants in organizing and documenting protests, also leave visible traces of activity, as they do in the Occupy Movement, where images such as Obama Hope become key players in mobilizing people to dissent. In such unfolding events when unconscious collective activity is common, traces of activity are actually hypervisible, making it possible to empirically account for the active role things play in collective life.

In the past, libraries, museums, and other institutional archives were scholars' main resources for discovering historical traces of collective activity. Today, however, thanks to the Internet, World Wide Web, and other media technologies, traces of collective activity can often be detected via digital research strategies in methods such as iconographic tracking. Interestingly, while such digital kinds of research are occasions in which the active rhetorical life of things can be brought to light, they are also occasions in which the things under study are catapulted back into action, demonstrating how a researcher's intra-actions with a thing play a role in its rhetorical becoming. Digital research, of course, does not just contribute to a thing's circulation and rhetorical becoming. Artifacts buried in libraries, archives, and other storage spaces for long periods of time can experience phases of little activity; however, excavation can suddenly catapult a thing back into circulation and action, making the paths in which it travels and transforms visible.

We see this phenomenon at work all the time as scholars find artifacts in library and digital archives that become impetuses for new investigations, evidence for forwarding theories and claims, and, in some cases, stimuli for years of scholarly production. In one moment a visual or material artifact is at rest, so to speak, then suddenly it is back in action on visible, multiple trajectories that could never have been imagined in its "original" moment of production. My own digital research with the Obama Hope image has intensified its flow as the image is now circulating in print articles, on my website, on my Facebook page, in this book, and so forth. But a better example relates to Edward Said's research. In *Edward Said on Orientalism* (1998), Said claims he began thinking about Orientalism, in part, when he noticed distorted representations of people from the Middle East in historical paintings by Delacroix and Flaubert. When these paintings entered into relations with Said and a host of other entities, not only did they play an active role in the rhetorical production of a new literary theory, they also began to circulate in new and innovative ways in various scholarly circles, which Flaubert and Delacroix could never have predicted. Thus, while archival and digital research affords the opportunity to detect important, and often unforeseen, traces of activity, research is also responsible for reanimating things in ways that perpetuate that thing's circulation, transformation, and consequentiality.

EMBRACING UNCERTAINTY

Such reanimation demonstrates how the world is "an open process of mattering" (Barad 2007, 141) and explains in part why researching the rhetorical life of things is always a complicated, if not impossible, affair. As previously touched upon, because tracing the collective activities of single multiple images such as Obama Hope is particularly messy, scholars must become comfortable with the uncertainty that constitutes much of the research process. As Fleckenstein et al. (2008) have drawn on John Law to argue, if researchers wish to understand a world (or an activity in the world) that is complex and messy, "then we're going to have to teach ourselves to think, to practice, to relate, and to know in new ways" (2), ways that are complex and messy. In particular, if we want to investigate how a wildly consequential a visual thing is, we cannot help but confront materiality's radical openness and flux no matter how much uncertainty such research creates.

For this reason, even though it may require much constraint, suspending interpretation for as long as possible is important during the research process as data is collected and organized. Interpretation is an act of realization, and, as Elizabeth Grosz (1999) draws on Henri Bergson and others to explain, "Realization is a temporal process in which creativity and the new are no longer conceivable" (26). Realization, in other words, is an act of closure signified in the words *I know*. In rhetorical study, when we interpret the rhetorical meanings of fixed, stable objects, we attempt to give certainty to an event that has yet to completely unfold. A new materialist rhetorical approach, on the other hand, recognizes that the impossibility of rhetoric lies in its unwillingness to be confined. After all, as meaning is identified, things are still circulating, transforming, and affecting consequences. Our interpretations are not divorced from this eventfulness. Therefore, a new materialist rhetorical approach acknowledges and embraces a thing's "unwillingness" to be captured by suspending interpretation and belief for as long as possible during the research process.

To further explain this point, it is useful to remember that rhetorical transformation is a dynamic process in which a thing's virtual potential is actualized with time through its unfolding relations. This spatiotemporal process is always marked by a degree of uncertainty because all matter is "a being *on the way* to identity (again)" (Massumi 2002, 232). "Every experience, as it happens," then, "carries a 'fringe' of active indetermination. Experience under way is a constitutionally vague '*something doing*' in the world" (232). This "rhetorical doing" does not stop just because we make an interpretation and fix the meaning of rhetoric in a particular context; nor, then, does the uncertainty and vagueness disappear. If we take seriously the becoming of rhetoric, we must get used to the impossibility of rhetoric—its refusal to be confined and defined. To quote a line from one of my favorite movies, *Almost Famous* (and thereby reveal my affinity for rock-band movies), we have to be aware that "it's all happening." A new materialist rhetorical approach throws up its hands and applauds this research disposition. And in doing so, it refrains from making interpretive judgments early on the research process. Instead, it opens itself up to a world of discovery and embraces the uncertainty that comes with any new research adventure.

Rather than rely on a quote from a fictional rock-band groupie to articulate this research disposition, perhaps it is best to describe this disposition by comparing it to dispositions taken up by other theorists and philosophers. A research disposition, as a reminder, can be thought of as the habits of behavior (or tendencies) acted out, often unconsciously, when performing research. As articulated in the introduction, representational, synchronic approaches to visual rhetoric typically entail reading visual things like stable, fixed texts within limited contexts; analyzing the strategies within a pictorial artifact as well as the rhetorical situation; practicing interpretation to identify how persuasion and identification happens; and so forth. A new materialist rhetorical approach, which is concerned with distributed ontology and ongoing materialization, attempts to disrupt such tendencies by following a circulating image, tracing its divergent rhetorical activities, and focusing on its exterior relations to investigate rhetorical transformation. Embracing the virtual is one disposition necessary for remaining open to the intransitive nature of visual things. As discussed in chapter 2, from a new materialist perspective, reality is change. Embracing the virtual, then, means acknowledging that visual things are "never in position, only ever in passing" (Massumi 2002, 5) and thus studying visual rhetoric as a distributed event always undergoing the process of change. Such disposition helps one remain open to the continuity of transformation and variation that visual things experience with time and space. However, in order to discover the multiple pathways of transformation and the wide spectrum of consequences that unfold during an image's circulation, researchers must also embrace chance, openness, and unpredictability throughout the research process, especially during early stages.

This mental disposition is similar to the one practiced by the situationists, who participated in the technique of *dérive* as conceived by Guy Debord. *Dérive* was developed when Debord started a revolutionary group called the Situationist International to interrupt cultural systems of advanced capitalism in the late 1950s in France. In particular, the situationists attempted to create ways of being in experiences or situations that were alternatives to those prescribed by the capitalist order of the

day.[7] Such alternative ways of being—such disruptions of social norms—
often entailed social-aesthetic practices that subverted the original or
intended purposes of public space and/or altered contemporary art
forms such as film to create alternative ways of experiencing and perceiving the world. One such practice developed by Debord is *dérive*, which
is a way of moving through and occupying public space in ways unimag-
ined by designers and planners. *Dérive* specifically entails letting go of
one's motives and letting oneself be drawn by the psychogeographical
effects that emerge as one wanders through an urban landscape. When
engaging in *dérive*, one might find psychogeographical attractions that
fixate people around certain axes to which they will constantly be drawn
back (Debord 2006a). Yet, in order to maintain the playful-constructive
practice of *dérive*, one must remain open to chance, openness, unpredictability. *Dérive*, as conceived by Debord, was imagined to be practiced in urban landscapes in order to undermine the spectacle of con-
sumerism at the heart of class struggles in France. Therefore, in terms
of twenty-first-century research practices, using this technique is far
removed from its intended purpose.

Yet, the technique of letting go of one's motives and letting oneself be
drawn by psychogeographical attractions offers a constructive disposition
for attending to rhetorical transformation. Psychogeography, as originally defined by Debord (2006b), is "the study of the precise laws and
specific effects of the geographical environment, consciously organized
or not, on the emotions and behavior of individuals." As he explains,
"The charmingly vague adjective *psychogeographical* . . . can be applied to
the findings arrived at by this type of investigation, to their influence on
human feelings. . ." Yet Debord (2006b) also claims that on a general
level, *psychogeographical* refers to any "situation or conduct that seems to
reflect the same spirit of discovery." In terms of new materialist research,
we can think of pyschogeographical effects as those influences that
impact our thoughts and emotions and constantly draw us back to a particular place or site. In order to avoid bounding a case study of a single
multiple image prematurely, it is especially important for a researcher to
resist the temptation to set down one particular research path so early as
to preclude multiple paths of rhetorical transformation from coming to
light. Instead, new materialist researchers must let go of their research
motives, follow the transformations and collective activities of an image,
and let themselves be drawn by the psychogeographical effects that keep
drawing their attention. Through such practice, researchers discover
data that they might never have stumbled upon and thus learn from their
research how to create appropriate boundaries for their case studies.

This research disposition is also similar to the disposition taken during the practice of what Jean-Francois Lyotard calls "peregrination"— the "philosopher's itinerant movement in the world of ideas" (Skordili 2001, 277). This movement is like "wandering among the clouds of ideas and a commitment to respect the ways in which they are constantly eluding our complete understanding" (277). This movement has no middle, beginning, and end in the traditional narrative account of things. Instead, the philosopher is always in the middle of things, engaging in events with an awareness that allows them to be sensitive to the unfolding of things around them. This awareness entails staying open to experience and possibility and suspending judgment for as long as possible. Rather than deciding early on what to zoom in on during the research process, peregrination encourages scholars to consider research as serious play—play with ideas, play with data, play with possibilities for productive inquiries. In addition, rather than engage in analysis, which often leads a researcher to draw conclusions early on in the research process, peregrination encourages tracing, observation, and rich description. Just as *dérive* helps a researcher resist the temptation to settle on a research path too early, then, peregrination helps a researcher resist drawing conclusions before the data-collection phase has been completed and specific transformations and collective activities reveal themselves to a researcher.

When taking a new materialist approach to visual rhetoric, such research dispositions may be uncomfortable for some scholars, yet scholars can accomplish a great deal when they learn how to "feed off uncertainties" (Latour 2005b, 115). Most important, perhaps, such uncertainties encourage us to ask research questions about matters of concern that do not already have the answers embedded in them. Rather than ask, then, for instance, how the Obama Hope image became an important political actor in the US 2008 election, we can ask in a more ambiguous sense how the Obama Hope image came to lead such a brief but wondrous rhetorical life? The first question assumes a matter of fact about the Obama Hope image's rhetorical purpose and meaning and thus leads a researcher to look for answers by focusing only on the Obama Hope image's political roles that unfolded in 2008. The second question, on the other hand, investigates a matter of concern, as no assumption is made prior to research about how it is or why it is that Obama Hope has become so rhetorically consequential. The outcome— that it indeed has led an extraordinary rhetorical life—is considered fact prior to research. However, embedded in the question is an uncertainty that demands investigation into the ways the image was able to spread and all the diverse transformations, activities, and consequences that have unfolded during this single multiple image's life span. Such uncertainty is nothing to shy away from; instead, it is welcomed as a challenge of diving into the great, unpredictable, rhetorical unknown to disclose how visual things become vital, material forces with time and space.

DE-SCRIBING

The principles of a new materialist rhetorical approach do not just constrain how data is collected during the research process, as I have been discussing. If you recall, *to disclose*, as I have been deploying that term, entails making transparent a single image's divergent actualizations as well as the diverse material consequences that emerge via a single multiple image's varied collective activities. To make transparent is an act of shedding light on something—an act made possible by research but extending into a written account. The principles of a new materialist rhetorical approach thus also constrain how research findings are written about in scholarly form. One metaphoric goal of this new materialist rhetorical approach is to create opportunities on the page for contemporary images to speak up about their own important and multifaceted contributions to collective life. Offering symmetrical accounts, as discussed in chapter 3, can help make transparent how visual things become rhetorically vital via their multiple relations. However, to make sure visual things are given their due on the page, such accounts must also rely heavily on descriptions that do not belie their rhetorical complexity.

Description, as understood here, is a composing act (de-scribing) that entails deploying visual actants as networks of mediation in such rich detail that little theoretical explanation is needed to account for how their actions are distributed across proliferating and fluctuating collectives. This point is difficult to accept, as the hypothetical student notes in Latour's (2005b) imagined dialogue presented in the interlude of *Reassembling the Social*. But as iterated previously, visual rhetoric scholars often choose an interpretive framework, grounded in print culture and representationalism, in which to study a visual text within preordained and limited contexts. The problem is that in overrelying on such representational frameworks, we not only, in Raul Sanchez's (2012) terms, "underestimate [visual things'] inherent and deep complexity" but also "mischaracterize their relations with other entities" (238). When we *preestablish* a limited context for our visual rhetorical studies and focus too much attention on the interiority of a picture, I would add, we also end up missing the multitudes of activities that any given thing becomes involved in when it circulates and engages in a multiplicity of associations.

When coupled with following, tracing, and embracing uncertainty, case-study descriptions are better suited to account for how images travel, transform, and acquire power as they both participate in and co-constitute dynamic networks of relations. Description, in this sense, entails foregrounding the actions that emerge from "*an association of actants . . .* in the process of exchanging competencies, offering one another new possibilities, new goals, new functions" (Latour 1999, 182). It entails, in other words, being fully attentive to the traces of activity that one discovers by following an actant intra-acting in a current state of affairs and making the connections, movement, and work of actants fully transparent on the page (Latour 2005b, 143–44). This composition of networked mediations can get quite messy and may seem impossible to follow, trace, and adequately describe, especially from a new materialist perspective that recognizes the ongoing materialization of visual matter. However, if diachronic, symmetrical accounts are constructed in which human and nonhuman entities are equally allowed to mediate action via their ongoing entanglements, good descriptions can adequately account for the rhetorical complexity we are after. Scholars simply need to trust that their rich, realist descriptions can do the work we tend to overrely on contextual explanations to do. "Deploy the content with all its connections," Latour (2005b) claims, "and you will have the context in addition" (146). The context, in other words, will manifest via the connections disclosed on the page.

Such emergent contextualization, if we want to call it that, is not always transparent, especially because during final publishing stages, scholars are often pushed to organize findings for the sake of coherence, word count, reviewer requests, and so forth. The challenge when writing, then, is how to describe a thing's complexity of relations and transformations without "taming" its wild eventfulness. From a new materialist perspective, this conflicting need to organize an image's collective activities and be faithful to its rhetorical abandon can be satisfied by foregrounding rich description and saving the bulk of insights for conclusions. In the case study that follows, for instance, I devoted the body of each chapter to the following descriptions related to Obama Hope's circulation, transformation, and consequentiality:

- Chapter 6 describes how the image was able to circulate broadly and become iconic due to a large number of contributing factors that took place during the 2008 election season.

- Chapter 7 describes how Obama Hope's unexpected collective activities around fair use intensified the image's circulation, diversified its actualizations, and exacerbated its rhetorical impact.
- Chapter 8 describes how Obama Hope experienced viral transformation as it took an ironic rhetorical turn to become a popular commodity, an enactment of parody and satire, and a new cybergenre.
- Chapter 9 describes how Obama Hope unexpectedly circulated across the globe to become a vociferous activist as it participated in a multiplicity of social movements.

While I introduce some concepts mid-description in these chapters to help identify Obama Hope's rhetorical transformation, in most instances I reserve insights for the final pages of each chapter. By privileging description over explanation in such a way, I was able to draw productive insights from the disclosed connections yet simultaneously generate realistic accounts of its movement, change, and consequentiality in the world. This move toward description is admittedly perhaps the greatest challenge of a new materialist approach to rhetorical study. Yet from a new materialist perspective, it is only with trust in this descriptive process that things in all of their rhetorical complexity can finally be given their due.

CONCLUSION

In Old Norse, the North Germanic language we depended on in the introduction to define *thing* or *ding*, *trust* means "confidence, help." In terms of research actions, to say we trust some *thing*, then, means we have confidence in its ability to assemble and reassemble collective life, to help bring a diverse array of entities into intra-action to address diverse matters. To a great extent, this trust requires relinquishing our representational, synchronic habits of reading, analyzing, and explaining a visual thing's diverse powers via methods and theories that have come to define who we are as visual rhetoric scholars. It requires, I would argue, turning to methods such as iconographic tracking and to theories such as actor-network theory and new materialism to create more room on the page for those visual things to make transparent their own multiple, divergent rhetorical becomings. This trust is, as mentioned above, especially difficult because it requires that we, as scholars, learn that actants themselves can "make everything, including their own frames, their own theories, their own contexts, their own metaphysics . . . even their own ontologies" (Latour 2005b, 147). As such, we must grow comfortable with visual rhetoric's refusal to be constrained, refrain from trying to overexplain, and trust that our descriptive symmetrical accounts can do the work necessary to disclose a thing's rhetorical transformations.[8] From a new materialist perspective, our responsibility as scholars is to give things their due by creating scholarship that does not undercut a visual thing's ontological becoming, complex relationality, and transformative thing-power.

When aligned with the new materialist principles articulated at the beginning of this chapter, the research practices of following, tracing, embracing uncertainty, and describing, as envisioned here, can help scholars negotiate these methodological difficulties so that more realistic accounts of visual rhetoric can be generated. Via methods such as iconographic tracking that demand embracing uncertainty throughout much of the research process, we can especially follow and trace how visual things exert force in the world as they circulate, experience multiple modes of existence, and catalyze divergent kinds of change. Such a method, I believe, is especially useful for disclosing how single multiple images such as Obama Hope make rhetorical history as they become important civic-actants both within and beyond US borders. I turn now to articulating how this particular research method can be deployed to do such important work.

Notes

1. Parts of this chapter are being published in "Dingrhetoriks," a chapter in *Thinking with Bruno Latour in Rhetoric and Composition*, edited by Paul Lynch and Nathaniel Rivers (Carbondale: Southern Illinois University Press, 2015).

2. For more on habitus of method, methodology, and accountabilities, see Phelps's "The Method in Theory: Reconstructing a Tradition of Theoretical/Philosophical Inquiry for International Writing Studies," a conference paper delivered at *Writing Research Across Borders II* (February 2011), as well as "How We Take Responsibility for Inquiry: An Account of Accountability," a conference paper delivered at the Conference on College Composition and Communication (March 2003).

3. This conditioning is the reason those familiar with process philosophies, actor-network theory, new materialism, contagion theory, and so forth will find the principles above familiar. All of these principles directly appropriate and build off other scholars' ideas; as such, they ought not be conceived as coming from me alone. The principle of consequentiality, for instance, is heavily informed by Kevin Porter's work with meaning consequentialism while the principle of virality takes up Tony's Sampson's work with assemblage and contagion theory. As with all remixes, the originality comes in synthesizing all of these principles into one research approach.

4. One would assume that a collective's length of duration and extension of space is commensurate. We cannot assume, however, that just because a collective is functioning for longer periods of time, it extends across larger spaces, and vice versa.

5. "Filter bubble" was coined by Eli Pariser (2011) in his book by the same name to refer to a personal ecosystem of information produced by algorithms detecting past click behavior, search history, and so forth. See also chapter 5.

6. For more on runaway objects, see pages 472 through 477 in Spinuzzi's (2011) article "Losing by Expanding: Coralling the Runaway Object."

7. In an article published by Citizen LA (n.d.), Shepard Fairey actually identifies his work as being situationist in its intent to disrupt public space and draw people out of their ordinary routines. According to Fairey, "They [the Situationists] believe that people's lives have become boring and people don't really question their condition as human domesticated livestock, and situations need to be created that snap people out of their boring day-to-day routine. The Situationists felt that art should be revolutionary and it should be part of everyday life, and that's a major rationale behind street art."

8. To read Latour's (2005b) perspective on explanation versus description, see the interlude in *Reassembling the Social.*

5
ICONOGRAPHIC TRACKING[1]

What is most important is that scholars and citizens alike become more engaged, thoughtful, and creative when arguing about the images that are part and parcel of public culture.
—Robert Hariman and John Louis Lucaites, *No Caption Needed*

In May of 2013, a new political scandal broke out when it was discovered that the IRS was targeting conservative groups seeking tax-exempt status during the months and years leading up to the 2012 elections. As we have since learned, President Obama and the White House had nothing to do with the IRS's decision to flag the Tea Party and other conservative groups for extra scrutiny.[2] However, within a week of the newsbreak, fundraising groups for the Republican Party such as American Crossroads (2013) were publishing headlines such as "From 'Hope' to 'Snoop'" mocking "Obama's transformation . . . in light of the recent IRS scandal." Accompanying this headline was no other commentary but a large remix of Obama Hope in which Obama was depicted with a pair of high-tech binoculars positioned over his eyes and the word "Snoop" sitting below where "Hope" typically resides (see Figure 5.1).

On that same day, Obama Hope materialized again on a blog titled *Obama Cartoons*—a personal blog aiming to "advance understanding of political, human rights, economic, democracy, and social justice issues." Surfacing in a political cartoon created by Glenn McCoy, a tattered version of an Obama *Hope* poster was half covered with a remix depicting Obama as an ominous autocrat and the words "Big Brother Is Watching You" (see Figure 5.2). The accompanying headline printed in bright red, bold caps read "Hope and change has gone to hell. Now we are learning that the fictional big brother is real and in the person of President Obama and he is watching you although he will never admit it." Again, on that very same day, Obama Hope materialized in a different political cartoon depicting Obama spying on the media on the blog *Powerline*. This time, it joined a host of other political cartoons intended by the author Steven Hayward to illustrate a current theme running

DOI: 10.7330/9780874219784.c005

Figure 5.1. Snoop *Obamicon,*
American Crossroads, 2013.

through the media about the Obama administration's encroachment on privacy.

This intensity of rhetorical activity took place in just one day of Obama Hope's life, and that single day's activity took place over five years after it first entered into circulation. Especially during 2008, but also throughout Obama's entire first term, Obama Hope was been involved in a storm of rhetorical activity not only in cyberspace but also on urban streets and in protests across the globe. How do we account for such intensity of distributed rhetorical activity? In the previous chapter, I articulated five principles that describe the habitus of method particular to a new materialist rhetorical approach and then discussed specific research actions scholars can take that are line with this approach's guiding assumptions:

Figure 5.2. Big Brother Is Watching You, *Glenn McCoy, 2013. Courtesy of McCoy.*

- embracing the virtual and following an image flow in and out of assemblages to see how it changes in form, media, genre, and function;
- embracing uncertainty and maintaining a radical sense of openness via the practices of *dérive* and *perigrination* in order to account for an image's rhetorical becomings (i.e., rhetorical transformation); and
- tracing an actualized image's exterior relations and committing to rich descriptions of its collective activities.

While useful in a general sense, such research actions do not identify a clear research method for gathering empirical data needed to account for the complex rhetorical life of a single multiple image such as Obama Hope. In terms of method, then, how can we actually collect, organize, analyze, and visualize data in ways that help disclose how a single multiple image flows and contributes to collective life as it materializes in divergent manifestations?

Answers to this question about method are obviously dependent on the image under study. Images move, transform, and reassemble collective space in particular ways depending on the potential afforded by the design, genre, and materiality of their actualized versions as well as the various intra-actions in which they become entangled. In addition, accounting for an image's circulation, transformation, and consequentiality is dependent on the traces of evidence it leaves in its wake and the tools and strategies with which scholars can access its collective activity. Twenty-first-century digital technologies both complicate and ease the study of the rhetorical life of visual things. In one sense, because digital technologies make it relatively easy for those with access[3] to produce, distribute, reproduce, remix, and redistribute images, the often-viral proliferation of images makes it difficult to keep up with their distributed ontology and consequentiality. On the other hand, the Internet, the World Wide Web, and especially social media sites such as Facebook, Flickr, and Twitter provide a vast space of exploration in which to find traces of rhetorical transformation and collective activity. Also, new data-collection and organization tools such as Zotero, in conjunction with mapping and visualization tools, can be useful in aggregating, visualizing, and making sense of research findings. In many cases, new materialist scholars simply need to be inventive in terms of method to track and disclose the rhetorical life of things.[4]

When it came time to study the Obama Hope image, for instance, I lacked a method at my disposal to account for this single multiple image's intense and distributed rhetorical becomings. Neither representational approaches, as they have been typically enacted in textual and rhetorical analyses, nor ethnographic studies that focus on a particular local site at a particular moment in time could account for the Obama Hope image's dynamic circulation and transformations. Nor could these methods account for the numerous rhetorical consequences that unfolded with time as the Obama Hope image entered into various networks of associations. Scholarship on the circulation of images, as discussed in chapter 1, does exist that could possibly be used to account for circulation, transformation, and consequentiality. Without identifying it as such, Hariman and Lucaites (2007) even practice a sort of iconographic tracking in *No Caption Needed* as they track nine iconic photographs across a wide range of media. In terms of method, these scholars explain in a footnote that they "reviewed thousands of books, Websites, museum shows, and related media regarding visual history and the history of photojournalism" (309). Yet so few details are included about how data were collected that I had little to draw on in terms of method when it came time to conduct my own study. The same is true for Lester Olson's (2004) work. Reading his book *Benjamin Franklin's Vision of American Community* reveals that much archival research went into tracking the transformations and circulations of Franklin's motifs, but a detailed description of this research process is not articulated. Clearly the research methods Hariman, Lucaites, and Olson employed yielded productive results in tracking the ongoing circulation of images beyond their initial moment of production. Yet in order for a method to be transferable, it must be transparently methodical (Phelps 2011). These scholars offer so few details about how they conducted their research that emulation was all but impossible. I thus needed to invent (or reinvent) a method I call *iconographic tracking* that could account for the rhetorical life of Obama Hope.

In this chapter, I describe this method and then offer a four-part case study to demonstrate the potential of both a new materialist approach and this method for visual rhetoric. To be clear, we can think of method[5] as "an aspect of a mode of inquiry, consisting of a more or less tightly coupled constellation of strategies for dealing systematically with phenomena as objects of study, according to a tradition of inquiry" (Phelps 2011). As a distinct method accountable to the principles of a new materialist rhetorical approach delineated in chapter 4, iconographic tracking is specifically designed to elucidate how images become rhetorical and iconic in the sense that once actualized in multiple versions, they become not only vital actants capable of catalyzing change and producing space (and time) but also readily recognized and culturally and/or politically significant to a wide cultural group. This method makes use of traditional qualitative strategies such as questionnaires, interviews, and field study as well as inventive digital research strategies to collect, organize, and visualize data. From this data, symmetrical accounts are generated to describe not only how images spread and transform but also how they reassemble collective life through a variety of rhetorical endeavors.

In this chapter I explain how iconographic tracking is conducted in different phases, or stages, of research I label R1, R2, and R3 so others may put it into practice for their own research purposes. Phases are only described as such to help readers develop a chronological sense of how this method works. When it comes to enacting this method, the phases of research do not necessarily unfold in a perfectly linear fashion. Iconographic tracking entails reciprocal research actions, as I try to demonstrate in this written account. In actuality, then, iconographic tracking should be understood as a messy research process that attempts to make sense of a very messy affair.

ICONOGRAPHIC TRACKING IN ACTION

The initial research phase of iconographic tracking (R1) begins by deploying digital research to collect a large data set using basic search engines with image-search capabilities. A big data set is necessary so researchers can identify patterns and trends in an image's materialization (form, medium, genre), location, collective activity, and consequentiality. With a large data set, researchers can also gain a sense of how broad the circulation of the thing under study has been as well as how expansive its collective activity has been. In the initial stages of research, the data set consists largely of web page snapshots made possible through software platforms such as Zotero. The goal of this initial research phase is to collect as much data as possible before conducting data mining and a close analysis of that data. *Data hoarding*, then, might be an appropriate term to describe this initial phase of research.

In order to generate a large data set, it is important not only to embrace the virtual, as suggested by a new materialist rhetorical approach, but also to embrace uncertainty and the spirit of discovery as articulated in the practices of *dérive* and *perigrination*. During the initial research phase, this sense of aimless wonder is vital as it helps a scholar remain open to an image's multiple transformations and intense, unpredictable, and divergent eventfulness. As researchers discover interesting data, they ought to let themselves be drawn by the psychogeographical effects that keep drawing their attention. However, while it is tempting to begin performing close analysis of specific data and thus head down a particular research path, it is essential during this stage of research for scholars to let go of their research motives and simply follow an image's diverse actualizations and transformations to collect as many web page snapshots as possible. Through such practice of wondering and following, scholars can discover data they might never have stumbled upon had they proceeded down a single research path too early even if they may have little idea at this point where their research is taking them.

Once a significant amount of data has been collected, a second phase of research begins—assembling data into a collection (R2). Scholars can think of the assemblage strategy at work here as data mining—a process of sorting through massive amounts of saved data to locate patterns, trends, and relationships. Data mining is advantageous because trends and patterns that might not otherwise be discernible and relations that might have been unknown often become apparent, providing information that can be used to provisionally bound a case study. Data mining often entails generating key terms, or tags, which function to make relationships and trends visible. As researchers identify such trends and patterns, they can begin to create a personal database, or collection of patterned information significant to their provisional research goals. To

assemble a data collection, software such as Zotero can help create folders to store and organize evidence of identified trends or patterns. For
organizational purposes, it is especially useful to create tags that indicate
different transformations in terms of form, media, location, genre, and
so forth and to create title folders with relevant terms that indicate an
image's collective activities and changing rhetorical functions.

For instance, early on in my initial research, I discovered a number
of murals and stickers on urban streets as well as pieces of art in which
different versions of Obama Hope materialized. With Zotero, I thus
took screen shots of websites where such data was evident and created
tags such as *street art, political art,* and so forth, which later helped me
identify some of the image's most popular manifestations. Data mining
also revealed that in addition to becoming a strong political actor in
the 2008 election, Obama Hope was also becoming a number of other
rhetorically powerful things, such as a new genre of critique, a touchstone for copyright debate, and a new media literacy tool. To assemble
evidence of such consequentiality, I created different folders with titles
such as *Critique, Copyright Debate, Education*—tag names for the patterns
of consequences identified during the initial data-collection stage. To
organize data, I simply dragged the tagged web source into the appropriate file, where it was stored via Zotero until I could go back to study
the source in more detail later. Even during this second research phase
(R2), it is important to save close analysis of data in the folders for the
latter stages of research; too often, researchers are inclined to draw conclusions before enough data has been collected. This phase of research
thus requires that scholars look at data only long enough to assemble
folders, set provisional research boundaries, and generate key terms and
tags that can be used as new search terms in the next research phase.

Once folders with data are established and organized, the next phase
of research begins (R3). This phase entails taking a more narrow, controlled approach in order to diversify and expand the data collection
by using new search terms (generated from previous findings) to follow
both visual and verbal threads in relation to each transformation and
rhetorical consequence identified during the data-mining phase. It is
useful here to utilize a diverse range of search engines, especially visual
search engines such as TinEye and Search Cube, as well as search-engine
options to narrow search by video, shopping, blogs, and so forth. This is
especially the case since, as previously mentioned, search engines such
as Google tend to act as vital actants in and of themselves and create
"filter bubbles"—Eli Pariser's (2011) term for indicating how information is edited out by algorithms based on personalized interests, search

history, and clicking behaviors. Because search engines limit exposure to certain data, they constrain our ability to follow a single multiple image and trace its various collective activities, and thus they ultimately influence the object of study itself. Considering such intervention, it is important to use different search engines throughout the research process, and I would even suggest using different computers.

During this research phase (R3), it is also productive to explore different social media sites such as Flickr, YouTube, Facebook, and Twitter as well as other independent organizations made accessible via the Creative Commons.org website. After collecting new data in relation to previously identified trends, researchers can simply data mine and organize new data, generating new folders if need be. Even though research during this phase is more narrow and controlled, it also demands staying open to finding as much data as possible and thus moving back and forth between in both visual and verbal form, tracing its collective activities, and assembling and reassembling data into appropriate folders. This phase of iconographic tracking (R3) can thus be described as a recursive process that fluctuates between data mining and assembling a collection, a process productive in that it helps discover an image's specific remixes and unintended consequences as well as particular networks of collectives in which the image has played a major role. These discoveries also open up divergent research paths necessary for gaining a deeper understanding of an image's eventfulness and rhetorical transformation. The wild rhetorical abandon of an image such as Obama Hope can only be disclosed by conducting a close study of specific collective activities, however. The data generated and organized during this third research phase (R3) is thus also useful in helping scholars decide which collective activities they want to study more closely during the next research phase.

RESEARCHING THE SEVEN PROCESSES

During this fourth research phase (R4), researchers conduct a close study of specific collectives to determine how an image intra-acts with humans and various technologies and other entities to materialize, spark change, and produce collective space. Such investigation entails attending to seven interrelated material processes[6]—composition, production, transformation, distribution, circulation, collectivity, and consequentiality. Mapping out these processes helps discover how many different happenings, desires, peoples, technologies, collective actions, and so forth come into play during an image's rhetorical becomings. By investigating how these processes overlap, it is also possible to see how a singular image undergoes recomposition, reproduction, redistribution, and reassemblage—all processes that intensify the circulation, transformation, and consequentiality of not only a particular image but also its derivatives. What exactly needs to be considered in relation to each process depends on the visual thing under investigation. However, to give readers some sense of how to conduct research during this phase (R4), I describe the kinds of, but certainly not the only, questions one can ask when studying these seven interrelated processes. These processes of study are not taken up in a linear, chronological fashion. Yet, in order to generate complex, messy, ontological accounts of how images circulate and become rhetorical with time and space, researchers ought to attend to all these interlaminated processes in a single case study.

COMPOSITION

Composition refers to an image's rhetorical design, while *production* refers to the techno-human labor involved in bringing a design into material construction. When studying an image's composition, researchers consider, if recoverable, the articulated exigence and purpose for rhetorical design as well as how visual elements, conventional practices, and design strategies work together, often multimodally, in an actualized image's composition. Especially when remix is a fundamental ingredient in an image's rhetorical life, scholars must pay close attention to intertextuality and identify how different rhetorical tropes and visual topoi are at work. They must also consider gazes to see what kind of relation is constructed not only between objects within a picture but also between the visual thing and viewers. Scholars explore such concerns to discover how design creates the potential for certain identifications, affects, persuasive messages, and/or propaganda to manifest. Yet such design issues are also studied in relation to the five other material processes. For example, researchers may ask, how does the rhetorical design create potential for rhetorical velocity and/or transformation? How does rhetorical design influence people to (re)assemble around an image? And how does a design spark specific consequences that can be empirically mapped out? Composition, then, is studied in relation to the other processes just as the other processes are studied in relation to composition.

To address such questions, rhetorical and semiotic analyses of a picture's interior relations are useful to help identify what signs, colors, styles, and so forth are at play within the frame that enables interpretation by those who encounter it. Yet composition (as well as production and distribution) is contingent on material resources, labor practices, cultural values, and cultural positioning. In her work with historical needlepoint samplers, for instance, Maureen Goggin (2004) shows how the content of needlepoint samplers changed from pictorial to verbal due to the influence of print culture and the rise of protestant religions as well as changes in class designations. Due to such kinds of exterior influence, scholars must move beyond studies of interiority to consider the conditions of design (again, as well as production and distribution) contingent on social, cultural, economic, political, and technological forces (106). In contemporary US culture experiencing a shift from literacy to electracy (Ulmer 1997) one might especially consider how digital technologies, copyright laws, new ideas about participatory culture, social media, and so forth are influencing design as well as the other material processes.

In addition, especially when images are remixed by people of different genders, cultures, races, and so forth or in ways that prevent a message from being clear, it is not always easy to tell why particular images are recomposed in certain ways, what designers intend, and/or how they designed and produced their reproductions. Qualitative research strategies such as questionnaires and interviews are useful here, and social media sites such as Flickr, Tumblr, Facebook, and Myspace make it is possible to easily gain access to designers. Such qualitative research is important for a number of reasons. First, it helps identify emotions, thoughts, actions, experiences, historical and personal backgrounds, and so forth, which, in turn, help explain why an image was composed and/or recomposed in particular ways. While one may argue that such information ought not be important to an approach mainly focused on futurity and consequentiality, such intentions help disclose what meanings an image has for the designer and perhaps others in their culture, which are important to consider, especially when trying to account for how single multiple images spark consequences in countries other than the United States. Second, such qualitative research can help uncover how visual design might have influenced other unintended consequences. For instance, as will become clear in part 1 of the Obama case study, while Fairey intended to create a single image to help garner votes during the 2008 presidential election, he did not foresee *just* how important this image would be to the official campaign. Yet in talking to Scott Thomas, one of the head designers of Obama's official 2008 campaign, I was able to learn why and how the design of the Obama Hope image came to play such an influential role in branding Obama during that election season. Finally, in talking to designers and others intimately involved in the composing processes, scholars can also learn more about the production and distribution processes that influence a visual thing's design and vice versa. Oftentimes, after all, such processes cannot be divorced from each other.

PRODUCTION

Studies of production are especially important to iconographic tracking as they help discover what materials, activities, people, technologies, institutional infrastructures, and bureaucratic forces are intra-acting to bring an image's design into actualized form. Activity theory is useful here to help understand what different kinds of interlaminated and distributed activities are involved in bringing a design into material form. In such studies, scholars pay attention to what kinds of technologies are involved as well as what kinds of human labor are enacted by various people taking on different roles. Historical production processes, circulations, and uses of images shape contemporary manifestations of images as designers and other folks bring that knowledge to bear on current designs and production processes (Bianchi 2012).[7] Thus, scholars want to ask if traditional kinds of production and distribution practices are being deployed and/or if innovative ones are being developed that deserve special attention.

Institutional factors also need to be considered, as many visual things come into being under the influence of particular industries. As Finnegan (2010) notes, "How one analyzes institutions will vary by case, but attention to institutions typically involves studying the economics of production, the ideological aspects of an institution's goals or ideals, and institutional forces that enable or constrain the production [process]" (253). Fairey, for instance, not only works in the graphic design industry but also in the industry of street art. As will become apparent in the following chapter, this latter line of work greatly influenced not only his design and production process but also the distribution tactics used to help Obama Hope achieve mass circulation. Genre, too, bears on production just as it does on design and distribution. As such, the histories of genre design, production, and distribution ought to be considered, especially in relation to institutional and other forces. Again, in the case of Obama Hope, historical influences as well as personal experiences working with the genres of political posters and street art influenced the design, production, and distribution of the Obama Works in which Obama Hope first manifested in its most recognizable form. More significantly, discussions of genre in relation to Obama Hope sparked a massive amount of metacultural activity, which I will later discuss, and thus can be directly attributed to accelerating the circulation of Obama Hope. Just as scholars need to study composition in relation to the other material processes, so then should production be studied in relation to all the others as well.

Researching the production of single multiple images can get pretty messy for several reasons. One, in relation to a specific actualization, the interlaminated activity of production often takes place across collectives as people with different objectives and goals come together for collaborative purposes to produce a specific design and picture. Two, because it is important to account for an image's divergent manifestations, studies of production ideally need to take place in relation to each actualized version. When an image such as Obama Hope goes viral, it is often difficult to locate the designers of each manifestation, which in turn makes it very difficult to learn about all the production processes that come into play during the rhetorical life of a single multiple image. Three, the various forces, especially historical ones, that influence design and production are often invisible and can only become transparent through qualitative research. Even if those involved in production can be tracked down and interviewed, various people often offer different stories about the contributing factors to the production process. Some, like Fairey himself, even distort their production stories in order to avoid economic, political, or social consequences. For all these reasons, rhetorical choices must be made about when it is most important to study the production processes of various transformations and what to include in such accounts. Researchers must also accept that in most cases of dealing with a single multiple image that has gone viral, the story of production will be incomplete. Therefore, for multiple reasons, many stories of production must go untold when accounting for the rhetorical life of an image.

TRANSFORMATION

Transformation is studied by following an image via digital research and paying close attention to how a circulating image changes in terms of design, form, medium, materiality, genre, and function as it enters into new associations. With the advent of the Internet and the expansion of participatory culture, in which remix is a foundational vehicle for communication (Lessig 2008), images transform at lightning speeds and in diverse ways. One only has to perform a simple Google Image search for *Obama Hope image* to find evidence of how contemporary images can

Figure 5.3. Obama Hope *Portrait made out of Illinois License Plates, Drew Shade. Courtesy of Shade.*

transform widely across different forms, media, and genres at viral rates. In terms of form, materiality, and medium, while an image such as the now-iconic pepper-spray meme largely changes across digital manifestations, other images such as Obama Hope often transform in a wide spectrum of physical manifestations in addition to digital ones. For instance, by 2009, in addition to the instantiations previously discussed, the Obama Hope image had been constructed out of a wide range of materials—dryer lint, colored credit cards, LEGOs, dried beans, pennies, and license plates, just to name a few (see Figure 5.3). Such detectable change in form and materiality makes it evident that images often undergo not only viral circulation but also viral transformation.

Studies of transformation are especially useful in tracking how images undergo change in ways unanticipated by the "original" image's designer and spark unexpected consequences. In early 2008, for instance, and as I describe in more detail in the following chapter, a PDF of the *Progress* poster with Obama Hope was made freely available for download on Fairey's Obey website to increase chances for the

Figure 5.4. Gratitude, *Lucas Long, 2012. Photograph Courtesy of Patter Hellstrom.*

image's mass reproduction. Within a short time, Obama supporters were reproducing and proliferating the poster at rates that one single organization could never achieve on its own. In such cases, Obama Hope reproduced to serve Fairey's intended functions, and in many renditions, Obama Hope's design barely transformed. Yet the image has transformed in ways that only those very familiar with the image would even recognize and has become consequential in ways far different than Fairey undoubtedly imagined. Obama Hope, for example, just recently transformed when it materialized in a mural Lucas Long designed as an ode to his school and in honor of recently deceased schoolmate— a far cry from the image's original intent of garnering Obama support (see Figure 5.4). Attending to such transformations makes evident how unforeseeably rhetorical and influential Obama Hope still is as it continues to circulate in diverse forms and genres and take on conjunctive and disjunctive purposes. Attending to transformation also helps elucidate how things continue to circulate long after the original designer's distribution efforts.

CIRCULATION AND DISTRIBUTION

Because circulation of a single multiple image is largely beyond a designer's control, and because it unfolds in nonlinear, divergent ways during an image's rhetorical lifespan, the movement of an image in and out of assemblages is nearly impossible to map out. However, from a new materialist perspective, the concern with circulation is less about generating a coherent map of where something moves than about trying to account for how something flows. When it comes to images, pictures, videos, ideas, concepts, etc. that circulate via the Internet, such inquiry increasingly demands becoming aware of the Internet and computer infrastructures' influence on their circulation. In recent years, scholars such as Beer (2013) and Nahon and Hemsley (2013), among others, have begun to pay close attention to how algorithms, cookies, coded software, etc. influence how media flows. As David Gunkel (2009) has argued in "Beyond Mediation," the computer is not a passive, neutral object. "Instead of functioning as a virtually immaterial and transparent channel through which human agents exchange messages, the computer participates in and contaminates the process. It acts on messages, significantly alters them, and delivers information that was not necessarily selected, composed, or even controlled by human participants" (63). While we are beginning to learn how website algorithms, built-in constraints in social media, and networked structures of blogs influence how images circulate thanks to the work of Beer and Nahon and Hemsley respectively, we need to expand our investigation into the socio-technical systems that influence circulation. While I neglected to do such research for my own case study, visual rhetoric scholars attending to circulation thus might begin to ask questions about the hidden materiality and structures of computers and the Internet, as well as the relevant economic, political, institutional systems, contribute to how images circulates on both the inter and outernet.

Asking specific questions about other material processes involved in an image's rhetorical transformation also helps to better understand circulation. Questions about transformation, for instance, which prompt a researcher to follow an image, help identify in what assemblages and locations an image has landed, as does asking questions about collectivity, which prompts scholars to trace an image's collective activity. Questions about distribution are also particularly useful. As James Porter (2009) suggests, we can think of distribution as the initial decisions made about how to package a message in order to send it to its intended audience (214). But distribution is also constituted by the intentional strategies deployed to transport that message to that audience(s) as well as the collective networks of human and nonhuman entities involved in putting those strategies into action. Distribution—conceived here as deliberate activity—is thus studied by investigating the intentional strategies deployed to disseminate an actualized image as well as the collaborations between participating human and nonhuman entities involved in that distribution process. With its ability to identify interlaminated activities involved in collaborative work, activity theory is useful in studies of distribution, especially when a tangled web of collectives is involved. This approach is particularly productive when coupled with Malcom Gladwell's (2002) epidemiological approach, which has been explored recently by Kristen Seas (2012) for its theoretical applications in rhetorical study. Via such research of social networks, it is possible to learn how various actors take on specific roles, often on their own accord, to help propagate an image's circulation in actualized versions.

Questions about metaculture are also especially useful in discovering how images flow between abstract and concrete forms. As Greg Urban (2001) explains in *Metaculture*, inertia generated by already-existing traditions and artifacts drives the production and flow of culture— that which is socially learned and transmitted. Yet, as Urban illustrates through a discourse analysis of movie reviews, culture, especially in late-capitalistic societies, accelerates through metaculture—"a set of cultural elements and objects, such as discourse, with the ability to represent or portray or refer to cultural elements and objects" (224). Metaculture, in other words, "carries an idea about culture" (224). To explain, Urban points out that culture has a "built-in propensity for change"; it is inherently dynamic, characterized by periods of acceleration and deceleration (3). The pace at which culture changes is driven by motion generated between the circulation of metaculture, or ideas and interpretations about culture, and that thing it comments upon. Metaculture often occurs at a faster rate than the actual cultural object circulates (Urban 2001, 227). As such, expressed interests, criticisms, rumors, and so forth can be totally detached from the cultural objects on which they comment. This explains the reasons people can know much about a certain image without even having encountered that image in the physical realm (226). It also explains why images themselves are "less the source of their own intrinsic self-definition and more the product of meanings emanating" from metaculture (226).[8]

While the circulation of things themselves is dependent on a number of factors—distribution, technologies, human labor, and so forth—the acceleration and deceleration of metaculture is driven by the intensity or lack of interest stimulated by both those things' novelty and their resemblance to things in the past, whether that resemblance relates to their form, design, genre, or some other characteristic. An image such as Obama Hope, then, circulates due to the distribution of its divergent

actualized forms—on the streets in murals, in various digital reproductions across websites, in pictures screen printed onto t-shirts, and so
forth. Yet, to a great extent, images circulate because of the metacultural
activity generated by talk about their actualized forms—in reviews, articles, blog posts, and so forth—that drive and often accelerate their flow.
As will become clear in the Obama Hope case study, such metacultural
activity, in turn, often stimulates the production of other actualized versions with the same image or derivatives that may resemble it in form,
genre, style, content, or function. As these new actualizations begin to
take on a life of their own, the recursive process between metaculture
and culture begins all over again in divergent ways. While I do not talk
about this much in the case study, a clear example of such recursivity
is evident in the case of the Obama Joker that began to spread widely
in 2009. The first known rendition of the Obama Joker was created
by some members of FSU College Republicans in 2008, who remixed
Obama Hope by depicting Obama as the Joker—the villainous character
played by Heath Ledger in the 2008 film *The Dark Knight*—on a white
poster with the words "Why so Socialist?" As reported by Rebecca Hertz
(2010), the students remixed Obama Hope to gain attention from the
college audience at a campus rally when Democratic vice president Joe
Biden was visiting. The following January, a similar "Jokerized" image of
Obama was photoshopped by Firas Alkhateeb, which began to stir a lot
of controversy when it was downloaded from the Internet, remixed with
the single word *socialism*, and began popping up on streets across the
United States (see Figure 5.5). Much metacultural activity arose about
the accusation that Obama had socialist leanings as well as about who
the author of this popularized version was, which also happened with
Obama Hope. In addition, Obama Joker itself began to spread, transform, and catalyze change widely as imitative behaviors were triggered
and it participated in much on-the-ground political activity.

   As is evident in this case, and as will become even more clear with
Obama Hope, the metacultural activity of single multiple images is
largely beyond any single person's control just as is the reproduction,
transformation, and circulation of the image itself. In a participatory
culture, this is the case no matter how much public relations tactics or
copyright laws might be used to constrain how something is reproduced,
appropriated, and redistributed. Evidence of metacultural activity is
especially hypervisible on the World Wide Web, not only in blog posts,
news articles, and editorials but also in the comments on such works.
Some comments are surely crafted by Internet trolls who purposefully try
to start arguments and debate; therefore, it is difficult to determine just

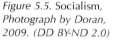

Figure 5.5. Socialism,
Photograph by Doran,
2009. (DD BY-ND 2.0)

how authentic the articulated opinions and concerns are that emerge in relation to a particular image. However, as Whitney Phillips (2012) has stated in the *Atlantic*, what matters most about trolling are the consequences. As we will see in the case of Obama Hope Mystery in chapter 7, oftentimes a conversation takes place on a blog for several days or weeks, and this conversation, in and of itself, stirs debate on other blogs and/or collective activity in which people actually respond and organize on the ground to address particular concerns. In such cases, whether trolls are involved are not, metacultural activity that arises in response to an image is producing change and space and ought to be accounted for in the rhetorical life of an image. When trying to account for how a single multiple image flows, then, it is important not only to gather as much information as possible about the intentional strategies used by various collectives to disseminate an actualized image but also to look at the ensuing metacultural activity that emerges, often unpredictably.

COLLECTIVITY AND CONSEQUENTIALITY

While the metacultural activity that emerges in response to an image is important for understanding how things flow, it is also important, as the above example demonstrates, for disclosing how images reassemble collective life. A new materialist rhetorical approach, if you recall, assumes that images have an ability to induce assemblage—a process in which an actor "bends space around itself" (Callon and Latour 1981, 286) by attracting various heterogeneous entities to assemble in open-ended collectives. These collectives, which leave traces of activity, take on unique spatio-temporal configurations and acquire the capacity to impact change via the emergent intra-actions that take place among varying entities. Thus, as articulated in chapter 4, during this final research phase (R4), iconographic tracking works hard to identify how different collectives emerge as human and nonhuman entities enter into various associations with an image. In regard to such collectivity, researchers rely on digital and qualitative research strategies to identify interrelated collectives that may be involved in the design, production, distribution, and/or circulation of an actualized image. Researchers then take an activity theory approach to study the specific intra-actions that take place within these collectives to see to what kinds of rhetorical activities unfold. Again, such research can become quite messy, especially for an image such as Obama Hope that goes viral and becomes wildly consequential in a short time via a plethora of collective activities. Yet it is only via such research that scholars can begin to identify the specific ways in which an image generates consequences via its divergent associations and thus becomes meaningful throughout its rhetorical life.

In order to account for an image's rhetorical eventfulness, it is important to study both intended and unintended consequences as well as to investigate as many consequences as possible to recover the nuanced ways an image contributes to collective life. In such investigation, rather than confine studies of an image's consequences to a specific context, it's best to account for how different events *are generated* via an image's collective actions. Especially in the case of a single multiple image such as Obama Hope that has materialized in so many unpredictable places across the world, it is also very important to consider emplacement. As Ronald Scollon and Suzanne B. K. Scollon (2003) have helped us understand with their work in geosemiotics, the location in which actualized images land matters to their meaning. First, images shape landscapes differently depending on whether they surface in governmentally or privately sanctioned places or whether they trespass into areas without permission. Second, images shape landscapes differently depending on what other signs they are interacting with not only within but also beyond a picture frame. When attending to collectivity and consequentiality, then, scholars ought to play close attention to emplacement and begin to ask questions such as, how does an image's appearance in this particular place bend space not only by inducing others to respond to and enter into relation with it but also by changing the purpose of that place where it temporarily appears? In the case of an image such as Obama Hope that shows up in places ranging from fields of grass on private farms, to tattoos on human bodies, to signposts in Paris, place matters. Therefore, we need to be asking how images produce rhetorical spaces[9]—how places become rhetorical when images penetrate them.

In terms of consequentiality, we must also be concerned with bodies, and we must explore the affective dimensions of visual rhetoric, as I have previously mentioned but want to reiterate here. By *affect*, I am referring to energy transfer and sense appeals that are material, autonomous, and dynamic and that register in bodily experience before cognition takes place. Affect is important to rhetoric in that it makes bodies vulnerable, a condition arising out of responsiveness to others (Marback 2008) that is necessary for persuasion and symbolic action to occur (Davis 2010). Affect is always transmitted in that it spreads, contaminates, and is absorbed by various bodies; as such, affect is contagious. As Nigel Thrift (2008) has drawn on Tarde and Deleuze to argue, affective contagions are transferred among a wide variety of human and nonhuman entities that are able to receive and transmit energy and affective messages. Such contagion often takes place via a complex process of desire, imitation, and invention. To be more specific, as Tony Sampson (2012) also draws on Tarde to explain, biological needs repeated in everyday life are transformed via encounters with social invention into a second kind of desire we can think of as cultural contagions (25). Such social desires and inventions then radiate outward into society, where they experience repetition, accumulation, and adaptation, which helps explain how small innovations can become quite large in terms of presence and impact within and across cultures. In relation to Obama Hope, for instance, we might say that people's biological drive for improved quality of life was appropriated, expressed, and transmitted via the social invention of Fairey's Obama Works that propagated desires for change, progress, and hope for a better future. Such image-inventions, we might call them, were repeated and imitated as various people tapped into these desires and came to believe in the actual potential of affective contagion as well as the idea that Obama could actually transform those desires into political action. In simplest terms, as people came to believe that hope, change, and progress could become contagious and actualized, they unconsciously (and consciously of course) jumped on the rhetorical bandwagon and began reproducing and adapting the image-invention of Obama Hope at viral rates. How, then, might we build on the work of Edbauer Rice (2005) and Seas (2012) and begin to account for how single multiple images such as Obama Hope alter bodies and space in ways that drive contagious rhetorical action?

While iconographic tracking, like any method, can never fully account for or keep up with all the rhetorical consequences a single multiple image cogenerates, it can at least help recover some of the most visible ways that a single image has influenced and continues to shape collective existence. In such recoveries, scholars must be careful not to generate asymmetrical accounts in which humans take on the center role of collective activities. This is not to say that human beings are not given their due. You will notice in the next chapter that Shepard Fairey, Yosi Sergant, and others sometimes steal the spotlight in accounting for the composition, production, and distribution of Obama Hope in relation to the 2008 presidential campaign. Yet, as much as possible, the image under study and its multiple relations with all kinds of diverse entities ought to take the leading role in descriptive accounts. In creating such symmetrical accounts of an image's consequentiality, all matter can come to play an important mediating role in collective life.

VISUALIZING AND RECORDING DATA

At the risk of overdoing this methodical discussion of iconographic tracking, I want to just briefly touch upon how visualizing and recording data can help researchers solidify what kinds of questions they want to tackle in a written case study. Data visualization, or what many refer to as *information visualization,* has several inventive affordances especially valuable for mapping transformations across genre, purpose, form, and location. As Colin Ware (2000), author of *Information Visualization: Perception for Design* explains, data visualization boosts several cognitive capabilities, which are beneficial for making sense of one's data. To name a few, data visualization enables rapid interpretation of high quantities of information; enhances perception of trends, patterns, analogies, and threads; leads to new revelations about data and the way it is collected; facilitates understanding; and leads to hypothesis formation. Rather than think of visualization as a means of delivering a final argument or research findings to a wider audience, researchers must think of visualization as an integral part of the research process when conducting iconographic tracking. It is research activity that is

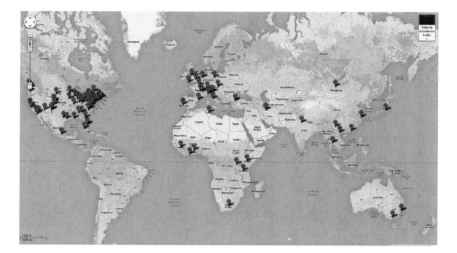

Figure 5.6. Obama Hope *Sightings Across the Globe, 2008–2009, Screenshot Created by* Laurie Gries, 2014. Google, *Reprinted with Permissions.*

co-responsible for producing research findings and is ultimately the object of study itself.

In the digital humanities, as is evident in Lev Manovich's (2001) work with cultural analytics, as well as Franco Moretti's (2007) and others' work with literary genres and spatial analysis, using data visualization as a research strategy is not uncommon. Visualizing data, as Richard White (2010) argues, is a productive "means of doing research; it generates questions that might otherwise go unasked, it reveals historical relations that might otherwise go unnoticed, and it undermines, or substantiates, stories upon which we build our own versions of the past." During iconographic tracking, new digital technologies that make use of concept mapping are useful in helping a researcher organize data, identify common trends in rhetorical functions, and identify periods of circulation intensity. Inventive affordances of geographical mapping are also useful for keeping track and making sense of the circulations and transformations of images as they manifest across the globe. During my research, for example, I made use of Google Maps to document where Obama Hope and its various transformations showed up around the world within its first eighteen months of circulation (see Figure 5.6). Admittedly, much more work could have been done here to use visualizations during the research process to map out, make sense of, and generate new inquiries about the various genres, media, and material forms in which the image surfaced.[10] However, geographic mapping, at the very least, can help identify where a single multiple image has circulated so researchers can begin to ask questions about the reasons an image materializes so often say in Africa rather than South America, as was the case with Obama Hope. Such inquiries often generate new directions for further research.

While data visualizations such as Google Maps are useful in helping generate new inquiries, visualizations can also help describe a single multiple image's transformation and consequentiality in ways that do not demand relation building. According to a new materialist rhetorical approach, remember, scholars must embrace description without overexplaining. When we try to account for certain relations or trends, we often overstep our new materialist boundaries and end up erasing a single multiple image's divergent eventfulness and consequentiality in favor of interpreting those relations or trends. Thus, during the early writing stages, it is useful to also create visualizations that can help describe research findings without a coherent explanation. Such visualizations can come in mapping form, as is evident in the map of Obama Hope's collective activities and networked relations included in this book's final chapter (see Figure 10.1).[11] Practicing ontography to generate lists similar to the lists described by Ian Bogost (2012) in *Alien Phenomenology* is also very useful in this regard. While ontology is concerned with theories of nature and existence, ontography is concerned with description (36). The kind of ontography Bogost introduces avoids developing a coherent map that details how heterogeneous entities are related to other entities. Ontography is more like the practice of recording juxtaposed things; the simplest example is a list that identifies a group of entities loosely joined by a comma (38). Latour is famous for creating such lists, which function primarily, in Bogost's words, as "provocations, as litanies of surprisingly contrasted curiosities" (38). Bogost likes such lists because they emphasize disjunction rather than flow—an emphasis that makes evident how entities involved in any given collective or system are always isolated, mutual aliens (40). As such, Bogost recommends ontographical cataloguing that abandons "anthropocentric narrative coherence in favor of worldly detail" (42). Such cataloguing might produce an incoherent mess, but listing objects without the need to explicate connections goes a long way, as Bogost argues, in generating greater awareness of and drawing attention toward them (45).

The kind of ontography enacted in the method of iconographic tracking during the visualization phase of research is similar in that it embraces rich description, lets go of any need for coherence, and favors a record of not necessarily connected things. However, the lists being generated here are less concerned with exploding the innards of things to reveal the hidden density of a thing as Bogost imagines the lists functioning (58). Instead, lists are concerned with generating a detailed map of places an image has surfaced around the globe; genres, materials, and media in which an image materializes; and rhetorical functions an image takes on during circulation. The Obama Hope image, for instance, has led a spectacular rhetorical life as it has transformed in terms of genres, media, and function. Cataloguing such transformations would include the following three lists, which are condensed here for illustrative purposes:

- murals, protest signs, advertisements, lesson plans, cartoons, commercial art, comic props, graffiti, political art;
- credit cards, dried beans, pennies, blades of grass, yarn, ink, thread, spray paint, paper, pumpkins, pencil lead, metal, acrylic paint, license plates, marshmallows, post-it notes, thumbtacks, canned beans, icing, pixels, LEGOs, cans of beans, dryer lint;
- political actor, commodity fetish, advertising strategy, novel cyber-genre, touchstone for contemporary debates about fair use, educator, advocate for remix commemorative theme, branding machine, transnational activist, social network generator.

During such cataloguing, scholars ought not be so concerned with making connections among these functions and/or among these functions and the genres and media in which an image materializes. These lists purely serve as a record to help researchers see, acknowledge, and attend to an image's diverse actualizations and the divergent kinds of rhetorical functions an image has taken on. In producing these lists, researchers can begin to solidify specific research questions based on their research findings and go back to the data or collect new data to find answers to their questions.

Before concluding this chapter, I just want to note that Bogost (2012) sees disjunctive listing produced by ontography as a remedy for what he and others invested in object oriented ontology (OOO) identify as the "problem with Deleuzean becoming, a preference for continuity and smoothness instead of sequentiality and fitfulness [and incompatability]" (40).[12] As such, appropriating ontography for iconographic tracking might seem contradictory to a new materialist rhetorical approach articulated herein. When conducting iconographic tracking, however, the genres, media, and functions in lists such as the ones above are based on trends and patterns identified during earlier research phases via the help of Zotero and mapping technologies. Some connections between items on the list therefore do exist, and when useful, these connections are attended to in accounts of research findings when it comes time to write a case study. Such written explication, as is evident in my multipronged case study of Obama Hope, however, does not necessarily result in a linear account of a thing's rhetorical life, nor does it result in the smooth explication of a thing's rhetorical becomings. As articulated in part 1, an image does not unfold in a single-threaded, sequential, continuous manner but rather along divergent and seemingly simultaneous spatiotemporal channels. As such, while identifying the rhetorical life of an image might be the main goal of iconographic tracking, what is actually generated via the help of ontographical lists is an account of a single multiple image's dynamic network of distributed, unfolding, and unforeseeable becomings. Such an account could never be anything but discontinuous, rough, and messy.

CONCLUSION

The Obama Hope image's complex rhetorical life did not emerge overnight. However, once actualized in cyberspace, the Obama Hope image did experience viral circulation and gain mass recognition in a matter of weeks. Within one short year, it also earned a reputation as one of the most iconic images to surface in recent years. Such intensity of eventfulness, which I discovered early on during research via iconographic tracking, raises important questions that the following case study ultimately and specifically aimed to take up: Just how did the Obama Hope image go viral and become a cultural icon, national symbol, and powerful rhetorical agent in such a short span of time? And just what kind of rhetorical impact has this single multiple image made since entering into circulation in early 2006?

In this chapter, I have articulated how to conduct iconographic tracking and, using the Obama Hope image as an example, I have demonstrated how it can generate data needed to develop[13] and address such questions. In the following chapter, I describe how specific distribution tactics, collective actions, and metacultural activity helped the Obama Hope image become a powerful rhetorical agent in the 2008 election. Once actualized in divergent digital and print forms, metaculture spread, and Obama Hope's circulation and transformation accelerated as it began to materialize in a diverse array of forms and media and become part of collectives in ways that far exceeded Fairey's expectations. In addition, many unanticipated consequences emerged in 2008 and beyond, which both complicate and deepen our understanding of the image's rhetorical impact. In the remaining chapters, I thus focus on a variety of unanticipated consequences that have emerged during the Obama Hope image's life and helped (a) accelerate the image's circulation and transformation; (b) diversify its rhetorical functions; and (c) manifest its potential to go viral and reassemble the social. My aim in this four-part case study is to not only paint a vivid picture of *how* this image gained iconic status in such a short amount of time but also how this image has come to and continues to lead such an extraordinary rhetorical existence as it circulates and contributes to collective life.

Notes

1. The term *iconographic tracking* is influenced by Jessica Enoch's work with historiographic tracking, a methodology she introduces to help scholars look beyond the immediate rhetorical situation to see how women's rhetorics survive and take on new rhetorical effects. See Jessica Enoch, "Survival Stories: Feminist Historiographic Approaches to Chicana Rhetorics of Sterilization," *Rhetoric Society Quarterly* 35, no. 3 (2005): 5–30.

2. For more on this IRS scandal that broke out in 2013, see Stein and Delaney (2013) "IRS Official: White House Was Not Involved in Targeting of Conservative Groups" (*Huffington Post*, June 18, 2013. http://www.huffingtonpost.com/2013/06/18/irs -scandal-washington_n_3460904.html). As later discovered, the IRS was also targeting progressive groups, although not to the same extent.

3. By access to (re)producing, distributing, and remixing images here, I mean more than simply proximity to various technologies. Instead, I draw on Adam Banks (2006), who explains that access entails being able to, individually and collectively, "use, critique, resist, design, and change technologies in ways that are relevant to [people's] lives and needs" (41).

4. For more on the invention or reinvention of method, see Sullivan and Porter's (1997) *Opening Spaces*.

5. As Phelps (2011) also notes, strategies of inquiry, such as interviewing, questionnaires, and observations, are not particular to a single method. Rather, strategies become constitutive of method when "they are habitually associated in a constellation of strategies and defined relative to a tradition of inquiry that legitimates and disciplines them" (5). What distinguishes one method from another, then, is the unique configuration of strategies typically employed in a method, or more precisely, "how tightly coupled strategies are in these constellations, and how impervious they are to strategies that are not habitual to that method" (5).

6. In "Studying Visual Modes of Public Address," Cara Finnegan (2010) identifies five approaches to analyzing images, which together, she argues, create "*a way of seeing* the role of visual images in public culture" (251). These approaches include production, composition, reproduction, circulation, and reception. The seven material processes I identify are different in many ways, and, unlike Finnegan, I suggest attending to all these processes in a single case study. Nonetheless, I am indebted to Finnegan's work as it has helped me think through the material processes I describe here. I recommend that readers take a close look at Finnegan's article.

7. I am grateful to Melissa Bianchi (2012), who taught me this point in her master's thesis, "Diagnosing the State of Rhetoric through X-Ray Images."

8. Urban actually argues that metaculture exists on a different plane than culture.

Such differentiation of planes works against my understanding of assemblage theory, which tries not to grant ontological status to different levels.

9. As Roxanne Mountford (2001) has argued in "On Gender and Rhetorical Space," we can think of rhetorical space as "the geography of a communicative event . . . and may include both the cultural and material arrangement, whether intended or fortuitous, of a location" (41).

10. I am currently working on a substantive data visualization project with Obama Hope in which I code 1000 different manifestations of Obama Hope around the world for genre, media, artform, function, place, and date as well as visualize metadata in a series of interactive maps such as heat maps, chronological bar graphs, bubble maps, etc. These visualizations are helping me generate new insights and develop new questions for a book length rhetorical biography about Obama Hope.

11. Digital interactive maps are best suited to help visualize the distributed rhetorical activities of a runaway object such as Obama Hope. I am currently working on a set of digital visualizations that can better capture Obama Hope's movement and transformation with time and space.

12. On his blog, Ian Bogost (2009) describes object-oriented ontology in this way: "Ontology is the philosophical study of existence. Object-oriented ontology ("OOO" for short) puts things at the center of this study. Its proponents contend that nothing has special status, but that everything exists equally—plumbers, DVD players, cotton, bonobos, sandstone, and Harry Potter, for example. In particular, OOO rejects the claims that human experience rests at the center of philosophy, and that things can be understood by how they appear to us. In place of science alone, OOO uses speculation to characterize how objects exist and interact.

13. My original research question was much more ambiguous, as I discussed in chapter 4. Yet, as my research uncovered more and more information about Obama Hope, my research questions became more specific according to my research findings.

PART III

Obama Hope Case Study

6

OBAMA HOPE, PRESIDENTIAL ICONOGRAPHY, AND THE 2008 ELECTION

The rhetorical life of Obama Hope is a complicated story with a humble beginning. As identified in the book's introduction, the image first actualized in one among hundreds of photos taken by Mannie Garcia at a national press conference in April of 2006 (see Figure 1.1). This photograph only appeared in a few online news sources and personal blogs between 2006 and early 2008. While it was intended to document the actual press conference, the Obama photo mostly served another purpose. In some online news sources, such as *Star Media Noticias*, the Obama photo depicts the relatively unknown senator from Illinois as a contender for the 2008 Democratic Party presidential nominee. In others, it offers a visual comparison to his opponents, Hillary Clinton and John McCain. Typical of news photos taken during an election season, then, Obama Hope initially helped online readers visualize the potential presidential candidate reading about him in the accompanying text. Because of its limited function and circulation, Obama Hope was largely inconsequential at the beginning of its life—an image, perhaps, doomed to be archived and lost among thousands of other news photos taken that year. In early 2008, however, that all changed when street artist and graphic designer, Shepard Fairey, located Garcia's Obama photo on Google Images. This encounter proved to be an important one as it jumpstarted Obama Hope's journey to becoming a cultural icon, a national symbol, and a dynamic actant with a rich rhetorical life.

Shepard Fairey is a Rhode Island School of Design (RISD) graduate who up until 2008 was most famous for his Obey sticker campaign (see Figure 6.1). This campaign, according to Fairey's (1990) manifesto, started as an experiment in phenomenology intended to achieve three goals: trigger the viewer's curiosity; evoke questions about what this ambiguous sign means to and requests of the viewer; and challenge the viewer to confront their own obedience. Fairey's Obey stickers are

DOI: 10.7330/9780874219784.c006

Figure 6.1. Obey *Icon, Shepard Fairey, 1995. Courtesy of Shepard Fairey-ObeyGiant.com.*

plastered all over the globe and have received mass amounts of attention. While not all may agree, Sarah Jaye William argues that the Obey sticker—a fixture at many urban and rural street corners—has become "an incitement for the uninitiated masses . . . to begin questioning and distrusting the images and slogans they face on daily basis" (Fairey 2009a, 12). At the very least, the Obey sticker campaign has inspired others to create their own sticker campaigns and has thus promoted the rhetorical value of this medium.

Fairey, especially now, is not just famous for the Obey campaign. After graduating from RISD, Fairey launched a small printing press called Alternative Graphics, where he designed t-shirts and stickers with various original designs. Eventually, Fairey started Studio Number One—a design agency that produces books, album covers, and other commercial work as well as promotional materials for nonprofit organizations and fund-raising materials for charity events. On his Obey Giant website, Fairey also sells a number of designs that appropriate older forms of propaganda to create new forms for contemporary contexts. As Fairey (2009a) explains, his work—what W.J.T. Mitchell would call "image-texts"—"uses people, symbols, and people as symbols to decon-struct how powerful visuals and emotionally potent phrases can be used to manipulate and indoctrinate" (139). Fairey especially likes to refash-ion images that have already had a history of their own (see Figures 6.2 and 6.3) to demonstrate not only how easy it is to manipulate sym-bols for different purposes but also how people can be "reconditioned through imagery" (99).

In this sense, Fairey is a quintessential example of Generation X media activists. According to Douglass Rushkoff (1996), Generation Xers are the first generation to grow up knowing they could manipulate digital technologies and already-circulating images in the media to influ-ence reality. As such, this generation is preoccupied with deconstructing and reexamining media and engaging in the techniques of recycling, juxtaposing, and recontextualizing existing imagery to activate change (32). In this context—what Lawrence Lessig (2004) might name a "read-write culture"—Fairey can be considered a productive activist in that he has developed a unique style of remixing older imagery to generate new visual designs. He also knows how to distribute those visual things so they are widely visible. Fairey often wheatpastes posters, paints murals, or plasters stickers of his work in cities around the world—a transgres-sive act that has resulted in some physical altercations and numerous arrests over his lifetime. Yet increasingly many of his images can also be observed in art galleries and books. In 2009, for instance, an art exhibit called *Obey: Supply and Demand* traveled across the United States accom-panied by a retrospective book celebrating the twentieth anniversary of the Obey Giant project. With his work continuing to be shown in art gal-leries at the same time it is still popping up on streets around the world, Fairey has, in many people's eyes, become one of the most influential contemporary street artists of his generation.

As evident in *Greetings from Iraq* and in much of the work in Obey, many of Fairey's designs are rhetorical in intent and work for political change. Titles of his work exemplify this rhetorical purpose. *Big Brother Is Watching You* (2007), *Two Sides of Capitalism* (2007), and *War for Sale* (2007) are just a few among many works that critique the political sta-tus quo. Such images are colored in intense hues of red and black and designed in the streamlined graphic style of the Russian Constructivist poster—a minimalist style of dynamic compositions with geometric lines, powerful typefaces, and blaring slogans that have come to define Fairey's subversive art. Designed with the revolutionary purpose of agi-tating the viewer and (re)constructing society, Fairey has produced a number of portraits in this style, which, in depicting dictators such

Figure 6.2. Yellowstone National Park, *National Park Service, 1938. Courtesy of Library of Congress.*

Figure 6.3. Greetings from Iraq, *Shepard Fairey, 2005. Courtesy of Shepard Fairey-ObeyGiant.com.*

as Che Guevara, Stalin, and Mao Tse-tung, warn viewers against blind obedience to political leaders. US politicians have not been spared as targets in Fairey's critiques. Richard Nixon and Ronald Reagan, for instance, have received their fair share of attention, but George W. Bush has, perhaps, been hit the hardest. In Fairey's designs for a 2004 anti-Bush campaign, for instance, President Bush is depicted not only as a bloodthirsty vampire but also as a modern-day version of Hitler. While such critiques are typical for Fairey, Obama inspired Fairey to change gears with his political activism and move from negative critique to positive support. Fairey's desire to create art to work for positive political change emerged when Obama ran for president. Obama offered Fairey a glimpse of a new era of politics—a politics of hope and progress. In the belief that Obama could offer the United States a brighter future, Fairey wanted to design a poster to help Obama win the 2008 presidential election. When searching for a reference to be used in this political poster, Fairey located Garcia's Obama photo on Google Images a couple of weeks before Super Tuesday (February 5, 2008). In this moment, Obama Hope, as we know it, stepped onto the rhetorical stage.

Obama Hope, like many other things, did not come into this world because of the desires or work of a lone artist, however. While his own motivation to help Obama get into office was a catalyst for his Google search, Fairey's actions were also motivated by publicist Yosi Sergant and others intent on making sure Republicans did not gain the presidential seat again after being in the White House for eight years (see Figure 6.4). Sergant helped found 008themovement.org—a Los Angeles-based grassroots organization consisting of young professionals with extensive experience in the entertainment industry and in politics. This group, as reported by James Kaelan, formed right after Bush was elected a second time in 2004 with aims to work for Democratic mobilization. From 2004 to 2007, Sergant and other organization members had been making plans to launch a political, visual assault on Republicans. When 2007 arrived and they suspected that every state would be a close call, they realized a viral campaign would be necessary. This assault, they realized, could come in the form of pro-Obama posters to be disseminated in battleground precincts across the United States (Kaelan 2009).

Around Halloween of 2007 at an Adidas event, Sergant is reported[1] as striking up a conversation with Fairey about who Fairey was supporting for president. Sergant "saw an opportunity" (qtd. in Kaelan 2009) and, according to Fairey, "thought it would be cool if [he] did something for Obama" (qtd. in Arnon 2008). By this time, Sergant had teamed up with Jennifer Gross's Evolutionary Media Group, which served as

Figure 6.4. Yosi Sergant with Hope *Posters,* Lite-Bright Idea, *2008. Photograph Courtesy of Yosi Sergant.*

media consultant to the Obama campaign. However, Seven McDonald (2009) from *LAWeekly* (September 11, 2009) reported that when Fairey approached Sergant the next day about his idea for producing a poster, "Sergant immediately realized the power an iconic image by Fairey could have and decided that he and Evolutionary Media Group could be more effective if they worked outside the confines of the official Obama campaign." Sergant thus teamed up with Fairey instead. "If Fairey would do a poster," he reasoned, "008themovement.org had both its virus and a population of self-selected hosts—namely Fairey's worldwide base of volunteer vandals who had been for years postering cities around the globe with Fairey's satirical propaganda" (Kaelan 2009).

Before moving forward with production, Fairey apparently hesitated, asking Sergant if the campaign would approve of a street artist such as himself creating and distributing a political poster of Obama. Fairey typically does not consult or gain permission from anyone to make social commentary via his artwork. However, as Fairey (2009a) explained, "I'm a street artist who's been arrested fifteen times, and I didn't want to be a liability to Obama's cause. I didn't want him to be seen as a radical or too outside the mainstream just because someone like me chose to support him." Therefore, in early December, Fairey broached the topic again with Hill Harper, a personal acquaintance of Obama's, and two weeks before Super Tuesday (February 5, 2008), Fairey received the go-ahead from Sergant (Arnon 2008) and, according to Fairey, presumably from "the highest levels" of Obama's campaign (qtd. in Booth 2009). The next day, Fairey designed *Obama Progress*—the first design in the Obama Works series that would widely circulate during the 2008 presidential election and into the inauguration (see Figure 6.5). It is in this rendition that Obama Hope first appeared to the public in its most recognizable manifestation.

THE OBAMA WORKS[2]

The *Progress* poster is an abstract rendition of Garcia's photograph of Barack Obama presented in a palette of reds, blues, and off-whites. The exact design and production steps taken to produce the *Progress* poster have been made public in "Reflections on the Hope Poster Case" published in the *Harvard Journal of Law and Technology* (Fisher et al. 2012). While quite involved, this process is fascinating. According to Fairey, he wanted to create a portrait "that was political in nature and that would deracialize Mr. Obama [by using] a red, white, and blue color palette that was patriotic." In addition, he wanted to "capture

Figure 6.5. Obama Progress, Shepard Fairey, 2008. Courtesy of Shepard Fairey-ObeyGiant.com.

Figure 1.1. Photograph of Barack Obama, Mannie Garcia, 2006. Permissions from the Associated Press.

Figure 1.2. Obama Hope, Shepard Fairey, 2008. Courtesy of Shepard Fairey-ObeyGiant.com.

a pose in Mr. Obama that was a classic political pose, something that would elevate him to iconic status in the vein of people who had [preceded] him and were held in high regard in politics" (qtd. in Fisher et al. 2012). He thus set out on a Google Images search with key terms such as *Obama* or *Barack Obama* to find a reference picture for his work that would depict Obama in a "three-quarters view" (Fisher at al. 2012). After locating Garcia's photograph on January 22, he began manipulating this picture in Photoshop by converting it to grayscale, cropping the photograph, blurring background images, and changing lighting to create more definition and contrast. He also generated four bitmaps in Photoshop, to each of which he assigned a particular color in Adobe Illustrator in order to create the layers of color for his final poster. After integrating these layers into a composite sketch to see what the final design would look like, he printed them out on black-and-white paper, which he used as a guide to cut rubylith—a masking film that has a red or orange gelatin on top of a clear surface that looks much like a transparency. Apparently, these sheets of rubylith were cut out for each layer of color in the illustration, then scanned into Photoshop and imported into Adobe Illustrator, where Fairey performed further editing such as adding color to layers, cutting back their edges, and adding final design touches.[3]

With portraits, Fairey does not change much in terms of facial features and body position so he can retain a recognizable image of the person. In the *Progress* poster, for example, the American flag in behind Obama in Garcia's photograph was omitted and replaced with a blue and red background, each receiving equal weight. Beneath Obama's face, the word *progress*, printed in all capital letters, was added in a sans serif Gotham font. A lapel pin with Fairey's Obey logo was added to Obama's suit, and Obama's tie appears red rather than blue. In addition, the color of Obama's skin in the *Progress* poster appears in red, white and blue tones that have come to dominate all of the Obama Works. However, little else in terms of content changed. Even the exact shadow lines on Obama's face captured in Garcia's photograph were left unchanged. Because of such concerted efforts to stick close to the reference photo when creating portraits, there was little chance viewers would not recognize Barack Obama in Fairey's posters if they were at all familiar with what Obama looked like.

Once the *Progress* poster was finished, Fairey got busy producing the next poster in the Obama Works Series—the *Obama Hope* design (see Figure 1.2). The *Hope* poster replicated the *Progress* poster but transformed it in two ways. First, the word *hope* replaced the word *progress*.

Fairey claimed in an interview with Jeff Beer that he actually preferred the word *progress*. "[I]t's more about the action," he says, "it's a verb, the realization of that hope" (qtd. in Beer 2008). But he changed the word *progress* to *hope* because hope is the message the campaign wanted to push (Beer 2008). Second, the official Obama campaign logo was inserted on Obama's lapel pin, which in the *Progress* poster had contained Fairey's Obey star logo. While some people accused Fairey of trying to highjack Obama's credibility in the *Progress* poster by inserting his own logo onto Obama's lapel pin, Fairey claims that he added his logo to the *Progress* poster "because [he] knew that [his] hard core collectors would feel they had to buy the poster just because it had an Obey logo. Therefore, [he] was more or less forcing [his] audience to fund further perpetuation of the image" (Arnon 2008). Presumably, Fairey changed the Obey star logo in the poster into the Obama campaign logo to fit more closely with the state and nationwide official Obama campaign.

During the remainder of the 2008 election, the distribution process of Obama Hope was multifaceted, dependent not only on deliberate guerilla distribution tactics and an online sales plan created by the official Obama campaign, but also on unforeseeable grassroots participation by concerned Obama supporters around the United States. Wide distribution was not difficult to achieve for Fairey and Sergant. Fairey has been quoted as being "the foremost biological engineer in the world of virally spread guerilla art" (Kaelan 2009), evidence of which is provided by his work having a visible presence on six continents, made possible through Fairey's unique graffiti-style distribution techniques. Sergant had realized he could make use of Fairey in their encounter at the Adidas event in October 2007 and, being what Malcom Gladwell would call the maven and connector that he was, Sergant was convinced Fairey would be a strong asset to the grassroots campaign. Sergant's intuition proved right. The deliberate distribution tactics Sergant, Fairey, and a network of volunteers deployed enabled Obama Hope to spread like a virus across the fifty states.

The distribution network that contributed to the spread of Obama Hope in relation to Fairey's Obama Works can be thought of as a complex, emergent ecosystem. As will become clear in the next section, a dynamic intra-action among a number of people, technologies, and structures involved in interlaminated activities in multiple environments enabled Obama Hope to circulate widely across a variety of mediums, forms, genres, and locations. The human actors involved included designers, artists, magazine editors, reporters, politicians, digital consultants, and everyday citizens, among others. The contributing nonhuman actors included websites, blogs, social media sites, and digital photo technologies, among a diverse array of others entities ranging from ink to paper to printing machines. The intra-actions among various actors that contributed to the reproduction, transformation, distribution and redistribution of Obama Hope were thus multifaceted. While Fairey and Sergant implemented a top-down approach, a bottom-up approach also emerged as smaller networks of distributed activity contributed to the larger network and enabled wide distribution and viral circulation of the Obama Works. As with all complex systems, the self-organizing, adaptive, dynamic, and often seemingly simultaneous intra-actions that ensued could never have been fully predicted. However, these intra-actions, both anticipated and unanticipated, helped generate one of the most iconic images that has surfaced in recent years in the national if not the global arena.

INITIAL DISTRIBUTION TACTICS

As this section will make evident, Fairey and Sergant deployed clever and effective tactics to spread the Obama Works widely across the United States. To set rhetorical velocity in motion, Fairey made a free, high-resolution download of the *Progress* poster available in black and white on his Obey Giant website, which gave broad access to the Obama Hope image and created potential for it to rematerialize and transform. Within a short time of uploading the *Progress* poster, for instance, people were downloading the picture and using it as email signatures or Facebook profile pictures. People were also printing the poster and taping it up in their offices and outside metro stations, among other locales, proliferating Obama Hope in ways and places that one single organization could not achieve on its own. In St. Louis, for instance, Richard Rodriguez downloaded the PDF from Fairey's website and projected the picture onto 9 × 6-foot canvas paint cloths he purchased from Home Depot. He then traced the image and painted it with Behr house paint, spending quite a bit of money from his own pocket as well as funds donated by other Obama supporters and sales from some of his reproductions at a gallery opening (see Figure 6.6). Rodriguez's first installation was a series of *Progress*, *Hope*, and *Change* canvases hanging side by side on the outside wall of the Royale in St. Louis. But in total, Rodriguez and other volunteers hung a total of seventy-eight large format pictures around St. Louis, which included lending them out to campaign offices, other media functions, and even large house parties aiming to generate support for Obama.

Figure 6.6. Obama Royale by Richard Rodriguez, 2008. *Photograph Courtesy of Jane Ollendorff.*

In Dayton, Ohio, David Esrati, owner of an ad agency, also took it upon himself to print and distribute the *Hope* poster. As Esrati explained, he downloaded a small JPEG from Fairey's website. Using a plugin for Photoshop, he created a vector file, which he printed on paper with his 42-inch HP printer. Esrati hung one poster in his own design agency window but also gave the campaign headquarters in Dayton a poster (see Figure 6.7). In addition, he gave one of his prints to Miami County Democrats for a demonstration they were hosting in the same square where Bush had spoken a few years earlier. After taking down his poster from the campaign headquarters at the end of the primary, Esrati, who was running for Congress at the time, held an election-night party where, with permission from Fairey, he auctioned off the print for charity, raising $200 for a local runaway shelter. Despite

Figure 6.7. Hope *Poster in Dayton, 2008. Photograph Courtesy of David Esrati.*

his intentions for wide distribution, when Fairey made the PDFs freely available for reprint, he never anticipated that so many varied uptakes of the posters would emerge nor the magnitude with which Obama Hope would go viral (Cohen 2008; Gambino 2009).

Of course, Fairey's distribution tactics did not stop there. In addition to making the PDFs free to the public, Fairey also generated funds from sales of his posters to mass produce more campaign materials, efforts that put Obama Hope into circulation in a variety of mediums. Fairey initially put a limited edition of 350 *Progress* posters up for sale on his website for forty-five dollars each and printed another 350 on thin paper to be distributed and wheatpasted on the streets. He also put up 1,400 of the 350,000 *Hope* posters he would eventually produce up for sale for thirty-five dollars (Fisher et al. 2012). According to Fairey, the proceeds from the poster sales, which sold out within minutes, funded the production of more posters. Fairey also noticed that almost immediately, his artwork was selling on eBay for over $1,000; therefore, he sold a few limited-edition prints to private collectors to raise more money to print posters and stickers for distribution.[4] In addition, Fairey granted

Figure 6.8. Obama Hope *Stickers in Production, 2008. Photograph Courtesy of Yosi Sergant.*

a free nonexclusive license to organizations that supported Obama and granted a free license to Sticker Robot to produce and distribute, at cost, large numbers of stickers bearing the Obama Hope image. In February 2008, Fairey also teamed up with Upper Playground to make t-shirts with the *Hope* poster image. Upper Playground—considered a leader in the US progressive art movement through its pioneering apparel line and popular art gallery—made the shirts available for sale for twenty-five dollars at Upper Playground stores, including its online store. All proceeds went to creating more campaign t-shirts, posters, and stickers in support of Obama (see Figure 6.8). Soon, these items were popping up not only in the United States but also across the globe. For instance, one Flickr member identified as Hellblazer! proudly announced that his *Hope* t-shirt arrived in his mailbox in Melbourne, Australia, as early as March 2008.

Many of Fairey's posters were also donated to local campaign head-quarters and auctioned off at fundraising events to help raise funds for Obama's campaign. Many individuals in Los Angeles took it upon them-selves to purchase posters from local campaign headquarters and hang them up in their own yards, increasing the visibility of Obama Hope.

And Fairey himself teamed up with others to throw fundraising events. For instance, Fairey and DJ Z-Trip hosted a couple of Party for Change fundraising events in Los Angeles and San Francisco. To attract people to the events, the first arrivals to the party were guaranteed to receive a *Hope* poster. Yet other Obama supporters also organized events and used the Obama Works to raise funds for Obama. On September 23, 2008, for example, the Barack Obama-rama was held at Spaceland in Silver Lake, California. At this event, the Obama campaign set up a booth and a voter-registration drive. *Hope* posters donated by Fairey hung over the main stage and around the event space, and many were raffled off to generate funds for the Obama campaign. That night alone raised over $4,000 (Koga 2008). Two nights later in West Hollywood, Magda Rod held an Obama or Bust fundraising party at an ecochique boutique on Melrose Avenue. Not only could you bid on an original *Progress* screenprint, but you could also buy limited editions of Fairey's *Hope* posters. Signed posters were available for one hundred dollars, unsigned for fifty dollars. According to Rod (2010), this event raised over $10,000 with much of this money generated by Fairey's work alone. As the poster transformed in function from simply a political poster to a productive fund-raising vehicle, Obama Hope's circulation escalated, as did, obviously, its financial contribution to the Obama campaign.

Another mass-distribution strategy, enacted just days after the *Progress* and *Hope* posters were created, entailed using volunteers to distribute the *Hope* poster at political rallies and on urban streets in California and across the United States. James Kaelan (2009) reports, for example, that Sergant was at a rally at the Avalon Club in Los Angeles distributing the *Hope* poster as early as January 31, 2008. The poster gained almost instant popularity with the crowd. When speaking about hope during his speech, in fact, Obama pointed to Sergant holding the *Hope* poster and said, "Very nice graphic, by the way," which prompted huge applause from members of the crowd already familiar with the picture (Kaelan 2009). That moment, Sergant explains, proved to him that the guerrilla campaign was working; the *Hope* poster was "perfectly in sync" with Obama's message (Kaelan 2009). Mass distribution was intensified in Los Angeles and across California, obviously to make Obama Hope as highly visible as possible. At the UCLA rally, Sergant himself was "running up and down the aisles rolling up posters and sticking them in the hands of people in the bleachers who would be in the camera shot" (Arnon 2008). Meanwhile, in Los Angeles and San Francisco, as documented by members of the Obama Street Art group, Obama *Hope* posters were being pasted on building walls and stuck to metal transformer

Figure 6.9. Shepard Fairey's Hope *Poster in Downtown Los Angeles, 2008. Photograph Courtesy of Sam Neira.*

boxes (see Figure 6.9). Fairey himself put up billboard-sized wheatpastes at locations such as Sunset Boulevard, Hollywood Boulevard, and Echo Park in Los Angeles, which he would also do later in cities such as Denver and Washington, DC (see Figure 6.10). With time, nearly three hundred thousand posters and stickers would be printed and distributed across the United States.

Mass distribution was made possible via volunteer participation by using several different connectors' abilities to build social networks around them. Fairey and Sergant were two such connectors; as Fairey

Figure 6.10. Shepard in DC, 2008. Photograph Courtesy of Yosi Sergant.

explained, by January of 2008 he had a list of three thousand people who wanted to help distribute the poster. Fairey and Sergant mailed posters out to people in places where the primaries or caucuses hadn't yet taken place. For instance, on February 25 alone, one thousand t-shirts and over ten thousand posters were sent to Obama supporters in Ohio and Texas to promote Obama's bid in their primary elections. But other connectors also played an important role in distributing the *Hope* posters. In describing his goal to get Obama elected, Sergant explained in a Radaronline.com feature article, "I'm gonna make sure anyone who wants one [a Fairey poster] at the University of Arizona has one available to them. I'm going to make sure anyone who's living in Florida who's a Barack Obama supporter has one available to them if they want it. If they need any piece of material to show their support and it may just convince one more person to vote for Barack Obama, it is our objective to make sure they have it" (qtd. in 4Rilla 2008).

To meet this objective, Sergant distributed the *Hope* posters to connectors within key voting states. In Philadelphia, for instance, Tayyib Smith, the creator of *215 Magazine* discussed in chapter 2, played a significant role in getting out Obama *Hope* posters and stickers. Smith was motivated to help not only by his anti-Bush sentiment but also by his desire for real change, which he believed Obama could bring to the country, as well as by his desire to participate in bringing about change. Smith began receiving pallets of posters six to eight weeks before the primaries in Pennsylvania. With much experience in event networking and promotion, Smith himself passed out Fairey posters in coffee shops, at music events, and in other noncorporate spaces. He also dropped off the posters at Obama's official campaign offices in Philadelphia. Smith also arranged for his employees and small group of friends to pass out posters, but, unexpectedly, family members and friends of friends soon began volunteering to distribute posters. Smith's father, for instance, targeted specific neighborhoods in Philadelphia while office janitors in Smith's office building covered rural Pennsylvania neighborhoods. Smith explains (pers. comm.) that the network just spiraled out as each individual took their own initiative to spread posters. Together, working as a collective, Smith and others distributed thousands of Fairey posters.

This self-organizing network was just one among many that assembled to contribute to the dynamic system that enabled the Obama Hope image to spread. While some, such as Smith's network, assembled as a direct result of Sergant's and Fairey's intended actions, others assembled on their own accord. Obama Hope especially inspired craftspeople to take up the image to work for political change. As is evident in photographs uploaded on Flickr by members of the Obama Craft Project group, throughout the entire election year, people were printing, sewing, and stitching the Obama Hope image onto various crafts for their own personal satisfaction as well as to help spread Obama's message. The Obama Hope image, for instance, was needlepointed onto cloth canvases, glazed onto pottery, tiled into mosaic prints, and crocheted onto women's bags. Interestingly, but perhaps not surprisingly in the craft world, people did not just make Obama crafts for their own sakes. Instead, several people made their designs available for others to reproduce.

Such availability created layers and layers of the Obama Hope image's reproduction, intensified the image's transformation across media, and contributed to the emergence of new associations between Obama Hope and various entities. In October of 2008, for instance, a Screen Printing for Change party was held in which friends came together and made their own t-shirts with the Obama Hope image printed in black and colored ink. Patterns for knitting the Obama Hope image onto sweaters were also made available for free downloads, as were tutorials for making bottle caps for Barack (see Figure 6.11). Many craftspeople obviously

Figure 6.11. Bottle Caps for Barack, K. B. Vanhorn, 2008. Photograph Courtesy of Vanhorn.

did not worry too much about copyright issues, believing instead in the importance of spreading hope for Obama;[5] as K. B. Vanhorn (2008), a self-proclaimed "manic thing-maker" and writer of *A Patchwork World*, said, "I doubt Shepard Fairey will sue me for wanting to further his propaganda." They even went so far as to document their work not only on the Obama Craft Project Flickr page but also in an Obama Craft Project blog spearhead by the blogging duo known as the Sewer-Sewist.

The Obama Street Art group was another collective whose self-organized efforts made the Obama Hope image more visible in digital form. The Obama Street Art group emerged in February 2008 when Dave Combs, editor of *Peel Magazine*, became fascinated by how much public dialogue the Obama *Progress* posters and stickers were stimulating. Knowing a Flickr group would help the Obama posters and stickers reach a worldwide audience, he started the group with the hope of expanding dialogue about Obama, whether fueled by positive or negative opinions (pers. comm.). Soon, hundreds of people joined this group and began uploading photographs documenting sightings of the Obama Hope image in various manifestations—stickers, posters, murals, t-shirts, and so forth. Not all members joined this collective for the same reasons, however, or even out of interest in helping get Obama elected. Street art tracker Lois Stavsky—a.k.a. *LoisinWonderland*—has

Figure 6.12. What Happened to Hope? *Lois Stavsky, 2009. Photograph Courtesy of Stavsky.*

documented numerous sightings of the Obama *Hope* poster in New York City and Boston, some of which have been defaced and are peeling away (see Figure 6.12). Her documentation was stimulated simply by of her fascination with the image's hypervisibility (pers. comm.). While perhaps not meeting Combs's intended goal of intensifying the debate about Obama, such efforts of Obama Street Art group members certainly intensified the circulation of the Obama Hope image in digital form.

This group's collective efforts also made visible just how widely the Obama Hope image was circulating in physical forms. Philadelphia, New York City, Boston, and Los Angeles were just few cities among hundreds inundated with posters and stickers during the election. A Google Map of Obama Hope image sightings presented in chapter 5 helps to visualize just how widely the Obama Works proliferated across the United States and beyond within eighteen months of surfacing in Fairey's *Progress* design. (see Figure 5.6). By July 2008, for instance, stickers could be found stuck to streetlight signs in Minneapolis, personal computers in Ohio, and car rear windows in Monterey. Large wheatpastes could be found plastered in Washington DC, Austin, Birmingham, and

Figure 6.13. Hope in Hanoi, *Steve Jackson, 2009. Photograph Courtesy of Jackson.*

San Francisco, while other renditions of Obama Hope would eventually surface in locales as far away as Africa, Turkey, and Vietnam (see Figure 6.13). Whether enacted on an individual or collective basis, exactly who distributed pictures of Obama Hope is uncertain. However, as a result of this volunteer distribution in conjunction with the other initial distribution tactics instigated by Fairey and Sergant, the Obama Hope image became more and more widely recognized in both urban and rural settings across the globe.

METACULTURE

As early as January 31, 2008, just shortly after Obama Hope entered into circulation, rhetorical consequences were becoming transparent as people generated metaculture responding to Obama Hope in various online and print sources. Such attention, especially in the blogosphere, was not consistent in terms of content, as Obama Hope sparked a wide spectrum of conversations and opinions. Surprisingly, perhaps, much of the metaculture emerged in response to the aesthetic design of the *Progress* and *Hope* posters, and it was not positive. On *Boingboing,* for example, David Pescovitz (2008) posted a copy of Fairey's *Progress* poster with the comment "Obama has a Posse Too," alluding to Fairey's Andre the Giant Has a Posse sticker. Eighteen visitors tagged this post as a favorite, and within a short time, thirty-seven people had made comments, indicating just how rhetorically provocative Obama Hope was becoming. Some responses expressed puzzlement over the *Progress* and *Hope* posters' designs in relation to peoples' skepticism of Obama. For instance, a visitor named Motisbeard (2008) wondered why *Progress* was included on the poster, claiming "Why Progress . . .? Obama isn't going to repeal the Patriot Act, or close Guantanamo, or stop us from acting like swaggering cops all over the world. Someone please shake the artist awake and point him to some sites where he can look at the voting records of candidates and see where they get their money." Other visitors expressed dismay about the "socialist" style of Fairey's posters and its reminder of Maoist propaganda. In particular, many worried the poster's Soviet Constructivist design style would do more harm than good in terms of generating support for Obama. As Liberalart (2008) commented, "I think the visual association with totalitarian leftist movements like Mao's and Stalin's are problematic for the campaign's message on one nation and unity given the Right is already overly concerned about the culture wars. This feeds that concern by associating his throngs of supporters with the Cultural Revolution, coming to your home soon to take your bibles and re-educate you." Fairey (2009b) explained that while he did not believe in the "content" of posters crafted under Mao or by early Soviet constructivists, he did think they were engaging aesthetically and thus presumably rhetorically effective (273). Unconvinced, many, as is evident in the comment above, feared the association between the Obama Works and these propaganda posters would do too much damage to Obama in the long run.

Obama Hope also provoked much metacultural response about Obama, especially as it surfaced in murals that began appearing on walls from Tehran to Seattle to Santa Fe during the election season. In each mural, Obama Hope transformed in some way and stimulated its own metacultural response, but in at least two cases, Obama Hope murals elicited commentary on Obama's campaign tactics and presidential potential. In Seattle, for instance, as reported by Brad Wong (2008), artist and muralist Shelly Farnham painted Obama Hope without accompanying text on her garage door in the Capital Hill district. Farnham installed a video camera over the garage door, which captured a large number of local residents taking photos of the mural. The Obama Hope mural also made local and national headlines. Evidently, the mural was initially painted as a ploy to ward off graffiti taggers who had for some time been hitting Farnham's garage door. Farnham believed that painting a symbol of hope and inclusiveness on the door would appeal to the taggers' empathy and prevent what she perceived to be destructive vandalism. As a general interest piece, this story caught the media's attention in October 2008 when Obama Hope first appeared on Farnham's door. The Obama Hope image on Farnham's garage door continued to circulate in digital forms in the media as several local and national new sources reported the ongoing saga of the Obama Hope mural's fate. Apparently, the picture of Obama did not have the appeal Farnham had wished for; a tagger spray-painted "I only care about dead presidents" over the image the next month (qtd. in Wong 2008). This story, in turn, stimulated a host of comments from online bloggers, who over the next month debated, among other issues, the "cult-like adulation" of Obama supporters and the future efficacy of Obama's presidency. Also, while some readers thought this tag was referring to a popular funk rock band, others assumed the tagger was making a threat to Obama. Such threats were not rare during the election season; after all, as reported that same month by Reuters, Obama's life had been threatened by "two white supremacist skinheads in Tennessee" who had plans to go on a killing spree and then target Obama (Charles 2008).

In Santa Fe, New Mexico, debates also emerged on blogs in response to a photograph of another Obama Hope mural (see Figure 6.14). This time, street artists Ratha Sok and Bimmer Torre from Koolhats Productions painted the Obama Hope image in Fairey's color palette onto a wall alongside the following Obama quote: "I'm asking you to believe not in my ability to bring about real change in Washington. I am asking you to believe in yours." While we do not have access to people's reactions to this mural on the streets of Santa Fe, we do have access to comments posted in response to a photograph of the mural uploaded by Seetwist on Flickr in March of 2008. In the heated debate that unfolded, some praised Obama for his promise to evoke change, while others vehemently argued that the US American public had been duped into thinking Obama was different from all the other politicians who had been in office. Accusations of Obama's relations to the New World Order also surface with aggressive tones—accusations that echoed in several remixes of Obama Hope and that still echo in posts on numerous blogs circulating today (Adolff 2008).

While the style and design of posters of Obama received much metacultural attention, Obama Hope also triggered considerable

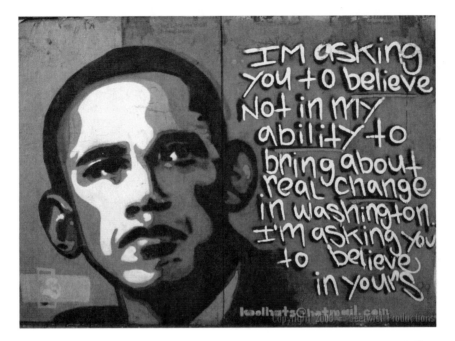

Figure 6.14. Barack Obeyma–2 Kool Productions, *2008. Photograph Courtesy of Adolff.*

commentary about Fairey himself. Indeed, some praised his ability to mass distribute nicely illustrated graphics. Yet, many called him out on his past "plagiarist" actions and decried his Obama posters as more evidence of this street artist's lack of creativity. Some critics, echoing sentiments disclosed above, also charged Fairey with creating propaganda, or what one critic called "Obamaganda." In his vehement March 12, 2008, post on *American Digest: Dispatches from the New America,* for example, a writer calling himself Vanderleun (2008) echoed Mark Vallen's (2007) now infamous rant against Fairey and charged Fairey with being a "one-trick pony" in that "there's one message and one method. It's art made by photoshop philosophy." Vanderleun also claimed that Fairey had managed to become nothing but a "Chief-Propagandist-in-Waiting among the Obamaites." "[F]or a mere $70," Vanderleun noted, "you too can have an Obamicon for your wall, your office, or wherever the worship of Obama wants to happen." In the next five days, over thirty-six people would enter into a dialogue commenting on Fairey's lack of creative talent and the poor design of his Obama Works.

Yet while such heated conversations were erupting early on in Obama Hope's political career and would later indeed come to haunt Obama

Hope and Fairey (as discussed in the next chapter), on the whole, Obama Hope's reputation was wildly positive. Many people, in fact, seemed completely rhetorically taken with Obama Hope. Consider the enthusiastic reactions of one visitor to *Creativity-Online* named Veiledsongbird (2008) as a quintessential example:

> I was driving down Georgia Avenue when I saw it. The sign was red, white and blew me away! The person holding it knew exactly what he had and that it stood for a lot more than mere endorsement. All the other people on the street corner idly stood with their Hillary and Ron Paul signs. But the man with the Obama sign held it high and eagerly. I couldn't help but grin and wave with enthusiasm! The poster and the person captured me in that moment. Of course, here I am able to linger longer and truly appreciate the poster. I love the waves of blue coming in from the left and washing over Obama's face. The red solid masses in the shadows on the right are struggles we currently face. Those struggles need to be brought to light, but cannot be dealt with in one fell swoop and will need waves of painstaking persistence in order to be resolved. Left and right can have their symbolism here, as well. I also like that he is leaning forward. This adds tremendous weight and depth to the poster. He leans into (blue waves) his strong conviction and values, which push him and give him strength to look toward the (red solid masses) present and future struggles our nation has with confidence. Awesome poster! Things are definitely looking up.

Because many shared such sentiments about Obama Hope and recognized its ability to generate national appeal, Obama Hope began earning the reputation as the 2008 election's hottest campaign poster. In surmising why the *Hope* poster was gaining such mass attention, historian Steven Heller (2008a) argued that the *Hope* poster was not particularly unique in its message, content, tone, or appeal when considered in a long line of historical political campaign posters. As evidence, he cited, among others, a poster for Eugene McCarthy by Ben Shan and an Andy Warhol design promoting Richard Nixon. In such posters, similar patriotic tones, portraits of candidates, and interactions between image and word send a short, powerful message. Yet, Heller argued, what the *Hope* poster had in common with all these historical posters, and what made all of them successful, was a message unique to the times and a fresh design with a youthful appeal.

While obviously not everyone agreed with its uniqueness, as evident in comments above, Obama's official campaign team was certainly convinced that Obama Hope was rhetorically in sync with the times and could indeed make powerful appeals to youth. This conviction was important as Obama's official campaign would prove to be one of the most important collectives in accelerating the Obama Hope image's distribution, circulation, and transformation. Yet before I move on to discuss that role, it's important to note here that no matter whether the metacultural response to Obama Hope was negative or positive, it played an important role in Obama Hope's circulation and transformation. As subsequent chapters disclose, as Obama Hope became widely discussed in and across various media and genres, a multiplicity of unexpected rhetorical consequences erupted as various individuals became interested in Obama Hope for different reasons. While some became invested in finding its origin, others desired to reproduce and remix it for divergent purposes—educational, political—and still others began to engage with it for legal reasons. In this rhetorical sense, Obama Hope, as we will see, began to take on epideictic, forensic, and deliberative functions as it commemorated, defended particular actions, and worked toward political and educational change. Such diversity in rhetorical function would not have emerged had its circulation and visibility not been intensified by the layers of metaculture that began emerging in response to it and circulating faster than the image itself.

THE OBAMA CAMPAIGN

As will be described in more detail in chapter 7, much controversy exists about the exact nature of the relationship among Obama's official campaign, Fairey, and Obama Hope. On February 22, 2008, Obama wrote a personal letter to Fairey thanking him for his work in support of Obama's election. Obama wrote that not only had Fairey's work "encouraged Americans to believe so they help change the status-quo," but it had also had "a profound effect on people, whether seen in a gallery or on a stop sign" (Fairey 2009a). According to Fairey, shortly thereafter, the Obama campaign officially asked him to create another poster to be sold on the Mybarackobama, or MyBO, website. But Fairey and Sergant both claimed that up until that point they were only loosely affiliated with the official Obama campaign. Many others suspected that the alliance between the Obama campaign and the Fairey-Sergant team was more calculated than Fairey and Sergant would have us believe. Fairey stated that the official Obama campaign "let" him produce the *Progress* poster "under the radar" (qtd. in Beer 2008). In a self-written blog post published in the *Huffington Post*, Fairey (2012) also stated that he "was politely asked" to change the word *progress* to *hope* in his initial poster design. Such claims have led many to think that the official campaign sought out Fairey (and others) for propagandistic purposes. While such intentions may never become fully known, the Obama campaign did eventually hire Fairey to produce three official posters for the campaign, and the MyBO website became a major means of distributing the Obama Hope image.

The Obama campaign's ability to widely distribute these posters can be attributed to the "fully networked campaign warfare" (Talbot 2008) launched by the Obama team, which provided wide access to the posters and increased their visibility. As is well known by now, much of Obama's victory has been attributed to his campaign's success in finding ways to create a buzz about Obama via social networking. As Karen Tumulty (2007) from *Time* magazine reported, "No campaign has been more aggressive in tapping into social networks and leveraging the financial power of hundreds of thousands of small donors." The Obama team was able to generate this buzz by using MyBO, which acted as a central networking platform, in conjunction with the use of Twitter, email, SMS (text messaging), and other phone tools. Such social networking devices enabled masses of people to easily volunteer, donate funds, and be contacted—all of which were necessary to deliver a strong campaign message and generate a strong network of supporters. Thanks to social media experts such as Facebook's Chris Hughes, MyBO was especially crucial in generating such support as it enabled, as Ellen McGirt (2008) pointed it, "Obamaniacs" to do all sorts of things that kept people working hard for Obama—link up their own blogs to discuss platform issues, submit policy recommendations directly to the campaign, set up, organize, and advertise mini fund-raising sites and other events, and even telecanvass from home. Visitors could also, of course, participate in online fund-raising events directly organized by the campaign itself.

One of the ways funds were raised on the MyBO website was to sell artwork, which came to be known as the Artists for Obama series. This series, produced by nine artists, entailed a run of ten limited edition prints available for sale on the Barack Obama online store. All sales were considered 100 percent contributions to the campaign and counted toward an individual's $2,300 contribution limit. In addition to the last poster of the series, Fairey donated the first poster in the series, which came to be called the Obama *Change* poster. While some of the art, such as the work produced by Scott Hansen, Antar Dayal, Jonathan Hoefler, Rafael Lopez, Lance Wyman, and Gui Borchert, sold for $60 to $70, other work produced by Lou Stoval and Robert Indiana sold for $1,000 or more. Within a short time, every piece of art sold out. This series[6] would thus prove to be quite lucrative for the Obama campaign, as it raised millions of dollars to help Obama get elected. By far though, the *Change* poster was the leading fundraiser for the series.

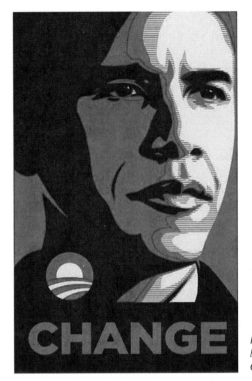

Figure 6.15. Obama Change, *Designed by Shepard Fairey for the 2008 Organizing for America Campaign.*

The *Change* poster marks a significant design transformation in Fairey's Obama Works. A different source picture provided by the official Obama campaign was used, but the style, color palette, and layout of Obama Hope bled into its interface (see Figure 6.15). The word *change*, which obviously replaced the word *hope*, also appeared in much smaller in print. In addition, Obama's logo no longer appeared as a lapel pin on Obama's left shoulder, appearing instead over Obama's neck on the left-hand side of the poster. Midday on March 12, 2008, the Barack Obama campaign sent out a tweet announcing that Artists for Obama items were going on sale. This tweet emphasized that a limited edition of Shepard Fairey's print would be sold on the Barack Obama online store, to which it provided a direct link.[7] The *Change* poster, five thousand of which were made available for seventy dollars each, sold out quickly, just as Fairey's posters did on his own website. Also, like Fairey's other posters, the *Change* poster sold for three times its value, at the very least, on eBay within a month. According to Fairey, this single poster raised between $300,000 and $400,000 for Obama's campaign (Sullivan 2008b).

The *Change* poster, in addition to the *Progress* and *Hope* posters, added to the metaculture of the Obama Hope image and solidified its importance in the Obama Campaign. Scott Goodstein, an external web strategist now considered the "digital guru" of the Obama campaign, had recognized the potential value of Obama Hope early on. Goodstein is credited with using his expertise in social networking to attract close to 2 million Obama supporters on Myspace, 6.5 million on Facebook, and over 1.5 million on Twitter (Talbot 2008). He also created Obama Mobile—the mobile communication strategy that used text messaging, downloads, interactive voice communication, and iPhone applications, among other technologies, to generate interconnected grassroots support. Goodstein understood that the Obama campaign needed to generate a wide community of activists who could generate support among US citizens. According to Goodstein, his first impression when he saw Obama Hope in one of its earliest poster manifestations was that the "image was what all of us were feeling around the campaign and why guys like me joined the campaign in early February when Obama was down by 20 points" (Edgers 2009). Goodstein says that Fairey's visual contributions, along with will.i.am's *Yes We Can* viral video, "were more valuable than the donation of money alone. What they gave us . . . was way more valuable. They gave us something that they as artists and musicians were able to craft—take our brand message and bring their artistic interpretation to it" ("How Obama Used Social Networking Tools To Win" 2009). With such affirmation of the value of Fairey' work, it is little wonder the official Obama campaign would later become a leading contributor in circulating various renditions of Obama Hope. In its role as a fundraising and branding machine, Obama Hope proved to play a significant role in creating the buzz Obama needed for victory. In this role, the image was also catapulted deeper into circulation.

RHETORICAL DESIGN

As is made clear in this case study thus far, the viral speed at which Obama Hope circulated was enabled by Fairey's and Sergant's intentional distribution tactics; emergent networks that assembled and self-organized; the metaculture surrounding the Obama Works; and the official Obama campaign. The rhetorical design of Obama Hope must also be credited with intensifying its circulation. In particular, the repetition of is visual elements helped brand Obama; thus, Fairey was asked to produce more art for the official Obama campaign, which only boosted Obama Hope's reputation. Also, the simplicity of the design made the image highly transferable to other mediums. Ease of transferability enabled the image to be mass reproduced in multiple genres, appropriated for political purposes, and emplaced in various settings across the Internet and in physical locations across the United States. Such mass reproduction, in turn, made the image hypervisible and widely recognized. To fully understand how this image reached iconic status and functioned as an important visual rhetoric during the election, then, both the consistency and transferability of the design must be attended to.

A comparison of Fairey's Obama *Vote* poster with other Fairey works illustrates just how integral rhetorical design was to helping Obama Hope reach iconic status. For the final work in the Artists for Obama series, Fairey was asked to produce a poster for the final campaign push. This Obama *Vote* poster would also be the last of the Obama Works designed specifically to garner political support for Obama during the campaign season of 2008. Like the *Change* poster, the *Vote* poster did not employ Garcia's news photo as a reference.[8] Instead, the *Vote* poster contains an image of Barack Obama taken by David Turnley, from whom Fairey obtained a proper license to use in his design (see Figure 6.16). In the *Vote* poster, Obama is smiling and *Vote* is positioned below his portrait in lieu of *Progress* or *Hope*. While earlier posters in the Obama Works depict a serious, confident, capable leader in order to achieve the goal of gaining support for Obama, the *Vote* poster depicts a more friendly, cheerful face. Also, in the middle of the *O* sits Obama's campaign logo, which in previous posters had been situated on a pin on his suit lapel or overlaid on Obama's neck.

The purpose of and message in the *Vote* poster is more direct than in previous ones. The *Progress* and *Hope* posters began, as Fairey claimed in an NPR interview with Terry Gross, with an initial concept—to divide Obama's face into tones of both red and blue signifying the divided Republican and Democratic parties and the need for unity. To actualize that concept, he needed, as described previously, to find an image that depicted a gaze of leadership and wisdom. He also needed an image with lighting that would allow him to play with shadows and tones to create the red, light beige, and blue values. The angle of Obama's gaze in Garcia's photos, Fairy explained, was popular among other historic photos of politicians and political figures, such as John F. Kennedy and Che Guevera. It is a gaze that looks off into the horizon as if confident the subject knows what lies in the future (Gross 2009). Thus, in the *Progress* and *Hope* images, as Fairey explained in an article in the *Washington Post*, the rhetorical purpose of the poster was to depict a leader gazing off into the future saying "I can guide you" (Booth 2009). In the *Vote*

Figure 6.16. Obama Vote, *Designed by Shepard Fairey for the 2008 Organizing for America campaign.*

poster, the purpose narrowed to help the official Obama campaign trigger actual votes for Obama in the US presidential election to would be held on November 4, 2008. Thus, whereas earlier messages conveyed abstract campaign themes of hope, change, and progress, the message of this poster, then, became a direct call to action—vote, and don't just vote, but vote for Obama. As such, the design was reprinted on many other posters with telephone numbers and websites informing voters as to where they could actually go to cast their vote.

Yet, despite the different messages communicated through play of image and word, the *Vote* poster, like the *Progress, Hope,* and *Change* posters, contained the same visual elements that had become Obama Hope's defining characteristics: a refined and simple design, a patriotic color palette, a stylized portrait of Obama, and a hierarchal arrangement between word and image. These signature design elements of Obama Hope created consistency not only across the Obama Works but also across the designs of the official Obama campaign. This consistency would prove to be very useful for cementing Obama's brand. As Scott Thomas (2010), designer of the Organizing for Obama website explained, the Obama campaign attempted to create consistent design themes constituted by four elements:

- simple and concise messaging,
- messages of hope and change,
- emphasis on the significant historical moment of this election, and
- consistency and balance in design elements.

This design consistency could certainly be seen across the official campaign literature being used to communicate certain messages and generate national appeals, such as the logo, signs, website, and so forth. But this consistency in design also translated to promotional products sold by the campaign such as umbrellas, stickers, jewelry, pins, water bottles, and clothing. Even as one of the brilliant moves made by the campaign was to let people remix the Obama brand to create their own campaign materials, the consistency across all things associated with the campaign helped brand Obama and earn him the title of "the best-designed identity of a U.S. presidential candidate" (Bhargava 2008). Yet while Obama's official campaign materials and social networking strategies certainly helped build a consistent identity for Obama, in terms of branding, none went so far as Obama Hope; the consistency of its design elements across the Obama Works helped generate a brand of hope and change that US citizens could buy into. Ironically, such branding only helped the Obama Hope image proliferate, as many went so far as to even brand the Obama Hope image onto their own bodies during the campaign season.

REPURPOSING

Because of its ability to raise funds, generate support for, and brand Obama, the *Hope* poster, of all the Obama works, was and still is considered the most rhetorically effective design produced during the election. By October of 2008, for instance, Fairey's *Hope* poster was being called "this election's poster child" in the *New York Times* (Heller 2008b) and "an important symbol in the political landscape of 2008" in the *Huffington Post* (Arnon 2008). Part of this fame was certainly established by the consistency of design in terms of color palette, graphic style, and layout across the Obama Works, along with other factors discussed thus far in this chapter. However, the ease of transferability of the Obama Hope image itself should also be noted. Because the design of Obama

Hope was so simple and its digital production made it so mutable and accessible, it could be easily incorporated in other pictures. It could also be reproduced in multiple mediums such as posters, t-shirts, stickers, and other goods—a possibility that was taken advantage of by the Obama campaign to generate funding and by others who, as we have seen, took their own initiative to reproduce the image in posters of their own. In chapter 8, it will become even clearer how the Obama Hope image transformed in unexpected ways across genres, forms, and mediums, which diversified its use, increased its circulation, and enhanced its recognizability. Yet, during the election season, Fairey and Sergant also repurposed the Obama Hope image to generate even more support for Obama. This repurposing of the design solidified Obama Hope's reputation as a political actor in and of itself, as is evident in the fact that it came to both commemorate and embody the entire Obama campaign.

Obama Hope's repurposing took place both before and after Obama was elected. The Obama Hope image, for instance, played a major role in generating interest for the Manifest Hope project that emerged on the campaign scene during the Democratic National Convention in Denver. Obey Giant, MoveOn.org, and the Service Employees International Union (SEIU) presented the Manifest Hope project. The Manifest Hope project offered an exhibit during the DNC showcasing some of the most influential and widely recognized art associated with the presidential campaign. To attract submissions, the event was billed to grass-roots and street artists in an online art contest for which artists were asked to submit art related to the major themes and grassroots energy driving the Obama campaign: hope, change, progress, unity, and patriotism. The top five winners of this contest had their art on display with other established, invited artists at Denver's Andenken Gallery between August 24 and 28, as well as on the Manifest Hope online gallery. Thirty-one other finalists' works were selected to be auctioned off on eBay, the proceeds of which were donated to progressive efforts aimed at helping Obama win the election. In those five days, over fifteen thousand people visited the gallery, and on the final night, a free public outdoor concert hosted by Denver mayor Gavin Newsom and comic Sarah Silverman attracted over eight thousand people.

The Obama Hope image was certainly on display at the Denver gallery among other contemporary work, as Fairey created a spray-painted stencil and collage of Obama Hope on paper (see Figure 6.17). In addition, the Obama Hope image helped advertise this event on the Internet and on posters, fliers, and wheatpastes distributed around Denver. Many

Figure 6.17. Shepard Fairey's Manifest Hope, Denver, CO, 2008. Photograph Courtesy of Yosi Sergant.

images could have been chosen to play this role; Ron English's *Abraham Obama* had certainly gained enough national recognition. Yet Obama Hope was chosen not only because Fairey was part of the event's organization but also because Fairey's work was often credited with inspiring other artists to generate their own art for the campaign. In addition, because of its hypervisibility during the election and its significant role in shaping political participation, toward the end of the election campaign, Obama Hope had become regarded as the most iconic image associated with Obama's campaign (Arnon 2008). Indicative of this status, Obama Hope was repurposed once again, this time to commemorate not only Obama's victory, but also the 2009 inauguration and the entire 2008 election campaign.

To commemorate Obama's presidential win, Obama Hope became part of the *Yes We Did* design for MoveOn.org (see Figure 6.18). MoveOn is a nonprofit organization that began in 1998 when Wes Boyd and Joan Blades came up with the idea to use technology to motivate people to participate in US politics. Since its inception, more than four million people have joined MoveOn, making it a powerful force in US politics today. In the 2008 election, MoveOn contributed close to one million volunteers to the Obama campaign who collectively worked over twenty million hours and helped generate over $80 million dollars to move

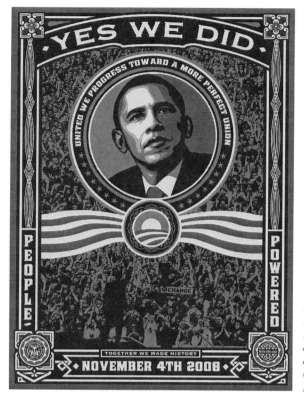

Figure 6.18. Yes We Did, Designed by Shepard Fairey for MoveOn. org, 2008. Courtesy of Shepard Fairey-ObeyGiant.com and MoveOn.org.

Obama toward victory (MoveOn 2010, 2–3). These efforts included online and offline organizing to register and recruit voters; producing some of the campaign's most memorable advertisements; mobilizing local councils to educate voters about Obama and McCain; and, as already noted, helping promote and put on the Manifest Hope project. As MoveOn executive director Eli Pariser remarked on election night, Obama's victory could not have happened without the incredible support of MoveOn members' collective action. Speaking to MoveOn members, he pointed out that Obama won because "in communities across the country, you stood up. We stood up. We found each other. We built a movement, and our voices got stronger. We talked to our neighbors, we enlisted our friends. And things began to change" (MoveOn 2010, 16). In an effort to thank members for their hard work, MoveOn hired Fairey to design the *Yes We Did* image and distributed over 3.25 million free *Yes We Did* stickers to their members.

In this design, the same color palette found in all of Fairey's political posters is used; however, Obama Hope interacts with several other images in the design to commemorate Obama's victory. The Obama Hope image is centered with the words "United We Progress Toward a More Perfect Union" encircling the central image. The words "Yes We Did" fill a banner that runs across the top of the image while the date Obama was elected, November 4, 2008, spreads across the bottom. Surrounding Obama Hope is a photograph refashioned by Fairey depicting Obama with hand raised in victory facing a cheering crowd. Written in small text below this image are the words "Together We Made History" while the words "People" and "Powered" sit on either sides of the bottom half of the image. In describing the purpose of this design, MoveOn.org told its members, "We wanted to say thank you to all of you who worked so hard in this historic campaign, so we joined with Shepard Fairey . . . to create a special piece of art commemorating this historic, people-powered victory" (*Art of Obama*, qtd. in "Free Victory Stickers by Shepard Fairey" 2008). In addition to receiving a free sticker, members could purchase additional stickers and limited edition posters, all of which were made available the day after Obama's victory in early November. The proceeds from the sales of *Yes We Did* prints would be used to launch a campaign to raise funds to pass Obama's progressive agenda once he entered office (MoveOn.org 2008).

During the inauguration, the Obama Hope image was again repurposed to take on yet another commemorative role as it surfaced in another design celebrating Obama's victory, which was created by Fairey for the Obama-Biden Presidential Inauguration Committee. This design is constructed in the same palette of colors, fonts, and theme as Fairey's other posters (see Figure 6.19). Yet, the words "Be the Change" hover horizontally over the Obama Hope image, which itself sits in the center of the poster between the images of the Capitol building and the White House in Washington, DC. The official inauguration seal sits beneath the Obama Hope image. Separating this part of the poster from the lower left- and right-hand corners of the poster is a red-and-white-striped ribbon. Beneath the striped ribbon, in the corners toward the bottom, the same image of the crowd found in the *Yes We Did* poster sits, with the inauguration date "January 20th, 2009" written below. Ten thousand copies of this poster were released by the Barack Obama Inaugural Committee to mark Obama's historical election. To no one's surprise, this poster design became a symbol of the inauguration itself. The design was reproduced on posters, lapel pins, t-shirts, and stickers and sold on the Inaugural Committee's online store. In addition, before sworn-in President Obama entered the stage at the Youth Inaugural Ball on the night of the inauguration, the inauguration poster hung over the

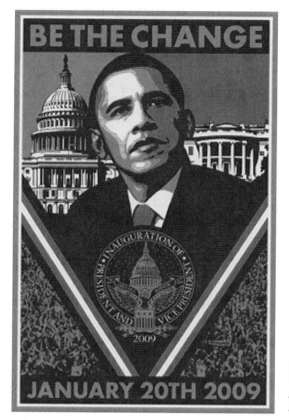

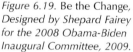

Figure 6.19. Be the Change, Designed by Shepard Fairey for the 2008 Obama-Biden Inaugural Committee, 2009.

stage as a symbol of a monumental milestone: the election of the first African American president in US history.

Due its wide circulation, high visibility, and ability to raise funds and motivate political participation, as well as its official recognition and use by the Obama campaign, Obama Hope came to commemorate more than Obama's victory and the inauguration. During inauguration weekend, one of Fairey's three mixed-stencil collages of Obama *Hope* was hung in the National Portrait Gallery in Washington, DC (see Figure 6.20).[9] In the past, official presidential portraits have been displayed in the National Portrait Gallery as presidents are leaving office. The Obama *Hope* stencil thus made history by becoming the first portrait to be hung in the gallery before inauguration weekend even ended. As justification for the acquisition of this collage, National Portrait Gallery director Martin Sullivan claimed that "Shepard Fairey's instantly recognizable image was integral to the Obama campaign"; it

Figure 6.20. Obama Portrait, *Photograph by Jacquelyn Martin, 2009. Permissions from Associated Press.*

was "an emblem of a significant election, as well as a new presidency" ("NPG Acquires Shepard Fairey's Portrait of Barack Obama" 2009). This official recognition sparked acceleration of the circulation of Obama Hope as newspapers around the world began to report the news. It also sparked more metaculture as people began to debate whether Obama Hope and Fairey were worthy of such a place in political history. Nonetheless, upon entering the US National Portrait Gallery, the Obama Hope image secured its status as *the* national symbol of the 2008 election campaign.

CONCLUSION

As this part of the Obama Hope case study has attempted to illustrate, whether people liked or disliked the Obama Hope image, during the 2008 presidential election campaign, the image became not just a cultural icon and brand but also a powerful rhetorical actor. This widespread recognition and political efficacy was made possible by the guerilla-distribution tactics initially enacted by Fairey and Sergant, which helped spread the image across a wide range of locations, forms, and genres. Fairey and Sergant were particularly strategic in making the Obama Works widely accessible in both print and digital forms, creating a network of volunteers to distribute the image in a variety of mediums, and harnessing the Obama Works' potential to raise funds and get out the vote for Obama. Such tactics instigated by Fairey and Sergant can, thus, certainly be credited for helping the Obama Hope image become the most recognized image of the 2008 presidential election.

The intentional tactics used by Fairey and Sergant, however, cannot be given full credit for the Obama Hope image's iconic status. As is evident in this chapter, many individuals took it upon themselves to reproduce Obama Hope and hang various, and often homemade, versions in private and public settings. Via such emplacement, Obama Hope transformed private homes and urban spaces into political spaces and became even more visible. Emergent collectives of people and technologies, whose intra-actions within certain collectives contributed to the image's mass distribution and reproduction, were also integral to the Obama Hope image's circulation and consequentiality. The official Obama campaign was one of the most important collectives that emerged during 2008. With the strategic implementation led by Goodstein and others, the MyBO website and other social networking sites especially became key actants in accelerating the image's circulation. Besides affording the opportunity for networks of volunteers to self-organize in geographical locations and in cyberspace to work for Obama, the MyBO website and Twitter teamed up to help orchestrate and maintain sales of the Obama Art series, which boosted the reputation of Obama Hope's design as a fundraising and branding machine as well as a political force.

Yet, as will become even clearer in art 2 of this case study, social networking sites such as Flickr enabled other networks to assemble and organize on their own accord. In some cases, as with the Obama Craft Project, certain members contributed to the collective effort to increase the visibility of Obama Hope for campaign-related reasons. In other cases, however, as with the Obama Street Art group, certain members contributed to the collective effort to increase the visibility of Obama Hope for reasons having nothing to do with helping bring Obama to victory. Instead, some citizens armed with cameras simply became fascinated with the Obama Hope image itself and wanted to help document in what locations the image was appearing and what kinds of transformations were emerging. Such participation illustrates how distributed networks of actants, which organized from both the top and the bottom, made possible the high visibility and intense consequentiality of Obama Hope.

In addition, we can clearly see how metaculture related to the Obama Hope image emerged in often surprising ways across a broad range of media sites from the *New York Times* to Flickr, Facebook, Twitter, and blogs. Much of the metaculture that accelerated the image's circulation and transformation was predictably filled with praise. The rhetorical design of the *Hope* poster alone sparked much inspiration and awe from reporters, other artists, and everyday citizens alike. Many even thought it had earned a place, alongside Norman Rockwell's *Rosie the Riveter* and John Fitzpatrick's Che Guevera posters, on the top-ten list of political posters that changed US history. Such praise increased the desire to own the image, document its locations and transformations, discuss its rhetorical design, and learn more about it. Yet, as will also become more evident in chapter 9, Obama Hope and its emergent praise also sparked unconscious feelings of relation and unconscious desires to get on the rhetorical bandwagon and create Obama-related work for political change—a contagious desire that catalyzed not only mass reproduction of Obama Hope but also the production of other imitative designs and distribution tactics.

As Fairey claims, viral circulation is dependent on how much an image is desired and admired; therefore, such metaculture, as Fairey initially hoped, helped intensify the circulation of Obama Hope. Yet much metaculture was actually filled with criticism expressing disapproval of the Obama Works' designs, Obama, and Fairey himself as well as with skepticism about the Obama Hope image's rhetorical potential. While most likely not wished for or appreciated by Fairey, this "negative" attention only contributed to the recognizability of Obama Hope. As chapter 7 makes especially clear, as more and more people shared their criticism via the Internet, particularly about issues related to "originality" and "creativity," Obama Hope's circulation in abstract, digital, and physical forms only intensified. Thus, as much as Obama Hope's viral circulation was dependent on people's admiration of its rhetorical potential to help Obama win the election, it was also dependent on a multitude of critical consequences that unexpectedly emerged on the metacultural scene during its circulation.

Obama Hope's circulation, transformation, and consequentiality were also made possible by its rhetorical design, the consistent style and content of which could be easily transferred across genres and media. In the Obama Works alone, we saw how in some cases the portrait of Obama would change yet the colors, tones, relation between image and word, and overall organization remained stable. In other instances, we saw how little changed except the word beneath Obama's portrait. While the consistency of style made the Obama Hope image more recognizable, the ease of content transferability also enabled the image to deliver various messages. With the help of the Obama Works, *hope* and *change* came to be *the* buzzwords associated with the Obama campaign. Through repetition of style and Obama's portrait, the Obama Works also helped brand Obama's image, which as Fairey himself explained, "promised utopia almost" (qtd. in Shapiro 2010). Because of such rhetorical potentials, in addition to the simplicity of design, which made it easy to replicate across a broad range of media by professionals and amateurs, Obama Hope came to be greatly valued as an actor for political change. As more and more people became interested in securing Obama's place in the oval office, they turned to Obama Hope to express their national identity, show support, and motivate political participation. Because of its ability to motivate action, Obama Hope would come to symbolize Obama's entire presidential election.

Such reliance on the image to do political work during the 2008 presidential election makes it fair to claim that the Hope image achieved its intended effects. Via its intra-actions with a wide spectrum of things—people, canvases, trees, signposts, websites, blogs, and so forth—it gained wide recognition, helped motivate political action in support of Obama, and helped persuade a wide audience that Obama had the wisdom to guide the United States toward progress and a more hopeful future. Such political reliance also certainly helps to explain why and how the viral circulation of Obama Hope occurred. Yet, as we have already witnessed to a small degree, unintended consequences emerge that accelerate the speed at which an image travels and intensify its rhetorical transformation. Such unintended consequentiality has enabled Obama Hope to not only become a cultural icon and cultural phenomenon, as Ben Arnon (2008) has argued, but also a rhetorical phenomenon that is still unfolding even today. In addition to what has already been made visible about the Obama Works in this chapter, then, any attempt to account for Obama Hope's rhetorical life must attend to such unforeseeable consequentiality.

Notes

1. I quote extensively from various reports in this account because, as will become evident in subsequent chapters, many people are suspicious about how and when Fairey became affiliated with Obama's official campaign.

2. Each time I introduce a new illustration in the Obama Works, the official name for each illustration is provided. From then on, the illustration name is abbreviated to avoid needless wordiness. For example, the Obama *Progress* poster is shortened to the *Progress* poster. The Obama *Hope* poster is shortened to the *Hope* poster.

3. See Fisher et al.'s (2012) "Reflections on the Hope Poster Case" for more exact details of Fairey's design and production process of Obama *Progress*.

4. Fairey did profit from some of his fine-art versions of Obama *Hope*. In fact, according to Fisher et al. (2012), together with his royalties from murals and designs commissioned by the Presidential Inauguration Committee and MoveOn.org, which I describe in this chapter, Fairey made more than $830,000 from sales of the fine-art editions of the *Hope* poster.

5. This belief was warranted, as Shepard Fairey is quoted as saying that the mass reproduction of his image was "exactly what [he] wanted to happen." See William Booth's (May 18, 2009) *Washington Post* article "Obama's On-the-Wall Endorsement."

6. This series can be seen for sale on an archived page of the Barack Obama online store: http://web.archive.org/web/20090317032142/http://store.barackobama.com/Artists_for_Obama_s/1018.htm.

7. Twitter was used by the Obama campaign throughout the election along with Facebook and YouTube, proving he was part of the Web 2.0 generation. As of November 2008, Obama had over 118,000 new followers on Twitter.

8. Like the *Change* poster, the *Vote* poster was also officially sold on the BarackObama website in late October/early November of 2008. The first run of these posters included five thousand and sold for twenty dollars while a second run of five thousand sold for forty-five dollars, again raising a lot of money for Obama.

9. Fairey had earlier donated another one of his three stenciled collages to be auctioned off at Russel Simmons's Art for Life charity auction; it sold for over $100,000.

7

OBAMA HOPE, COPYRIGHT, AND FAIR USE

Obama Hope, it could be said, was born into politics. Most well known for its political role in the 2008 presidential election, Obama Hope became somewhat of a hero in US national politics. Yet, like many political actors, the image has also led a rather scandalous life. As this part of the case study will make evident, Obama Hope became plagued with skepticism when its origins became a matter of national debate and accusations of plagiarism and copyright infringement flooded the blogosphere. Rather than stunting its popularity, though, such metacultural activity intensified the image's circulation, diversified its actualizations, and exacerbated its rhetorical impact. In particular, as it became the subject of an intense copyright investigation, it induced a multiplicity of collectives to assemble, and it became a touchstone for intellectual property debates. This entanglement, in turn, sparked more unforeseeable consequentiality as Obama Hope took on an educational role in scholarship about remix, new media, and fair use.

THE OBAMA PHOTO POSTER MYSTERY

As the transformation and circulation of the Obama Hope image became ubiquitous during the presidential season, so did people's fascination with it. As illustrated with the Obama Street Art group, much interest and collective activity emerged as people, intrigued by its mass circulation, committed to documenting Obama Hope' materialization in the United States and around the world. Just before the inauguration, much interest also emerged in where Fairey had obtained the original reference photo for his by-then-iconic Obama *Hope* poster. As mentioned in chapter 2, when pressed about the reference icon for his poster, Fairey said he could not recall where he found the reference photo. James Kaelan (2009) quoted Fairey saying, "I just basically went on the internet and looked for a good photo of Obama to work

DOI: 10.7330/9780874219784.c007

from. . . . So, I found an image that I felt had the right gesture, and then, of course, did my thing to it—re-illustrated and simplified it to this really iconic, three-color image." Unsatisfied with this response, Obama Hope became the subject of an intense, two-month-long investigation in late 2008 to find the original source of the *Hope* poster. This collective action, which entailed the intra-actions of journalists, bloggers, art collectors, computer programmers, and a variety of digital technologies dissipated once the actual source photo was found, but this collective work intensified Obama Hope's circulation and transformation and stirred debates about copyright, giving rise to new collectives that focused their attention on issues of fair use. The Obama Hope Photo Mystery was thus a brief but monumental stage in Obama Hope's rhetorical life that demands close attention.

The Obama Hope Photo Mystery case began when Tom Gralish, a photographer for the *Inquirer* in Philadelphia, and James Danziger from the *Daily Beast* began trying to locate the reference for the *Hope* poster in late December. Traces of activity that unfolded during the brief but intense investigation were visible on both their blogs. On December 22, for instance, Gralish (2008) posted a photograph of several *Hope* posters that he took in West Philadelphia in early 2008. He also posted information about where his viewers could go to download a copy of the Obama *Hope* poster for free and provided two sites where they could go to "Fairey-ize" their own images. Gralish also expressed confusion as to why the photographer who shot the reference photo for Fairey's poster had not stepped up to claim credit. After all, Gralish (2009a) wrote, "When fifteen nurses and twice that many sailors can claim to be subjects of Alfred Eisenstaedt's V-Jay Day hug in Time Squares Photo [sic], you'd think a whole bunch of photographers would step forward . . . claiming to have shot the Obama photo." He asked his viewers if any of them had any idea of who took the reference photo, but he received no replies.

In an effort to solve this mystery, Gralish contacted Danziger, who responded that he too had been trying to find out what reference photo Fairey had used. Danziger said he would ask around in the journalism and photography worlds, and both committed to finding the answer before the inauguration. On January 19, Danziger was the first to report that he thought he had solved the mystery. Mike Cramer, a computer programmer, had traced the Obama Hope image back to a Getty picture supposedly shot by Jonathan Daniel. Daniel insisted in an email to Danziger, however, that he was not the photographer who took the photo Danziger believed to be the reference photo. After contacting *Time*, in which the news photo was identified, Danziger found out that Jim Young, a freelance photographer for Reuters, was the one who should actually be credited. Coincidentally, on the same day on Tom Gralish's blog, Gralish (2009b) reported and illustrated how he and Mike Cramer had just confirmed Jim Young's photo to be the original reference. After locating Young's photo via Google Images, Cramer had imposed the Obama Hope image over Young's photo using Photoshop, causing Obama Hope to transform yet again (see Figure 2.4). As Cramer explained, he used the "flip canvas horizontal" rotate image command . . . and made a quick mask using the 'photocopy' sketch filter" (qtd. in Gralish 2009b). Gralish followed suit and claimed on his own blog that "while the ears weren't quite right, everything else about the two images lined up pretty darn close." Satisfied with the match, he reported on his blog that the mystery had been solved.

For a short while, Gralish, Danziger and even Jim Young were convinced Young's photo was the reference for the *Hope* poster. While Young appeared to be unalarmed by Fairey's use of his photo (one might say he was even flattered), Danziger (2009) reported on his blog that Reuters was slightly taken aback that they had received no credit for what was, as Danziger put it, "the presidential campaign's most enduring visual image." Yet, since no laws were broken, Reuters did not stir trouble over copyright. Nonetheless, Danziger raised an inquiry on his blog about fair use of the reference photo. In thinking Young's picture was the reference, Danziger argued that enough transformation existed to be considered fair use. Blog visitors did not all agree, however, claiming that lack of proper accreditation warranted further debate. On his own blog, for example, Mike Johnston (2009) uploaded a post in which he reported Danziger's findings and then added the following commentary: "Danziger notes late in his article that the Fairey rendering is technically a 'derivative work' and Fairey's use of the photo therefore falls under Fair Use, but how would you feel if you were the photographer, Jim Young? And does it make any difference that Shepard Fairey appears to have donated the work to the world without asking for or receiving any compensation for it?" Such invitation to debate sparked thirty comments within one day in which folks argued as to whether Fairey's production of derivative work ought be considered fair use.

After one commenter with the initials MJ posted an AP photo on top of the *Hope* poster for all to compare, however, people also began to debate whether Young's photo was actually even the correct reference photo. Over on Gralish's blog, visitors were having a similar debate as several people expressed doubt as to whether Young's photo actually was the reference. Just hours before Obama was to be sworn in at the

Original Source?   A virtual perfect match.

Not original source...   Note the eyes don't line up.

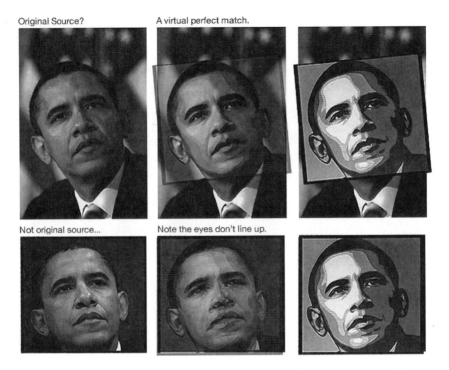

Figure 7.1. Photo Manipulation of Obama Hope, Steve Simula, 2009. Courtesy of Simula (CC BY-SA 2.0).

inauguration, visitors such as Anon were insisting the Young photo was not the right one while TomG, SteveS, Michael Kariuki, and others were posting links to an AP photo found on several different websites, claiming it was the source photo. Steve Simula confirmed such claims by working with Photoshop to create visual evidence that illustrated how the AP photo was a much better match than Young's. This visual comparison was originally posted to his Flickr site, but Gralish created links to it for others involved in the case to observe (see Figure 7.1). This manifestation of Obama Hope soon began to circulate, as it appeared on Gralish's blog and even *Wikipedia*, which was developing interest in the investigative activities of this collective. On his blog, *Amblon*, Nathan Lanstrum also posted visual evidence to confirm the AP photo was a perfect match to the Obama Hope image in Fairey's *Hope* poster, as did Chris Perly. Additional new remixes of the Obama Hope image thus entered into circulation on a small network of blogs as people were determined to find the right source.

Interestingly, the photographer of the AP photo was still unknown, prompting Gralish to conduct more investigation to locate the actual photographer. As he reported in yet another blog post, after finding the same AP photo on pennlive.com, he was able to access the IPTC caption file, which identified the AP photo as belonging to Mannie Garcia. Finally, nearly, one year after the *Hope* poster entered into circulation and nearly two and one-half years after Garcia's news photo first entered into circulation, the original source for the *Hope* poster was clearly identified. When Garcia was contacted by Gralish and told of the news, Garcia claimed he was first confused; then it "hit" him, and he thought "Wow. That's why it always seemed so familiar" (qtd. in Gralish 2009b). Later, after the news sank in, Garcia also said he was not angry with Fairey, nor did he intend to sue. He explained, "I know artists look at things; they see things and they make stuff. It's a really cool piece of work. I wouldn't mind getting a signed litho or something from the artist to put on my wall" (qt. in Gralish 2009b). Garcia even expressed pride for having the image captured in his news photo now hanging in the Smithsonian.

As soon as it was confirmed that Garcia's news photo was the original source image, Obama Hope's circulation accelerated even more as Garcia's Obama photo was catapulted back into circulation, especially as the Associated Press caught wind of Fairey's use of an AP photo and people began a rigorous debate about fair use. The visual evidence making comparisons between the Obama photo and Fairey's *Hope* poster created by Simula, Lunstrum, and Perley also began to circulate on the World Wide Web. In response, as the next section makes clear, a multitude of people—scholars, lawyers, educators, artists, journalists, radio talk-show hosts, and everyday people—were lured into conversations that are still ongoing today about copyright law in a digital age. Thus, even though the Obama Hope Photo Mystery case lasted for only a few intense weeks, the intra-actions between the Obama Hope image, those people involved, and various technologies sparked a constellation of new rhetorical consequences in relation to Obama Hope that reverberated for years to come.

POSTER CHILD FOR FAIR USE

In some ways, Obama Hope was perhaps destined to become embroiled in conversations about fair use because Shepard Fairey produced it. As mentioned earlier, tensions about fair use in relation to Fairey's work—what some call "Fairey use"—had been building long before

Obama Hope began to circulate. Fairey's most vehement critic, pre-Obama Hope, was Mark Vallen (2007), artist and author of the blog *Art for Change*. Writing in 2007 after he saw Fairey's Los Angeles 2007 solo exhibition, Vallen argued that Fairey was nothing short of a plagiarist. Despite Fairey's full disclosure that appropriation was part of his artistic process, this critique of Fairey's work stemmed from what Vallen saw as Fairey's "brazen, intentional copying of already existing artworks created by others—sometimes duplicating the originals without alteration—and then deceiving people by pawning off the counterfeit works as original creations." Not everyone goes so far as to call Fairey a plagiarist, as many accept that appropriation and remix are common artistic practices. However, especially after Garcia's photo was identified as the reference, a slew of people around the world began weighing in on issues of authorship, copyright, and fair use in relation to Obama Hope. Entire websites such as the Fair Use Lab even emerged to discuss matters of fair use in a free or participatory culture with the Obama Hope image front and center in the debate. Such conversations were so prolific that, at least for a short while, Obama Hope became the poster child for fair use in the United States.

To understand the crux of these debates, it is important to know some basics about copyright and fair use. According to Stanford University's Libraries and Academic Information Resources (SULAIR), creative works protected by copyright must meet three specific qualifications:

- a work must exist in some physical form for some period of time, no matter how brief that time period is;
- a work must be original, i.e., independently created by an author, not copied from someone else's work; and
- a work must be a result of some creative process enacted by the author (Stanford 2010).

Under copyright law, fair use of copyright works permits copying a work for a limited and "transformative" purpose without permission from the copyright owner. What entails "transformative use" is ambiguous, of course, and, consequently, many lawsuits emerge over disputes as to what counts as "transformative." In addition, because creative needs and practices differ with technology, time, and fields, copyright law does not dictate specifically how fair use should be applied; therefore, the Fair Use Doctrine is flexible and case dependent. Whether a practice such as remix is considered fair use, then, is dependent on what lawyers and judges decide is fair according to a "rule of reason" for a practice enacted in a certain field such as art, education, music, and film.

In each case, judges consider four factors to decide a contested case over fair use:

- the purpose and character of use, often referred to as the "transformative factor,"
- the nature of copyrighted work,
- the amount and susbstantiality of the taken portion, and
- the effect of the new work's use upon copyrighted work's potential market. (Stanford 2010)

As Deleuze and Guattari (1987) help us understand, all things undergo constant transformation. Repetition always entails differentiation on some level. Yet, at issue in the "transformative factor" is whether the new work helps to create something new and of some value or has merely copied the copyrighted work without permission. In terms of the nature of copyrighted work, at issue is whether that work is factual or fictional and published or unpublished. The scope of fair use is narrower for unpublished, fictional works. At issue with the third factor is how much and what portion was taken. The scope of fair use is narrower in most cases when less is taken and when the "heart" of the copyright work is not copied. Lastly, fair use is granted more often in cases in which the copyright owner's income is not deprived by the new work or the copyrighted work's potential market is not undermined. Also important to note is that proper accreditation for a source work does not always make using a copyrighted work permissible. Formal permission by the copyright owner is the surest way to fully avoid trouble with copyright law (Stanford 2010).

In the case of Obama Hope, lawyers, artists, journalists, and a plethora of concerned citizens debated whether Fairey's use of Garcia's news photo without permission was fair use. Some argued for fair use, pointing out that the purpose of Fairey's artistic efforts was to generate support for Obama was far different than Garcia's purpose of documenting a news conference. Others, however, thought Fairey took the "heart" of Garcia's news photo without permission and with so little artistic transformation that Fairey's rendition of Obama Hope entailed no more than sheer copying. Unaware of Fairey's complete process, many people saw Fairey as "merely" adding some shade lines, patriotic colors, a lapel pin, and the words *hope* and *progress*—adjustments that were not substantial enough in their minds to be considered fair use. Still others, such as Eric Frazier (2009) commenting in *Evil Monito* magazine in February 2009, pointed out that on *Fresh Air*, Garcia admitted he couldn't even recognize his photo as the reference for Fairey's work since he had snapped so many photos that day at the press conference, calling attention to the lack of creativity that went into the design of Garcia's photo. In addition, Frazier points out, Fairey's Obama designs with Obama Hope as the star player were far more valuable than Garcia's work ever would have been, and even Garcia himself stood to make more money because of the photo's use by Fairey. Lastly, Frazier pointed out, Garcia sold the photo to the Associated Press anyhow. Such arguments only present a small sample of the hundreds boiling in cyberspace on various online sources. Accompanying these verbal arguments was usually Obama Hope depicted in Garcia's Obama photo, or Fairey's Obama *Hope* poster, and/or the manipulated, Photoshop versions of both layered over one another. These debates, therefore, fueled the circulation of Obama Hope and heightened its recognition.

This circulation was only intensified when Fairey took preemptive measures in early February 2009 and sued the Associated Press to vindicate his rights to the Obama Hope image when he learned of their threat to sue him for copyright infringement—a threat that emerged just two days after Fairey's Obama Hope collage was hung in the National Portrait Gallery. Lawyers from the Stanford Center for Internet and Society, housed at Stanford Law School and founded by Lawrence Lessig, took up Fairey's case. In the complaint filed on behalf of Fairey and Obey Giant against the Associated Press in the US district court in New York, Fairey and Obey Giant argued that Fairey's use of Garcia's photo should have been protected by the Fair Use Doctrine for the following reasons:

- Fairey used the Garcia photograph as a visual reference for a highly transformative purpose; Fairey altered the original with new meaning, new expression, and new messages; and Fairey did not create any of the Obama Works for the sake of commercial gain.
- The Garcia photograph had been published well before Fairey used it as a visual reference, and is a factual, not fictional or highly creative work.
- Fairey used only a portion of the Garcia photograph, and the portion he used was in light of Fairey's expressive purpose.
- Fairey's use of the Garcia photograph imposed no significant or cognizable harm to the value of the Garcia photograph or any market for it or any derivatives; on the contrary, Fairey has enhanced the value of the Garcia photograph beyond measure. (Fairey et al. v AP 2009, 11)

As one might expect, all images involved in the case, including Garcia's photograph and each of the pictures constituting Fairey's Obama Works, could be found in the Appendix of this court filing.

Fairey's preemptive lawsuit was met with resistance from the AP, who immediately filed a countersuit. While it is beyond the scope of this case study to account for the complexity of the AP's arguments, the AP claimed that, among other things, Fairey (a) did gain from commercial profits off the Obama Works; (b) took not just a substantial part of the AP photo but "engaged in a form of computerized 'paint by numbers' with the AP's copyrighted image—taking the work in its entirety; (c) did not transform the purpose greatly since the AP photo "conveys a defining impression of President Obama"; (d) had patriotic themes as so many AP presidential photos have had in the past; and (e) impaired the potential market for the photo by preventing the AP from being able to license its use to other commercial and noncommercial customers (Fairey v. AP "Answer" 2009, 38–39). The AP also charged Fairey for acting in bad faith by illustrating a historical record of copyright infringement in previous work and, among other reasons, misinforming the court about which Garcia photo he used as the reference. This latter argument is important, as decisions made about fair use in courts of law are often contingent on an unspoken fifth factor: the judge's or jury's sense of right or wrong (Stanford 2010). Fair use involves subjective judgments, which ground the rationale for each final decision over fair use.

In his complaint, Fairey claimed to use and entered as evidence in his legal claim the Clooney photo, which captured a similar Obama pose yet from a more distant perspective. Fairey later admitted that he realized early on in the court case that he had actually used the Obama photo and had concealed this mistake by submitting false pictures and deleting others. Fairey (2009c) also apologized in public for this "lapse in judgment," stating he was sorry to have hurt not only colleagues, friends, and family but to have distracted attention from what should have been the "real focus" of his case—"the right to fair use so that all artists can create freely." When the mainstream media caught wind of his cover-up, however, sympathy was difficult to find. Headlines reading "Why Did Fairey Lie?" as well as "Shepard Fairey is a Liar" and "Artistliarthief"—most often accompanied by pictures of the *Hope* poster in comparison to Garcia's Obama photo—inundated online news sources and blogs. Many folks seemed surprised and visibly upset with what they saw to be a complete "ripoff" of Garcia's work. For others, such as a mysterious group of academics and artists who playfully called themselves Americans for Visual Literacy, the news of Fairey's cover-up only fueled their suspicions of a person they already deemed to be an untrustworthy figure.

As this scandal erupted, Obama Hope's circulation and rhetorical transformation only continued to escalate, of course. The Americans for

Visual Literacy, for instance, actually used the news of Fairey's cover-up and "bust" as ammunition for their attempts to expose what they called the "Obama Hope Scam." In October of 2008, the Americans for Visual Literacy had created a flyer with a picture of Obama Hope titled *2008 Obama Poster Facts*. This flyer was emailed out to art critics, bloggers, and others in the art world, but it eventually found its way to the (Free Republic n.d.) website—"the premier online gathering place for independent, grass-roots conservativism on the web . . . working to roll back decades of governmental largesse, to root out political fraud and corruption, and to champion causes which further conservatism in America." The flyer claimed that the *Hope* poster generated by a "graffiti-vandal" was neither unique nor original as it "was plagiarized from historic, Soviet, and Maoist propaganda posters" (see Figure 7.2). It also asked a series of "Do you know?" questions revealing Obama's "support for totalitarian messages," Obama's history with "criminal associates" such as Antoin 'Tony' Rezko, and his support for illegal graffiti." "Only Fools," the fact sheet reads at the bottom, "Find 'Hope' in Empty Statesman, Hollow Opportunists and Vile Imagery." In November of that same year, the Americans for Visual Literacy had also created a website with the homepage headline "What Everyone Needs to Know about 'Obama's Hope Scam.'" The Americans for Visual Literacy's ObamaHopeScam website, which was updated through May of 2010, posted links to numerous online articles announcing Fairey's "bust" and fraud and asked a series of charged questions as to why Obama was in cahoots with such a "petty career criminal." The site also tried to alert readers about what the AVL called "Obama's Hope Scam."

According to an interview with one of its founders, "Obama's Hope Scam" refers to the calculated yet hidden efforts of the Obama campaign to use Fairey to hand over an entire constituency of youth who would not only vote for but also work for Obama.[1] As discussed in chapter 2, Fairey claimed that even though the official Obama campaign approved of the production of the original *Progress* poster's being "under the radar" and asked him to change the word *progress* to *hope* in his second poster design, the official campaign was only loosely involved in the design of Obama Hope. The Americans for Visual Literacy, however, used Fairey's admittance that he had received the go-ahead to produce the first Obama *Progress* poster from "the highest levels" as ammunition to persuade readers that the Obama campaign manipulated Fairey and others to produce propaganda for them. Based on Obama's political record in Chicago with activists such Bill Ayers, the Americans for Visual Literacy believed that Obama, like Fairey, would go to any lengths

2008 OBAMA POSTER FACTS

Do You Know This 2008 Barak Obama Poster Does Not Proclaim 'Hope', 'Change' Or 'Democracy'?

This Poster Is Not Even Unique or Original...

A PRO-SOVIET PROPOGANDA POSTER...
- *DO YOU KNOW this poster design was plagiarized from historic Soviet and Maoist propaganda posters?*

NOT 'CHANGE', BUT 'ANARCHY'...
- *DO YOU KNOW this poster is the 2008 Democratic equivalent of the 'Che Guevara Poster' (with all that implies).*

ON NOVEMBER 4TH VOTE FOR PUTIN!
- *DO YOU KNOW the designer's fascination and reliance upon Communist imagery is so well known that Time called upon the designer to do a portrait of Vladimir Putin?*

LOOK AND THINK: REDS!
- *DO YOU KNOW most astute observers see this 2008 Obama 'HOPE' poster and think: REDS!*

VOTE FOR MAO!
- *DO YOU KNOW, in visual terms, this poster actually says, "MORE MAO!"*

LONG-STANDING HISTORY OF UN-AMERICAN IMAGERY...
- *DO YOU KNOW the designer, like Obama's Rev. Jeremiah Wright, has a long record of incendiary remarks and images against the United States government?*

OBAMA'S SUPPORT FOR TOTALITARIAN POLITICAL MESSAGES...
- *DO YOU KNOW that Obama, on February 22, praised the poster designer for his "encouraging political message"? What political message is that exactly, Senator Obama? Unoriginality, Communism, Maoism, or Revolution?*

ANOTHER OBAMA CRIMINAL ASSOCIATE...
- *DO YOU KNOW the poster was designed by one of America's leading graffiti vandals? Like another Obama criminal associate, Antoin 'Tony' Rezko, this career criminal was arrested again on August 25 at the DNC for graffiti.*

AMERICA'S $12 BILLION 'WAR AGAINST GRAFFITI'...
- *DO YOU KNOW that America's 'War Against Graffiti' costs American taxpayers and cities $10 - $12 billion dollars a year?*

OBAMA'S PUBLIC SUPPORT FOR ILLEGAL GRAFFITI...
- *DO YOU KNOW that Obama, on February 22, proudly supported the graffiti vandal's images littering America's "stop signs".*

AMERICA'S LEADING ADVOCATE OF GRAFFITI TO YOUTH...
- *DO YOU KNOW the poster designer is one of America's leading graffiti advocates to America's teenagers and youth? In his recent book, the graffiti-vandal urges Young American's to take up illegal graffiti and consider public buildings as acceptable targets. How much will this new crime wave cost American taxpayers?*

Only Fools Find *'Hope'* In Empty Statesmen, Hollow Opportunists and Vile Imagery.

*** PAID FOR BY AMERICANS FOR VISUAL LITERACY ***

For More Information Please Contact: AmericansForVisualLiteracy@yahoo.com

Figure 7.2. 2008 Obama Poster Facts, *Americans for Visual Literacy. Courtesy of Americans for Visual Literacy.*

to garner political support. They thus aggregated a number of quotes from various sources in an attempt to expose how Obama purposefully adopted Fairey's Communist iconography to, as one blogger put it, "utilize the skills of a career street vandal to appeal to the youth in the United States" (Sherwin 2009). Why else, one of its founders asked, would the Obama team want to be associated with a known vandal and plagiarist who used Communist propaganda techniques to deliver political messages?

The members of Americans for Visual Literacy were not the only ones who had been concerned with this issue before Fairey admitted his cover-up about the reference photo. In early February 2009, just after the lawsuit had erupted, Brian Sherwin posted a lengthy post titled "Was Shepard Fairey's Obama Posters Officially Endorsed by the Campaign or Not?" with a comparison of Garcia's Obama photo and Fairey's *Progress* and *Hope* posters on his blog *MyArtSpace* (which is cited on the ObamaHopeScam website). Sherwin cites a number of articles that present conflicting answers to this question and charges the mainstream news media with not working hard enough to get to the bottom of the matter. "The public deserves to know," he wrote. "[S]tudents reading the art history books of tomorrow deserve it. We deserve to know what exactly happened, who was involved, and how it was funded. Don't we?" Sherwin also claimed that the proper individuals needed to take responsibility for the confusion as to who was behind the production of the Obama Hope image. "Is the mainstream press at fault? Are former members of the Obama campaign at fault? Should Shepard Fairey take some responsibility? What about President Obama himself?"

Unfortunately for Sherwin, many people reporting and talking about the lawsuit were not interested in such questions about Fairey's early ties to the official Obama campaign. Many online news articles with headlines such as "Obama's Hope Poster a Rip Off?" and "Hope Poster Determined to be a Rip Off" simply reported the news of Obama Hope's involvement in Fairey et al. v. AP (2009a). In other cases, bloggers, lawyers, and artists drew on their expert knowledges to debate whether Obama Hope ought be considered fair use. Some blogs such as the *Marquette University Law School Faculty Blog*, the *Wall Street Journal Law Blog*, and Peter Friedman's blog on *Geniocity.com* even ran a series of posts about the Fairey et al. v. AP case, intensifying both the debate over fair use and the circulation and consequentiality of Obama Hope. This debate, as well as Obama Hope's rhetorical transformation, only continued to skyrocket as Garcia joined the lawsuit, Fairey admitted his wrongdoing, Fairey's lawyers from Stanford dropped him, and Fairey's artistic reputation came under further dispute. Many online news sources such as the *Huffington Post* and the *New York Times*, which had been interested in Obama Hope since its inception, printed numerous stories to keep their readers updated about Obama Hope's troubled affairs. Especially ironic were the number of Obamicons that began to surface with a

Figure 7.3. Liar *Obamicon, Dino Ignacio, 2009. Courtesy of Ignacio.*

portrait of Fairey in place of Obama with "Dolt," "Liar," and "Plagiarism" screaming beneath (see Figure 7.3).

TOUCHSTONE FOR INTELLECTUAL PROPERTY DEBATES

As discussions about fair use of Garcia's Obama photo escalated, Obama Hope became a touchstone for debates over intellectual property and the value of remix as a form of media literacy. Many people actually became excited about the lawsuit involving Obama Hope for its potential to settle intellectual property legal issues in a high court. Writing before the Fairey et al.v. AP case settled out of court, Evelyn McDonnell (2010) even went so far as to write that "'Hope' may not have merely helped the United States elect its first African-American president. It could set new legal precedents for one of the most important issues of the digital age: intellectual property." Intellectual property debates are increasingly heated in the current age of participatory culture and are made especially complicated by new media technologies. As Henry Jenkins (2009) succinctly explains, in a participatory culture "patterns of media consumption have been profoundly altered by a succession of new media technologies which enable average citizens to participate in the archiving, annotation, appropriation, transformation, and recirculation of media content." In a participatory culture, consumers demand and expect the "right to participate in and contribute to the creation and distribution of media" (Jenkins 2009). Media consumers, in other words, want to become media producers, and technologies such as low-cost copiers, scanners, and movie cameras as well as open-source software are making participation not only possible but also easy and inexpensive. Such assumed rights to and the value of production are very different than assumptions about intellectual property that emerged in the Industrial Revolution, which rested on the belief that "cultural value originates from the original contributions of individual authors" (Jenkins 2009). Of course, all creation builds on that which has come before it, whether that borrowing comes in the form of ideas, genre conventions, tropes, archetypes, style, and so forth. Yet, Industrial Revolution-era perceptions of intellectual property rested on the assumption that a creation is the "property" of that designer in the sense that they own it and have the power to control who uses it, and that nobody else can take it or use it unless the designer approves. Such conflicting ideologies, admittedly simplified here, underlined current debates over intellectual property that surfaced in relation to Obama Hope.

Lawrence Lessig has done perhaps more than anyone to draw attention to what he deems as a "property fundamentalism" reigning over current intellectual property laws in mainstream US culture. Thus, it should be of little surprise that Lessig became a staunch supporter of Fairey and Obama Hope early on when the controversy of fair use began to escalate. In *Free Culture*, Lessig (2004) makes comparisons between governing intellectual property systems and the Anglo-American tradition of feudalism. Under feudalism, property was held and controlled by a small number of individuals and entities. These property rights were extensive and powerful, and in order to protect them, property owners took concerted efforts to make sure the system of feudalism was not weakened by a free-market economy (267). Lessig draws on Peter Drahos and John Braithwaite to argue that right now, as an information society, we are making the decision about whether to be free or feudal. Lessig argues that media conglomerates have so much lobbying control that we are operating under a feudal system, which translates to an "all rights reserved" attitude, an enlargement of copyright, and a demonization and penalization of those who share, remix, and appropriate without formal permission. Rather than choose a "no rights reserved" attitude, for which some would argue, Lessig advocates for a revision of copyright law that protects designers but does not inhibit innovation and creation, at the heart of which is remix.

Current copyright laws are especially destructive, Lessig argues, because they are curbing new media literacies such as remix that have much value in a free, participatory culture and, as was evident in the case of Obama Hope, have real potential to work for democratic change. Remix, to be clear, is often defined as "collage, a recombination of existing, reference images or music or video clips from popular digital culture, elements of which are mashed up into something new" (Stepanek 2009). As Johndan Johnson-Eilola and Stuart Selber and also James Porter and Dánielle DeVoss, among others, have made clear, all writing is and always has been remix (Johnson-Eilola and Selber 2007; DeVoss and Porter 2006). "Writing is an act of sharing and borrowing as well as of creating. Whenever you write, you borrow ideas, phrases, images, sounds, details from others—and then you weave those pieces into a new cloth and onto new fabric and with new threads and *that* becomes 'your' writing" (DeVoss and Porter 2006, 200). Yet, while remix is not particular to digital culture, digital technologies are escalating the sharing of mashups and remixes online and accelerating the speeds at which ideas and images spread across genres, networks, and forms. As DeVoss and Porter (2006) argue, "Writing in the digital age increasingly requires remixing." As a consequence, while remix may be a historical practice, laws regulating remixes such as Obama Hope are negatively impacting more and more people who practice remix on a daily basis.

For Lessig, what is especially problematic is that for the first time in the history of the United States, copyright laws—historically reserved for professionals—are regulating and even criminalizing the media production of ordinary citizens. Whereas before 1909, Intellectual Property (IP) laws only limited the exclusive right to "copy" professional works such as statues, since then copyright law has increasingly limited virtually every technology that "cop[ies]" (Lessig 2008, 101). Today, because much creative work by amateurs (sampling, remix, mash-ups, etc.) produces a copy, more and more uses of creative works technically become entangled with copyright law. As the range of digital technologies has increased ordinary citizens' ability to copy, then, so has the scope of regulation expanded (101). Not just professionals such as Fairey are being taken to court, Lessig points out. In many instances, young amateurs are not only being taken to court but are being so heavily fined for their creative works that their own as well as their families' financial securities are undermined. At the very least, in classrooms, students who practice remix are often charged with plagiarism. Such criminalization for creativity, Lessig, Jenkins, and others argue, threatens new media forms of literacy enacted by ordinary citizens to participate in the production of their culture and democracy. Rather than perpetuate laws that curb new media literacies, they argue, we ought to recognize the public good of creative works such as the Obama *Hope* poster and foster the innovative creations that young people such as Fairey are crafting and using to make their voices heard. While media conglomerates obviously would disagree in order to maintain their IP rights, revising IP laws to support such new media literacy is a battle that Lessig, Jenkins, and other educators insist we all ought to be fighting.

Obama Hope is front and center in such debates as it circulates in work published by Lessig and others about intellectual property in relation to both legal action and education. For a short while before Fairey and the AP settled out of court, in fact, as McDonnell (2010) explains, the lawsuit related to Obama Hope were considered "a test case for the changing rules of IP and a case study in what media studies scholar Henry Jenkins et al. have described as the new media literacy of appropriation" (qtd. in Jenkins et al. 2006). Obama Hope's role as a touchstone about IP was particularly evident in its visibility in a number of articles written by lawyers about the Fairey/AP/Garcia lawsuit. On March 24, 2010, Sonia Katyal and Eduardo Penalver remarked on the irony of Obama Hope's destiny, pointing out how an image that "captured an entire political generation—inspiring so many to move forward in sweeping Obama into office—has sparked one of the most controversial and high-profile copyright suits in recent history." As Katyal and Penalver (2010) also pointed out, the lawsuit was about more than the unauthorized use of a news photo; it also drew attention to the problems with the doctrine of fair use and "the concomitant failures of the legal doctrine that courts have developed to surround and defend the doctrine's dwindling power." One such problem is a lack of legally defined boundaries between lawful fair use and unlawful infringement, a boundary at the heart of the dispute over Fairey's use of Garcia's photo in the Obama Works.

Unfortunately, as several articles with Obama Hope at the center claimed, Fairey's cover-up attempt jeopardized the chances of this lawsuit making it to court and a definitive ruling about fair-use boundaries being set in law. While Obama Hope has indeed become a touchstone for debates about fair use, then, its chances to go down in history as not only the symbol of the 2008 presidential election but also the symbol of changing rules in twenty-first-century IP law were ruined by

Fairey's admitted misjudgments and his settling with the AP out of court in January of 2011. Still, in both verbal and visual form, Obama Hope would spark public debate about copyright, the lawsuit, and Fairey himself for years to come. Rhetorical consequences from these debates are still hypervisible on the World Wide Web today, especially as online news sources and a plethora of blogs kept up with Fairey's fate after he was charged with a federal crime for destroying documents, falsifying evidence, "and other misconduct" in his civil litigation with the Associated Press—a crime for which he was eventually put on probation and required to pay a fee of $25,000 and serve community service. In addition, scholars such as Shelly Rosenfeld (2011) are still writing about how courts would have ruled had Fairey and the Associated Press not settled out of court. Such discussions, along with its educational role to be discussed in the following section, leave little doubt that, even though its significance was not foreseen, Obama Hope has become the twenty-first-century poster child for fair use and a touchstone for contemporary debates over intellectual property, remix, and visual culture.

EDUCATOR

While Obama Hope's chances to become the star in a precedent case over IP laws diminished with Fairey's legal troubles, Obama Hope's chances to make an educational impact interestingly did not. Today, Obama Hope can be found in countless books and online websites serving a variety of educational roles. Besides appearing in my own scholarship, for instance, Obama Hope is showing up in work produced by scholars in rhetoric and composition and visual culture studies to educate folks on theories of design, visual contributions to politics, and theories of noetic space. For instance, in his webtext "The Annotated Obama Poster," which won a 2009 *Computers and Composition* Michelle R. Kendrick Award, Ben McCorkle (2009) analyses the visual rhetoric behind Fairey's *Hope* poster in light of current copyright and intellectual property concerns. In this webtext, viewers can click on various parts of the Obama *Hope* poster and learn about design choices, production techniques, copyright concerns, aesthetic comparisons, and so forth. In Jeff Rice's scholarship, on the other hand, we see Obama Hope educating readers on how images acquire noetic value and create noetic space. As Rice (2011) draws on Walter Ong to explain, noetic figures are heroic, rhetorical characters who enact memorable deeds in public, leave emotional impressions on people's bodies, and organize public space. Obama Hope acquired noetic value as it "generated an emotional and personal connection (the promise of hope and change, the excitement for a new type of leader, the convergence of American flag colors with the promise of an African American president) that a different type of display would likely not generate" (11). In addition, the space of the campaign became "greatly organized" by Obama Hope as did both the physical and internal space of Obama supporters "who internalized and personalized Obama as their own sense of hope" (11). What Obama Hope teaches us about contemporary rhetorical organization, then, Rice argues, is how images such as Obama Hope actually "invent and arrange expression through space in the age of media" (11).

Besides playing a role in rhetorical education, Obama Hope also makes appearances in books aiming to educate the general public on the role of political art in presidential campaigns. Admittedly, one book, *Art for Obama*, was produced by Fairey and others, but Obama Hope also makes appearances in Hal Wert's (2009) *Hope: A Collection of Obama Posters and Prints*, Scott Thomas's (2010) *Designing Obama*, and most recently in *Presidential Campaign Posters* put together by the Library of Congress (see Figure 7.4). This latter book, filled with 11 × 14 color prints, illustrates how since 1828 with Andrew Jackson's election, political art has played a major role not only in selling campaign messages but in selling images of America to Americans. As Brooke Gladstone (2012) notes in the preface to this poster collection, Americans tend to cast their votes for candidates based on character, not a candidate's policies. "We vote for the person whom we want to be our public face for the next four years, the face the nation sees when it looks in the mirror." In terms of 2008, Gladstone argues that Fairey's Obama *Hope* poster and its stylized red, white, and blue portrait of Obama was able to "visually overcome the 'otherness' of being black in America" (4). As a mirror, he argues, the Obama *Hope* poster depicted an "evolved, postracial America" (4). While certainly many would not agree with Gladstone's (2012) interpretation of this rhetorical function, most would agree with the Library of Congress's claim in the final pages of the book that the Obama *Hope* poster mirrored the desires for change and hope that many Americans felt in the midst of continuing wars in Iraq and Afghanistan (206). So intense were these feelings, the authors claim, that it is plausible to say that Obama was the first to attract a "cult" (202). This devotion, the authors maintain, was largely due to the fact that much of the art for Obama produced images of Obama "as an almost God-like figure" with one-word messages that operated much like "subliminal billboard messages" (202). While some, as we will see throughout this case study, thought such artwork and utter devotion was "creepy," overall, the pro-Obama messages in political art

Figure 7.4. Presidential Campaign Posters *Book Cover, 2012. Courtesy of Library of Congress/Quirk Books.*

such as the Obama *Hope* poster were well received and succeeded in moving voters to help Obama achieve victory.

While Obama Hope has functioned to educate readers about rhetoric, design, and presidential campaign history, most of its educational role has been involved, unsurprisingly, with issues about fair use and remix. Educational lessons involving Obama Hope are growing so popular in secondary and higher education that it is not outlandish to claim, in fact, that Obama Hope is becoming a staple in education about fair use. In graphic design and in writing and rhetoric courses taught by scholars such as Jim Ridolfo, for instance, Obama Hope helps students inquire into the role, ethics, and responsibilities of remix in the composing process. In journalism classes, Obama Hope helps students explore the definitions of copyright and fair use so they can better determine how to use and adapt online media in their own work. Obama Hope is even beginning to show up in scholarly textbooks to educate readers on copyright issues. For instance, in *Videojournalism: Multimedia Storytelling*, Obama Hope makes an appearance as "the most famous recent example" of how journalists can get into trouble with copyright infringement by not obtaining the license to use someone else's work (Kobre 2012, 233). In Wayne Overbeck and Genelle Belmas's *Major Principles of Media Law*, on the other hand, Obama Hope shows up in a chapter devoted to copyrights and trademarks to address whether creative works should be "locked as they are, without permission for others to transform them, to mix and 'mash' them into new creative works" (Overbeck and Belmas 2012, 235). As these authors note, such questions are especially pressing as the growth of the Internet creates more opportunities for remixing creative works and thus creating more complexities for copyright law.

Obama Hope also plays a key educational role on the New Media Literacies Project (NML) website. NML is an online resource devoted to a research initiative funded by the MacArthur Foundation and based within USC's Annenberg School for Communication. The mission of this initiative is to investigate ways to "best equip young people with the social skills and cultural competencies required to become full participants in an emergent media landscape and raise public understanding of what it means to be literate in a globally, interconnected multicultural world." One feature of the website is the Learning Library, where visitors can upload challenges to test their knowledge about rights to download and use content from the web. One key literacy young people must have, after all, according to NML, is to understand copyright/fair-use law so they know the boundaries of creating and distributing remix material. The Obama Hope image plays a major role in offering visitors an opportunity to think critically about copyright law. NML created three challenges related to the Obama Hope image—"Mannie Garcia and Copyright," "Shepard Fairey and Fair Use," and "Optimus Prime and Creative Commons." In the challenge "Shepard Fairey and Fair Use," visitors are introduced to the key arguments made by Fairey and the AP; shown the two images under dispute; introduced to arguments made on the *Colbert Show* about Fairy's use of Garcia's Obama photograph; and asked to take a side and submit their opinions. One important consequence that has emerged as a touchstone about IP law, then, is Obama Hope's role in educating ordinary citizens about copyright law and fair use.

While its appearance on the NML website and the Fair Use Lab seems rather neutral, its educational role in *Remix: Making Art and Commerce Thrive in the Hybrid Economy* put on at the New York Public Library in February of 2009 was much more loaded. This event, moderated by cultural historian Steven Johnson and featuring Lessig and Fairey, presented a provocative but one-sided argument about why remix should not be criminalized but should instead be promoted as an important literacy. At the heart of their argument was the fact that remix and appropriation are key to sharing ideas, which makes innovation possible. In addition, they echoed Porter, DeVoss, and others' arguments that remixing is a creative practice but not a new practice. As evidence, both Johnson and Lessig illustrated how politicians such as Thomas Jefferson and Benjamin Franklin and various artists such as Andy Warhol have long practiced appropriation and remix. What is new, they argued, are contemporary reactions to it. In a hilarious mockery of demonizations of remix by artists such as Fairey, Lessig presented a slide show of just how common remix is as a practice among designers of music, cartoons, paintings, and photographs. Lessig even showed how other artists have remixed images of Obama. The lawsuit over Obama Hope was offered as the quintessential example of how potentially devastating the current copyright war is to creative innovations such as the Obama *Hope* poster. As Lessig stated in making an argument for deregulating remix rather than criminalizing it, "The terrorists in this war [the copyright war] are our children. This wave of terrorism is threatening artists like Shepard Fairey. It's threatening kids. The RIAA is suing more than 28,000 kids for using material on the 'net illegally, according to the RIAA, but to no effect because the one thing we know about P2P filesharers is that they don't read Supreme Court decisions" (qtd. in L. Johnson 2009). As evident in such arguments, the Obama Hope image not only played a key role in advertising the event in print and digital mediums, but it also had a front and center role during the presentation as the quintessential example of how remix is both a creative act and one that has been demonized as a criminal act (see Figure 7.5).

This event, in turn, sparked more rhetorical consequences as bloggers and online journalists reported and responded to it. One such blogger was Mike Edwards, a fellow composition and rhetoric scholar, who on his blog *Vitia* summarized the event and expressed doubt about whether Lessig's solution to this issue—deregulation—is really the best option. On other sites, such as *Deep Media*, where the Obama Hope

Figure 7.5. Photograph of Obama Hope *at NYPL Remix Event, Peter Foley, 2009. Courtesy of Peter Foley/the New York Public Library.*

image accompanied a post titled "Hope and Theft," bloggers expressed agreement with Lessig's ideas, stating "the copyright panic that media companies are experiencing today is less about theft than about the rise of participatory culture—and the challenge it poses to the way they do business" (Rose 2009). Still on other sites, bloggers such as Jennifer Schuessler (2009) writing on the *New York Times* blog *Paper Cuts* expressed concern about remix artists profiting from bloggers' and others' work as "news organizations struggle to survive in the era of free content." Voicing worries as a freelance journalist, Schuessler wrote, "Information wants to be free, but my writing wants to cost money," implying that remix artists like Fairey jeopardize journalists' and news photographers' ability to profit from their own work. Such metacultural activity, of course, only accelerated the circulation of Obama Hope, making it more and more widely recognized. Incidentally, such metacultural activity also solidified Obama Hope's unexpected place in many education courses, where scholars ask students to watch the New York Public Library lecture, read the actual AP and Fairey claims, and debate about Fairey's use of Garcia's now-famous photo.

CONCLUSION

The metacultural and collective activities in relation to fair use, copyright, and remix that I have presented in this chapter are, perhaps, the most visible unintended consequences that have unfolded during

Obama Hope's rhetorical life. While Fairey desired for Obama Hope to become widely recognizable, he clearly did not anticipate the image's becoming so familiar to others because of the scandals that ensued around intellectual property issues, nor the educational role it would take on as a consequence of this involvement. Fairey has argued that in order for viral circulation to occur, an image not only must be made widely accessible to a broad audience but must also be highly desired, presumably because it is well liked and appreciated. What we learn here, however, is that as unintended consequences proliferate throughout an image's unfolding journey toward iconicity, an image often establishes an ambiguous ethos during circulation. In rhetorical theory, ethos has long been associated with personal character, ethics, and trust. Most often discussed in relation to humans, ethos is understood to be dynamic; ethos changes as human identities, locations, and aspirations transform in response to various circumstances. Ethos is also understood not to be solely dictated by a human rhetor; as Nedra Reynolds (1993) draws on Karen Burke LeFevre to explain, ethos emerges from one's intersection with a listener or reader and thus requires that writers negotiate how to identify their own positions in relation to others (333). Yet despite its dynamic, negotiated nature, ethos is still something identifiable that shapes how rhetors and their messages will be received. From most common understandings, if human rhetors establish trust with audiences, their chances for rhetorical success are increased.

While the ethos of images has not been heavily explored, we might think of an image's ethos in a similar fashion. An image's ethos is determined by several factors related to the pictures in which it emerges: the quality of design, production, and presentation; the content; the reputation of the image and picture established through metaculture; the reputation of the artist; the exchange value; and so forth. Not all these factors must be on the same playing field. For instance, a painting of a highly violent image that is offensive to many may earn a credible ethos if the quality of design and presentation is strong. Or the content of the image may trigger such strong emotional and logical appeals that the poor quality of the actualized image may not weaken its ethos. Yet, no matter what contributes to its strong ethos, one would assume that if an image establishes a trustworthy ethos, it would become more desirable and thus increase its chances for going viral and becoming iconic.

Obama Hope teaches us, however, that the credibility of an image's ethos may not influence its chances to go viral and become iconic as much as we may think. In the case of Obama Hope, this image, as we saw in chapter 6, initially acquired a credible ethos as it became an important rhetorical actor that shaped much political participation during the 2008 election season. And as will become apparent in chapters 8 and 9, as its credibility was established, more and more people desired to own, reproduce, and remix Obama Hope as well as appropriate it for their own uses. Whether Obama Hope was supposed to generate support for Obama, sell commercial products, make people laugh and/or think, or work to mobilize political action, it has been trusted to do the rhetorical work it was appropriated to do. Yet, as Obama Hope's origins came to be known, its ethos became much more ambiguous. In some sense, as we saw in Evelyn McDonnell's (2010) comments, in addition to becoming an important political actor during the 2008 campaign season, its ethos was enhanced as it demonstrated potential to change copyright law and provided a rich education about fair-use issues and the value of remix. In others' eyes, however, as it became a poster child for fair use, it acquired a shocking reputation for being a fraud. And as Fairey came to be thought of as a liar and thief in the eyes of many, so too did Obama Hope become charged with being a rip-off. Such conflicting, inconsistent perceptions about this image ought not be surprising for an image born into politics; rarely has the life of a political actor—even one who has made an impact on a national/international scene and established a respectful reputation—been scandal free. But more important, conflicting, inconsistent perceptions about Obama Hope's character did not seem to decelerate its circulation nor thwart this image's ability to be rhetorically powerful in its capacity to reassemble the social. On the contrary, the mystery and controversy that erupted over Obama Hope's design only seemed to accelerate its journey to becoming widely recognizable and significant. This image's viral circulation and iconicity, then, did not just depend on its desirability in the positive sense. As is evident in the unintended collective and metacultural activities presented in this chapter, Obama Hope went viral and became iconic because it also sparked much controversy, negative criticism, and public debate.

The unintended metacultural and collective activities presented in this chapter also indicate just how capable new media images such as Obama Hope are in inducing a distributed network of people and technologies to assemble to work toward collaborative goals. In part 1 of this case study, we saw people assembling in relation to Obama Hope to help Obama become the forty-fourth president of the United States—a phenomenon that chapter 9 will show became even more complex. But as with Obama himself, people were unsatisfied with the stories being told about the origins of Obama Hope. Thus, as we saw in this part of the case study, a group of strangers united for a brief period to work alongside a variety of technologies to find the truth about Obama Hope's ancestry. While such collective action may seem incidental, any attempt to describe Obama Hope's eventfulness would need to account for this short-lived but intense activity, especially if it wants to account for this image's distributed ontology. For not only was Obama Hope's transformation and circulation intensified by this collective experience and the metaculture that emerged in response to it, but it's involvement in the mystery case also sparked a spectrum of other collective activities and consequences in relation to fair use and media literacy. Much of this distributed activity occurred in cyberspace as people assembled on various blogs and online news sites to discuss matters of fair use and copyright. Yet much collective activity unfolded across multiple geographical, physical spaces as others assembled to work both for and against Fairey in a number of lawsuits or jumped on board to defend the production of Obama *Hope* posters and Fairey's remix practices. As is evident in regard to Obama Hope's educational role, much of this collective activity is ongoing as Obama Hope teaches people in online and physical spaces about the complex issues of remix, copyright, and fair use.

In and of itself, Obama Hope surely cannot receive sole credit for sparking this dynamic network of interrelated collective activities. As Jane Bennett (2010) reminds us, "An actant never really acts alone. Its efficacy or agency always depends on the collaboration, cooperation, or interactive interference of many bodies and forces" (21). And as Jenny Edbauer Rice (2005) insists, we can never attribute the exigence for any rhetorical activity to just one element that is part of a broader affective ecology. Yet, as one actant intra-acting in an assemblage with others, we ought at the very least to acknowledge Obama Hope's unique contributions to reassembling collective life. As this chapter has made clear, in addition to become a valued political actor, Obama Hope has become a poster child for fair use, a touchstone for contemporary debates about intellectual property issues and remix, and a popular educator. In these roles, various people's lives are transformed as they investigate, debate, learn, and work for educational and legal change during their engagements with Obama Hope. Such unexpected contributions are just a small sample of how influential Obama Hope has been to collective life since it began to circulate in its "Faireyized" version in early 2008.

Note

1.   This representative of Americans for Visual Literacy was interviewed by phone and chose to remain anonymous.

8

OBAMA HOPE, PARODY, AND SATIRE

Just as the scandalous affairs in which Obama Hope would become embroiled were unpredicted, one could never have anticipated how wildly Obama Hope would transform as it entered into diverse associations throughout and since early 2008. While certainly other iconic images—Uncle Sam, the Mona Lisa, the Last Supper, and most recently the Pepper Spray meme—have undergone intense transformation, no image designed for presidential campaign purposes has experienced reproduction, appropriation, and transformation on such a mass scale. In this chapter, I illustrate how the image experienced mass commodification and fueled what some call *Obamamania*. Yet, I mostly focus on how it took an ironic rhetorical turn to become a popular enactment of parody and satire, and, in the eyes of many, a quintessential political meme. In addition, I disclose how Obama Hope has inspired a novel cybergenre called *Obamicons* that has become a staple in political participation on the World Wide Web. When we zoom in on such divergent transformations, it becomes undeniable that Obama Hope has experienced a constant process of rhetorical becoming as it has taken on unexpected functions and has actualized in surprising and sometimes disturbing forms. Via this focus on rhetorical transformation, it also becomes even more clear how this single multiple image was able to achieve viral circulation and become iconic in such a short time is it drew many people into collective activity.

COMMODIFICATION

During the 2008 election season, Obama Hope's transformation and circulation accelerated as its commodification became rampant and online news sources began reporting about the "Obamabilia craze" that was sweeping the nation. As discussed in chapter 6, Obama Hope surfaced on merchandise sold by the official Obama campaign and items Obey Giant and other companies such as Sticker Robot produced and distributed. Yet,

DOI: 10.7330/9780874219784.c008

Figure 8.1. Obama Change *Print Dress, Alessandra Tarantino, 2009. Permissions by Associated Press.*

at street fairs, flea markets, political rallies, and online stores, those in the private sector also began producing Obama Hope on a plethora of diverse merchandise. In addition to its appearance on the expected t-shirts, sweatshirts, and hats, it has surfaced in typical commemorative fashion on coins and medals. Yet in a more random show of artifacts, Obama Hope has also turned up on action toys, silver business-card holders, cell-phone stickers, coffee cups, water bottles, and a variety of accessories such as tennis shoes, purses, earrings, watches, ties, barrettes, and lapel pins. Obama Hope even showed up on tote bags in Ghana while its red, white, and blue style, which influenced Fairey's *Change* poster, appeared on a woman's haute couture dress in Milan, Italy (see Figure 8.1). While such commodification certainly intensified when the US National Portrait Gallery acquired the *Hope* collage and cemented Obama Hope's national stardom, its commodification did not begin then. In fact, its commodification began as soon as people realized they could profit from sales of original posters that they paid for through Fairey's Obey website.

The "eBayification" of the Obama Hope image became especially popular when people who had gotten hold of Fairey's original *Progress* posters began selling them on eBay for prices as high as $1,000. These auctions began in February 2008, shortly after their initial publication on the Obey website. Ebay had become such a central location for circulating the Obama posters early, in fact, that the *Wall Street Journal* began tracking the prices of the Obama *Progress* poster on eBay during the Obama campaign (Lewis 2008). Its interactive "Obama's 'Progress' Report" illustrates how prices on eBay were driven by news and events throughout the campaign. Just after Hillary Clinton conceded in June of '08, for instance, the poster's price shot up to over $4,000 (Lewis 2008). Such eBay sales accelerated the circulation of the Obama Hope image in ways Fairey neither expected nor approved of. In fact, as soon as the eBay transactions began occurring without his permission, Fairey (2008) expressed disappointment on his Obey website, calling the eBay profiteers "greedy." He claimed all the proceeds from the *Progress* poster's sales on his own Obey website were intended to generate support for Obama, not enhance the pockets of people looking to make a profit off his work. The reality is, however, that the desire for Obama Hope had become so strong that Fairey could not produce enough prints to satisfy US Americans' desires for it. The prices of the *Progress* posters were thus driven up because of a lack of supply and high demand. Fairey tried to keep the prices of the *Hope* posters down by putting them up for sale on his website for thirty-five dollars. Yet, by April of 2008, even these posters were up for auction on eBay for over $300.

At the time of writing, sales of Obama Hope in a variety of manifestations can still be found on eBay. An original Obama *Hope* poster distributed at the 2008 Democratic National Convention has gone down to the thirty-five-dollar price Fairey was originally asking on his own site. But some of the items are priced quite high. While a signed edition of the *Hope* poster is going for $500, for instance, a limited edition of the *Progress* poster is up for international auction for over $13,000. A brand-new, unused, and unopened Obama Hope action figure is also available for $150, over six times its original price. Such items and others are also easily accessible on Amazon.com, other online stores, and entire websites devoted to the sales of Obama products and gifts. On Etsy, for instance, Obama Hope can be currently found stamped onto rings, magnets, and phone covers as well as crocheted, beaded, and weaved with dryer lint onto cloth canvases, the latter of which is on sale for $250. While it is unclear how much profit has been gained from the image's sales on various products, it is clear that even though the campaign is

long over, Obama Hope's commodification is still ongoing and is perpetuating its continued circulation.

Desires for ownership of Obama Hope in the United States, which
are both a stimulant for and a consequence of its mass commodification,
vary with individuals. Obviously, people purchased Obama Hope goods
to identify as Obama supporters, build alliances with other Obama
supporters, and commemorate this monumental moment in US history. Yet individuals also consumed Obama Hope for a wide range of
other personal reasons. George Clooney, for instance, is reported to
have an Obama poster hanging in his home as a reminder of his work
with Obama on behalf of Darfur and the fact that he was sitting next
to Obama when Garcia's photo was taken (Gardner 2012). Young artist Anna Jacobs, on the other hand, claims (pers. comm.) she bought a
t-shirt printed with Obama Hope simply because it was a powerful image
in and of itself. Others such as Gene Mackles (pers. comm.) explain
they tried to purchase a *Progress* poster on eBay because they liked the
image and thought it would become important in the future. Still others such as artists Andy Howell and Ginger Che (pers. comm.) were convinced "this iconic image served to help unify a voting public in changing the course of history." Obama Hope thus reminded these artists of
the power visual things can have on an entire populace. As for myself,
I obtained a signed, original print of the *Hope* poster as inspiration to
work on this research project. Hanging over my desk, the picture serves
as motivation to keep writing.

As is evident in such testimonies, no single cause for the rampant
commodification and consumption of Obama Hope can be identified.
Yet, interestingly, once Obama Hope's mass reproduction began, people
began to speculate as to why this image had become so desired. Some
argued the commodification was a smart campaign choice and political
strategy, as the campaign team knew that selling posters, limited-edition
prints, stickers, and so forth with depictions of Obama Hope (and other
designs) would help Obama achieve victory. Bruce Newman, associate
professor of marketing at DePaul University and author of *The Marketing of
the President*, argues that such commodification of Obama was, in fact, one
of the best strategies the Obama campaign could have used (Malooley
2008). Apparently, such strategy in marketing is called *attribution theory*.
According to this theory, "If Obama gets you to make a definite financial
commitment, it's hard for you not to support him down the road. Even
if it's just a $15 T-shirt" (Malooley 2008). This marketing strategy likely
worked, as Obama Hope helped generate hundreds of thousands of dollars, and presumably votes, for Obama.

Some would argue, however, that the commodification of Obama Hope was much less politically and economically motivated than is often surmised. In writing for *Global Comment*, for instance, Sarah Jaffe (2009) quipped, "Obama's image is salable in part because he is a black man. The first black president. History being made. Get your slice." As artists Godfied Donkor and Hank Willis Thomas, as well intellectuals Michael Dyson and bell hooks, among countless others, have argued, the commodification of black bodies is a longstanding historical practice in Western settings, beginning perhaps with the slave trade and continuing today throughout the mainstream media. Such commodification contributes to an erasure of human qualities from the black body and an equation of blackness with a mass-produced, unspecialized product that can be controlled and owned. Jaffe argued Obama is no different. Many, in fact, are most comfortable with Obama as a commodity that can be controlled, bought, or sold (Jaffe 2009).

Others would argue that such rampant reproduction is indicative of Obama Hope's fetishization in that it came to embody Obama's "magical" political qualities and demonstrated people's excessive, irrational, and unswayable commitment to Obama's candidacy. Fouad Ajami, for instance, is one among many scholars who have commented on Obama's charismatic ability to lure crowds of people who tend to "project their needs onto an imagined redeemer." In a *Wall Street Journal* article, "When the Obama Magic Died," Ajami (2013), a MacArthur-fellowship-winning senior fellow at Stanford University's Hoover Institution, likens the spectacle of adoration for Obama to the followers who clung to Egyptian leader Gamal Abdul Nassar. In Ajami's words, Nassar became a "demigod, immune to judgment" even when he led Arabs to a catastrophic military defeat in the Six-Day War of 1967. Nassar's reign, like Obama's, was never about policies and performance, Ajami says, but rather about political magic. As evidence, he asks readers to recall how the Obama coalition was formed back in 2008. "There were African Americans justifiably proud of one of their own. There were upper-class white professionals who were drawn to the candidate's 'cool.' There were Latinos swayed by the promise of immigration reform. The white working class in the Rust Belt was the last bloc to embrace Mr. Obama—he wasn't one of them, but they put their reservations aside during an economic storm and voted for the redistributive state and its protections." Such assemblage, he argues, illustrates that this coalition was not formed by economic or cultural bonds. People simply rallied around "the new leader, who was all things to all people."

Many have labeled such unquestioning adulation as *Obamamania*, a term that exploded in popular discourse during the 2008 election season. In the most conservative sense, Obamamania is defined as "the condition of being a very enthusiastic support of . . . [Barack Obama]" (Maxwell 2008). Yet Obamamania is commonly defined in more extreme terms, such as the zealous and cult-like support for Obama that escalated when he ran for president. Lisa Lerer (2008) from *Politico* describes Obamamania in this way: "[Obama's] most fervent backers fall in love with his idealistic message of change . . . his youth, and his powerful presence on the stump. For some, the affair can border on obsession. . . . And activist Democrats aren't the only ones swept up in *Obamamania*" [my emphasis]. His campaign events are filled with first-time voters, self-described political slackers, and even a few Republicans who now zealously back the first-term senator from Illinois." Some, such as Sean Hannity (2010) from *Fox News*, even went so far as to describe Obamamania as a "hypnotic trance, the feeling of omnipotent ecstasy and euphoria at the sight of the Anointed One during the campaign."

This ability of Obama to hypnotize US citizens was not an uncommon accusation, and in some cases, Obama Hope was inculcated in this process. Jason Mattera, for instance, has visually implied that an entire generation of people was turned into Obama Zombies with the help of branding machines such as Obama Hope. In *Obama Zombies: How the Liberal Machine Brainwashed my Generation*, Mattera (2010) describes Obama zombies as members of his own generation who have public "O-gasms" (242) at the site of Obama, drink up the promise of change like their favorite adult beverage (x), and experience nothing short of "mental mummification" (xi) when exposed to Obama marketing strategies. Such easily swayed people did more than simply identify with Obama, Mattera claims. They actually believed that Obama could save humankind and renew our faith in both American politics and government. As examples of such Obama Zombies, young adults with a hypnotized gaze are depicted in the style of Obama Hope on the cover of Mattera's book (see Figure 8.2).

Obamamania triggered much response from people disturbed by the supposed fervent, blind admiration for Obama, and many of these responses came in the form of Obama Hope remixes. In a sticker designed by Byron Durham, a.k.a. BigMini, for instance, Obama Hope surfaced in a black-and-white version with a bar code stamped onto Obama's forehead (see Figure 8.3). The actual design, which was distributed on stickers all over Chicago, was intended, according to Durham (pers. comm.) to "poke fun at the fringe elements of the Christian right that believe the bar code is the 'mark of the beast' due to use of '666,' and/or believe that Obama is the antichrist." Yet, Durham made and distributed these

Figure 8.2. Obama Zombies at Table, *Book Cover Designed by Ruth Lee-Mui, Photograph by Blackhorse 17, 2010. Photograph Courtesy of Blackhorse 17.*

stickers after the inauguration because he also wanted to "raise questions about the current excess of adulation for a political figure, which is always dangerous." Durham further explained, "It is unhealthy in a democracy to not question our leaders, no matter how enamored we are of them." While appearing to critique Obama, then, this actualized version of Obama Hope also circulated as a critique of US responses to Obama, whether hyperbolically negative or positive. Durham says his critique obviously aroused a lot of response. His sticker was torn down almost as quickly as it was put up, a response in Durham's eyes that offers evidence of the very unquestioning support he was critiquing.

Despite such critical responses to Obamamania, if we want to call it that, others capitalized on Obama Hope's commodification. Some organizations such as Canstruction capitalized on it for nonprofit purposes. Canstruction is a nonprofit organization that hosts annual design-and-build competitions to raise food for local food banks. Each year, a contest is held in different cities in which participants construct large structures made entirely out of cans of food. In each city, the winning constructs go on view for the general public as giant art exhibits, and at the close of the competitions, all canned food used in the structures is donated to local food banks for distribution to emergency food programs. In 2009, a group of ACE high-school students teamed up with GBD Architects, Glumac Engineering, and Brightworks to build an eight-foot-tall can sculpture of Obama Hope in Portland, Oregon. To create their winning sculpture, titled *Yes We Can*, Google's 3D software

Figure 8.3. Obama Anti-
Christ, *Bryon Durham, 2009.
Courtesy of Durham.*

program, SketchUp, was used to design the model and 2,583 cans of olives and black, green, and kidney beans were arranged according to the pixels on different can labels. In combination with other constructions in Portland, this event generated thirty thousand pounds of food and $25,000 dollars for the Oregon Food Bank (Carter).

Yet while Obama Hope was able to work without profit in such ways, it was also capitalized on for profit. In addition to surfacing on the range of products mentioned earlier, Obama Hope also became a popular advertising strategy for a number of products, services, and events both within and beyond US borders. Here in the United States, the image has been remixed on signs selling everything from coffee to cookies to haircuts, while in Italy, Obama Hope has worked to lure people to see music and to sell haute couture on fashion runways. In Istanbul, Turkey, on the other hand, renditions of Obama Hope have worked to promote a low loan interest rate for the Turkish bank Garanti as well as clothes for the company T-Box (see Figure 8.4). While other depictions of Obama certainly appear in various advertisements, this small sampling, in addition to the evidence below, discloses how Obama Hope has become a leading figure in making Obamamania work for profit in the global arena.

Figure 8.4. Blue Mosque and Obama, 2009. Photograph Courtesy of Matthew Shaw.

OBAMAMANIA IN AFRICA

Obamamania has been especially intense in Africa—a continent in which many, especially Kenyans, take pride in Obama's ancestry. President Obama's father, if you remember, was born in Kenya, where, after attending the University of Hawaii and Harvard, he worked as an economist for a couple of different Kenyan ministries before falling into a life of poverty and alcoholism. As Edwin Okong'o (2008) explains, in most tribal cultures in Kenya, "a child belongs to the father"; thus, "the fact that his [Obama's] father was Kenyan . . ., according to our tradition, makes him one of our own." This patrimonial ancestry has generated much, if not absolute, support for Obama across Kenya and many other countries in Africa. Kenyans believe in Barack Obama so much in fact, Okong'o claims, that if Obama were to run for the presidency there, he would win, even though Obama has never lived there. This blind support is amplified not only because Obama has had a successful career in the United States—a country deemed to be the most powerful nation in the world—but also because many hope and seem to believe Obama could deliver Kenya, if not the world, from its miseries (Okong'o 2008). Many reporters targeting an African audience, such as Charlotte Bauer (2008), warned against such naïve hope. "Obama may be the best thing that's happened to global morale since Nelson Mandela," she wrote, "but he is someone else's president, in another country, however much clout that country has. Expectations that he will cure racism, end poverty, reverse climate change and bring bout world peace quicker than a beauty queen, appear to be global, yet they seem impossibly high, not least from an African perspective." Many Africans, of course, agreed and did not buy into such idealist notions about Obama's potential to catalyze change on a global scale. However, even those Africans who didn't believe in his messianic potential considered Obama a source of hope and pride.

African support for Obama came in many forms both before and after the 2008 election, and Obama Hope often played a major role in generating such support (see Figure 8.5). Most often, perhaps, Obama Hope showed up on t-shirts and tote bags with slogans such as "A Change You Can Believe In" and "Yes We Can." But Obama Hope has also surfaced on flip-flops in Guinea featuring a slogan that claims Obama is "the face of change" and on clocks in South Africa made out of recycled records. In many instances, such as its appearance on murals on the backs of busses in Tanzania, Obama Hope appears by itself. In others cases, Obama Hope appears with words such as *African*, with other popular pictures of Obama, or alongside portraits of other important persons in Africa. In Kenya, for example, Obama Hope surfaced on a black "O3" t-shirt with sepia-tone portraits of other supposed saviors: Raila Odinga, the Prime Minister of Kenya, and Dennis Oliech, a Kenyan professional football player (see Figure 8.5, bottom left). In his explanation of why such "Messianic inclinations" lean toward Obama on this t-shirt, George Oloo wrote on his personal blog:

> Here in Kenya, with our love for the sensational and the peculiar, [Obama has] become an absolute source of enchantment. In many people's minds, an Obama presidency means an instant upshot in our lives—not

Figure 8.5. Collection of Obama Hope Artifacts from Africa. Courtesy of The Melville J. Herskovits Library of African Studies, Northwestern University.

only economically, but also the ease with which we can all travel to the United States (land of milk and honey) whenever we feel so inclined. In fact, we're so passionate about this K'Ogello man that just last week, we deported some American author who'd dropped by to launch an anti-Obama book. We have truly become "The Obama Nation" ("The O3").

Such devotion to Obama is obvious on things other than simple totes and t-shirts. Across Africa, primary and high schools have been named after Obama as have restaurants, lollipops, and brandy.

Obama has even had biscuits produced in his name with Obama Hope front and center on the packaging (see Figure 8.5, bottom row, center). These biscuits were produced by Marc Skaf, the managing director of United Biscuit, Ltd. Skaf, who explained that, like him, many entrepreneurs were inspired to produce and market Obama goods after seeing how much inspiration Obama sparked when he visited Ghana in 2009. During Obama's visit, "hundreds of shops, bars, restaurants and hotels across the continent adopted the Obama name" and "dozens of companies put Obama on their products, including bottled water, bubble gum, and beer" (Connors 2010). A year later, many of the products were still selling well, marking a definite "African consumer trend that could be termed 'brand Obama'" (Connors 2010). As such, Skaf began selling Obama biscuits in a number of different flavors such as ChocObama. As of 2010, the sales of the biscuits were beginning to taper off, but Obama still continued to be enormously popular, and at least for a short while, his name and image were appropriated for multiple purposes. Obama Hope, of course, is often the image to which entrepreneurs like Skaf turn to market their products and gain business profit.

Interestingly, in 2007, Obamamania caught the attention of David Easterbrook, curator of Northwestern University's Melville J. Herskovits Library of African Studies, on a trip to South Africa. Easterbrook was so fascinated with this unfolding bit of African history that he began collecting various artifacts on which Obama's picture was plastered. As he explained, "You couldn't miss the Obama industry that was proliferating across the continent. The use of Obama's portrait on products in Africa isn't just about making money. It's also about a message of hope that Obama's life story bestows on many Africans" (qtd. in Leopold 2010). Upon returning home, Easterbrook sent out word to scholars, students, and contacts in Africa that he was collecting artifacts to document "the African response to Obama's candidacy and election" (qtd. in Leopold 2009). This collection, he realized, could help document African history and culture. "Future scholars will want to see how Africa responded to the Obama election at the popular level," he added (qtd. in Leopold 2009). The response to the collection was remarkable as people began sending him t-shirts, photographs, artwork, CDs, and other artifacts; "Never before," in fact, "had so many people so eagerly collected for the library" he said (qtd. in Leopold 2010). Today, the collection has over five hundred items, and it and related exhibits have caught national attention in news articles written for BBC, the *New York Times*, and multiple local sources. As is evident in the collection depicted in Figure 8.5, Obama Hope appears on many of the artifacts. Thus, once again, as we saw in chapter 7, Obama Hope began to take on educational significance as it became part of an important archive of African material culture.

POLITICAL SATIRE

Like most political adulations, the Obamamania that swept across the United States and the globe was bound to diminish sometime. During 2011 and 2012, while Fairey's own ethos came under suspicion as online news sources updated readers about each new development in his legal case, Obama himself also came under scrutiny for failing to fulfill his campaign promises of change and progress, especially in regards to the economy. Obama entered office during an economic downturn—according to many, the worst economic downturn since the Great Depression. During his first term, Obama pressed Congress to pass the American Recovery and Reinvestment Act (AARA) in an attempt to save and create jobs and worked hard to pass comprehensive health insurance and Wall Street and tax reforms. Among other things, he also made great efforts to end the Don't Ask Don't Tell military policy, pass the Hate Crimes Bill, fight Al-Queda terrorism, and withdraw troops from Iraq and Afghanistan. Despite such accomplishments, many citizens in the United States on both ends of the political spectrum grew frustrated with Obama. Among other accusations, liberals claimed he was not aggressive enough in ending corporate influence in Washington nor in eliminating tax privileges for the wealthy, while conservatives accused him of being a "big-government liberal," too concerned with social policies and not concerned enough with economic ones. Citizens also grew uneasy about the proliferation of drones under Obama's administration as well as his support of the controversial National Defense Authorization Act, which broadens US military arrest and detention powers. As trust in Obama wavered during his first term, Obama Hope's messages of progress, hope, and change came to be seen as naive and misguided, and remixes of Obama Hope began to comment on such shifting attitudes toward Obama.

Some of this frustration and commentary appears in political art. Matt Sesow, for instance, has produced a series of Obama Hope paintings in which Obama Hope materializes in various renditions with different words such as *rhetoric, power, drones,* and so forth (see Figure 1.3). In one painting, actually, Obama Hope sits next to a barrage of political injustices that Sesow believes have continued or emerged under Obama's watch: Afghanistan (Obama's war), foreclosure, BP, Patriot Act, drones, healthcare, Gitmo, and Iraq (see Figure 8.6). Sesow, an artist from Washington DC, plans to keep generating such political art until Obama is out of office, as he feels (pers. comm.) it is important for people to question popular perceptions and the actions of our president. Dana Ellyn is another DC resident and artist who has generated

Figure 8.6. Balance of Power, *Painting by Matt Sesow, 2010. Courtesy of Sesow.*

Obama art for similar reasons. Ellyn first began painting Obama in early 2008. Like many others discussed in this case study, Ellyn (pers. comm.) felt skeptical about Obamamania and Obama Hope from the onset. Her first Obama painting (produced in early 2008), titled *Winning Smile,* for example, was intended to remind viewers of how coercive posters and icons can be, while her second painting, *Selling Hope,* which depicts a depression-era paper boy peddling Obamabilia in front of Obama *Hope* posters, comments on the extreme capitalism indicative in the hypercommercialization of Obama Hope and other Obama merchandise. Ellyn's 2001 painting *Hope and Change,* on the other hand, comments on the changing image of Obama over the course of his first term (see Figure 8.7). As is depicted in this painting, the Obama *Hope* posters that had been wheatpasted and painted all over urban America were beginning to fade and peel. The economy was struggling, and, as Ellyn put it, "All the 'hope and change' that were

Figure 8.7. Hope and Change, *Painting by Dana Ellyn, 2011. Courtesy of Ellyn.*

promised during [Obama's] election weren't panning out so well for many Americans." As part of a series responding to current news stories, Obama Hope thus surfaced in this painting to comment on the failed promises of Obama's campaign.

Besides surfacing in a wide range of political art, a variety of political cartoons began to use Obama Hope to lampoon both Obama's campaign promises and the duped US Americans who fell prey to those promises. In one of Paul Laud's cartoons published in 2012, for example, we see a before and after shot of Obama *Hope* posters printed in black and white (see Figure 8.8). In the before panel, as Laud himself describes it (pers. comm.), a slightly sullen Obama is depicted in the Obama Hope style; in the after panel, we see Obama staring in wide-eyed shock from behind a high stack of papers representing the federal budget over which he can barely see. Below Obama in the before panel, the word "Hope" is listing and sinking, which gives way to "Do" in the second panel. Beneath this illustration is the caption "By the time my first term is through I'll have cut the deficit in two. But at a trillion or so it just goes to show the difference between hope and do." Laud explains (pers. comm.) that he wanted to depict the changing emotions

Figure 8.8. Hope vs. Do, *Political Cartoon by Paul Laud, 2012. Courtesy of Laud.*

of Obama due to some overwhelming event, and when the request for the 2012 federal budget came about, the opportunity presented itself. In Fairey's posters, he explains, "The word Hope is a noun, that Obama is our hope for the future. In my side-by-side comparison, I twist this around a bit and use Hope as a verb (and a passive one at that) and set it side by side to the more action-oriented 'Do.' In other words, hoping won't solve the budget dilemma; only doing will." Here in this cartoon, then, Obama Hope emerges to point out a disconnect between Obama's campaign promises and his actual political actions.

This example of Obama Hope's role in political cartoons is just one among many that popped up during Obama's first term. In many cartoons, Obama Hope satirized the diminishing faith US Americans had in Obama. In some cartoons, for instance, a faded Obama *Hope* poster appears on a wall on a city street with onlookers saying "Hope's fading," while in others, an illustrator's hand or a young citizen can be seen revising the word "Hope" beneath Obama's portrait to say something such as "Nope" and "Hopeless." In others, we see a series of Obama *Hope* posters lined up in a row on which the word *hope* gets smaller and smaller on each subsequent poster. Or we see single versions of the *Hope* poster with the words "Mope" or "Hype" or "Want Some More Hope?" In many of these cartoons, very little change to Obama Hope has been made. Yet, in other examples, the Obama Hope image has transformed substantially. In one of Robert Matson's cartoons titled *Hope and Change* created early on in Obama's first term, for instance, we see side-by-side Obama *Hope* posters (see Figure 8.9). The first is pretty much an exact copy of Fairey's Obama *Hope* poster, but in the next, Obama's face morphs into George W. Bush's face and the title reads *Change* rather than *Hope*.

In true editorial-cartoon style, this cartoon was published on the editorial page in the *St. Louis Post-Dispatch* alongside an editorial calling for the US armed forces' withdrawal from Afghanistan. "The editorial board" Matson explains (pers. comm.), "had also written editorials suggesting that President Obama's circle of economic advisers, coming from Wall Street, would ensure that as little as possible would be done to reregulate the financial industry and that the culture of deregulation that began under President Clinton and prevailed during the George W. Bush administration would continue." Working in response to this claim, Matson's cartoon suggested "that being in office would change President Obama as much as, and perhaps more than, his being in office would change U.S. policy." In morphing Obama's face into Bush's, he wanted to communicate a "feeling of resignation that things might not change very much during an Obama presidential administration." Using Obama Hope to make such commentary was appropriate because it was "the best visual representation of the Hope and Change slogan during the 2008 campaign and it was the best way to represent the slogan after the campaign while also evoking memories of the campaign." Iconic images are an editorial cartoonist's stock in trade, and because of its familiarity and cultural significance, Obama Hope, at least during Obama's presidency, has become a go-to image to craft political and social commentary.

Besides being so iconic, the Obama *Hope* poster has become part of cartoonists' "cartoon inventory" for at least three other reasons. First, the simplicity of Obama Hope's design makes it easy to manipulate and transfer. Second, when it comes to the *Hope* poster, as Taylor Jones notes (pers. comm.), word play is fun and easy, especially as *hope* can be easily replaced with other four-letter words such as *fear*. *Hope*, of course, is also easy to rhyme with words such as *nope* and *dope*. Third, Obama Hope often shows up in political cartoons because it can function as what Janis L. Edwards and Carol K. Winkler call a *visual ideograph*. According

Figure 8.9. Hope and Change, *Political Cartoon by Robert Matson, 2009. Courtesy of Matson.*

to Edwards and Winkler (2005), visual ideographs have four defining characteristics. First, visual ideographs are ordinary images found in political discourse aimed to influence the beliefs and actions of both the political elite and their nonelite constituents (126). Second, visual ideographs are high-order abstractions that represent collective commitments to particular yet ambiguous and ill-defined goals (128). As such, multiple interpretations of an image can be surmised. Third, visual ideographs warrant certain uses of power; excuse certain beliefs and/or actions that might be deemed eccentric or antisocial; and guide behavior and beliefs deemed acceptable and laudable by a relevant communities (128). Fourth, visual ideographs are, and must be, culture bound (131). Functioning in these characteristic ways, visual ideographs assist political cartoons in using satire, parody, and irony to spark people's emotions, thoughts, and behaviors. To do so, of course, an image that functions as a visual ideograph must be easily recognizable to a relevant community, even as it can exist in multiple forms in different cartoons. As such, as Edwards and Winkler note, only a few images in US culture, such as the Iwo Jima images, the *American Gothic* painting, and the *I Want*

You poster of Uncle Sam can function as visual ideographs. To this list, we can add Obama Hope; for by the time Obama began his first term, it had become so widely and highly visible that it could easily function as a visual ideograph in many political cartoons to satirize Obama's administration and US Americans' responding sentiment.

In addition to its more recent manifestations in political cartoons responding to current events such as the NSA surveillance leaks (see Figure 8.10), Obama Hope's emergent function in political cartoons continued throughout (and beyond) the 2012 campaign season as Obama Hope began to make political commentary about Obama's chance for reelection. In one cartoon, for instance, we see Obama's portrait, redrawn with oversized, Dopey-like ears, talking to various independent voters and saying such things as, "I guess your vote is out of the question." In another, we see Obama with Dopey ears staring straight at the viewer saying, "I'm going to run for re-election, but this time I'm a little older and a little wiser." Next to this panel is a panel with a 2012 placard and a tilted Obama *Hope* poster with the words "No Hope, No Change, No Promises." Cartoonist Mike Flugennock even went so far as to produce a variety of t-shirts, stickers, and other products with a cartoon in the Obama Hope style depicting a worn out Obama with a cigarette in his mouth, a 2012 lapel pin, and the words "Aw, C'Mon," which Flugennock advertises as "anti-Obama gear for the discerning irate Leftist." As the next section will make clear, such humorous, critical remixes of Obama Hope were far from rare.

A POPULAR PARODY OR MEME

Much of the visual play we see with Obama Hope in political cartoons can also be found in a number of remixes of Fairey's Obama *Hope* poster produced by everyday citizens across the globe. So many of these remixes emerged at viral rates, in fact, that Obama Hope has come to be considered by many as one of the most popular memes to surface in recent years, if not the most popular one. While I prefer the previously discussed epidemiological theories introduced by Tarde and extended by Sampson (2012) to help account for how things become contagious via repetition, imitation, and invention, memes have become a common means of describing how a variety of things replicate via imitation. The term *meme* became popular with Richard Dawkins's work in *The Selfish Gene*, where he introduced the term— an abbreviated form of the Greek root *mimeme*—to signify the name for a "unit of cultural transmission, or a unit of imitation" (192). As

Figure 8.10. Ever Get that Feeling? *Political Cartoon by David Pope/the* Canberra, *2013. Permissions from Pope/the* Canberra.

examples, Dawkins (1989) suggests we think of tunes, ideas, or clothing fashions, all of which propagate from mind to mind when people
copy one another. Scholars such as Susan Blackmore (1998) have
extended Dawkins's work with memes to emphasize that imitation
must be understood as "a behavior that is learned by copying it from
someone else." According to this definition, anything copied through
learned behavior is a meme, no matter whether it spreads itself in useful, neutral, or harmful ways (Blackmore 2000, 7). Blackmore suggests
that memes are also selfish in the sense that they work to get themselves copied rather than operate according to their original author's
or designer's wishes (8). Similar to Bennett's (2010) claims that things
have thing-power, Blackmore claims memes have replicator power
(5). Memes also have variations, as things rarely pass on and duplicate
without some kind of change. As Blackmore puts it, "Copying is rarely
perfect" (14). New memes, in fact, Blackmore argues, come about
through variation and combination of old memes (15).

Memes, according to Douglas Rushkoff, are also part of media
viruses that have become such a vital force in the digital age, which
Yosi Sergant realized when launching the 008 movement as discussed
in Chapter 6. Media viruses, Rushkoff (1996) argues, are protein shells

that contain memes, which infiltrate the way we act, interact, and perceive reality (19). Media viruses generally come in three kinds: intentional ones produced specifically to spread a product or ideology; co-opted or "bandwagon" ones, which are not necessarily launched intentionally but rather are appropriated by others; and self-generated viruses that elicit interest and spread on their own accord because they resonate or evoke a dramatic response from others (19–20). In the case of Obama Hope, if we consider it through a mimetic framework as many people do, we see all kinds of media viruses at work. The Obama Works that were intentionally launched by Fairey and Obama's official campaign, and which carried the Obama Hope meme, were obviously intentionally launched. As a meme within that particular media virus, Obama Hope was supposed to infiltrate people's minds with the important messages of progress and hope. Yet, as we have seen, once Obama Hope began to circulate and enter into various associations, it began to emerge in different renditions, media, and genres and take on various political roles not imagined by Fairey. As such, it also became self-generating and rhetorical in divergent ways that few presidential images have done before. In many eyes, then, Obama Hope has become a quintessential political meme not so much because of its role in the 2008 election but rather because it has been copied, cut, and pasted by people who have figured out how to generate parodies of Obama Hope to critique politicians, the political system, and/or the political climate.

Many of the digital parodies or spoofs of Obama Hope, which began circulating almost as soon as the Obama *Hope* poster hit the streets, were obviously intended to entertain. A popular spoofing trend in the style of Obama Hope, for instance, emerged in January 2009 when Jared Moraitis created the now-famous Obama *Brains* zombie spoof (see Figure 8.11). As Moraitis (2009) explained, most of the Obama Hope parodies circulating at that point simply had words that rhymed with *hope* beneath the portrait of Obama or other figures. At that time, for instance, once could find remixes depicting Sarah Palin with the word *nope* beneath them or portraits of George W. Bush with the word *dope*. "At the risk of coming across as an Obama-hater and attracting the FBI's attention," Moraitis wanted to move in a different direction and "parody those parodies." So he chose to go with the zombie theme that was so hypervisible at that time in popular culture to create "Zombama." The slogan Brains was "easy," he notes. "What other slogan would a zombie choose for his campaign?" This design, which Moraitis drew from scratch rather than use photo manipulation, helped accelerate Obama

Figure 8.11. Zombama Brains, *Obamicon by Jared Moraitis, 2009. Courtesy of Moraitis.*

Figure 8.12 Zombie, *Obamicon by Azael Solis, 2010. Courtesy of Solis.*

Hope's circulation, as many people began to share the design on their own blogs. The design was so popular that, like many other Obama Hope parodies, it was also made available on online stores such as TeeFury.com and Café Press, among others, which enable artists such as Moraitis to print their designs on various products and sell them for profit. In addition, since that image entered into circulation, many other zombie spoofs have been generated as artists and designers both generate their own designs and remix Moraitis's spoof in playful jest (see Figure 8.12). The comic book *President Evil* created by David Hutchison (2010) even got on the rhetorical bandwagon to remix Obama Hope for one of its covers. Thus, in a sense, Obama Hope can be said to have inspired a humorous spoofing trend with its own offshoots of visual play.

Zombie-themed parodies, of course, are not the only spoofs that have been generated. As soon as Obama Hope gained mass attention in early 2008, digital posters of all different kinds began popping up in the *Hope* poster style. Besides Bush and Palin, Ralph Nadar, Hillary Clinton, and John McCain were obvious targets because of the election season, as were not-so-obvious faces such as Bill Clinton, Hitler, Rush Limbaugh,

WEB POSTER EXHIBITION - *Shepard Fairey posters for Barack Obama*

Original Obama poster by Shepard Fairey

In 1989, Shepard Fairey (b. 1970) began to paste stickers all over town with a face and the mysterious message "Andre the Giant Has a Posse" or "Obey Giant" . Since then, his palette, geographic range and activities have increased enormously, and when he offered to support Barack Obama's campaign with some posters in January 2008, he readily got permission from Obama to do so. Within a day, he had finished a design, one with the text "PROGRESS", and another with "HOPE".

A first print run of 350 was sold out within minutes for $ 45 a piece, and, much to Fairey's annoyance, resold on ebay for a lot more. Wall Street Journal began to track the ebay prices, they quickly shot up to $ 3'000, and reached $ 10'000 in June. In July, a mixed media painting done by Fairey in the same style as his "Hope" poster, sold for $ 108'000. By July 31, about 200'000 sticker versions of the original Obama poster had been printed.

Meanwhile, Fairey and his fans continued to wild post their Obamas all over the United States, and Fairey was promptly arrested, like many times before, and spent a night in jail. Ironically, this happened in Denver during the Democratic National Convention that won Obama the nomination of his party.

The strong, simple poster hit the nerve of many graphic designers. Fairey, who had been accused of copying style and content of communist propaganda posters, found himself suddenly imitated with numerous versions of his original design. Tutorials and plugins began to appear in the web on how to make your own Fairey/Obama poster, even ready made solutions where you can just enter your own text instead of HOPE.

Not all of the imitations are pro-Obama, some are below-the-belt, many require detailed knowledge of the campaign events or american folklore to be understandable, some, like the "Marxism" or the "Yes we can" are jewels of satyre, only a few are probably printed or displayed in the streets. Out of curiosity and fascination, I began to look for them in the web: www.thepeoplescube.com, www.obamaartreport.com and flickr are particularly rich sources. Many people also sent me links and explanations, thank you all!

Below are 149 posters inspired by the original Shepard Fairey poster at left. The authors are not always identifiable, but clicking on the picture will bring you to the page where I found it. Most of the persons depicted are in Wikipedia.

Barack Obama won the election on November 4, 2008.

Amy Winehouse   Sarah Palin   Pope Benedict 16   Bob Hope   Bill Clinton

Figure 8.13. Rene Wanner Exhibition, Shepard Fairey's Posters for Barack Obama, *Screenshot taken by Author, 2014. Courtesy of Wanner.*

and even Reverend Manning. In addition, celebrities such as Bob Hope, historical figures such as Jesus, and fictional characters such as Luke Skywalker and *Mad Magazine*'s cover boy Alfred Neuman also surfaced. By October of 2008, such spoofs of Obama Hope were so popular, in fact, that people began documenting this phenomenon. Rene Wanner, for instance, created a web poster exhibition called *Shepard Fairey's Posters for Barack Obama* (see Figure 8.13). News sources such as *Wired* and the *Village Voice* also began reporting about the phenomenon, the latter of which going so far as to present a slide show of the "25 best parodies out there." Such metacultural activity, of course, only fueled Obama Hope's popularity and circulation.

Today, this phenomenon of remixing Obama Hope has taken on a more serious role in collective life than anyone might have foretold. In an educational sense, it helps inform people as to what memes are and how they go viral. Know Your Meme, for example, is a site specifically designed to research and document Internet memes and viral phenomena. On this website, a gallery of Obama Hope remixes, which includes over three hundred pictures, is accessible, as is a written entry that, among other things, briefly (and incompletely) articulates how Obama Hope came into existence and how this meme started. As articulated in the entry, new digital technologies created potential for Obama Hope to transform and circulate at viral speeds. As soon as Obama Hope gained mass attention, in fact, people began creating tutorials, plugins, and ready-made solutions and making them accessible via the Internet so others could create their own remixes in the style of Obama Hope. For instance, Ed Alkema, owner of the domain pendego.com, built a platform called Do it Yourself Barack Obama. On this website, visitors find the Obama Hope digital image reproduced in Fairey's poster style with a blank blue space beneath it where typically the word *hope* appears. Viewers can type in a word of their choice and click the "Make Poster" button. The new image appears in seconds with a URL link to a jpeg of the visitor's new design, which can be dragged onto the viewer's desktop. Interestingly, then, Obama Hope has inspired the development of technologies that have ensured its own circulation, replication, and transformation. This unintended consequence perhaps best explains why Obama Hope earned its reputation in many people's eyes as *the* quintessential political meme of the twenty-first century.

Yet, in many cases, as the next section will make even more clear, Obama Hope remixes take on a satirical role as they respond critically to Obama and his policies. On his blog, for instance, Matt Cornell, an artist, performer, and film programmer from Los Angeles, uploaded a whole series of Obama Hope spoofs beginning in early 2008. When he first encountered the *Hope* poster on the streets of Los Angeles, Cornell (pers. comm.) was struck by Fairey's unabashed propaganda, especially in light of the "messianic tenor of the Obama campaign" and the "naïve sense" among liberals that Obama would be "a progressive hero." To poke fun of Fairey and subvert the seriousness of the *Hope* poster, Cornell created his *Obey Daddy* design for San Francisco's Folsom Street Fair, an annual celebration of BDSM and leather subculture (see Figure 8.14). In his eyes, *Obey Daddy* was a "funnier, sexier, and darker" version of Obama *Hope* that would show people "how easily the poster could be altered to create a different image of leadership, power, and (implied) state violence." Since then, Cornell has created a number of different spoofs to remind people that while Obama was sold to them under the banner of hope and change, Obama's actual political practices have

Figure 8.14. Obey Daddy,
*Obamicon by Matt Cornell, 2008.
Courtesy of Cornell.*

been far from progressive. Cornell, for example, made versions that used logos from major campaign contributors like Chase Manhattan Bank and AT&T to remind people that Obama accepted large donations from corporations, donations that could not help but be reflected in his policy positions about telecom immunity and Wall Street bailouts. Such spoofs may seem like "a symptom of our meaningless political culture," Cornell claims, but they are also "an expression of the frustrated desire for a better process." According to Cornell, many artists were co-opted by Obama's campaign to work for his election. "There was very little place for leftist critique of Obama." Spoofers such himself want a meaningful politics and to participate in genuine political dialogue. Obama Hope parodies are thus important in Cornell's and many others' eyes for their ability to articulate dissent, spark political dialogue, and engage both artists and everyday citizens in the democratic process. As I discuss in the next section, user-created remixes of Fairey's Obama *Hope* poster, or what have come to be commonly called *Obamicons*, might thus best be thought of as a new cybergenre.

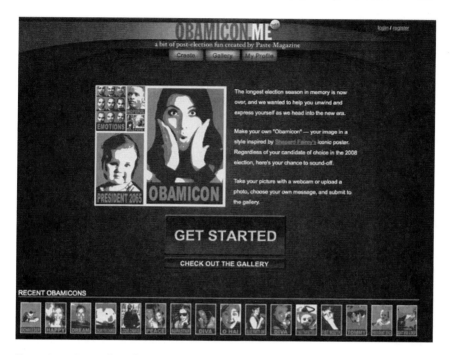

Figure 8.15. Screenshot of Obamicon.me website, 2009. Permissions by Paste Magazine.

OBAMICONS

As a term, *Obamicon* was coined by *Paste Magazine* when, just before the inauguration in 2009, and with the help of Tim Regan-Porter, it developed the obamicon.me website, which allowed visitors to create digitally born pictures modeled in the style of Obama Hope (see Figure 8.15). To create Obamicons via the Obamicon technology, a visitor could simply upload a picture or take an instant picture with their webcam, the captured image of which would appear in the red, white, and blue colors found in Obama Hope. Once a picture was uploaded into obamicon.me, the saturation of the color palette could be adjusted and the captured image could be zoomed in on and/or rotated. To generate captions, visitors could then select from several preset slogans, or insert their own as was possible via other ready-made digital technologies made available by Alkema and others. Yet obamicon.me differentiated itself from other Obamifying technologies in allowing Obamicons either to be saved onto visitors' computers via a simple right click and then uploaded to Flickr or Facebook, which many people have done, or archived and shared in the obamicon.me gallery so that comments can be made in response to an image and links can be established. By January 28, just three weeks after the site went live, obamicon.me had "garnered seven million page views . . . with more than one million unique visitors and 200,000 registered users" (Magee 2009).

While this website was taken down in 2013, Obamicons, whether generated on the obamicon.me website or not, can still be found circulating not only on streets across the world but also across cyberspace. As previously mentioned, many Obamicons function as playful parodies as they express allegiance to certain celebrities, movie or televisions shows, and even sports teams. Many Obamicons also clearly function for personal enjoyment, as people upload pictures of themselves and insert silly captions obviously intended to entertain. Obamicons also, however, often act satirically as they criticize various politicians and articulate dissent about official government authorities and their political practices. US political figures were especially popular targets in 2008, as alluded to earlier, but since then foreign figures such as David Cameron, Vladimir Putin, and Muammar Gaddafi have also received their fair share of attention. In this latter capacity, Obamicons have proven their potential to stir public debate and thus ought be considered to be an important new cybergenre inspired by Obama Hope.

To be clear, in using the term *genre* here I am thinking about genre as "typified rhetorical actions based in recurrent situations" (Miller 1984, 159). Such situations are not static, material sets of circumstances that can be objectively identifiable. As Jenny Edbauer Rice (2005) has argued, a rhetorical situation actually and always encompasses a wide sphere of historical and lived processes (8). Nonetheless, we recognize a situation has occurred that is comparable to a previously occurring situation based on a stock of social knowledge acquired through enculturation (Bazerman 1994; Berkenkotter and Huckin 1995; Yates, Orlikowski, and Rennecker 1992; Miller 1984). Genres are put to use by people who realize that it might be appropriate and effective to address the exigence that arises in that perceived situation. While recurring for this reason, rhetorical genres are also dynamic; they evolve, are sustained for certain time periods, and dissolve or fade from popular use (Bakhtin 1986; Bazerman 1994; Berkenkotter and Huckin 1995; Miller 1984). The evolution of genres, as well as the creation of new genres altogether, is often a result of innovations in communication media (Sheperd and Watters 1998; Yates, Orlikowski, and Rennecker 1997). The combination of the computer and the Internet, especially, has triggered, for instance, the emergence of a new class of genres called *cybergenres* (Sheperd and Watters 1998), to which Obamicons belong.

Obama, of course, has been the main target of many Obamicons produced by citizens both within and beyond US borders. In some cases,
as with the zombie-themed parodies, such visual play seems innocent
enough—a fun, amateur form of participation in what many refer to as
Internet meme culture. Yet, many remixes of Obama Hope circulating and
still visible on the World Wide Web today are drenched with racial under-
tones. Some of these are strikingly blatant, such as one remix that shows
Obama hanging from a noose with the word *rope* beneath. Others are
more implicit. As early as March of '08, for example, some of the earliest
parodies of Obama Hope were posted on a prowhite discussion board[1]
started in 1995 by a former KKK member and white nationalist activist.
The first parody to appear was an exact digital replica of Fairey's Obama
Hope poster, but instead of "Hope," the word read "Nope." In response
to the image, another member asked, "How about 'dope' or 'dupe'?"
while another responded, "Why not Pope? The presidency is too small
for Obama. He might as well go for the big prize." Such questions triggered verbal responses calling Obama everything from a Muslim to an
Uncle Tom. One responder even said that Obama Hope shouldn't be
reworked at all. This person wrote, "This poster can stay 'as is' with only
one thing added. This poster needs one of those fake bullet hole stickers
(the ones people put on their cars to make it look like their car was shot
up). 'Hope' with one of the bullet hole decals would look pretty good."
As one member surmised about the emotional consequences triggered
by Obama Hope, "I guess there's a large anti-Obama sentiment that others feel when seeing the original." Such an understatement on a website
devoted to prowhite sentiments is clearly meant to be sarcastic. Yet, it
illustrates just how much racial tension Obama's candidacy was generating, a tension that was clearly fueled by Obama Hope.

Not surprisingly perhaps, a spoof of Obama Hope depicting Obama
as a zombie with a hole in its head actually came to fruition sometime later, indicating how even if generated for humorous purposes,
many Obama Hope remixes sparked more serious consequences as
they took on a life of their own. The design of this spoof titled *Obama
as Zombie* (see Figure 8.16)—which appears to be a remix of Moraitis's
remix of Fairey's rendition of Obama Hope—was credited to a designer
who chooses to stay anonymous. People familiar with zombies know
that the only way to render a zombie immobile is to destroy its brains.
Therefore, Obama Hope in this remix is simply intended to entertain,
as it takes the Zombama theme one step further. Yet no matter the intention, this remix, which most people saw as Obama with a bullet in his
head, caused an uproar among Washington politicos and others when

Figure 8.16.
Obama as Zombie,
Obamicon Credited to
XXDinkMeekerxx, Reprinted
with Permissions².

it surfaced in a Halloween event flyer emailed by Virginia's Loudoun County Republican Committee in October of 2011. In this flyer, *Obama as Zombie* sits alongside a zombified image of Nancy Pelosi and other zombie rhetorics. Once bloggers got hold of the mailer, this remix of Obama Hope evoked different anxieties in viewers depending on where people located themselves on the political spectrum. People on the right worried that it would hurt the Republican Party, which was already at risk for coming across as constituted by extreme fundamentalists. Others worried it would fuel hate and disrespect for Obama, not to mention racism. In this zombie version, then, Obama Hope unintentionally found itself embroiled in yet another scandalous affair that captured much media attention and sparked heated debate.

Obama Hope would also come to spark heated conversations when it surfaced in Obamicons commenting on Obama's religious affiliations and ethnicity. In these Obamicons, Obama is often depicted with a turban or keffileh on his head above the word *Arab* or *Muslim* (see Figure 8.17). As reported in the *Los Angeles Times* piece "Smears 2.0" (2007), accusations about Obama's secret devotion to Islam first began

Figure 8.17. Arab, *Obamicon by Oleg Atbashian, 2008. Courtesy of Atbashian.*

to surface when Obama ran for the Senate, but the circulation of such accusations escalated first during a viral e-mail campaign in 2006 and again in 2007 when Obama began his campaign for president. By 2008, claims that Obama is both a secretly practicing Muslim and an Arab could be heard loud and clear in the blogosphere, and Obamicons often acted to reinforce such claims. In a post titled "Rush Limbaugh says Obama is Arab, 'not Black'" (2008) published on the blog *Undercover Black Man*, for example, an Obamicon depicting Obama with a keffileh on his head and the word "Arab" sits next to a statement that details Obama's ethnic lines, reported as "50% Caucasian, 43.75% Arab, and 6.25% Black African." Such posts stirred a slew of comments in which some expressed disgust with Limbaugh while others commented on the absurdity of the claims about ethnicity. As one commenter named Jess said, "This is just so hilarious to me. . . . They hate him because he's black, but that's not scaring enough people away so they now claim he's Arab and will try to re-draw geography to try to do so, pathetic. . . . These people couldn't understand the social construct of race if it hit them in the face." Still others commented on the Obamicons themselves. One commenter named Anais referred to it as an "idiot poster" and wrote, "You can always spot white racists by their poor (non-existent) reasoning, and their underestimation of black people."

While such metaculture has often unfolded on blogs in response to various Obamicons, much dialogue emerged on the obamicon.me website itself, especially when the site first emerged. Figures 8.18 and 8.19 show a couple of opposing viewpoints that unfolded in response to two different Obamicons published in 2009. In the first conversation, visitors discussed the redistribution of wealth, which became a heated topic in October of 2008 when Obama was captured in a video telling Joe Wurzelbacher, a.k.a. Joe the Plumber, that he thought it was good to "spread the wealth around." Such conversations bled into fervent critiques about Obama's "socialist" ideals in which Obamicons accusing Obama of socialism scream loud and bright. Many of these socialist Obamicons ended up on blogs in posts with headlines such as "Interesting: Socialist World Supports Obama, Our Military Supports McCain" or "Is Obama Really a Marxist Socialist? Yes." While such Obamicons began escalating in 2009, they were still popping up in 2012 and, in fact, are still circulating and sparking dialogue today.

Jan 21, 2009 9:51 PM pervier said: Share the wealth.

Feb 05, 2009 1:49 PM precised said: I am not going to give up what I have worked so hard for so some degenerate can get it . . .

Feb 20, 2009 9:23 PM 3nails4holes said: Obama—because everyone else deserves a slice of what you've worked hard for, comrade.

Mar 07, 2009 4:55 AM cellulat said: I hope you didn't pay tax when Bush was in power Bush stole billions and gave it to the rich. Lets see how republican plans work for the economy, oh wait, we just did! . . .

May 29, 2009 11:28 PM wiildkat26 said: Funny thing about the Republican plan . . . it was socialism. Redistributing wealth, trying to play master to the economy. They're all a bunch of statists, Republicans and Democrats alike. They're just

Figure 8.18. Redistributor, Obamicon Uploaded by Pervier, 2009. Courtesy of Paste Magazine.

in different packages: supply-side and demand-side, but they both reak of the same socialist stench. If somebody is stupid enough to think that a large deficit doesn't hurt the economy right now, at this moment, then they know nothing about economics. I'm sick of Keynesians running our economy into the ground. Redistribution, aka centralization, has never worked. And never will. There's no such thing as the Aggregate Demand. John Maynard Keynes was a crack. So was Hoover. So was FDR. So is Bush. So is Obama.

Jan 20, 2009 10:31 PM realchange said: Socialism disguised as "hope" and "change"—hang onto your wallets, your bibles, and your guns. H's civilian police force will be coming for you soon.

Jan 25, 2009 12:50 AM jprg196 said: The only socialist I know who's pitching tax cuts.

Feb 03, 2009 10:56 PM realchange said: Are you kidding me? Tax cuts? That was only campaign rhetoric to seize the entitlement vote from cool aid drinkers. Have you read the stimulus package—it's chuck full of pork that neither cuts taxes or creates jobs. He promised tax cuts for 95% of Americans, and he said he wouldn't hire lobbyists—neither of these have happened. Not only did he hire a lobbyist, he elevated a tax cheat and thief to the head of the IRS. Daschle was tarnishing his crispy clean image so they got rid of him and Nancy, the other tax cheat. Where the hope and change you can believe in?

Figure 8.19. Socialist, Obamicon Uploaded by Realchange, 2009. Courtesy of Paste Magazine.

New government. It's the same old thing. The only thing that's new is the fact that H is biracial. Big deal.[3]

Obamicons linking Obama with socialism are especially evident in the People's Cube, a satirical conservative news website generated by Oleg Atbashian, author of *Shakedown Socialism*. Atbashian grew up in Ukraine under a totalitarian regime and was later employed by the Communist Party in Siberia to produce propaganda posters. In his book *Shakedown Socialism*, Atbashian (2010) argues that many US policies implemented by Obama and other politicians are similar to those he was subjected to under communist rule. On the People's Cube, Atbashian generates his own Obamicons, as well as uploading ones made by others, to provoke thought about how various political figures from Obama to Biden to Palin to Hillary Clinton are duping the US American masses. In his Obamicons depicting Obama, the words *utopia, cowbell*, and s*pread the wealth around* sit under various portraits of Obama (see Figure 8.20). These Obamicons have been mass reproduced and have appeared waving at rallies, such as the Restore Sanity rally held in Washington, DC, in 2010 and circulating on conservative blogs and online new sources.

Figure 8.20. Cowbell,
Obamicon by Oleg Atbashian,
2008. Courtesy of Atbashian.

In fact, the People's Cube is responsible for generating many of the Obamicons circulating in cyberspace today.

SodaHead is another website on which Obamicons have stirred and continue to stir much public debate. SodaHead is an online community in which visitors are encouraged to discover, debate, and discuss contemporary hot-button issues. Cofounded by social media veteran Jason Feffer, SodaHead caters to a global audience of eight million visitors, which doesn't even include the "'tens of millions' of users reached by major publishers, news organizations (*Fox News,* 'Good Morning America') and bloggers using SodaHead technology as embeddable poll widgets for their websites and social media platforms" (Miguel 2012). On the website, Obama Hope has made a presence in several remixes that function in various ways. In some instances, Obama Hope shows up in posts next to questions intended to stir debate such as "What were the key selling points in the marketing of Barack Obama to American Public?" or "Is it sad that we have people here who hate America so much that they will vote to put Commie Obama back in the WH?" In many cases, people respond not only with verbal comments but also visual ones, as we saw in the forum thread discussed previously. For example, in one post, a person wrote, "The artist whose poster of Barack Obama became a rallying image during the hope-and-change election of 2008 says he understands why so many people have lost faith"—a line taken directly from an article written by Aamer Madhani (2010). Accompanying this line is Nick Anderson's political cartoon with two side-by-side pictures—one the Obama *Hope* poster and another showing Obama sinking chest high in water with the word "Help!" written beneath. In response, alongside verbal comments, people uploaded remixes of Obama Hope, such as one picture of six Obama *Hope* posters that progressively fade in color from the first to last. While many of these remixes were downloaded from Google Images and social media sites, many were undoubtedly created by SodaHead visitors using the various technologies previously discussed. Either way, as is evident here, Sodahead, like the People's Cube, became a major player in helping Obama Hope circulate widely and become a popular cybergenre with potential to stir public debate.

Blogs, of course, should also be credited for playing a major role in spreading Obamicons. Many Obama Hope remixes have been specifically designed by or have been appropriated by bloggers to critique Obama and his policies. On one blog written by a firefighter from Philadelphia, for instance, a homemade remix of Fairey's poster with the Obama Hope image and the word *dope* is located in a post titled *Obama: In Big Pharma's Pocket* (2009). Beneath the Obamicon sit the words, "Well, well, well, look at this. Barack Obama is making back-room deals with the pharmaceutical companies, all to get his disastrous ObamaCare passed." In another example, we find a design created by Ben Heine in which a germ-prevention mask is covering Obama's face and "H1N1" is written in place of "Hope" (see Figure 8.21). On his Flickr page, this spoof interacts with an article titled "H1N1 Swine Flu: Barack Obama and the First Deadly Mistake" to critique Obama for his refusal to enforce social separation to prevent the spread of swine flu. This same spoof designed by Heine also circulates on other blogs, where it functions for completely different purposes when put into action with different verbal arguments. For instance, the Obama Hope image in the *H1N1* poster can be found on the blog of homeopathic practitioner Sonya McLeod (2009) from Vancouver. McLeod argues the hype of H1N1 is exaggerated, most likely constructed by pharmaceutical companies who stand the chance to make billions off the swine flu vaccine. Interestingly, then, as Obama Hope

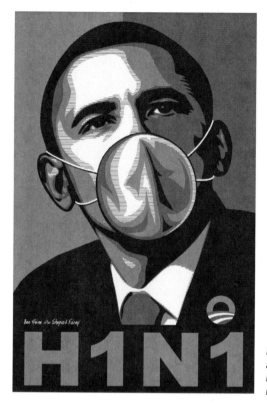

Figure 8.21. H1N1: Ben Heine after Shepard Fairey, *Obamicon by Ben Heine, 2010. Permissions by Heine.*

began to take on a life of its own, so did some of the Obamicons that it inspired into existence.

Today, Obamicons seem to have become a mainstay in popular culture, as is evident in their ongoing surfacing in response to current events. Some of this activity is surely humorous and seems rhetorically insignificant, such as when a PhotoFunia-generated montage fooled many people into thinking an enormous mural depicting an Obamicon of *Game of Thrones* character Tyrion Lannister, with "Pimp" written below, had been painted last year on a London street urban wall (see Figure 8.22). Yet more often than not, Obama Hope materializes for more serious purposes. During the primary election in 2012, Obama Hope played a role in both garnering support for and launching critique against nearly all the candidates. Subsequently, during the presidential election, it surfaced on dresses, banners, pins, and posters in support of Obama at the Democratic National Convention; in political cartoons satirizing both Obama and the public; and in articulations of support and dissent for both Romney and Ryan. Perhaps

Figure 8.22. [P]imp,
Obamicon by Jan Jesko
Mantey, 2012. Courtesy of
Mantey.

the most hilarious Obamicons to emerge during the 2012 election season depicted a chair and Big Bird in response to the gaffes in Clint Eastwood's bizarre Republican National Convention performance and Romney's now-infamous debate remark about cutting subsidies for PBS. Jim Lennox even went so far to spraypaint another enormous Obamicon onto his field, this time with "Help" under a portrait of a very concerned Big Bird (see Figure 8.23).

As it continues to circulate and transform, Obama Hope, perhaps unsurprisingly, most often shadows political affairs associated with Obama's administration. When Obama came out in early 2012 to make his own views clear about same-sex marriage, for instance, Obama Hope was remixed in various Obamicons to comment on this landmark political move. And, of course, when Obama's 2012 victory was announced, a plethora of Obama Hope remixes surfaced in political cartoons, on personal blogs, and in other venues expressing joy and fear, victory and defeat. Yet, as we saw in the Obamicon produced on the American Crossroads website in response to the IRS scandal (see Figure 5.1), and in perhaps its most recent appearance in a remix of

Figure 8.23. Help Big Bird, *Field Painting by Jim Lennox, 2012. Courtesy of Lennox.*

the *Yes We Did* design by Fairey for MoveOn.org responding to the NSA scandal (see Figure 8.24), Obama Hope is still following Obama's every move. In light of such parallel movement between Obama and Obama Hope, one cannot help but wonder if another president will ever go down in history with a single image so attached to their political persona and career. In its rhetorical transformations over the past five years, Obama Hope, it seems, has not only become the face of the 2008 election, the Obama art movement, and contemporary deliberations over fair use and remix, but also the face of the Obama administration itself. Obama, America, and the world just can't seem to escape Obama Hope.

CONCLUSION

In order to help explain how this image went viral and became wildly consequential in unforeseeable ways, my goal in this part of the case study has been to describe just a few of the multiple transformations and functions Obama Hope has experienced and taken on since entering into circulation. As Hariman and Lucaites (2007) have argued, "The circulation of images is one basis for the foundation of contemporary publics" (303).

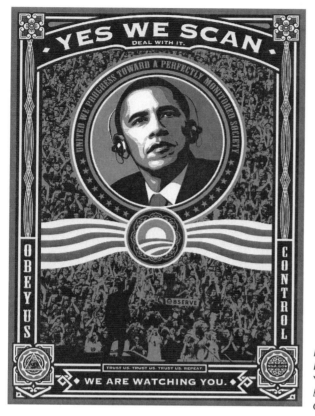

Figure 8.24. Remix of Fairey's Yes We Did. Yes We Scan, *Design by Rene Walter, 2013. Courtesy of Walter.*

Images come to ground collective life as they "are taken from mass media into many smaller circuits of private consumption, social display, retail distribution, subcultural articulation, political advocacy, and so forth, and back again into other public arts and media such as cartoons and books, and then again reproduced in major media retrospectives, celebrations, and other performances" (303). As this chapter begins to make clear, Obama Hope has certainly moved in such ways, all the while experiencing a constant process of rhetorical becoming as it has been reproduced, appropriated, and redistributed for a variety of political reasons far beyond its role as an image-invention in the 2008 election.

As part of a complex rhetorical ecology, while Obama Hope entered into associations with many who identified with Obama's affective desires and policies, those who disidentified with Obama were also moved to action in relation to Obama Hope. We witnessed Obama Hope's rhetorical transformation especially as it acted as a visual parody and satire to critique Obama and his policies as well as those people who seemed to fall in "Obama-love." Such critiques were not limited to one genre; as this chapter has disclosed, Obama Hope emerged in political cartoons, paintings, and digital webicons to make nuanced critiques and spark public debate. Nor was the image limited to specific contexts, as Obama Hope surfaced to make political commentary in response to a wide range of unfolding events relating to everything from political gaffes to political scandals to the exposure of political secrets. In helping to frame and reframe people's identifications and disidentifications with Obama, Obama Hope thus seems to have produced a great deal of political enchantment[4] as people felt moved to respond to the image itself as well as to deploy it in response to contemporary affairs.

As such visual play escalated, one of Obama Hope's most unforeseeable but significant contributions to collective life surfaced with the emergence of the Obamicon as a new cybergenre—a genre that, as the next chapter will make even clearer, has been taken up by citizens across the globe to work for change in various ways. As Michael Sheperd and Carolyn Watters (1998) explain, cybergenres can be extant or they may be novel. Extant genres emerge when genres existing in other mediums migrate to a new medium, while novel cybergenres, to differentiate from extant ones, can be particularly new to a medium in that they have developed within a particular medium with no real counterpart in another medium. Novel genres can also be emergent in that they have evolved so far from the original that they can be classed as entirely new genres (Sheperd and Watters 1998). Obamicons are similar in content and form to the Obama Hope posters, yet Obamicons ought be considered as belonging to this latter category of novel cybergenres. For what began as a digitally born campaign poster intended to deliver campaign messages, present an idealized image of a candidate, and garner support for a presidential candidate has evolved into a novel, popular genre for parody, satire, and dissent.

Obamicons, as I have tried to explain in this chapter, stimulate dialogue about a number of political issues as they articulate disidentifications with Obama as well as other political figures. Identification, as Kenneth Burke (1969) has taught us, is rhetorically achieved when people recognize others as sharing properties (ideas, attitudes, feelings, visions) and become consubstantial even as they might retain some divisions that prevent them from being totally aligned in all perspectives and actions. Obama Hope has undoubtedly been widely recognized for its ability to instill faith in Obama's messages of progress, hope, and change during the 2008 campaign. So effective was this ability, in

Obama's own words, "to encourage Americans to believe they can help change the status quo" that it was chosen, as discussed in chapter 5, to commemorate not only Obama's inauguration and victory but also the entire 2008 presidential election campaign. As such, it is fair to say that Obama Hope became one of the most important political and rhetorical actors in generating positive identifications with Obama during that campaign. This and subsequent chapters make evident, however, that since entering into circulation, Obama Hope has also sparked a multiplicity of disidentifications, which complicate our rhetorical understanding of this single multiple image. Many of these rhetorical disidentifications are verbally expressed in the metaculture that emerged in cyberspace on blogs, digital news outlets, and social media platforms, as we saw in this and previous chapters. However, Obamicons have also become a popular novel cybergenre of dissent for everyday citizens both within and beyond the United States who disidentify with Obama and other politicians' politics. As such, while Obama Hope played an important role as a political actor to help bring Obama to victory, it has been just as active in expressing and triggering dissenting opinions about Obama's as well as other politicians' policies and agendas.

Interestingly, the mass reproduction, remix, and appropriation of Obama Hope that surfaced in Obamicons, political cartoons, and other genres only enhanced its unique aura—a phenomenon that counters Walter Benjamin's (1968) argument in "The Work of Art in the Age of Mechanical Reproduction." Writing in 1936, Benjamin argued that the status of artwork changed with the advent of capitalist mass production, which dispelled art's unique aura and revered standing by devaluing the concept of the 'original'" (1164). As Benjamin explains, a work's aura issues from the presence it has from being situated squarely in a particular space and point in history, or in other words, its authenticity. The ceiling of the Sistine Chapel, for instance, has a strong aura. This authenticity, which gives it authority, certainly derives from its formal qualities, its materiality. However, its aura also derives from its presence in the Vatican, its survival through five centuries of exposure to potentially harmful elements, its brushstrokes by Michelangelo, and its lack of ability to be duplicated. Any replica of that ceiling printed on various products is, thus, totally *without aura* as it lacks the tradition and history of the "original." The Obama Hope image, however, illustrates that mass reproductions of an "original" image can also establish the authority of that image by generating and enhancing its aura. In fact, when it comes to images such as Obama Hope that start out largely unnoticed as one among hundreds of similar photographs taken by a digital camera, it seems that mass reproduction is necessary for creating the aura and authority necessary for becoming iconic. Mass reproduction triggers mass transformations that spark a multiplicity of rhetorical consequences, which, in turn, begins the process all over again. This recursive process of circulation, transformation, and consequentiality enables an image to become widely recognized and gain the aura necessary for becoming a cultural icon.

For reasons discussed in the previous chapter, the AP would disagree, of course, arguing that the Obama Hope image stole the aura from Garcia's news photo and thus diminished its value. In fact, in the lawsuit claims filed by the AP to countersue Fairey, the AP's attorneys essentially argued just that. In their answer to Fairey's complaint, the AP specifically claimed that Manny Garcia's Obama photo conveyed a "defining impression of President Obama," which created a unique narrative about him, just as many of the creative photos taken by countless AP photographers have become iconic (Fairey et al. v. AP 2009b, 38). The AP argued that Fairey's work simply conveyed what was "already present" in the Obama photograph. It was the distinctive qualities that created the photo's essence, in fact, they argued, that persuaded Fairey to select this photo among thousands of others on Google Images to use as a reference for the Obama Works. Garcia would most likely side with the AP on this point, as he claimed he "made the most iconic image of our time" in an interview with John Harrington. Yet others responding to Garcia's comment, such as Harrington (2009) himself, have argued that "the poster was iconic, the photograph was not." While it is not my intention to enter into this debate here, it seems that my research proves that the latter point is accurate. It was only with viral circulation, divergent transformation, and intense consequentiality that Obama Hope became widely recognized, developed an aura, and gained its iconic status.

As this case study has thus far disclosed, Obama Hope could only become widely recognized so quickly because diverse collectives constituted by digital software, websites, online news sources, genres, cartoonists, bloggers, forum members, and so forth assembled in relation to Obama Hope to participate in democratic, political life. Obama Hope was not just a means for others to become politically active, however. In multiple ways, Obama Hope became a civic actant in its own right as it experienced a distributed ontology in a variety of Obamicons and triggered people to assemble on blogs, forums, and other online outlets to discuss a number of hot-button issues. If ever there was a doubt than an image could be considered "equal or superior to discursive media for enacting public reason or democratic deliberation" or emancipatory for its ability to constitute identity (Hariman and Lucaites 2007, 40),

Obama Hope proves otherwise. As the following chapter will make clear, Obama Hope's civic actancy is not just confined to the United States nor to Internet culture. Working as an international activist, Obama Hope has also become a transnational, rhetorical actant on the world stage.

Notes

1.   To protect the anonymity of people participating in this prowhite discussion forum, I have chosen to withhold the name of the discussion board and member names, even as I have received permission from some to print these comments.

2.   This *Obama as Zombie* Obamicon has been cropped, and the designers and copyright owners of this design have chosen to remain anonymous. Permissions to reprint this design have been granted, however.

3.   This quote is copied directly from the Obamicon.me website, which is no longer available. No changes in spelling have been made. While not positive, I believe "H" refers to Barack Hussein Obama, which as previously discussed is a name commonly used by people who believe and/or accuse Barack Obama of being a Muslim and an Arab.

4.   In speaking of political enchantment here, I am thinking of Jane Bennett's (2001) definition of enchantment as "a mixed bodily state of joy and disturbance, a transitory sensuous condition dense and intense enough to stop you in your tracks and toss you onto new terrain, to move you from the actual world to its virtual possibilities" (paragraph 1).

9

OBAMA HOPE, REMIX, AND
GLOBAL ACTIVISM

This case study has thus far concentrated largely on the national implications of Obama Hope's rhetorical life as it has become a single multiple image—one that has a distinct identity yet also exists in a plethora of different versions that take on various roles that often cause it to stray far from its original function. As is evident in numerous sightings of Obama Hope abroad not only in Africa but also Vietnam, Turkey, New Zealand, Mexico, Liberia, China, Spain, and Italy, just to name a few, Obama Hope's circulation and collective activities have not been confined by US borders. As this chapter discloses, Obama Hope has become an entity that people across the world can count on for its ability to inspire hope, catalyze change, and (re)assemble the social. Its entanglement in various social movements perhaps best illustrates the important rhetorical contribution Obama Hope has made to collective life. To be clear, social movements, from a new materialist perspective, can be thought of as networks of actants that assemble to take collective action in an effort to challenge existing power relations. As many scholars have noted, social movements are dependent on communication activism—strategic interventions and actions that use information, media, and communication to effect social change (Carroll and Hackett 2006; Meikle 2002; Stein, Notley, and Davis 2012). Manuel Castells (2009) has argued, in fact, that the success of a social movement in acquiring power and influence is dependent on its communication capacity—its ability to design, produce, access, and distribute messages over communication networks. Digital technologies and social media have become key players in contemporary social movements because they afford communication capacity; in particular, as Stein, Notley, and Davis (2012) note, they afford (a) the production of messages as, well as their circulation to local and transnational audiences; (b) the development of strategic relationships among various constituents with shared interests and goals; and (c) the generation and activation of distributed collective actions (Castells

DOI: 10.7330/9780874219784.c009

2009, 55, 302; Meikle 2002, 24; Stein, Notley, and Davis 2012, 1). Yet, we should also not forget to give proper credit to the communicative things in and of themselves—the slogans, the pictures, the signs—that work hard alongside a variety of human and nonhuman actants to bend space around them and catalyze change. As this chapter will make clear, Obama Hope has acquired this thing-power as it has materialized not only in various remixes within specific local movements but also across transnational movements that are distributed with time and space.

ART ACTIVISM

The first social movement in which Obama Hope became an active participant was the Obama art movement, which, for this case study's purposes, refers to the art, people, technologies, organizations, and events that assembled during the 2008 election season in support of Obama's presidency. The Obama art movement was generated by the contributions of many different human and nonhuman players who became part of the movement at different times and in different locales across the United States. The movement certainly included the efforts of nine artists, including Fairey, who generated the Artist for Obama series for the official Obama campaign. This art series, which began with Fairey's *Change* poster and ended with his inauguration poster, generated millions of dollars for the campaign. The Obama art movement also included the contributions made by different collectives of artists and designers, who worked during the election season to generate support for Obama. The nine hundred or so members of one such group called Artists for Obama, for instance, hosted over four hundred events; made over forty-six thousand phone calls; knocked on over 450 doors; and, collectively, generated over $350,000 for Obama's campaign.[1] Another important player was Design for Obama—an online forum designed by Aaron Perry-Zucker and Adam Meyer on which artists and designers uploaded their artworks with the intention of their being downloaded by others for free. As art historian Steven Heller (2009) notes, the posters on the Design for Obama website gave artists and designers "a chance to take part in the electoral process, to make their feelings known, and perhaps even impact others" (21). Now documented in a coffee-table-style book, the Design for Obama poster collection helps us visualize just how integral the visual creativity and rhetorics of the Obama art movement were in facilitating Obama's victory.

The plethora of work created by individual artists who were early players in the Obama art movement must not be omitted from this descriptive account. Sculptor and professor Michael Murphy, for instance, began creating Obama artwork in 2007 when a buzz emerged about the young senator from Illinois. He did some research on the Internet to see if others were creating Obama art and only found one example—David Cordero's *Blessing*, a sculpture that depicts Obama as the Messiah dressed in a white robe with neon blue halo. Murphy began listening to Obama's speeches for inspiration and produced the first of many Obama nail portraits (see Figure 3.4). His work, in addition to a gallery full of other artists' work, was included in the Manifest Hope Project that emerged on the campaign scene during the democratic national convention in Denver, as well as the second Manifest Hope show that was on display in Washington, DC, during the inauguration. The Manifest Hope DC show was similar to the show in Denver; however, now that Obama was the president elect, artists were challenged to create art related to three new themes: healthcare reform, workers' rights, and the green economy. While many artists generated art specifically for these shows, Murphy is just one artist among many others who contributed on their own accord to the Obama art movement months before Obama Hope was even conceived.

While such art played a significant role in generating support for Obama, Obama Hope is the image that came to embody the Obama art movement in many people's minds. Jennifer Gross, Yosi Sergant, and Megan Rollins, who helped organize the Manifest Hope Project, justified this embodiment by implying that the Obama Hope image was largely responsible for sparking the entire movement. They specifically claimed (Gross, Sergant, and Rollins 2009) that although it was "unexpected," "as Shepard Fairey's image took off, it was as though a fire had been ignited, motivating other artists to create and organize" (13). The Manifest team was not alone in such implications. In her blog post "Shepherding in a New Era," for instance, artist Gwenn Seemel (2009), writing in early 2009, said, "Everyone is trying to be like Shepard Fairey." Citing artists such as Ron Englishman, Ben Hazard, and especially William Everly as evidence, Seemel remarked, "Not to be outdone by a street artist from Los Angeles, all the usual (and unusual) suspects are trying to catch up with Fairey." In fact, she wrote, "It seems that few artists have **not** tried their hands at making an Obama." While Seemel's claims were obviously hyperbolic, Obama Hope certainly did propagate affective desires for change, hope, and progress and inspire other artists to become politically active and produce Obama art. With her production of *Believe* stencils, twenty thousand of which were printed on bicycle-spoke cards and distributed in Portland, Oregon, ahead of the primary, Margaret

Figure 9.1. Wings of Hope, *Sculpture by Jim Lennox, 2009. Photograph Courtesy of Lennox.*

Coble was one such artist who testified to being inspired to generate her own art by Obama Hope and its noticeable contribution to Obama's campaign efforts (see Figure 3.2). Among countless other examples, Simon Gardinar was inspired by seeing an Obama *Progress* sticker on the streets of New York to create his own digitally born portrait titled *Obama Inauguration 2009* to celebrate "history in the making." Others such as Shine Chisolm created a hope-themed glazed bowl after being inspired by Obama Hope, while still others such as Jim Lennox built winged sculptures with Obama Hope front and center (see Figure 9.1).

Yet despite many artists' claims and testimonies that Obama Hope catalyzed them to generate art for Obama, many insist both Fairey and Obama Hope have received far too much credit for the movement. Murphy (pers. comm.), an assistant art professor at Georgia College, reminds us that grassroots movements "consist of ordinary people taking action to support a specific cause for the sake of that cause." We should also keep in mind that movements often gain momentum when people unknowingly work toward similar goals on their own accord without awareness that a movement is even happening, especially when the movement is a bottom-up, emergent event. As is evident in the work of Murphy and Ray Noland that came out before Obama Hope was even conceived, this is exactly what was happening with the Obama art movement as they, and perhaps others, were producing art for Obama simply because they thought it was a cause worth fighting for.

Noland, a Chicago native and African American designer and printmaker, for instance, began designing, printing, and pasting Obama poster art on the streets of Chicago in 2006 under the pseudonym CRO. In November of that year—around the same time the Obama for American campaign was announced—Noland created the GoTellMama! campaign in collaboration with Rebecca Berdel. As explained on the campaign website's "About" page, Noland's idea was to use nontraditional tactics such as street art and a viral video campaign to create a parallel campaign to boost awareness of Obama and inspire the public (Noland 2009). In the two years leading up to the 2008 general election, Noland, a.k.a CRO, drove over twenty thousand miles to paste screenprinted posters in cities during important caucuses and primaries (see Figure 9.2). He also created multiple videos viewed by thousands on YouTube and hosted ten art exhibitions in nine cities; the art he created is now housed in collections of the Library of Congress and the Smithsonian. Because of such intense involvement, CRO claims that even as he has the utmost respect for Fairey and the Manifest Hope team, he is the one who secured his place in history as a major "creator of the Obama Art Movement"—a claim supported by art historian Hal Wert (2009), who began following Noland's artwork early on in the movement and subsequently put together the beautiful art collection titled *Hope: A Collection of Obama Posters and Prints.*

As evidence for such claims, Noland recounts (pers. comm.) a series of events he experienced in relation to the Obama campaign that are certainly worth disclosing here.[2] Throughout 2007, he points out, the Obama campaign was only circulating its Change You Can Believe In Obamabilia and Hope placards, and Fairey's Obama Works were yet to be unleashed. During that year, Noland was not only distributing his own designs on streets across the United States but also deliberately placing his posters near Obama campaign offices and in strategic places he knew campaign workers would see them. In July 2007, Scott Goodstein (New Media Director, Obama for America) contacted Noland in an email and asked to meet, exclaiming, "It [GoTellMama!] is amazing and captures the true emotion of the campaign." According to Noland, when they actually met to initially discuss Noland's designs, Goodstein didn't seem overly impressed with his artwork. However,

Figure 9.2. Ray Noland Posters in San Francisco. Photograph Courtesy of Ray Noland.

around October of that same year, one month before Fairey began talking with Yosi Sergant (who at that time was consulting with the Obama campaign via the Evolutionary Media Group), the Obama campaign contacted Noland again and asked him to officially design a poster for their New York City rally. "This is where the story gets good," Noland (2009) insists. After communicating with the campaign team on possible designs, he "started to realize they really didn't enjoy seeing Obama's image as a black man. . . . They kept asking me for ways to not focus on his skin." As an artist who had been trying to depict Obama as accurately as possible (see Figure 9.3), this request frustrated Noland so much that finally during an email correspondence with Goodstein, he sarcastically wrote, "Why don't you just make him, red, white and blue?" After that, Noland claims, he never heard back from the campaign. Two months later, though, Shepard's red, white, and blue versions of Obama in the *Progress* and *Hope* posters were released.

While Noland never quite came out in our personal correspondence to accuse the Obama campaign of influencing the initial design of Obama's portraits, he certainly implied so. Others have surmised so as well, especially since Fairey admitted that the campaign "politely asked"

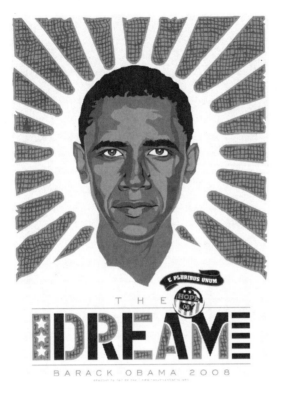

Figure 9.3. Obama Dream,
Design by Ray Noland, 2006.
Photograph Courtesy of Ray
Noland.

him to change *progress* to *hope* (Fairey, "I'm Voting" 2012).[3] In an April 24, 2008, *New York Post* article, for instance, Maureen Callahan reported that "Fairey worked in such close coordination with campaign communications director Scott Goodstein that they discussed the color palette for Fairey's limited-edition Obama print." When asked to comment on this reported "fact," Yosi Sergant denied it, claiming, "If Shep talked with Scott [Goodstein] it was about his CHANGE poster, not the progress nor the hope ones. I'm quite literally the only one who ever saw those before they went to print. I'm an unpaid, grass roots volunteer and never consulted with anyone from the campaign on any of this" (qtd. in "Obama Inspires Art, Again" 2008). Sergant recounted the story about running into Fairey at a party and Fairey coming up with the initial design, and then claimed that Obama's campaign simply "saw it take off and hopped on the train" (qtd. in "Obama Inspires Art, Again" 2008). But Noland claimed "that is just the 'official story'" told by Sergant, Fairey, and the Manifest Hope team to explain how Fairey got involved with the Obama campaign and sparked the entire grassroots movement.[4] Ultimately, he insisted, "This issue as to what or who started the Obama art movement is about who takes credit historically. . . . They [the campaign] don't want you to know about me, and what I was doing throughout 2007. I destroy their timeline."[5] Implying that the campaign was indeed heavily involved with Fairey's poster designs from the onset, Noland insisted, "The campaign used Shepard Fairey to catch up. The campaign felt the visual movement growing under their feet and wanted to take control of it and its message."[6] That message, as he put it so succinctly, was "Obama's not black, he's post racial. He's Red, White and Blue."[7]

While Murphy might not have agreed that Noland started the movement any more than Fairey did, he did agree with Noland in thinking that the Obama campaign and Democratic Party used artists to create art for Obama that they hoped would influence people to identify with and ultimately vote for Obama. Murphy claimed that from the perspective of "the first person in the country to create Obama art," it seemed pretty clear that the official campaign used their contacts with the press to give artists attention so that other artists would be "lured" into producing more Obama art. Echoing many of the claims made by the Americans for Visual Literacy discussed in chapter 7, Noland's testimony and Murphy's beliefs challenge scholars, historians, and rhetorical scholars to make visible the full story about the Obama art movement and to uncover the official campaign's exact role in Obama Hope's inception in Fairey's Obama Works. Obviously, contradictory opinions exist as to who deserves credit for the significant contribution art made to Obama's election. Was it the grassroots efforts of artists around the country, such as Noland and Murphy, who took their own initiative to produce art for Obama? Was it members of the official Obama campaign who decided to hire Fairy "under the radar," lured other artists into selling Obama's brand, and thus, as Noland and Murphy claim, took the reins of a grassroots art movement that had actually begun on its own accord? Was it, as Brian Sherwin (2009) has claimed, that Sergant had ties to the campaign all along and, thus, the art movement was nothing short of a propaganda machine "fostered by artificial means—a playing of the system by individuals with the right (in this case left) press connections, controversial funding, and the know-how of implementing a strategic and stealthy art campaign"?[8] Such conflicting opinions contradict narratives about the Obama art movement in the popular media and illustrate the difficulty of pinpointing how an art movement begins and unfolds. Such opinions even complicate the narrative created thus far in this case study as to not only why the Obama campaign got involved in the distribution of the Obama Works but also why and how Fairey created the *Progress* poster in the first place. To find definitive answers to such inquiries, if it is possible at all, a more thorough investigation of the Obama art movement must be conducted in the future. Yet, even as doubt exists pertaining to the whys and hows of the Obama art movement, there is no doubt that whether deserved or not, Obama Hope did become the most widely recognized image associated with the Obama campaign, even as Noland and others received their fair share of attention.

Obama Hope's embodiment of the Obama Art movement intensified its circulation, especially as a number of websites devoted to documenting the proliferation of Obama art gave much attention to Obama Hope. Besides the *Obama Art Report* blog administered by Ken Hashimoto, *The Art of Obama* blog also emerged as an important site for documenting not only Obama-related graphics and graffiti but also remixes of Obama Hope. This website began when, much like Hashimoto, Gabriel Nagmay noticed the sudden proliferation of political art around her in Portland, Oregon. Much of the work materialized in posters, tags, and extensive works of spray-painted graffiti, and while much was pro-Obama, much was not. Still, Nagmay was struck by the sheer amount of president-related art on the streets. Photographs of such work taken by Nagmay, along with the Obama *Hope* poster and other official works distributed by Fairey and the official campaign, initially constituted the content of *The Art of Obama*. But soon, artists began sending Nagmay submissions of their own work as well, including others like her who photographed Obama-related art on the streets; as many as forty emails a day flooded Nagmay's inbox. Given the overabundance of Obama art produced, Nagmay admitted (pers. comm.), "It is silly how much attention was given" to Obama Hope. But as Carolyn Carr, deputy director and chief curator of the National Portrait Gallery, stated when asked why it was chosen for inclusion, "Everyone knows it. They recognize it. It is part of our popular culture." Obama Hope was so ubiquitous, she also notes that "when people think of a portrait of Obama, they think of this image" (qtd. in Zonker 2008). At least in her and many others' minds, then, Obama Hope earned its position as the face of the Obama art movement because it was the most hypervisible and iconic image of the 2008 presidential campaign—*the* campaign, we should note, in which the first African American president came into office.

ENVIRONMENTAL ACTIVISM

While Obama Hope played an important, if not controversial, role in the Obama art movement here in the United States, Obama Hope

Figure 9.4. Adaptation of Hope, 2011. *Photograph Courtesy of Chelsea Marie Hicks (CC BY 2.0).*

spread its wings in social movements far beyond US borders. Since early 2008, Obama Hope has actually become involved as a visual activist in a number of local protests across the globe. Here in the United States, for instance, remixes of Obama Hope have played a role in protests against Proposition 8 in California and strikes at the Smithsonian museums in Washington, DC, to name a few. Remixes of Obama Hope have also surfaced in protests against fraudulent parliamentary elections in Russia, in poster campaigns to speak out against Toronto's mayor Rob Ford, and to ridicule candidates such as Henry Tang in Hong Kong (see Figure 9.4). Sometimes, as Eric Parker, the illustrator of the *Ford-o-lini* remix of Obama Hope (see Figure 9.5) explains (pers. comm.), designers create their own remixes "with no conscious reference to the Obama HOPE image," even as they "must have seen it." Yet, in other instances, Obama Hope is deliberately taken up as activists realize it has the ability to generate identifications and spark public reaction. Such was likely the case when Obama Hope became involved in a number of interrelated environmental campaigns organized by Greenpeace in its transnational social movement to influence global environmental policymaking.

To understand its role as an environmental activist, it's useful to keep in mind that Obama Hope came into existence at a time when

Figure 9.5. Ford-o-lini: Rob Ford as Mussolini, *Designed by Eric Parker, 2011. Photograph Courtesy of Parker.*

pressing environmental issues such as climate change were sparking a number of image events across the globe. As John Delicath and Kevin DeLuca have explained, image events can be thought of as "staged acts of protest designed for media dissemination" (Delicath and DeLuca 2003, 315). Image events are central argumentative practices for radical ecology groups such as Earth First and Greenpeace, who often deploy subversive tactics to infiltrate public consciousness and take collective action. These staged acts of protest are often enacted at sites appropriate for raising ecological consciousness. Sites may be at places such as Niagara Falls or the Glen Canyon Dam, whose ecosystems demand strong defense against destructive practices such as damming rivers. Or sites for image events may include international conferences such as the World Trade Summit or UN Climate Change Conferences. Yet image events should also be understood as fragments in that photographic and video captures of these protests are then disseminated by mass media (325). As fragments, dramatic pictures "advance indirect, incomplete, and unstated propositions; refute unstated assumptions; operate

Figure 9.6. Sarkobama, 2008. Photograph Courtesy of Pascale Mestdagh.

as evidence for claims; or otherwise serve as inventional resources for future deliberation" (323). As such, image events often do not deliver immediate arguments; rather, because these events are staged acts of protest, audiences who encounter these arguments either in person or via the media are responsible for constructing the arguments as they deliberate with others about the meaning of these events (328). Image events, then, are often elusive in one way or another, even as many may be conducted at sites with more familiar kinds of protest occurring at simultaneous times.

Perhaps one of the most exciting image events in which Obama Hope became involved occurred in late 2008 when a number of *Sarkobama* posters began showing up en masse on the streets of Paris (see Figure 9.6). In the Obama Hope style, all *Sarkobama* posters featured a red, white, and blue portrait of Nicolas Sarkozy above the comment "Yes, We Can"—a slogan used by Obama's 2008 presidential campaign. On different posters beneath this slogan sat one-line questions such as "Clean and lasting energy in Europe?" or "Allow every household to save 1000 Euro a year?" or "Making polluters pay?" Within days, news of the poster campaign spread across France, Europe, and the United States, leading some such as blogger Andrew Sullivan (2008a) to call Sarkozy "shameless" as he, presumably alongside others, identified it as a pro-Sarkozy publicity stunt. Bloggers also began to debate about copyright issues, since the posters so closely resembled Fairey's posters, as well discuss the overall efficacy of Greenpeace's Sarkobama campaign.

Most of all, though, people were curious as to who had launched this campaign and what its exact purpose was because, at first, nobody took credit for this image event. Therefore, on its website, the news organization *L'Express* started a readers' appeal to solve what would come to be known as the Sarkobama Poster Mystery. In response, those responsible for the posters began to post a series of online clues, such as photos of themselves with their faces masked behind *Sarkobama* posters. Soon after Sarkozy denied any responsibility, the culprits finally confessed by posing another image of Sarkozy in the Obama Hope style, this time with the words "Commit now to a 30% reduction in greenhouse gas emissions in Europe by 2020? Yes you must!" Accompanying this demand was a Greenpeace logo. As just one of many image events to be produced in the coming months, this campaign was launched by Greenpeace apparently to persuade European heads of state to review the climate/energy plan at the upcoming European Summit to be held that December in Poznan, Poland. Sarkozy was targeted in the campaign because, according to the head of Greenpeace France, Pascal Hustin, Sarkozy was "hugely responsible for watering down the Climate and Energy package" needed to fulfill the EU's goal to cut European emissions (Wilson 2008).

Such image-event involvements diversified Obama Hope's influence across the globe far beyond its use in selling Obama's messages to the US public and garnering support for his presidency. It also further proved Obama Hope's ability to generate a very loud buzz, trigger collective action, and make a strong rhetorical impact. Sarkozy, of course, is not the only politician to become "Obamafied" by Greenpeace's environmental tactics or in other public campaigns. *Obamafy* (also commonly spelled *Obamify*) is a neologism that came into popular use during Obama's presidential campaign as a reference to the process of generating pictures in the style of Obama Hope. In 2008, for instance, Dubi Kaufman created the Obamafy Photo Booth Plugin along with an online version, which, much like the Do It Yourself Barack Obama and obamicon.me sites, allowed visitors to generate Obamicons in a red, white, and blue palette. Such sites became so popular during 2008 and 2009 that today, many apps[9] exist that allow you to create Obama *Hope*-style posters on your own smart phone. Obamafication, in this sense, often entails copying the tricolored theme, portrait style, and the layout of the Obama *Hope* poster. While in some cases, such as the *Sarkobama* posters, politicians are Obamafied in the same color palette as Obama

Hope, in other cases, the color palette changes, even as Obama Hope's aesthetic influence is still apparent.

In 2009, for example, German Chancellor Angela Merkel became Obamafied in three interrelated activist tactics orchestrated by Greenpeace in Europe. This time, however, Obamafication occurred in the black, red, and gold colors of the German flag, and often with more direct messages written beneath Merkel's portrait. In the first instance, an Obamafied image of Merkel appeared in Indonesia on banners that said, "Climate change starts here. Less talk, more money." These banners were unfurled in a recently cleared peatland forest in the Kampar Peninsular—a region whose ecosystems are being threatened, according to Greenpeace, by pulp and paper and palm-oil industries. In another instance, Obamafied Merkel appeared on an enormous banner with the words "Climate Protection Now! Copenhagen 2009." This banner appeared ahead of the United Nation climate talks to be held in Copenhagen[10] in December of that year. It was hung from the main central railway station in Berlin next to another banner that said "Ms. Merkel—Save the Climate Now or Never."

In perhaps the most outrageous image event of the three, however, Obamafied Merkel was part of an Angie You Can campaign implemented in Germany earlier in the year on the day of the NATO summit in Kehl. This summit marked the sixtieth anniversary of NATO's establishment; as such, it was expected to be not only a big celebration but also an important summit for discussing a number of urgent topics such as the ongoing Afghanistan War, Western relations with Russia, and France's reintegration with the NATO military command structure. Greenpeace, of course, also wanted climate protection to be on the agenda. More particularly, they wanted to convince industrialized countries to invest in adapting measures for climate change and virgin forest protection. The signal of both German and US commitment could be an important starting point for reducing carbon emissions and taking action on climate change (Totz 2009). In this image event, then, an Obamafied Merkle showed up on posters plastered around Berlin with the words "Angie You can" and "Not only Banks, Save Also the Environment." A 7 × 10-foot "Angie You Can" banner was even hung from a hot-air balloon, which floated over Kehl on the morning of April 4 (see Figure 9.7). As the biodiversity expert at Greenpeace Corinne Hoelzel explained, while the economic crisis demands attention, the "climate crisis threatens us all . . . far more than the economic crisis" (Totz 2009). Remixes of Obama Hope thus worked in this particular fragmented image event to urge politicians such as Merkel to ward off

Figure 9.7. Angie You Can, *2008. Photograph Courtesy of Andreas/ Varnhorn Greenpeace.*

"climate chaos" that would undoubtedly ensue, according to Hoelzel, if no government action was taken (Totz 2009). Interestingly then, as is evident here, in each local Greenpeace campaign, Obama Hope played a nuanced activist role to mobilize collective action even as it fought for common international goals.

Such activity, of course, only accelerated Obama Hope's rhetorical transformation, as media outlets began reporting these image events. As already noted, the *Sarkobama* posters themselves sparked a plethora of metacultural activity that lasted for days on end. Yet, Obama Hope's participation in other Greenpeace image events also captured the imagination of the public eye. As was typical with other Obama Hope remixes, Obama Hope sparked unintended conversations about its design in addition to a variety of other topics. In response to its actualization in the Angie you Can campaign, for example, some such as Zohar Efroni (2009) at the Center for Internet and Society at Stanford Law School wondered if anyone else besides him had copyright reservations about the design, while blogger January Lachnit (2009) wondered why Greenpeace thought such an "unimaginative" design would provoke collective action. Others, however, marveled at Obama Hope's continued proliferation and divergent use. As one blogger put it, "Just when you were starting to forget the iconic Shepard Fairey Obama poster, it gets resuscitated to support another cause" (Urban 2009). Such resuscitation would only continue to unfold in years to come. As the next makes clear, for instance, besides working to influence environmental policy in the transnational social movement orchestrated by Greenpeace, Obama Hope took up yet another cause to confront economic and political concerns via its involvement in the Occupy movement.

OCCUPY ACTIVISM

As an ongoing international protest movement aimed to create more just economic structures and power relations, in many ways, the Occupy movement came into existence much like Obama Hope in that once the idea for it was unleashed, it began to take on a life of its own. The Canadian activist group, the Adbusters Media Foundation—most well known for its anticonsumerist magazine and culture-jamming practices—is credited for conceiving the idea behind the Occupy movement when it issued a call for a peaceful occupation of Wall Street in mid-2011. As articulated in a post signed by Culture Jammers HQ (2011) on the *Adbusters* blog on July 13, *Adbusters* was inspired by the fresh tactics deployed in both Tahrir Square and the *acampadas* of Spain to generate, in Raimudo Viejo's words, a "big swarm of people" to organize in physical settings and virtual assemblies to make revolutionary demands. As reported by Andrew Fleming (September 27, 2011) in the *Vancouver Courier*, *Adbusters* was simultaneously "frustrated by a growing disparity in wealth" and the absence of legal actions taken against those responsible for the 2007 global financial crisis that sparked several significant events: the collapse of large financial institutions, large numbers of bank bailouts issued by national governments, and stock market downturns across the globe. Yet, while *Adbusters* is credited for starting this movement, Micah White, the senior editor of *Adbusters*, claims that *Adbusters* actually just "floated" an idea that was "spontaneously taken up by people around the world" who learned about it via social media outlets and "made it their own" (qtd. in Fleming 2011). Today, the Occupy movement is considered a leaderless resistance movement that has erupted on a global scale with no real centralized authority controlling its growth and evolution. Much like Obama Hope, then, the Occupy movement

Figure 9.8. Anonymous,
*Adbusters Poster for Occupy
Movement, Ben Sliver, 2011.
Photograph Courtesy of Sliver.*

has experienced a rhetorical transformation that has gone wild beyond its conceptual designer's imagination.

As is evident in the design of the *Anonymous* poster Ben Sliver designed for *Adbusters*, Obama Hope first became part of the Occupy movement to urge people to assemble on Wall Street on September 17, 2011 (see Figure 9.8). Obama Hope was also remixed into a variety of signs including one of its most unusual actualizations, an enormous chalkup produced by Fresh Juice Party in Oakland's Frank H. Ogawa Plaza, a.k.a. Oscar Grant Plaza[11] (see Figure 9.9). Fresh Juice Party is a collective of artists and musicians who work with various citizens across the United States to create music and happenings for various causes. They also create unique stencil designs and organize "chalk-upy" parties in which various chalk designs are laid out and colored. In its chalkup version, Obama Hope materialized in an approximately 25 × 25-foot design depicting Obama with a police hat and the words *Dear Leader.* Such manifestations on urban streets worked to keep local

Figure 9.9. Dear Leader, 2011. *Photograph Courtesy of Craig Casey/Fresh Juice Party.*

spaces politicized. Grant Plaza was the first site of Oakland's main protest encampment. It was raided by local authorities, rebuilt by protestors, and then raided again, forcing Occupy protestors to find other spaces. Despite such moving of the encampment, Grant Plaza remains a hot spot of Occupy activism thanks to the work of groups such as Fresh Juice Party. As explained by Fresh Juice Party (pers. comm.), their chalkups were washed away every week by local authorities during the heat of the movement.[12] Therefore, every Friday for nine months, Fresh Juice chalked up a fresh design in Grant Plaza to keep the Occupy momentum going. During the week of July 23, 2012, when Obama was visiting for a fundraising event at a local theater, Obama Hope played that politicizing role as it occupied Grant Plaza in a gigantic way.

Despite such an enormous presence in local Occupy protests, Obama Hope became most visibly involved in the Occupy movement when Shepard Fairey remixed his iconic poster design to create the first of two *Occupy Hope* designs. In the first poster design, which he posted on his Obey website, we find a portrait of V, a character from a series of Alan Moore comics who enacts spectacles of violence to revolt against a totalitarian government. In the poster, V is covered with a smiling Guy

Figure 9.10. Occupy Hope, *Design by Shepard Fairey, 2011.*

Fawkes mask, which had become the face of the Occupy movement, and a logo that reads, "We are the 99%. Occupy Wall Street." Beneath this portrait sit the words "We Are the Hope." Just after this Obama Hope remix was made public, Fairey revised the design based on responses he received from various people involved with Occupy, including an organizer of Occupy Wall Street. Fairey (2011) explained that he conceived of Obama as an ally of the Occupy movement. He designed the poster to urge outsiders like himself, as well as insiders like Obama, to stand up against corruption and the imbalance of power and to work toward creating a democracy that represents and helps average Americans. Respondents to the poster, however, questioned whether Obama was really that strong of an ally and worried that Fairey's original design would generate a pro-Obama statement and send a message that Obama was co-opting Occupy Wall Street. In response, Fairey, who insisted that he did not intend to create a pro-Obama message, changed the main line from "We Are the Hope" to "Mister President, We Hope You're on Our Side" (see Figure 9.10). This revised design, in which the direct call

Figure 9.11. There's Still Hope, *Doran, 2011. Photograph Courtesy of Doran.*

to Obama is loud and clear, was made available for free download on Fairey's Obey Giant website much like the original *Progress* posters were made available during the 2008 election. Obey Giant and Sticker Robot also teamed up again as they did in 2008 to give away free silkscreen stickers until supplies ran out.

Throughout the ongoing Occupy movement, Obama Hope has been found in its Occupy version wheatpasted to city walls and stuck on car bumpers and metal signs across the United States (see Figure 9.11). It has also been deployed in protests, such as when a coalition of labor, community, and environmental groups met outside the American Legislative Exchange Council (ALEC) in Chicago in August of 2013 (see Figure 9.12). Yet, *Occupy Hope*'s presence in cyberspace has been much more diverse and perhaps much more consequential, as it experienced a fate similar to the Obama Hope version. As soon as it was unleashed, for instance, metaculture spread quickly in cyberspace about the production of *Occupy Hope*, and many people praised *Occupy Hope*'s design and Fairey's efforts. A small amount of Ebayification also emerged as people began to auction off stickers and t-shirts with the *Occupy Hope* design. In addition, remixes of *Occupy Hope* such as Mike Estee's Occupy

Figure 9.12. Mr. President, We HOPE You're on Our Side, *Mike Slivka, 2013. Photograph Courtesy of Slivka.*

Fairey were created. As Estee (2011) explains on his blog, he chose to remix Fairey's *Occupy Hope* design because he did not agree with Fairey when Fairey (2011) wrote on his Obey blog that Obama is "the closest thing to 'a man on the inside' that we [the Occupy movement] have presently." Estee (2011) feels that, in actuality, Obama "is a President who has taken the Bush doctrine, and just *run with it.* Instead of turning around our erosion of civil liberties, he's accelerated them." Estee, therefore, chose to depict the tent in his version because to him, the tent represents "all the people who lost their homes. All the people who lost their jobs. It represents a protest movement of people committed to being heard by their voices, and not their fists. My hope is that someday when we've moved on from parks and bank lobbies to congressional seats & mayoral offices, that an idea will take a new place in American history as a symbol of hope, instead of a politician." Like other remixes of Obama Hope, this picture too began to take on a life of its own as it circulated both on the streets and on a variety of blogs about diverse Occupy-related issues.

In addition, just as Obama Hope initially spurred much frustration with its design and designer, many people, in addition to Estee, seemed disgruntled with *Occupy Hope*. Many, in fact, seemed to have altogether rejected the intended message of *Occupy Hope*, complaining that even with the second version, Fairey got it all wrong in trying to affiliate the movement with Obama in any shape or form. As both Bucky Turco and Maura Judkis articulated on different blogs, the NYC General Assembly's (2011) "Statement of Autonomy" claims "Occupy Wall Street is not and never has been affiliated with any established political party, candidate, or organization." And, unlike Fairey, many Occupy protestors did not believe in Obama's potential to work for economic justice nor trust him to represent their concerns. As Pham Binh (2012), a self-titled socialist activist, explained in a blog post accompanied by *Occupy Hope*, "Only we can truly represent ourselves; elected representatives can easily misrepresent their constituents; trust no one to do anything on your behalf, do it yourself." In light of such critiques, it may not be that surprising to learn that Obama Hope did not become the face of the Occupy movement as it did with the Obama art movement. While certainly *Occupy Hope*'s cool reception can be partly to blame, as Michael Beirut (2012) has argued, no poster came to be credited for launching or perfectly embodying the Occupy movement. Beirut surmises that this fact had less to do with the quality of design and more to do with the fact that the participatory democracy in action overshadowed any graphic design that could mobilize collective action. If any image were to really focus public attention on the movement, he argues, it is the live-video capture of the protestors in Manhattan being pepper-sprayed by police officers. Obama Hope did not have a chance to become the face of the Occupy movement, he might argue then, because "sometimes, the key to political change isn't designing a logo or poster. It's simply having the courage to show up and make your voice heard, no matter what the cause— and no matter what the risk."

Despite the fact that Beirut may be right about this point in regard to the Occupy movement, as well as I would argue the Arab Spring, which I discuss below, *Occupy Hope* did become a widely recognized visual activist in this important movement alongside a plethora of other posters, some of which have been bought by the MOMA in New York to document this important moment in New York's history. And while it did encounter much resistance, *Occupy Hope* also stirred up conversation in the blogosphere about a wide range of issues, such as the movement's choice to adopt V and Guy Fawkes iconography and about the new role of American protest art. Obama Hope even emerged in one blogger's post as "a clarion call to Mr. Obama—the very people he reached out to in 2008 are ready to turn away from him unless he "changes" ("Power of Art" 2011). It also, of course, functioned to show people's allegiance to the movement and mobilize people to action for the Occupy movement. As one young person, Brad Barrish (2011), wrote above a picture of *Occupy Hope* uploaded to his blog, "Stop wondering what you can do, and just start taking action. You have time and it's not difficult." Or as another blogger put it more forcefully above an uploaded picture of *Occupy Hope*, "Get the hell out there and occupy something, Occupy everything, before all you're allowed to occupy is a cell. And who knows, besides just pissing off the cops, you might even do some good."

Some people such as Steven Fitzgerald must have heard[13] such demands in the blogosphere, as on his own blog he explains how he printed out a copy of *Occupy Hope*, turned it into a mask, added a black hooded sweatshirt and cargo pants, and took a four-hour bus drive to Washington, DC, to participate in an Occupy Congress rally. While such action may seem silly, Fitzgerald (2012), a healthcare professional, claims that it was a transformative experience:

> In that time and in that place, this mask felt like . . . my "real face." At the foot of the hill that led up to the Capitol, a group of protesters were holding various banners and what not with the iconic government building in the background. I went and stood next to them and held my "RISE UP" sign over my head with all of the forceful, completely earnest intent I could radiate. I knew exactly what I was doing putting [on] this mask, with this black hoodie look from the Fairey poster together with these particular words on this sign and standing in front of this historic, symbolic, photogenic building. To me, this image was everything that this event was about (for me) and everything (in my opinion) that it should project to the world in a nutshell. From my perspective, this was quintessential. So instead of waiting for someone else to do it, I just did it myself.

Here in the flesh, then, Obama Hope was taking political action as it became a vibrant actant in a multitude of others fighting for a similar cause. Such activism, as the remainder of this chapter discloses, was just one enactment among many in which Obama Hope would come to intra-act with others to protest against unjust political causes. Yet is it is a quintessential moment that illustrates Obama Hope's constitutive power—its ability to spark incorporeal transformation as it entered into relations with everyday US citizens.

ARAB SPRING ACTIVISM

In addition to becoming part of the Obama art and Occupy movements, Obama Hope has worked as a political activist in a variety of events related to the Arab Spring movement. There has been much debate as to when, where, and how this broad movement started. Many claim the movement is a recent phenomenon involving a contagious wave of revolutionary demonstrations, protests, and civil uprisings that have occurred in Arab-speaking states such as Tunisia, Egypt, Libya, Yemen, and Syria over the last five years. As Lisa Anderson (2011) has argued in *Foreign Affairs,* Arab revolts began to spread back in 1919 as Arab nationalist networks enacted civil disobedience throughout the Arab-speaking region post-World War I. Thus, she, like others, insists that the recent spread of popular movements most define as the Arab Spring is actually not that new. In addition, many claim the Arab Spring movement began in Tehran in 2009 during the Iranian green movement, while others claim it was actually sparked in December of 2010 in Sidi Bouizid, Tunisia, after Mohammed Bouazzi committed self-immolation to protest police corruption and brutality. Interestingly, despite such debates, most agree that in addition to military might and outside intervention, much of whatever success can be claimed in the Arab Spring is attributed to strong grassroots activism that emerged via a distributed network of actants. From a postcolonial perspective, as Dhanashree Thorat has reminded me (pers. comm.), it is important to recognize the distributed network of human agents responsible for Arab Spring activism—agents both on the ground in the forementioned countries and agents abroad who worked to build and show solidarity. But from a new materialist perspective, we also need to acknowledge how this activism was enabled by digital technologies and social media working in cahoots with brave citizens on the ground fighting for justice. No matter how small its contributions, Obama Hope, I would argue, ought be recognized for its work among this distributed network of actants.

Important to realize is that the protest rhetoric that emerged in relation to the Arab Spring did not just take place within, nor target those in power of, countries where local revolutions were exploding on the ground. Rather, in countries such as the United States, England, and Turkey, protests also emerged to convince Western leaders to intervene in the often-violent uprisings going on in places such as Libya and Iran and to both promote and demonstrate solidarity for local revolutions. In addition, protestors on the ground in countries such as Egypt, Libya, and Iran, where media outlets were blocked off, also generated and found ways to distribute protest rhetoric invented for similar purposes.

Figure 9.13. Obama Hope remix in Mubarak Protest Sign, Photograph by Murad Sezer, 2011. Permissions from Reuters.

It is in these particular kinds of protest actions that Obama Hope left traces of significant rhetorical activity.

In 2011, for instance, Obama Hope became politically active in Istanbul, Turkey, as it surfaced in a protest poster depicting an Obamafied Mubarak with the words "No You Can't" written in English (see Figure 9.13). While it is unclear who was responsible for these posters, it is clear that protestors holding these signs wanted to show support for regime change in Egypt and gain the attention of an international audience and foreign media. Such targeting of an international audience was not rare in the Egyptian revolution. Along with Alex Ortiz, Rayya El Zein has curated a collection of protest signs, graffiti, and street art that surfaced during the Egyptian revolution. As El Zein and Ortiz (2011) note, because of the regime's crackdown on journalism and live coverage, it became increasingly important for protestors' resistance to be witnessed despite their fears of being noticed by local authorities. Such resistance, at least in Egypt, became largely an aesthetic endeavor (4). Many signs that worked to change the dominant narrative, demand political goals, articulate personal expressions, and commemorate losses were created in words, phrases, and pictures only fellow Egyptians could understand. Yet many translated such messages into signs that were internationally legible (25) and recognizable so that people around the world could identify with the protestors and be impacted. As is evident

Figure 9.14.
Hopeless, 2011.
*Photograph
Courtesy of Joan
Pantsios.*

with the "No You Can't" Mubarak sign, remixes of Obama Hope played an important rhetorical role alongside other signs in this communicative endeavor.[14]

Obama Hope worked in this capacity for regime change not only in regard to Egypt but also to Libya. During 2011, Obamafied versions of Gaddafi began to surface in Obamicons and circulate on the Internet to articulate opinions about Gaddafi and mobilize pressure against his regime. In some cases, the word *Libya* is written beneath Gaddafi's portrait while in other cases, the words *evil, mad, nuts,* and *hopeless* appear. Remixes of Obama Hope also emerged to protest against Gaddafi in the Enough! Gaddafi campaign in 2010–2011 (see Figure 9.14). Enough! Gaddafi (n.d.) was an activist campaign created by Libyan exiles to raise awareness about the injustices of the Gaddafi regime and as a call to action to spark change in Libya. Organizers of this campaign certainly wanted to express dissent against the Gaddafi regime. Yet they also wanted to bolster grass-roots organization, which helps Libyan people actualize their aspirations to overcome limitations placed upon them by what this campaign saw as an illegitimate and unjust government (Enough! Gaddafi n.d.). Enough! Gaddafi, cofounded by Libyan American activist Abdulla Darrat, origi-nally had a website to organize protest efforts and keep folks informed, but because it was hacked, it was only accessible for a short time. Twitter and YouTube thus became major players in keeping people informed about what was happening within Libya during the uprisings against Gaddafi in 2011.

Enough! Gaddafi also produced and distributed campaign materials to be taken up by others across the globe. In 2010, Enough! Gaddafi produced a portrait of Gaddafi in the Obama Hope style and the red, white, and blue palette. On top of the portrait the words "Enough! Gaddafi" were written above "enoughgaddafi.com," while on the bot-tom, the word "Hopeless" appeared in blue with the *less* emphasized in red. All words were printed in English, except for the name Gaddafi, which was written in Arabic. This poster, which was uploaded to Flickr in June of 2010, would come to be waved the following year in protests near the White House in Washington, DC, on the streets in Chicago, and outside the Libyan embassy in London. Homemade remixes of this poster with airplanes and weapons of mass destruction exploding from behind Gaddafi's Obamafied portrait could also be seen at protests in San Francisco. Photographs showing this Obama Hope remix at work in various protests also began to circulate in online news sources in which it worked to depict growing international opposition and protests against Gaddafi and to generate a response. Such visibility led many folks to marvel at Obama Hope's continued political activism. One blog-ger, for instance claimed, "As the revolution sweeps across the Middle East, art and graffiti have played a big role in communicating attitudes and making change happen. A major guiding artistic light seems to be Shepard Fairey and his patterned prints as well as his iconic 'HOPE' poster. . . . The ironic deployment of his style for Gaddafi is nothing less than delicious" (Ritchie 2011). Yet, more importantly, as this remix of Obama Hope circulated in various news sources and blogs, it helped to, among other things, induce people to follow Enough! Gaddafi's (n.d.) Twitter feed to keep up with what was going on in Libya; promote the Libyan Day of Rage announced by the National Conference for the Libyan Opposition (NCLO) and Libyan political activists on February 17, 2011; and spark conversation about how the United States might influence the actions of the Qaddafi regime.

Interestingly, for a short while before such enactments related to Libya, Obama Hope also became embroiled in the Iranian Green movement that emerged after the 2009 Iranian presidential reelection of Mahmoud Ahamadinejad when protestors demanded the annulment of what they perceived to be a fraudulent election. This movement escalated, if you recall, when Neda Aghar Soltan was killed in June of 2009 during the Iranian election protests. Neda's death on the streets of Tehran was recorded on video and spread across the world via social media sites such as Facebook and YouTube. Much as the Obama Hope image became an icon for the 2008 election, in a matter of hours, as reported by CBS correspondent Dan Farber (2009), Neda became "an icon for the Iranian protest movement." In his article "Naming Neda: Digital Discourse and the Rhetorics of Association," Bradford Gyori (2013) crafted a thorough rhetorical analysis of the online discourses that centered on Neda's death. As he noted, people instantly began to juxtapose the footage of Neda's death with words, texts, photographs, drawings, and music in attempt to make sense of both Neda's life and her death. While other images of Neda surfaced in such mashups, the image of Neda's blood-streaked face in particular circulated and transformed widely across a wide range of genres and locations.

As may not be surprising by now, this image was Obamafied and began to circulate in various media outlets and blogs not only to document the tragic event and memorialize Neda but also to galvanize the Iranian Green movement, which by that point had spread across the globe. The most widely circulating Obamicon that incorporated Neda's blood-streaked face was one produced by graphic designer Shahab Siavash, who as is evident below, has since produced a number of different Obamicons for various rhetorical purposes. This particular Obamicon incorporated a close-up of Neda's blood-streaked face with the words "Neda, We Will Never Forget U." This Obamicon not only materialized on a diverse array of online English-speaking news sites and blogs but also on blogs written in Arabic, Polish, Spanish, Bulgarian, Persian, Italian, and French, just to name a few. In addition to working in the rhetorical ways described above during 2009, this Obamicon later worked, among other ways, to critique the UN's 2010 decision to elect Iran to the Commission on Women's Rights and to critique the United States' refusal to confront Iran. In addition to calling for political change in Iran, then, this Obama Hope remix also surfaced to call for change in US policies toward Iran by reminding an international audience of Iran's ill treatment of its own female citizens.

Figure 9.15. Her Name Was Neda, *Obamicon by Shahab Siavash, 2011. Courtesy of Siavash.*

Interestingly, just after Neda's death, another Obamicon created by the same Iranian graphic designer surfaced to make a similar call to action (see Figure 9.15). In this Obamicon, Siavash inserted nuclear symbols into Obama's eyes and omitted the Obama campaign logo from Obama's lapel. The word "Hope" was replaced with "Her Name Was Neda." While the blood-streaked image of Neda is small, it appears in a circle between the words *was* and *Neda*. As Siavash explains in his own words,[15] his intention was to communicate a strong critique. "We here in Iran think that President Obama has forgotten about Democracy and acts of barbarism of the Iranian Regime against people of Iran & only thinks about Nuclear Danger of IRAN. I added two Nuclear icons in his eyes in this poster and also wrote 'HER NAME WAS NEDA!' to remind Obama that NEDA . . . was an innocent person. . . . WHEN the Iranian regime CAN kill an Innocent person from its own country, it easily can KILL thousands of Americans if they reach Nuclear bomb capabilities. . . . Restrictions and prohibitions against regime don't affect [the regime]. . ., only buy them TIME. . . . Obama should destroy this regime so BOTH we have FREEDOM and USA has confidence." Initially, Siavash uploaded this site to Flickr, explaining that creating such posters and uploading them to such sites is a productive way for graphic designers such as himself to make their voices heard. In Iran, Siavash explained, he and others feel scared to speak out and against "the Iranian regime," especially because it instituted an extensive media blackout when the protests began. While social networking sites such as Twitter and Facebook have been acknowledged for their role in helping Iranian's voices be heard, Siavash explains that Flickr also became a useful outlet for voicing Iranian concerns so they could be heard in the international media. As reported in Octavia Nasr's (2009) CNN article "Tear Gas and Twitter," social media outlets "offer the world a unique voice: free, unfiltered and very different from what the Islamic Republic of Iran's media propaganda offers viewers and readers." Because landlines, mobile phones, and emails are not trusted for fear of messages being traced, sites such as Flickr, if accessible, are considered "safe" spaces to voice opinions.

During 2009, the Obamicon website, discussed in the previous chapter, also become a safe haven for voicing Iranian opinions, and many people across the world began generating their own Obamicons in relation to Iranian politics. On June 19, 2009, in recognition that Obamicons were an important means for circulating Iranian perspectives and a productive way to garner support for Iran's green movement for democracy, Pastemedia began enabling viewers to make Iranicons—webicons generated in the Obama Hope-image style yet in the colors of Iran. While various images of Neda became especially popular, Mahmoud Ahmadinejad also received his share of attention in Iranicons. In addition, many people have simply uploaded their own photos and inserted phrases such as *Free Iran* and *Where's My Vote?* Like many Obamicons, Iranicons began to circulate in both cyber and physical spaces. While Iranicons depicting Neda often showed up on blogs reporting about Neda's life and martyrdom, Iranicons with the word "Nope" beneath Ahmadinejad's portrait showed up on stickers on the streets of Berlin in 2009, on protest signs in San Francisco, and even on t-shirts sold by Café Press (see Figure 9.16). Thus, just as Obama Hope experienced mass circulation and reproduction, so did some of the Arab Spring related Obamicons,[16] whose invention and distribution Obama Hope so fervently inspired.

Figure 9.16. Nope *Iranicon*
by Jochen Friedrich, 2011.
Courtesy of Friedrich.

CONCLUSION

In previous chapters, we witnessed Obama Hope's commodification
both in the United States and abroad, as is evident in its actualizations
in a variety of advertisements and merchandise that raised money not
only for Obama's campaign but also for private businesses and individual artists. This commodification is perhaps not all that surprising. In
consumer cultures, art often becomes a commodity. In fact, art "deliberately admits that it is [a commodity]; art renounces its own autonomy
and proudly takes its place among consumption goods" (Horkheimer
and Adorno 1972, 157). Such commodification often leads to passive
consumption, the dulling of the imagination, and a lack of spontane-
ity (Horkheimer and Adorno 1972, 126–27). And, to be sure, Obama
Hope probably did impact some people in this way, as we saw Jason
Mattera arguing in the previous chapter. Yet, as is evident in this chapter, the intra-actions between Obama Hope and the various people who

reproduced and remixed it in the United States and abroad for political purposes make evident that even as it became part of the culture industry, Obama Hope did not participate in the squandering of energy, the dulling of the senses, or the enervation of people's will to work for things in which they believed. Instead, Obama Hope helped energize, politicize, and mobilize thousands of people to work feverishly for political and social change.

Obviously, Obama Hope cannot take full responsibility for the widespread political devotion and labor disclosed in this chapter, as a wide ecology of events, feelings, institutions, motivations, moods, and so forth contribute to any rhetorical action. Artists in the Obama art movement, for instance, testify that not only Obama but also the eight years of the Bush administration inspired and motivated them to work for change. Yet, as is evident in the testimony of many such as Margaret Coble (2009) and Scott Fitzgerald (2012), Obama Hope clearly played an affective role in inducing people to organize and mobilize to help Obama get elected during the 2008 election season and to confront a perceived unjust political system. In *Arts of the Political*, Ash Amin and Nigel Thrift draw on Tarde to remind us that collective life is constituted by a circulating flow of affective imitations, which constantly move through individuals in semiconscious ways and produce microvariations along the way (Amin and Thrift 2013, 160). Imitations, as studies have confirmed, are not only rapid, automatic, and semiconscious but also involve emotional contagion. While it is something many of us would like to deny, people, and other entities capable of affective response, have little individual agency as affective forces heavily influence their thoughts, dispositions, and actions (160). Especially in the political realm, people's actions are shaped by semiconscious thoughts (160) and unconscious perceptions of how others around them are feeling and what they are doing. While charismatic figures such as Obama are able via their rhetorical prowess to generate affective imitations and catalyze a specific political mood, visual things such as Obama Hope also acquire that ability as they circulate, enter into various affective encounters, and work in various capacities. Via affective labor,[17] then, we might say, visual things especially acquire the ability, if even for a short time, to induce incorporeal and rhetorical transformations, as we saw in the case of food-service workers, artists, craftspeople, and others who began to identify and act as political activists during the 2008 election season and the ongoing Occupy movement via their relations with Obama Hope. In fact, I would argue, it is because of such recognized thing-power that this image-invention not only went viral but also continues to circulate so broadly. As people witnessed its ability to induce such transformations, it contagiously passed on as it was reproduced and appropriated for a wide range of divergent purposes.

This contagion quickly spread across the globe, as is evident in the various protests and social movements in which Obama Hope remixes materialized. Such adoption of Obama Hope for political activism in the Occupy movement and the Arab Spring was not simply the result of pure coincidence. As Manuel Castells (2012) explains in *Networks of Outrage and Hope*, one of the common threads in the different uprisings that sprung up across the globe between 2009 and 2011 was an emotional mobilization triggered by not only outrage and blatant injustice but also by hope, hope for possible change (220). Each of the protests described in this chapter were local in the sense that they were fighting on the ground for their own reasons in response to regional and national injustices. However, each of these protests was also global in that (a) people were connected to other protests or movements through communicative messages; (b) people learned from others' experiences; and (c) people were inspired by others' experiences to mobilize for their own causes (223). Obama Hope was one of those communicative threads and actants of change that helped mobilize and connect the various movements across the globe. As people witnessed Obama Hope's power to help bring the first African American man to the US presidential office and bring change to US politics, they realized its power to revolutionize and embraced it for their own causes, whether that was rebelling against Gaddafi, working to confront economic corruption, or agitating for environmental change. All these interrelated movements ultimately wanted to achieve similar things: "To raise awareness among citizens at large, to empower them through their participation in the movement and in a wide deliberation about their lives and their country, and to trust their ability to make their own decisions in relation to political class" (Castells 2012, 236). With its ability to raise awareness and trigger political action, Obama Hope was an important actant in helping people across the globe reach this common goal.

Today, as different protests and movements emerge, Obama Hope is still fighting for justice in nuanced, unforetold ways. In 2013 alone, Obama Hope not only made appearances in Mexico and Arizona in protests against US deportation policies but also in tent protests in the West Bank against Israeli occupation. In London, on the other hand, Obama Hope emerged outside the embassy to protest against drone attacks in Pakistan. Obama Hope also surfaced in protests against the US National Security Agency in various countries across the globe. In Germany, for instance, remixes of Obama Hope made a loud appearance in a couple

Figure 9.17. Germany NSA Spying, *Photograph by Markus Schreiber, 2013. Permissions from the Associated Press.*

of different protests against the NSA. If you recall, media reports came out shortly beforehand claiming the US National Security Agency was eavesdropping on several EU offices not only in Washington, DC, and New York but also in Brussels. Outraged about what some claimed to be "cold war practices," in June, protestors took to the streets in Hanover and used Obama Hope to show their disapproval. In this particular instance, Obama Hope showed up in a remix of Fairey's MoveOn *Yes We Can* design, but this time, Obama is wearing a pair of earphones over his ears (see Figure 8.24). And instead of saying "Yes We Did," the poster reads "Yes We Scan" on top with the words "United We Progress toward a Perfectly Monitored Society" around Obama's portrait and the words "We Are Watching You" at the bottom. In another remix of Obama Hope, as one might expect, Edward Snowden has been Obamafied with abbreviations such as "ASYL" beneath Snowden's portrait (see Figure 9.17). This rendition showed up in protests outside the German parliament building in Berlin after Snowden offered to help Germany investigate NSA spying activities in exchange for asylum. Signs made out of Obamicons depicting Barack Obama with earphones and a satellite logo on his lapel have also surfaced in protests in Hong Kong and Washington, DC, as have Obamafications of Snowden with the word "Hero" printed beneath his portrait.

Figure 9.18. Remix of Hope *Poster in Response to 2009 Bombing in Gaza, Art by Southpaw.org for Jewish Voice for Peace, 2009. Photography Courtesy of Code Pink Women for Peace (CC BY-SA 2.0).*

Such instances of ongoing activism demonstrate how remix has become a popular transnational political practice with Obama Hope being a reliable go-to image for catalyzing change. Eduardo Navas (2012) has argued that the remix ought be recognized as a "global activity consisting of the creative and efficient exchange of information made possible by digital technologies" (65). In his book *Remix Theory*, Navas demonstrates how remix (the activity of locating and combining preexisting materials into new forms) is ubiquitous across the globe in art and music (65). And writing studies scholars have done good work in studying remix in genres such as video and music (Banks 2011; Kuhn 2012) as well as exploring how remix has become a popular practice in small-screen and participatory culture (Dietel-McLaughlin 2009; Hodgson 2010). Yet, as Obama Hope teaches us in this chapter, remix is not just a practice taken up by artists and musicians or US citizens concerned with who gets into office or making their voices heard on YouTube. Remix, in the twenty-first century, has also become a ubiquitous political practice for activating change, reaching out to international audiences, and building alliances of protest across the globe (see Figure 9.18).

As a way to bring this chapter and case study to a close, I just want to note that as Obama Hope surfaces to work for change in global enactments of activism, one can't help but be impressed with Obama Hope's ongoing rhetorical flexibility and dependability. From news photo to political poster to educator to novel cybergenre to political activist, Obama Hope is an image that constantly emerges to take on new responsibilities with each divergent encounter. As such enactments continue to unfold almost a decade after it first appeared in Mannie Garcia's photograph, one also cannot help but wonder how long this single multiple image will continue to circulate and play an active role in collective life. Will its circulation and transformation slow down once Obama is out of office? Will it, like so many of the *Hope* posters still hanging on urban walls, fade slowly into history to become an archival relic that speaks only to a particular historical moment? Or will it, like the Mona Lisa and the Raised Fist, experience a long and active rhetorical history of varied and divergent collective activities? Only time, of course, will tell us the answers to such questions. But as for now, one thing is clear. Like the iconic Energizer Bunny©, Obama Hope is simply a rhetorical tour de force whose consequential impact just keeps going and going.

Notes

1. These statistics for Artists for Obama activities are taken from the Activity Summary page for the Artists for Obama community on the *Organizing for America* blog. See https://my.barackobama.com/page/group/ArtistsforObama.
2. Ray Noland, in e-mail correspondence with Laurie Gries, January 2014.
3. Such surmisings are likely bolstered by Fairey's admittance that he was trying to "deracialize" Obama in his original design of the *Progress* poster (Fisher et al. 2012).
4. Ray Noland, in e-mail correspondence with Laurie Gries, September 2009.
5. Ibid.
6. Ray Noland, in e-mail correspondence with Laurie Gries, January 2014.
7. Ibid.
8. Such charges, some might argue, are especially plausible due to the emergence of a scandal that broke out in August 2009 when Yosi Sergant, who was then working as Director of Communications for the National Endowment for the Arts, was caught on tape with United We Serve allegedly trying to influence artists to cre-

ate work to support the Obama administration's domestic policy. While the NEA denies the allegations, Sergant did resign as the Director of Communications in late September 2009, and accusations against the NEA and Sergant persist.

9.   While 3DTOPO, Inc. invented the HOPE Poster Photo Filter for the iPhone, the Obama HOPE NOPE CAM is now available for Androids.

10.   Interestingly, at the actual protests in Copenhagen, Obama Hope also showed up in protest signs with a picture of Obama and the words "Hope Nhagen" written beneath.

11.   Oscar Grant Plaza is the name given to the Frank H. Ogawa Plaza by Occupy protestors. They renamed it in honor of the young man from Haywood who had been shot while lying on his back by a Bay Area Rapid Transit police officer in 2009.

12.   Ultimately, Fresh Juice Party claims (pers. comm.) that this obligation to wash the plaza every week benefited Fresh Juice as they could then mobilize to generate new designs each week. While the first encounter with the wash crew was adversarial, Fresh Juice Party and the city's power washers formed a truce, and the washers would even take pictures of Fresh Juice Party's work before washing over each design.

13.   I mean *heard* figuratively. There is no actual evidence that Fitzgerald's actions were directly motivated by Barrish's directions to take action.

14.   The "No You Can't" sign appears on page 23 of S*igns of the Times* (El Zein and Ortiz 2011) along with other images written in Hebrew and French.

15.   Shahab Siavash, in e-mail correspondence with Laurie Gries, November 6, 2009.

16.   These Gaddafi Obamicons became so popular in 2011 that, much like Obama *Hope* posters, they became commodified and began to appear on a diverse range of commercial products: t-shirts, hats, coffee mugs, key chains, mouse pads, pins, aprons, and even iPad and iPhone cases.

17.   As defined by Michael Hardt and Antonio Negri in *Multitude: War and Democracy in the Age of Empire*, affective labor is "labor that produces or manipulates affects" (Hardt and Negri 2005, 108).

10

FUTURE MATTERS
A Conclusion

A true invention is an object that precedes its utility. . . . An invention is an in situ plumbing of potential rather than an extrapolation of disengaged possibility. It is a trial-and-error process of connecting with new forces, or in new ways with old forces, to unanticipated effect. Invention is a plug-in to the impossible. It is only by plumbing that connection that anything truly new can arise.

—Brian Massumi, *Parables for the Virtual*

I begin this final chapter with this quote about invention, potential, and novelty from Brian Massumi (2002) for two reasons. The first is to make a final note about the Obama Hope image. As both an invention in photojournalism and an invention in political art, Obama Hope preceded its utility and its own possibility. First imagined to function as a documentary photo and then as a political poster, Obama Hope exceeded these functions to take on a multiplicity of diverse rhetorical roles throughout its ongoing life:

> Protest, critique, satire, parody, advertising, fundraising, branding, education, commemoration, inspiration, entertainment, propaganda, commodification, embodiment, call to action, political enchantment, civic engagement, social and political commentary, environmental/political activism, rhetorical (dis)identification, and touchstone for debate.

These functions, disclosed in the four-part case study, came about as the image entered into divergent relations with a surprising range of human and nonhuman entities and became embroiled in various collective activities (see Figure 10.1). Mapping out this messy network of loosely affiliated entities and collectives illustrates just how complicated Obama Hope's rhetorical life has been. An image-invention with such an extraordinary rhetorical existence has a lot to teach us if we just take time to listen.

DOI: 10.7330/9780874219784.c010

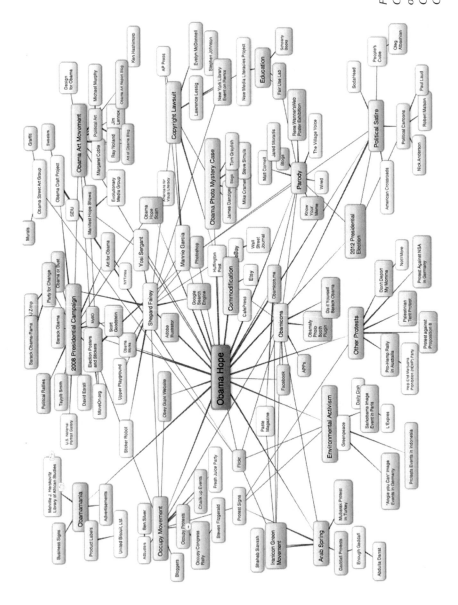

Figure 10.1. Map of
Obama Hope's Network
of Loosely Affiliated
Collective Activities.
Created by Author.

In the conclusion of each case study chapter, I touched upon the many lessons Obama Hope has to offer, especially in relation to an image's rhetorical transformation. Here, I want to synthesize a few of those implications for those interested in researching, producing, and teaching visual rhetoric. Yet I also want to discuss the broader implications of what Obama Hope has to teach us about studying other things from a new materialist rhetorical perspective. For while Obama Hope challenges us to think more deeply about what we mean by viral circulation and delivery, it also inspires us to become more attuned to the ways things rhetorically matter to collective life and to become more inclusive of those things in rhetorical history.

ON GOING VIRAL

First, Obama Hope challenges us to rethink what we mean by the term *going viral* and how we think about delivery from a rhetorical perspective in the digital age. In the introduction to this book, I described commonly understood assumptions about what going viral means and how things go viral, including Shepard Fairey's perspective that things go viral because they are made widely accessible and become greatly admired and desired. In *Spreadable Media*, Henry Jenkins, Sam Ford, and Joshua Green have recently argued that we might abandon viral metaphors when trying to account for circulation because of their inability to accurately describe how media texts actually spread from person to person in a networked culture. The term *viral media*, they insist, "is at once too encompassing and too limiting, creating false assumptions about how culture operates and distorted understandings of the power relations between producers and audiences" (Jenkins, Ford, and Green 2013, 20). *Spreadability*, they argue, is a much more useful term to describe how technical resources make circulation of media content possible, how economic structures support or restrict circulation, how attributes of a media text might motivate community members to share materials among themselves, and how social networks contribute to such sharing (4–5). While I agree that such factors are important to consider in any account of circulation, I also believe that, as we saw with the concept of circulation itself, the term *viral* gets blamed for consequences that are actually a methodological matter. As I attempt to demonstrate throughout *Still Life with Rhetoric*, if we develop new research approaches that look to futurity and account for a thing's ongoing rhetorical transformation, we can develop adequate insights into how things become contagious within and across various communities due to a complex

network of technologies, human actors, distribution strategies, economic structures, political institutions, social media, moods, desires,
affects, and so forth.[1]

Nonetheless, Obama Hope does challenge us to interrogate our
assumptions about how things spread and to develop questions that
complicate our own understanding of viral circulation. Does going viral
mean that a visual thing has been seen by a certain number of people
in a specific amount of time? Does going viral require that visual things
actually travel, or move from place to place, as the progressive tense verb
going insinuates? Does going viral require that things are reproduced
and adapted for various uses on mass levels and/or that they produce
metaculture about themselves? For instance, should we refer to a video
on YouTube as *viral* if it attracts a million viewers but does not actually move from YouTube to other sites nor undergo much transformation across genre, media, and form and thus encourage other things to
become more like itself? Rather than abandon the term, then, I think we
need to pause and think more deeply about what we mean by *going viral*,
especially before it becomes a useless cliché deployed too frequently to
actually retain any significant meaning.

As a case in point, in early 2012, I was watching Rachel Maddow
talking about the so-called war on women and Virginia Governor Bob
McDonnell's push for legislation that would mandate women getting
transvaginal ultrasounds before undergoing an abortion. As reported
by Laura Bassett (2012) from the *Huffington Post* and made hypervisible
by the media, many citizens and politicians alike critiqued the bill not
only for being medically unnecessary but also for being an "egregious
government overreach into personal medical decisions that women
should make with their doctors." This critique came in the form of
debates in the Senate, citizen-generated petitions, and satire produced
by the likes of John Stewart and others. In talking about this legislation
as well as the ensuing backlash, Maddow showed a parody of a white
transvaginal probe that she claimed had "gone viral," as photoshopped
pictures of the probe were popping up on Facebook and other places.
On these probes, folks had written things such as "I can see the White
House from here" or "If you can read this, your government is too
close." Interested, over the next few days I tried to track the image to
see just how widely it had circulated and how many transformations
of the photoshopped image I could find. After some time, I was only
able to find a few instances in which the probe was reproduced and
had transformed with different sayings. Surely, on Facebook, blogs,
and online news sites, the news of McDonnell's legislation had spread

like wildfire. And a couple of YouTube users were having fun producing videos such as *I'm Your Transvaginal Probe* depicting a cartoon probe singing a satirical bit. But, by and large, while plenty of folks were talking about probes, far fewer reproductions and transformations of the probe were circulating. In such cases, can we really say that the probe had gone viral?

Drawing on lessons learned from Obama Hope, I suggest we reserve the descriptor *going viral* for things that are highly mobile, contagious, replicable, metacultural, *and* reflexive.[2] While *mobility* refers to a thing's ability to move and spread and *contagious* refers to a thing's ability to trigger affect and influence others in an infectious manner, *replicable* refers to a thing's tendency to be reproduced and imitated with varying intensities of transformation. In addition, to say something is *metacultural* and *reflexive* refers to a thing's ability to spark cultural response in relation to itself, a response that might manifest in a verbal and/or visual form of critique, praise, analysis, review, parody, satire, and so forth. According to this definition, and as is made visible in this multipronged case study, visual things such as Obama Hope go viral in a digital age for a variety of interrelated reasons:

- Effective distribution strategies make a visual thing easily accessible to a mass audience.

- Digital technologies (social networking websites, pictures and video hosting websites, image editing software, search engines, computer infrastructure, etc.) afford easy manipulation of and access and response to visual things.

- Simple visual design makes reproduction and remix easily possible.

- An abundance of metaculture (positive and/or negative) emerges in response to a visual thing, which helps accelerate its flow in verbal and nonverbal threads.

- Imitation-suggestibility is present, which stimulates others to imitate and appropriate a visual thing's design, production, and/or distribution strategies.

- Collectives emerge in relation to a visual thing, diversifying its function and consequentiality and enabling it to spread.

Such contributing factors, you will notice, are not always under the control of a designer, but especially when it comes to composition, production, and distribution, they are not an afterthought either. We can learn to spread our messages more widely by thinking more carefully about how circulation unfolds in a digital age and making delivery a forethought in our composing practices.

In an advanced undergraduate course at the university where I teach, for instance, I offer a course I call Public Culture, Writing, and (Viral) Circulation. The challenge I set forth for students is to create a social campaign with the goal of creating a buzz about it and assembling a public of interested parties on our campus. Throughout the semester, we read about theories of distribution, circulation, rhetoric, and design, and, inspired by Obama Hope, students are encouraged to put these theories into action as they design and produce with delivery and collective formation in mind. Such forethought about delivery prompts them to consider not only rhetorical velocity throughout the design process but also how they might deploy distribution tactics via social media and on-the-ground strategies to accelerate the spread of their campaign messages and generate and maintain collective formation in relation to their campaigns. Such attention to delivery heavily impacts the design and production of campaign materials (flyers, websites, Facebook pages, public relations notices, etc.); thus, while delivery is often thought of as a final presentation of already-produced material, here, delivery becomes a vital means of invention, not to mention the other canons of arrangement, style, and even memory.

In such regard, Obama Hope challenges us to continue to explore what delivery means for rhetoric not only in theory but in our classrooms. As Ben McCorkle (2012) argues in *Rhetorical Delivery as Technological Discourse*, the canon of delivery has been remediated by technological and cultural shifts and various appropriated uses of a given communication technology. In the face of electracy, networked culture, new media, shifting publication politics, and "advances in our understanding of language, semiotics, human development, technology, and society" (Prior et al. 2007, 2), scholars such as James Porter, Collin Brooke, John Trimbur, Paul Prior, and others have argued that rhetorical theory must reimagine the canon of delivery for rhetoric. In light of new media, Brooke (2009) himself has argued for reconceiving delivery as performance, a conception that allows us to move away from thinking of rhetoric in the intransitive sense. Obama Hope, if it could speak in our traditional understanding of that verb, might second this move toward an intransitive understanding of delivery. For scholars interested in what Sid Dobrin (2011) calls "post-composition," this move is productive in that it helps draw attention away from products generated by a "producing subject" to a "never-ending (re)circulation" in which visual things take place within a larger ecology (77). Yet, it is also, and perhaps especially, important for our students to develop an intuitive and ecological sensibility toward rhetoric that recognizes its enduring vitality, materiality, and spatiotemporality—its capacity to be both impacted by external influences and to impact material consequences as it intra-acts with humans and other nonhuman entities during circulation. Such notions can help students better understand not only how rhetoric functions as event once released into the world but also, and perhaps more important, how their own discourse actually comes to matter—that once let go, it can transform their communities and environments in ways they have perhaps never even imagined. To be convinced that rhetoric is a vital, generative force—a performance that actually has potential to catalyze change and reassemble society—students must be given an opportunity to set their own discourse in motion and to witness how it circulates and activates others around them. Emphasizing delivery as performance is useful, then, in that it can help students realize why delivery matters to the communities in which they themselves circulate.

As a supplement to delivery, performance, however, is etymologically tied to notions of accomplishment, execution, completion, and fulfillment—all outcome-oriented actions that discount the unpredictability and unforeseeability of rhetoric's ongoing rhetorical transformation. As Obama Hope has showed us, visual things (as well as texts, artifacts, etc.) often exceed their intended goals and do not stop moving, transforming, and triggering change once they are unleashed into the world. Not all things, of course, move, change, and catalyze such a wide range of consequences so quickly and intensely as Obama Hope. Yet, things are not as outcome-oriented and still as we make them out to be either. If we actually take time to trace things as they circulate and enter into various relations, we can come to discover that many things are unpredictably active and still on the rhetorical move. We might think of delivery, then, as an ongoing activation that is ironically signified in the word *still*. Etymologically, the verb *activate* has ties to the adjective *active*, which itself means "given to worldly activity," "energetic," and "lively." In this vitalist sense, rhetoric is not something that has already been delivered nor is it fulfilling or executing some preplanned act. As an ongoing activation, rhetoric is a distributed event, an energetic and generative process in which single things become multiple and vital as they experience rhetorical transformation. From this perspective, composition, production, distribution, circulation, transformation, collectivity, and consequentiality are all and always at play in a thing's ongoing rhetorical activation. Obama Hope challenges us to rethink delivery in these terms, not in a chronological sense but in a new materialist sense so we can better understand how things are always energetically and rhetorically at play in co-constructing this complex world.

ON BECOMING INVENTIVE

Obama Hope also challenges us to become inventive with our methodologies to help account for rhetoric's dynamic and distributed dimensions. This challenge brings me to the second reason I began this chapter with Massumi's quote about invention—to reiterate that the impetus for this methodological project was to supplement representational, synchrotic approaches with an approach that can better disclose how things-in-flow transform collective life. This new materialist rhetorical approach is particularly useful in tuning us in to rhetoric's enduring materiality, distributed activity, and unforeseeable consequentiality—an attunement necessary for disclosing how things become rhetorical with time and space as they enter into divergent associations and spark a wide range of often unforeseeable consequences. As I discussed in chapter 4, such disclosure demands embracing the virtual, and even as uncertainties may arise, following the transformation of things-in-flow. Such disclosure also demands tracing a thing's collective activities and enacting rich description to create symmetrical accounts of how rhetoric, actancy, and meaning materialize within and across dynamic assemblages. In order to do such accounting, I particularly argue for taking our eyes off the still life of rhetoric and turning to futurity to account for rhetorical transformation. Such methodological moves, I hope I have demonstrated, can open up new directions for not only visual rhetoric and circulation studies but also rhetorical studies at large.

The new materialist rhetorical approach I have introduced in this book has been informed by a complex array of interdisciplinary theories and philosophies that are productive in that they help account for how things generate change, assemblage, and event. In part 1 of this book, I remixed these productive theories to generate six principles, which act as research guidelines, or accountabilities, for the new materialist rhetorical approach herein.

PRINCIPLE OF BECOMING

Becoming is an opening up of events into an unknown future. Reality is change, an open process of mattering and assemblage. From such perspectives, a new materialist rhetorical approach recognizes that things constantly exist in a dynamic state of flux and are productive of change, time, and space.

PRINCIPLE OF TRANSFORMATION

Rhetorical transformation is virtual-actual process of becoming in which rhetoric unfolds in unpredictable, divergent, and inconsistent ways. To account for a thing's distributed ontology, a new materialist rhetorical approach tries to disclose the rhetorical transformations that things experience as they materialize in differing spatiotemporal configurations.

PRINCIPLE OF CONSEQUENTIALITY

The meaning of matter is constituted by the consequences that emerge with time and space via its relations with other entities. These consequences emerge before, during, and after a thing's initial physical production and delivery. Turning to futurity, a new materialist rhetorical approach focuses the most attention on the consequences that emerge once matter is initially produced, has been perceived as relatively stable, and enters into circulation.

PRINCIPLE OF VITALITY

Things have lives of their own and exert material force as they move in and out of various assemblages and trigger diverse kinds of change. A new materialist rhetorical approach tries to account for a thing's distributed, emergent materializations in a nonteleological fashion and disclose the complexity of unsurprising and unpredictable ways it impacts collective life.

PRINCIPLE OF AGENCY

Agency, better thought of as actancy, is a distributed, dynamic dance enacted by diverse entities intra-acting within and across assemblages. To cultivate a fluid sense of collective life and to explore how rhetoric emerges from the distributed relations and activities of mutually transforming entities, a new materialist rhetorical approach focuses on a thing's emergent and unfolding exterior relations and intra-actions.

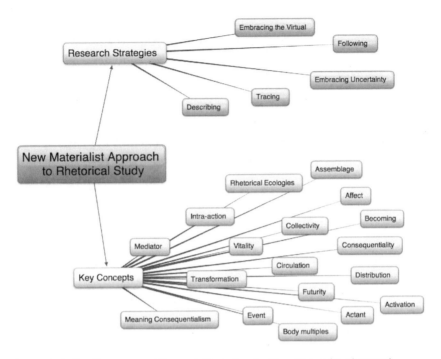

Figure 10.2. Key Concepts and Research Strategies of a New Materialist Rhetorical Approach. Created by Author.

PRINCIPLE OF VIRALITY

Virality—the tendency of things to spread quickly and widely—is a consequence of a thing's design, production, distribution, circulation, transformation, collectivity, and consequentiality. Things are especially contagious when they propagate affective desires that induce unconscious collective identifications and unconscious imitative feelings, thoughts, and behaviors.

From these principles, we can extract key concepts and research strategies that are both indicative of the new materialist rhetorical approach herein and productive for inventing new research methods such as iconographic tracking (see Figure 10.2).

Iconographic tracking, to recap, is a research method that draws on traditional qualitative and digital research strategies to (a) follow the multiple transformations an image undergoes during circulation and (b) identify the complex consequentiality that emerges from its divergent, collective encounters. In chapter 5, I offered a rich description of how this method can be conceived as operating in different phases so that others can employ or adapt it for their own purposes or simply be inspired to invent their own methods that take a new materialist rhetorical approach. In *No Caption Needed*, Hariman and Lucaites (2007) tracked the circulation of photographic images that had already become iconic in US mainstream culture and investigated how they had been appropriated through generations to help citizens negotiate civic life in a liberal-democratic society. Iconographic tracking can be a useful research method to contribute to such research. Yet iconographic tracking can also help explain *how* an image such as Obama Hope becomes iconic in the first place. Furthermore, beyond that function, one of Obama Hope's most important potential contributions to rhetorical and circulation studies might just be its ability to help us visualize how visual rhetoric is a driving, immanent force in collective life that refuses to be bound by a presupposed context.

In *The Ends of Rhetoric*, John Bender and David Wellbery point out that we can no longer conceive of rhetoric as it was conceived in ancient Greece or in Enlightenment-era Europe. In today's day and age, they point out, "Rhetoric is no longer the title of a doctrine and a practice, nor a form of cultural memory; it becomes instead something like the condition of our existence" (Bender and Wellbery 1990, 25). Bender and Wellbery specifically challenge us to think in terms of rhetoricality, which positions rhetoric as the general "condition of human existence and action." While this conception of rhetoric is enticing, part of the problem in accepting it is a lack of ability to visualize rhetoric as such. It is difficult, in other words, to think about rhetoric as a general condition of our existence when we cannot actually envision how it creates the material conditions of our daily lives in multifaceted and divergent ways. Yet, what we learn in taking a new materialist rhetorical approach to track the Obama Hope image is that rhetoric is a distributed process whose beginning and end cannot be not easily identified. Like a dynamic network of energy, rhetoric materializes, circulates, transforms, and sparks material consequences, which, in turn, circulate, transform, and stimulate an entirely new divergent set of consequences. It is, in simple terms, a distributed, and unending, process of becoming in which divergent consequences are actualized with time and space. As such, rhetoric is all around and within us; it permeates our lives and shapes the material realities in which we find ourselves entwined.

While such permeation might seem impossible to visualize, iconographic tracking illustrates that a new materialist rhetorical approach can help map out a complex network of rhetorical transformations involved in the life of a single multiple thing such as Obama Hope. Certainly the entire complexity of rhetorical contributions involved in any single thing's life cannot be fully mapped out. As a distributed event, always constituted by change, rhetoric is always doing, happening; as such, the complex rhetorical life of any single thing can never be fully captured. However, methods such as iconographic tracking can help identify a visual thing's emergent rhetorical flexibility—its ability to transform in purpose, function, and form with each relation it enters into. With an eye on futurity, these methods can also make transparent how rhetoric unfolds with time and space among a constellation of dynamic actor-networks, where rhetorical situations are blurred, initial intensions are often left behind, and agency is distributed among images, pictures, media, humans, technologies, various forces, and other physical and abstract, virtual and actual entities.

In the four-part case study presented in part 3 of this book, I have tried to demonstrate the affordances of a new materialist rhetorical approach and iconographic tracking for making a single thing's rhetorical flexibility and transformation transparent. This case study is surely limited in scope. The final chapter on Obama Hope's transnational activities especially needs to be fleshed out by zooming in more closely on the specific collective activities of the various protests and transnational social movements in which Obama Hope has become embroiled. While it is useful to identify the unexpected collectives enrolled, mobilized, and transformed in their intra-actions with a single image, we need to learn more about how the Obama Hope remixes were actually designed, produced, and distributed within this loose network of collectives as well as how people reacted to its use in these important events—details that would help us develop a more nuanced account of Obama Hope's rhetorical transformation. Nonetheless, this case study makes evident that if we take up Obama Hope's challenge to become inventive with methodology and method, it is possible to trace the rhetorical life of runaway objects such as Obama Hope, even if we can never predict the utility or outcome of the inventions under study.

ON BECOMING RHETORICAL

Finally, Obama Hope challenges us to do a better job of acknowledging the rich and varied rhetorical contributions things makes to collective life, not just because of their representative powers and ability to persuade and trigger (dis)identifications but also because of their ability to reassemble collective life as they inspire people to feel, think, and act in divergent ways. To say that things such as Obama Hope have material consequences in our lives is an understatement at best. As iconographic tracking of Obama Hope makes clear, as things enter into relations with us, our lives are mutually transformed. Through its intra-actions with other entities, for instance, Obama Hope transformed from political poster to novel cybergenre to environmental activist, among many other things. Through these same intra-actions, not only has collective space been transformed but also people's individual lives. As Obama Hope surfaced in Berlin, Indonesia, and Paris in a number of Greenpeace campaigns as well as in Occupy protests in cities such as Oakland, for instance, it helped transform train stations, peatlands, and urban streets into politicized spaces with distinct environmental and political messages. And via their relations with Obama Hope, among other incorporeal transformations, everyday citizens transformed into active political participants; graphic designers transformed into empowered critics; and service workers transformed into important players in a powerful art movement. Perhaps most important of all, because of their relations with Obama Hope, at least in part, one senator transformed into the first African American president in the history of the United States while one graduate student transformed into an academic with a deeper understanding of how images become rhetorical with time and space. As is evident here, any agency we claim in our lives is indebted to those things we come into relation with. We can do a better job of acknowledging just how entangled our lives with things are and work harder to disclose how they actually reassemble collective life.

As the four-part case study in part 3 aims to demonstrate, we can especially make visible how things mobilize civic engagement if we take the time and energy to follow their divergent transformations and trace their collective activities. Via iconographic tracking, for instance, we have been able to witness how Obama Hope became a powerful actant as it intra-acted with various people engaged in social movements across the globe. We have been also been able to witness how, through their encounters with Obama Hope, people were provoked to assemble and debate as well as act alongside other entities toward many common goals. Whether these collectives entailed assembling to discuss hot-button issues such as copyright or Obama's policies, or working to bring people into office, or collaborating to discover certain truths, people and other entities assembled in relation to Obama Hope on numerous occasions. No activity or transformation, of course, can be attributed to a single element; a complex rhetorical ecology of historical, contemporary, virtual, physical, and internal and external factors motivates all

Figure 10.3. Obama History, *Design by Shepard Fairey, 2009. Printed By StickerRobot.com, Courtesy of Shepard Fairey/ ObeyGiant.com. Photograph of Sticker by Author.*

change. Digital technologies and social media, as demonstrated earlier, especially enable a thing and the people it encounters to mutually transform. But as things such as Obama Hope circulate, engage in various collective activities, and work to catalyze change, they also become important movers and shakers in the world.

Typically, in rhetorical history, human figures have received much of the focus as historians have worked hard to recover the voices of both canonical and underrepresented people. In such studies, scholars often focus on how humans use things to influence rhetorical change and/ or become active members of their communities. Yet too little *sustained* attention in rhetorical history has worked to recover how single multiple images and other distinct artifacts are legitimate and important rhetorical actors in their own right. Obama Hope teaches us that as they circulate and become involved in various activities, things shape collective life in multifaceted ways and thus deserve a more prominent role in rhetorical history. What might we learn about rhetorical history if we create more symmetrical accounts to disclose how things circulate, transform, and generate a multiplicity of changes via their various encounters? If we make things such as Obama Hope the main characters in, say, rhetorical biographies? If we produce social histories that work hard to recover not only the rhetorical activities of underrepresented peoples but also of underrepresented things that have played an important rhetorical role throughout history?

As *Still Life with Rhetoric* has specifically aimed to demonstrate, images are important members of communities that have a rhetorical life of their own, take on multiple civic roles, introduce new values into the world, and shape collective life in multifaceted ways. Many of these rhetorical contributions are unpredictable as they emerge with each new encounter in nuanced ways, but as they actualize in different versions and become embroiled in various activities, images do leave traces of their collective activity that can be disclosed. Unfortunately, as W.J.T. Mitchell (2005) has argued, most visual things are subalterns whose voices simply have not been invited to speak (33). From a new materialist perspective, we can give images their due by making visible their complex rhetorical lives and disclosing how they collectively engage to produce new perceptions, behaviors, and arrangements of the world. Such disclosure is important because these perceptions, behaviors, and arrangements constitute the fabric of collective life. Obama Hope specifically challenges us to produce rhetorical histories that enrich our understanding of how images function rhetorically to reassemble our economic, political, and cultural lives.

But, as a way to bring closure to *Still Life with Rhetoric*, what other things have also earned their place in rhetorical history? And what other methods might we invent to study how those things come to rhetorically matter to collective life? As rhetorical studies takes the nonhuman turn and as our lives becomes more and more entangled with digital images, smart technologies, robots, GPS, AR technologies, persuasive technologies, and so forth, we especially have a responsibility to ask such questions. The goal here is not to replace humans as the focus of rhetorical study. From a new materialist perspective, we simply need to create more room in our studies for those things in collective life that become rhetorically savvy alongside us.

Notes

1. Readers interested in circulation, new media, and culture especially ought consult David Beer's (2013) *Popular Culture and New Media: The Politics of Circulation.* Beer's work, which I discovered in the late stages of this book's publication, is especially usefully in mapping out how archives, algorithms, data play, and the body influence circulation, which, as Beer argues, is central to the production of culture.

2. See also Karine Nahon's and Jeff Hemsley's *Going Viral* for more on what virality is and how viral events are made possible by a wide range of factors: human attention, gatekeepers, invested networks, bandwagon effects, and so forth.

REFERENCES

4Rilla. 2008. "Bombing for Obama-Shep Article in Radar Magazine." Comment on the Giant .org Discussion Board. September 16. http://forum.thegiant.org/viewtopic.php?f=6&t =12787.

Adam, Barbara. 2004. *Time*. Cambridge, UK: Polity.

Adam, Barbara. 2007. Forward to *24/7: Time and Temporality in the Network Society*, edited by Robert Hassan and Ronald E. Purser, ix–xii. Palo Alto, CA: Stanford University Press.

Adolff, Eric. 2008. Comment on "Barack Obama—Santa Fe Art District." *Seetwist PhotoStream*, Flickr, March. http://www.flickr.com/photos/seetwist/2311174232/.

Ajami, Fouad. 2013. "When the Obama Magic Died." *Wall Street Journal*, November 14. http:// www.wsj.com/articles/SB10001424052702304243904579196440800552408.

Amin, Ash, and Nigel Thrift. 2013. *Arts of the Political: New Openings for the Left*. Durham, NC: Duke University Press. http://dx.doi.org/10.1215/9780822399056.

Anderson, Lisa. 2011. "Demystifying the Arab Spring." *Foreign Affairs* 90 (3): 2–7.

Arnon, Ben. 2008. "How the Obama 'Hope' Poster Reached a Tipping Point and Became a Cultural Phenomenon: An Interview with the Artist Shepard Fairey." *Huffington Post*, March 13. http://www.huffingtonpost.com/ben-arnon/how-the-obama-hope-poster_b_13387 4.html.

Atbashian, Oleg. 2010. *Shakedown Socialism: Unions, Pitchforks, Collective Greed, the Fallacy of Economic Equality, and Other Optical Illusions of "Redistributive Justice."* Lebanon, TN: Greenleaf.

Bakhtin, Mikhail. 1981. "Forms Of Time And Of The Chronotope in the Novel." In *The Dialogic Imagination*, edited by Michael Holquist, 84–258. Austin: University of Texas Press.

Bakhtin, Mikhail. 1986. *Speech Genres and Other Late Essays*. Edited by Caryl Emerson and Michael Holquist. Translated by Vern W. McGee. Austin: University of Texas Press.

Banks, Adam J. 2006. *Race, Rhetoric, and Technology: Searching for Higher Ground*. Mahwah, NJ: Erlbaum.

Banks, Adam J. 2011. *Digital Griots: African American Rhetoric in a Multimedia Age*. Carbondale: Southern Illinois University Press.

Barad, Karen. 2007. *Meeting the Universe Halfway: Quantum Physics and the Entanglement of Matter and Meaning*. Durham, NC: Duke University Press. http://dx.doi.org/10.1215 /9780822388128.

Barnett, Scot. 2010. "Toward an Object-Oriented Rhetoric." *Enculturation* (7).

Barnett, Scot, and Casey Boyle. 2015. *Rhetorical Ontologies: Rhetoric through Everyday Things*. Tuscaloosa: The University of Alabama Press.

Barrish, Brad. 2011. "Stop Wondering What You Can Do to Support the Occupy Movement." *Whatevernevermind* (blog), November 19. http://whatevernevermind.com/post /13030689177/stop-wondering-what-you-can-do-to-support-the-occupy.

Barry, Anne Marie Seward. 1997. *Visual Intelligence: Perception, Image, and Manipulation in Visual Communication*. Albany: State University of New York Press.

Barthes, Roland. 1982. *Camera Lucida: Reflections on Photography*. New York: Hill and Wang.

Bassett, Laura. 2012. "Bob McDonnell, Virginia Governor, Signs Mandatory Ultrasound Bill into Law." *Huffington Post*, March 3. http://www.huffingtonpost.com/2012/03/07/bob -mcdonnell-virginia-mandatory-ultrasound-bill_n_1327707.html.

Baudrillard, Jean. 1999. *Fatal Strategies*. London: Pluto. First Published 1983 as *Les stratégies fatales* by Editions Grasset, Paris.

DOI: 10.7330/9780874219784.c011

Bauer, Charlotte. 2008. "Barack's Popularity Balloons." *Mail & Guardian*, November 9. http://mg.co.za/article/2008-11-09-baracks-popularity-balloons.

Bazerman, Charles. 1994. "Systems of Genres and the Enactment of Social Intentions." In *Genre and the New Rhetoric*, edited by Aviva Freedman and Peter Medway, 79–101. London: Taylor & Francis.

Beer, David. 2013. *Popular Culture and New Media: The Politics of Circulation*. New York: Palgrave Macmillion.

Beer, Jeff. 2008. "Shepard Fairey: Obey Obama." *Advertising Age*, January 30. http://adage .com/article/behind-the-work/shepard-fairey-obey-obama/124743/.

Beirut, Michael. 2012. "The Poster That Launched a Movement (or Not)." *Design Observer*, April 30. http://designobserver.com/feature/the-poster-that-launched-a-movement-or-not/32588.

Bender, John B., and David E. Wellbery. 1990. *The Ends of Rhetoric: History, Theory, Practice*. Stanford: Stanford University Press.

Benjamin, Walter. 1968. "The Work of Art in the Age of Mechanical Reproduction." In *Illuminations: Essays and Reflections*, edited by Hannah Arendt. Translated by Harry Zohn, 219–14. New York: Harcourt Brace & World.

Bennett, Jane. 2001. "Commodity Fetishism and Commodity Enchantment." *Theory and Event*. 5 (1): 1–28.

Bennett, Jane. 2010. *Vibrant Matter: A Political Ecology of Things*. Durham, NC: Duke University Press.

Bennett, Jane. 2012. "Systems and Things: A Materialist and an Object-Oriented Philosopher Walk into a Bar." A Plenary Lecture for the Conference on the Nonhuman Turn, Milwaukee, WI, May 4. https://www.youtube.com/watch?v=pYxy-MlypUU.

Bergson, Henri. 2007. *The Creative Mind: An Introduction to Metaphysics*. Mineola, NY: Dover. First published 1946 by The Philosophical Library.

Berkenkotter, Carol, and Thomas N. Huckin. 1995. *Genre Knowledge in Disciplinary Communication: Cognition /Culture/Power*. Hillsdale, NJ: Erlbaum.

Berlin, James. 1996. "Cultural Studies." In *Encyclopedia of Rhetoric and Composition*, edited by Theresa Enos, 154–56. New York: Routledge.

Bhargava, Rohit. 2008. "How Obama's Brand Helped Him to Win the Election." *Rhohit Bhargava* (blog), November 4. http://www.rohitbhargava.com/2008/11/how-obamas -bran.html.

Booth, Wayne. 1974. *Modern Dogma and the Rhetoric of Assent*. Chicago: University of Chicago Press.

Bianchi, Melissa. 2012. "Diagnosing the State of Rhetoric through X-Ray Images." Master's Thesis, University of Florida. http://ufdc.ufl.edu/UFE0044270/00001.

Biesecker, Barbara A. 1989. "Rethinking the Rhetorical Situation from Within Thematic of Difference." *Philosophy & Rhetoric* 22 (2): 110–30.

Binh, Pham. 2012. "Occupy Sees Rebirth of American Radicalism." Anticapitalist Initiative. http://anticapitalists.org/2012/05/11/occupy-rebirth-of-american-radicalism/.

Blackmore, Susan. 1998. "Imitation and the Definition of a Meme." *Journal of Memetics— Evolutionary Models of Information Transmission* vol. 2. http://cfpm.org/jom-emit/1998 /vol2/blackmore_s.html.

Blackmore, Susan. 2000. *The Meme Machine*. New York: Oxford University Press.

Blair, Carole. 1999. "Contemporary U.S. Material Sites as Exemplars of Rhetoric's Materiality." In *Rhetorical Bodies*, edited by Jack Selzer and Sharon Crowley, 15–67. Madison: University of Wisconsin Press.

Bogost, Ian. 2009. "What is Object-Oriented Ontology? A Definition for Ordinary Folk." Bogost.com. December 8. http://bogost.com/writing/blog/what_is_objectoriented_ ontolog/.

Bogost, Ian. 2012. *Alien Phenomenology, or What It's Like to Be a Thing*. Minneapolis: University of Minnesota Press.

Borić, Dušan. 2010. "Becoming, Phenomenal Change, Event: Past and Archaeological Re-presentations." In *Eventful Archaeologies: New Approaches to Social Transformation in the Archaeological Record*, edited by Douglas J. Bolender, 48–67. Albany: SUNY Press.

Booth, William. 2009. "Obama's On-the-Wall Endorsement." *Washington Post*, May 18. http://www.washingtonpost.com/wp-dyn/content/article/2008/05/16/AR2008051601017.html.

Brennan, Teresa. 2004. *The Transmission of Affect*. Ithaca, NY: Cornell University Press.

Brooke, Collin Gifford. 2009. *Lingua Fracta: Toward a Rhetoric of New Media*. Cresskill, NJ: Hampton.

Brooke, Collin. 2015. "Bruno Latour's Posthuman Rhetoric of Assent." In *The Object of Rhetoric: Assembling and Disassembling Bruno Latour*, edited by Paul Lynch and Nathaniel Rivers. Carbondale: Southern Illinois University Press.

Brummett, Barry. 1976. "Some Implications of 'Process' or 'Intersubjectivity': Postmodern Rhetoric." *Philosophy & Rhetoric* 9 (1): 21–51.

Bryant, Levi. 2011. *The Democracy of Objects*. Ann Arbor, MI: Open Humanities Press. http://dx.doi.org/10.3998/ohp.9750134.0001.001.

Burke, Kenneth. 1969. *Grammar of Motives*. Berkley: University of California Press.

Callahan, Maureen. 2008. "Paint Misbehavin' in Team O's 'Street Art.'" *New York Post*, April 24. http://nypost.com/2008/04/24/paint-misbehavin-in-team-os-street-art/.

Callon, Michel, and Bruno Latour. 1981. "Unscrewing the Big Leviathan: How Actors Macro-Structure Reality and How Sociologists Help Them to Do So." In *Advances in Social Theory and Methodology: Towards an Integration of Micro- and Macro-Sociologies*, edited by Karin Knorr-Cetina and Aaron V. Cicourel, 277–303. Boston: Routledge & Kegan Paul.

Campbell, Karlyn Kohrs. 2005. "Agency: Promiscuous and Protean." *Communication and Critical/ Cultural Studies* 2 (1): 1–19.

Carroll, William K., and Robert A. Hackett. 2006. "Democratic Media Activism through the Lens of Social Movement Theory." *Media Culture & Society* 28 (1): 83–104. http://dx.doi.org/10.1177/0163443706059289.

Castells, Manuel. 1996. *The Information Age: Economy, Society, and Culture*. In Vol. 1 of *The Rise of the Network Society*. Malden, MA: Blackwell.

Castells, Manuel. 2009. *Communication Power*. New York: Oxford University Press.

Castells, Manuel. 2012. *Networks of Outrage and Hope: Social Movements in the Internet Age*. Cambridge: Polity.

Charles, Deborah. 2008. "Skinheads Held Over Plot to Kill Obama." *Reuters*, October 28. http://www.reuters.com/article/2008/10/28/us-usa-politics-plot-idUSTRE49Q7KJ20081028.

Citizen LA. n.d. "Shepard Fairey: Obey" CitizenLA. http://citizenla.com/?p=4149.

Clark, Andy. 2008. "Where Brain, Body and World Collide." In *Material Agency: Towards a Non- Anthropocentric Approach*, edited by Carl Knappett and Lambros Malafouris, 1–18. New York: Springer. http://dx.doi.org/10.1007/978-0-387-74711-8_1.

Coble, Margaret. 2009. "Press Release." *The Art of Obama* (blog), June 29. http://www.artofobama.com/2009/01/29/margaret-coble/.

Cohen, Alex. 2008. "What's With That Obama Poster?" *National Public Radio*, April 7. http://www.npr.org/templates/story/story.php?storyId=89431734.

Connors, Will. 2010. "African Brand Is Sweet on Obama." *Wall Street Journal*, October 7. http://online.wsj.com/news/articles/SB10001424052748703843804575534760942191000.

Coole, Diana, and Samantha Frost. 2010. "Introducing the New Materialisms." In *New Materialisms: Ontology, Agency, and Politics*, edited by Diana Coole and Samantha Frost, 1–43. Durham, NC: Duke University Press. http://dx.doi.org/10.1215/9780822392996-001.

Cooper, Marilyn. 1986. "The Ecology of Writing." *College English* 48 (4): 364–75. http://dx.doi.org/10.2307/377264.

Cooper, Marilyn. 2011. "Rhetorical Agency as Emergent and Enacted." *College Composition and Communication* 62 (3): 420–49.

Crick, Nathan. 2010. *Democracy and Rhetoric: John Dewey on the Arts of Becoming*. Columbia: University of South Carolina Press.

Crowley, Sharon. 2006. *Toward a Civil Discourse: Rhetoric and Fundamentalism*. Pittsburgh: University of Pittsburgh Press.

Culture Jammers HQ. 2011. "#OCCUPYWALLSTREET." *Adbusters* (blog), July 13. https://www.adbusters.org/blogs/adbusters-blog/occupywallstreet.html.

Danziger, James. 2009. "The Obama Hope Photo Mystery! Continues." *The Daily Beast* (blog), January 19. http://www.thedailybeast.com/blogs-and-stories/2009-01-19/who-took-the-presidential-campaigns-most-famous-photo.

Davis, Diane. 2010. *Inessential Solidarity: Rhetoric and Foreigner Relations*. Pittsburgh: University of Pittsburgh Press.

Dawkins, Richard. 1989. *The Selfish Gene*. Oxford: Oxford University Press. First published 1976 by Oxford University Press.

Debord, Guy. 2006a. "Theory of the Derive." Bureau of Public Secrets. Previously published in *Situationist International Anthology*, edited and translated by Kenn Knapp. http://www.bopsecrets.org/SI/2.derive.htm.

Debord, Guy. (1955) 2006b. "Introduction to a Critique of Urban Geography." Bureau of Public Secrets. Previously published in *Situationist International Anthology*, edited and translated by Kenn Knapp. http://www.bopsecrets.org/SI/urbgeog.htm.

Dietel-McLaughlin, Erin. 2009. "Remediating Democracy: Irreverent Composition and the Vernacular Rhetorics of Web 2.0." Special 2.0 edition, *Computers and Composition Online*. http://www2.bgsu.edu/departments/english/cconline/Dietel/.

De Landa, Manuel. 2006. *A New Philosophy of Society: Assemblage Theory and Social Complexity*. New York: Continuum.

Deleuze, Gilles. 1994. *Difference and Repetition*. Translated by Paul Patton. New York: Columbia University Press. First published 1968 as Différence et Répétition by Presses Universitaires de France.

Deleuze, Gilles, and Felix Guattari. 1986. *Nomadology: The War Machine*. Translated by Brian Massumi. New York: Semiotext(e).

Deleuze, Gilles, and Felix Guattari. 1987. *A Thousand Plateaus: Capitalism and Schizophrenia*. Translated by Brian Massumi. Minneapolis: University of Minnesota Press.

Delicath, John W., and Kevin Michael DeLuca. 2003. "Image Events, the Public Sphere, and Argumentative Practice: The Case of Radical Environmental Groups." *Argumentation* 17 (3): 315–33. http://dx.doi.org/10.1023/A:1025179019397.

DeLuca, Kevin, and Anne Demo. 2000. "Imaging Nature: Watkins, Yosemite, and the Birth of Environmentalism." *Critical Studies in Communication* 17 (3): 241–60. http://dx.doi.org/10.1080/15295030009388395.

DeLuca, Kevin, and Joe Wilferth. 2009. Forward to *Enculturation* 6 (2). http://enculturation.net/6.2/foreword.

Derrida, Jacques. 2002. "Artifactualities." In *Echographies of Television: Filmed Interviews*, edited by Jacques Derrida and Bernard Stiegler, 1–28. Cambridge: Polity.

DeVoss, Dànielle Nicole, and James Porter. 2006. "Why Napster Matters to Writing: File-sharing as a New Ethic of Digital Delivery." *Computers and Composition* 23 (2): 178–210. http://dx.doi.org/10.1016/j.compcom.2006.02.001.

Dobrin, Sidney I. 2011. *Postcomposition*. Carbondale: Southern Illinois University Press.

Dobrin, Sidney I., and Christina Weisser, eds. 2001. *Ecocomposition: Theoretical and Pedagogical Approaches*. Albany: SUNY Press.

Dolphijn, Rick, and Iris van der Tuin. 2012. "The Transversality of New Materialism." In *New Materialism: Interviews & Cartographies*, 93–114. Ann Arbor, MI: MPublishing.

Edbauer Rice, Jenny. 2005. "Unframing Models of Public Distribution: From Rhetorical Situation to Rhetorical Ecologies." *Rhetoric Society Quarterly* 35 (4): 5–24. http://dx.doi.org/10.1080/02773940509391320.

Edgers, Geoff. 2009. "Shepard the Giant." *Boston Globe*, January 25. http://www.boston.com/ae/theater_arts/articles/2009/01/25/shepard_the_giant/.

Edwards, Janis L., and Carol K. Winkler. 2005. ""Representative Form and the Visual Ideograph: The Iwo Jima Image." In *Readings in Rhetorical Criticism*. 3rd ed.. Edited by Carl R. Burgchardt, 487–508. State College, PA: Strata.

Edward Said on Orientalism. 1998. Directed by Sut Jhally. Northampton, MA: Media Education Foundation.

Efroni, Zohar. 2009. "Copyright Reservations, Anyone?" *The Center for Internet and Society* (blog), April 2. http://cyberlaw.stanford.edu/blog/2009/04/copyright-reservations-anyone.

El Zein, Rayya, and Alex Ortiz. 2011. "Signs of the Times." *Shahadat* (April): 1–37. http://www.arteeast.org/2012/02/21/signs-of-the-times-the-popular-literature-of-tahrir/.

Engeström, Yrjö. 2006. "Values, Rubbish, and Workplace Learning." In *Critical Perspectives on Activity: Explorations Across Education, Work, and Everyday Life*, edited by Peter Sawchuk, Newton Duarte, and Mohamed Elhammoumi, 193–207. Cambridge: Cambridge University Press. http://dx.doi.org/10.1017/CBO9780511509568.011.

Engeström, Yrjö. 2007. "From Communities of Practice to Mycorrhizae." In *Communities of Practice: Critical Perspectives*, edited by Jason Hughes, Nick Jewson, and Lorna Unwin, 41–54. New York: Routledge. http://dx.doi.org/10.4324/NOE0415364737.ch4.

Enough! Gaddafi. n.d. Change.org. https://www.change.org/organizations/enough_gaddafi.

Estee, Mike. 2011. "I Made a Poster." *mike estee* (blog) November 20. http://www.mikeestee.com/blog/2011/11/i-made-a-poster/.

Fairey, Shepard. 1990. "Manifesto." Obey. http://www.obeygiant.com/articles/manifesto.

Fairey, Shepard. 2008. "Obama Ebay Disappointment." Obey Giant Website. http://www.obeygiant.com/headlines/obama-ebay-disappointment.

Fairey, Shepard. 2009a. "Birth of Hope." In *Art for Obama: Designing Manifest Hope and the Campaign for Change*, edited by Shepard Fairey and Jennifer Gross, 7–12. New York: Abrams Image.

Fairey, Shepard. 2009b. *Obey: Supply and Demand: 20th Anniversary Edition*. Berkeley, CA: Gingko.

Fairey, Shepard. 2009c. "Statement by Shepard Fairey on Associated Fair Use Case." Obey. http://www.obeygiant.com/headlines/associated-press-fair-use-case.

Fairey, Shepard. 2011. "Occupy Hope." Obey. http://www.obeygiant.com/headlines/occupy-hope.

Fairey, Shepard. 2012. "I'm Voting for Barack Obama Because I Believe Progress is Possible." *Huffington Post*, October 30. http://www.huffingtonpost.com/shepard-fairey/im-voting-for-barack-obam_b_2045171.html?.

Fairey et al. v. AP. 2009a. "Complaint for Declaratory Judgment and Injunctive Relief." (Civil Action No. 09–01123 (AKH), United States District Court Southern District of New York)." *Filing* 1 (February): 9. http://docs.justia.com/cases/federal/district-courts/new-york/nysdce/1:2009cv01123/340121/1.

Fairey, et al. v. AP. 2009b. "Answer, Affirmative Defenses, and Counterclaims of the Defendant, the Associated Press." (Civil Action No. 09–01123 (AKH)), Filing 13, Feburary 9. http://www.docstoc.com/docs/4817783/Answer_and_Counterclaims_of_Associated_Press-1.

Farber, Dan. 2009. "Neda: An Unintended Symbol." *CBS News*, June 21. http://www.cbsnews.com/news/neda-an-unintended-symbol/.

Finnegan, Cara. 2003. *Picturing Poverty: Print Culture and FSA Photographs*. Washington, DC: Smithsonian Books.

Finnegan, Cara. 2010. "Studying Visual Modes of Public Address." In *The Handbook of Rhetoric and Public Address*, edited by Shawn Parry-Giles and J. Michael Hogan, 250–70. Malden, MA: Wiley-Blackwell. http://dx.doi.org/10.1002/9781444324105.ch10.

Fisher, William W., III, Frank Cost, Shepard Fairey, Meir Feder, Edwin Fountain, Geoffrey Stewart, and Marta Sturken. 2012. "Reflections on the Hope Poster Case." *Harvard Journal of Law and Technology* 25 (12): 243–338.

Fitzgerald, Scott. 2012. "The Occupy Wall St Movement—January 17, 2012 'Occupy Congress.'" *American Autumn: A Report from the Frontline* (blog), February 4. http://americanautumnrevolution-sfitzgerald.blogspot.com/2012/02/occupy-wall-st-movement-january-17-2012.html.

Fleck, Ludwik. 1979. *Genesis and Development of a Scientific Fact.* Chicago: University of Chicago Press.

Fleckenstein, Kristie S., Sue Hum, and Linda T. Calendrillo. 2007. *Ways of Seeing, Ways of Speaking: The Integration of Rhetoric and Vision in Constructing the Real.* Anderson, SC: Parlor.

Fleckenstein, Kristie S., Clay Spinuzzi, Rebecca J. Rickly, and Carole Clark Papper. 2008. "The Importance of Harmony: An Ecological Metaphor for Writing Research." *College Composition and Communication* 60 (1): 388–419.

Fleming, Andrew. 2011. "Adbusters Sparks Wall Street Protest." *Vancouver Courier*, September 27. http://www.vancourier.com/news/adbusters-sparks-wall-street-protest-1.374299.

Fleming, David. 2003. "Becoming Rhetorical: An Education in the Topics." In *The Realms of Rhetoric: Inquiries into the Prospects for Rhetoric Education*, edited by Deepika Bahri and Joseph Petraglia, 93–116. Albany: State University of New York Press.

Frazier, Eric G. 2009. Comment on Allicia, "Manny Garcia's Obama Photograph." *Evilmonito*, January 26. http://evilmonito.com/2009/01/26/manny-garcias-obama-photograph/.

Free Republic. n.d. "About." Free Republic. http://www.freerepublic.com/home.htm.

"Free Victory Stickers by Shepard Fairey." 2008. *The Art of Obama Blog.* November 7. http://www.artofobama.com/2008/11/07/free-victory-stickers-by-shepard-fairey/.

Gambino, Megan. 2009. "Shepard Fairey: The Artist Behind the Obama Portrait." Smithsonian.com.http://www.smithsonianmag.com/ist/?next=/arts-culture/Shepard-Fairey-The-Artist-Behind-the-Obama-Portrait.html.

Gardner, Amy. 2012. "Obama Hangs with Clooney in L.A." *Washington Post*, May 11. http://www.washingtonpost.com/blogs/post-politics/post/obama-hangs-with-clooney-inla/2012/05/11/gIQABH0DHU_blog.html.

Gibbs, Garron. 2013. "The Influential: Tayyib Smith of 215 Magazine." *Concrete Cakes* (blog). http://www.concretecakes.com/tayyib-smith-215-magazine/.

Gladstone, Brooke. 2012. Preface to *Presidential Campaign Posters*, by the Library of Congress. Philadelphia: Quirk Books.

Gladwell, Malcom. 2002. *The Tipping Point: How Little Things Can Make a Big Difference.* New York: Back Bay Books.

Glenn, Cheryl. 1995. "Remapping Rhetorical Territory." *Rhetoric Review* 13 (2): 287–303. http://dx.doi.org/10.1080/07350199509359188.

Goggin, Maureen. 2004. "Visual Rhetorics in Pens of Steel and Inks of Silk: Challenging the Great Visual/Verbal Divide." In *Defining Visual Rhetoric*, edited by Charles Hill and Marguerite Helmers, 87–110. Mahwah: Erlbaum.

Gralish, Tom. 2008. "That's My Picture! (Not)." *Scene on the Road* (blog), December 22. http://blogs.phillynews.com/inquirer/sceneonroad/obama_poster_photo_mystery/ (site discontinued).

Gralish, Tom. 2009a. "A Last Word—Hopefully—and Updates on the Obama Poster Photo Mystery." *Scene on the Road* (blog). http://blogs.phillynews.com/inquirer/sceneonroad/2009/01/a_last_word_hopefully_and_upda_1.html (accessed May 15, 2009; site discontinued).

Gralish, Tom. 2009b. "MYSTERY SOLVED! The Obama Poster Photographer ID'd." *Scene on the Road* (blog), January 14. http://blogs.phillynews.com/inquirer/sceneonroad/2009/01/mystery_solved_the_obama_poste.html (site discontinued).

Gries, Laurie. 2011. "Agential Matters: Tumbleweed, Women-Pens, Citizens-Hope, and Rhetorical Actancy." In *Ecology, Writing Theory, and New Media: Writing Ecology*, edited by Sidney Dobrin, 67–91. New York: Routledge.

Gross, Jennifer, Yosi Sergant, and Megan Rollins. 2009. "The Evolution of a Revolution." In *Art for Obama: Designing Manifest Hope and the Campaign for Change*, edited by Shepard Fairey and Jennifer Gross. New York: Abrams Image.

Gross, Terry. 2009. "Shepard Fairey: Inspiration or Infringement." *National Public Radio*, February 26. http://www.npr.org/templates/transcript/transcript.php?storyId=101182453.

Grosz, Elizabeth. 1999. "Thinking the New: Of Futures Yet Unthought." In *Becomings: Explorations in Time, Memory, and Futures*, edited by Elizabeth Grosz, 15–28. Ithaca, NY: Cornell University Press.

Gunkel, David J. 2009. "Beyond Mediation: Thinking the Computer Otherwise." *Interactions: Studies in Communication and Culture* 1 (1): 53–70.

Gyori, Bradford. 2013. "Naming Neda: Digital Discourse and the Rhetorics of Association." *Journal of Broadcasting & Electronic Media* 57 (4): 482–503. http://dx.doi.org/10.1080/08838151.2013.845826.

Hannity, Sean. 2010. "Waking up the 'Obama Zombies.'" *Fox News*, March 26. http://www.foxnews.com/story/2010/03/26/waking-up-obama-zombies/.

Haraway, Donna. 2003. *The Companion Species Manifesto: Dogs, People, and Significant Otherness*. Chicago: Prickly Paradigm.

Hariman, Robert, and John Louis Lucaites. 2007. *No Caption Needed: Iconic Photographs, Public Culture, and Liberal Democracy*. Chicago: University of Chicago Press.

Harman, Graham. 2011. *The Quadruple Object*. Winchester, UK: Zero Books.

Harrington, John. 2009. "10 Questions for Mannie Garcia." *Photo Business News and Forum* (blog), February 5. http://photobusinessforum.blogspot.ca/2009/02/10-questions-for-mannie-garcia.html.

Hardt, Michael, and Antonio Negri. 2005. *Multitude: War and Democracy in the Age of Empire*. New York: Penguin Books.

Hawk, Byron. 2011. "Curating Ecologies, Circulating Musics: From the Public Sphere to Sphere Publics." In *Ecology, Writing Theory, and New Media: Writing Ecology*, edited by Sidney Dobrin, 160–79. New York: Routledge.

Hawk, Byron. 2007. *A Counter-History of Composition: Toward Methodologies of Complexity*. Pittsburgh: University of Pittsburgh Press.

Hekman, Susan. 2010. *The Material of Knowledge: Feminist Disclosures*. Bloomington: Indiana University Press.

Heller, Steven. 2008a. "Beyond Red, White, and Blue." *Campaign Stops* (blog), *New York Times*. http://campaignstops.blogs.nytimes.com/tag/shepard-fairey/.

Heller, Steven. 2008b. "This Election's Poster Child." *Campaign Stops* (blog), *New York Times*. http://campaignstops.blogs.nytimes.com/2008/10/21/this-elections-poster-child/.

Heller, Steven. 2009. *Design for Obama, Posters for Change: A Grassroots Anthology*, edited by Steven Heller, Aaron Perry-Zucker and Spike Lee. Cologne, Germany: Taschen.

Herndl, Carl G. 2012. "Rhetoric and the New Materialism." A Paper presented at the 15th Biennial Rhetoric Society of America Conference, Philadelphia, PA, May.

Herndl, Carl G., and Adela C. Licona. 2007. "Shifting Agency: Agency, Kairos, and the Possibilities of Social Action." In *Communicative Practices in Workplaces and Professions: Cultural Perspectives on the Regulation of Discourse and Organizations*, edited by Mark Zachry and Charlotte Thralls, 133–154. New York: Baywood.

Hertz, Rebecca. 2010. "Obama Jokerface is an FSU Original." *The Yeti*, 2 (December): 5. http://issuu.com/theyeti/docs/theyeti_december/4.

Hodgson, Justin. 2010. "Reculturalizations: 'Small Screen' Culture, Pedagogy, & YouTube." *Enculturation* 8. http://www.enculturation.net/reculturalizations.

Holding, Cory. 2007. "Review Essay: Affecting Rhetoric." *College Composition and Communication* 59 (2): 317–29.

Horkheimer, Max, and Theodor W. Adorno. 1972. *Dialectic of Enlightenment*. Translated by John Cumming. New York: Herder and Herder.

"How Obama Used Social Networking Tools to Win." 2009. *INSEAD Knowledge.* July 10. http://knowledge.insead.edu/innovation/how-obama-used-social-networking-tools-to-win-1600.

Hum, Sue. 1996. "Semiotics." In *Encyclopedia of Rhetoric and Composition*, edited by Theresa Enos, 666–68. New York: Routledge.

Hutchison, David. 2010. "Yes We Cannibal," *President Evil.* Issue 4. January 27. Antarctic Press.

Jaffe, Sarah. 2009. "Superhero President: the Commodification of Barack Obama." *GlobalComment.com*, January 13. http://globalcomment.com/superhero-president-the-commodification-of-barack-obama/#.

Jenkins, Henry, Ravi Purushotma, Margaret Weigel, Katie Clinton, and Alice L. Robison. 2006. *Confronting the Challenges of Participatory Culture: Media Education for the 21st Century.* Chicago: MacArthur Foundation.

Jenkins, Henry. 2009. "Quentin Tarantino's Star Wars?: Digital Cinema, Media Convergence, and Participatory Culture." Henry Jenkins Publications. http://web.mit.edu/21fms/People/henry3/starwars.html

Jenkins, Henry, Sam Ford, and Joshua Green. 2013. *Spreadable Media: Creating Value and Meaning in a Networked Culture.* New York: NYU Press.

Johnson, Lynne. 2009. "Should Art Be Outlawed if It's Remixed, Mashed-Up, or Sampled?" *Fast Company* (blog), February 27. http://www.fastcodesign.com/1191678/should-art-be-outlawed-if-its-remixed-mashed-up-or-sampled.

Johnson-Eilola, Johndan, and Stuart A. Selber. 2007. "Plagiarism, Originality, Assemblage." *Computers and Composition* 24: 375–403.

Johnston, Mark. 2009. "James Danziger Finds the Source of 'HOPE'." *The Online Photographer* (blog), January 20. http://theonlinephotographer.typepad.com/the_online_photographer/2009/01/james-danzinger-finds-the-source-of-hope.html

Kaelan, James. 2009. "Popaganda: The Obama Hope Poster." Flatmancrooked. http://theliteraryunderground.org/flatmancrooked/?p=938.

Katyal, Sonia, and Eduardo Penalver. 2010. "Introducing the Atlaw: The Shepard Fairey Obama 'Hope' Poster Controversy." Findlaw.http://writ.news.findlaw.com/commentary/20100324_katyal_penalver.html.

Kitchen, Rob, and Martin Dodge. 2014. *Code/Space: Software and Everyday Life.* Cambridge, MA: MIT Press.

Kobre, Kenneth. 2012. *Videojournalism: Multimedia Storytelling.* Waltham, MA: Focal.

Koga. 2008. "Barack Obama-rama W/ Wolfkin, The Polyamorous Affair, Electrocute, Willoughby, The Bird & The Bee, Hard Place, and The Lady Tigra @ Spaceland, 9/23/08." LAist: Los Angeles News, Food, Arts & Events. http://laist.com/2008/10/02/wolfkin_the_polyamorous_affair_electrocute_willoughby_the_bird_and_the_bee_hard_place_the_lady_tigra.php#photo-1.

Krause, Stephen. 1996. "The Immediacy of Rhetoric: Definitions, Illustrations, and Implications." PhD diss., Michigan State University. http://people.emich.edu/skrause/Diss/.

Kuhn, Virginia. 2012. "The Rhetoric of Remix." In "Fan/Remix Video," edited by Francesca Coppa and Julie Levin Russo, special issue, *Transformative Works and Culture* 9. http://journal.transformativeworks.org/index.php/twc/article/view/358/279.

L'Eplattenier, Barbara. 2009. "An Argument for Archival Research Methods: Thinking Beyond Methodology." *College English* 72 (1): 67–79.

Lachnit, January. 2009. "Can We Stop It?" *mind-funk.de* (blog), May 21. http://www.mind-funk.de/index.php/random-jazz/can-we-stop-it/.

Latour, Bruno. 1993. *We Have Never Been Modern.* Cambridge: Harvard University Press.

Latour, Bruno. 1996. "On Actor Network Theory: A Few Clarifications plus More than a Few Complications." *Soziale Welt* 47: 369–381.

Latour, Bruno. 1999. *Pandora's Hope: Essays on the Reality of Science Studies.* Cambridge: Harvard University Press.

Latour, Bruno. 2004. "Why Has Critique Run out of Steam? From Matters of Fact to Matters of Concern." In *Things*, edited by Bill Brown, 151–73. Chicago: University of Chicago Press. http://dx.doi.org/10.1086/421123.

Latour, Bruno. 2005a. "From Realpolitik to Dingpolitik—An Introduction to Making Things Public." In *Making Things Public: Atmospheres of Democracy*, edited by Bruno Latour and Peter Weibel, 14–41. Cambridge: MIT Press.

Latour, Bruno. 2005b. *Reassembling the Social*. New York: Oxford University Press.

Latour, Bruno, and Albena Yaneva. 2008. "Give Me a Gun and I Will Make All Buildings Move: An ANT'S View of Architecture." In *Explorations in Architecture: Teaching, Design, Research*, edited by Reto Geiser, 80–89. Basel: Birkhäuser.

Lavin, Chad, and Chris Russill. 2010. "The Ideology of the Epidemic." *New Political Science* 32 (1): 65–82. http://dx.doi.org/10.1080/07393140903492142.

Law, John. 2005. *After Method: Mess in Social Science Research*. London: Routledge.

Lefebvre, Henri. 1991. *The Production of Space*. Translated by Donald Nicholson-Smith. Malden: Blackwell.

Leopold, Wendy. 2010. "Africa Embracing Obama." Northwestern University.. http://www.northwestern.edu/newscenter/stories/2010/11/obama-exhibit.html.

Leopold, Wendy. 2009. "Obama Collectibles from Africa on Display and in Scholarly Collection." Northwestern University. http://www.northwestern.edu/newscenter/stories/2009/01/obamacollection.html.

Lerer, Lisa. 2008. "Obamamania Verges on Obsession." *Politico.com*. February 20. http://www.politico.com/news/stories/0208/8605.html.

Lessig, Lawrence. 2004. *Free Culture: How Big Media Uses Technology and the Law to Lock Down Culture and Control Creativity*. New York: Penguin.

Lessig, Lawrence. 2008. *Remix: Making Art and Commerce Thrive in the Hybrid Economy*. New York: Penguin. http://dx.doi.org/10.5040/9781849662505.

Lewis, Christina. 2008. "Picturing Obama" *Wall Street Journal*, July 17. http://online.wsj.com/news/articles/SB121625710569060513?mod=tff_main_tff_top.

Liberalart. 2008. Comment on Pescovitz, "Shepard Fairey's Obama Poster." *Boinboing* (blog), February, 1. http://boingboing.net/2008/01/31/shepard-faireys-obam.html#comment-116468.

Lucaites, John Louis, and Celeste Michelle Condit. 1999. "Epilogue: Contributions from Rhetorical Theory." In *Contemporary Rhetorical Theory: A Reader*, edited by John Louis Lucaites, Celeste Michelle Condit, and Sally Caudill, 609–13. New York: Guilford.

Madhani, Aamer. 2010. "Famed Obama 'Hope' Poster Artist Losing Hope." *Common Dreams*, September 25. https://www.commondreams.org/headline/2010/09/25-3.

Magee, Joan R. 2009. "Obamicon Me!" *Upstart Business Journal*, January 28. http://upstart.bizjournals.com/news/wire/2009/01/28/obamicon-me.html?page=all.

Mailloux, Steven. 2006. "Places in Time: The Inns and Outhouses of Rhetoric." *Quarterly Journal of Speech* 92 (1): 53–68. http://dx.doi.org/10.1080/00335630600696868.

Malafouris, Lambros. 2008. "At the Potter's Wheel: An Argument for Material Agency." In *Material Agency: Towards a Non-Anthropocentric Approach*, edited by Carl Knappett and Lambros Malafouris, 19–36. New York: Springer. http://dx.doi.org/10.1007/978-0-387-74711-8_2.

Malooley, Jake. 2008. "Barackonomics: Local Businesses Hop on the Change Train to Profitsville." Time Out Chicago. http://chicago.timeout.com/articles/shopping/42441/barackonomics (site discontinued).

Manovich, Lev. 2001. *The Language of New Media*. Cambridge: MIT Press.

Marback, Richard. 2008. "Unclenching the Fist: Embodying Rhetoric and Giving Objects Their Due." *Rhetoric Society Quarterly* 38 (1): 46–65. http://dx.doi.org/10.1080/02773940701779751.++

Massumi, Brian. 2002. *Parables for the Virtual: Movement, Affect, Sensation*. Durham, NC: Duke University Press. http://dx.doi.org/10.1215/9780822383574.

Mattera, Jason. 2010. *Obama Zombies: How the Liberal Machine Brainwashed my Generation*. New York: Threshold Editions.

Maxwell, Kerry. 2008. "Definition of Obamamania." *Macmillan Dictionary*, November 13. http://www.macmillandictionary.com/us/buzzword/entries/obamamania.html.

McCorkle, Ben. 2009. "The Annotated Obama Poster." *Harlot: A Revealing Look at the Arts of Persuasion* 2. http://harlotofthearts.org/index.php/harlot/article/view/29/18.

McCorkle, Ben. 2012. *Rhetorical Delivery as Technological Discourse: A Cross-Historical Study*. Carbondale: Southern Illinois Press.

McDonald, Seven. 2009. "Yosi Sergant and the Art of Change: The Publicist Behind Shepard Fairey's Obama Hope Posters." *LA Weekly*, September, 11. http://www.laweekly.com/2008-09-11/columns/yosi-sergant-and-the-art-of-change-the-publicist-behind-shepard-fairey-39-s-obama-hope-posters/.

McDonnell, Evelyn. 2010. "Never Mind the Bollucks: Shepard Fairey's Fight for Appropriation, Fair Use, and Free Culture." *Confessions of an Aca-Fan* (blog), January 13. http://henryjenkins.org/2010/01/never_mind.html.

McGirt, Ellen. 2008. "The Brand Called Obama." *Fast Company*, April 1. http://www.fastcompany.com/754505/brand-called-obama

McLeod, Sonya. 2009. "(Swine) Flu Vaccine and Treatment Is Not Safe or Effective." *Homeopathy Vancouver BC* (blog), August 17. http://littlemountainhomeopathy.wordpress.com/2009/08/17/swine-flu-vaccine-and-treatment-is-not-safe-or-effective/.

Meikle, Graham. 2002. *Future Active: Media Activism and the Internet*. New York: Routledge.

Miguel, Renay San. 2012. "Social Media Company Sodahead: Politics, People Power Opinions." *Splashmedia*, January 6. http://wayvs.com/2012/01/06/social-media-company-sodahead-politics-people-power-opinions/.

Miller, Carolyn. 1984. "Genre as Social Action." *Quarterly Journal of Speech* 70 (2): 151–67. http://dx.doi.org/10.1080/00335638409383686.

Miller, Carolyn. 2007. "What Can Automation Tell Us About Agency?" *Rhetoric Society Quarterly* 37 (2): 137–57. http://dx.doi.org/10.1080/02773940601021197.

Mitchell, W.J.T. 2005. *What do Pictures Want?: The Lives and Loves of Images*. Chicago: University of Chicago Press.

Mitchell, W.J.T. 2009. "Four Fundamental Concepts of Image Science." In *Visual Literacy*, edited by James Elkins, 14–30. London: Routledge.

Mol, Annemarie. 2002. *The Body Multiple: Ontology in Medical Practice*. Durham, NC: Duke University Press. http://dx.doi.org/10.1215/9780822384151.

Motisbeard. 2008. Comment on Pescovitz, "Shepard Fairey's Obama Poster." *Boinboing* (blog), February, 1. http://boingboing.net/2008/01/31/shepard-faireys-obam.html#comment-116399.

Moraitis, Jason. 2009. "Zombama is Hungry!" Pop-Monkey Stuff. 3 Jan. Accessed online Sept. 10, 2014.

Moretti, Franco. 2007. *Graphs, Maps, Trees*. London: Verso.

Morton, Timothy. 2012. *The Ecological Thought*. Cambridge, MA: Harvard University Press.

Mountford, Roxanne. 2001. "On Gender and Rhetorical Space." *College Composition and Communication* 31 (1): 41–71.

MoveOn. 2010. *People-Powered Politics 2008: Post-Election Report*. http://s3.moveon.org/pdfs/moveon_postelectionreport_ah14.pdf.

MoveOn.org. 2008. "Yes We Did—Victory! by Shephard Fairey." https://pol.moveon.org/shepstickers/leposters.html.

Nahon, Karine, and Jeff Hemsley. 2013. *Going Viral*. Cambridge, United Kingdom: Polity Press.

Nakasone, Marisa. 2008. "Ken Harman Hashimoto of the Obama Art Report." *Examiner.com*, October 30. http://www.examiner.com/x-533-SF-Art-Examiner~y2008m10d30-Ken-Harman-Hashimoto-of-The-Obama-Art-Report.

Napier, James. 2008. *Western Scottish Folklore and Superstitions*. Maple Shade, NJ: Lethe Press.

Nasr, Octavia. 2009. "Tear Gas and Twitter: Iranians Take Their Protests Online." CNN, June 15. http://www.cnn.com/2009/WORLD/meast/06/14/iran.protests.twitter/index .html?iref=allsearch.

Navas, Eduardo. 2012. *Remix Theory: The Aesthetics of Sampling.* New York: Springer-Verlag/ Wein. http://dx.doi.org/10.1007/978-3-7091-1263-2.

Noland, Ray. 2009. "About." GoTellMama! http://gotellmama.org/?About.

"NPG Acquires Shepard Fairey's Portrait of Barack Obama." 2009. Face to Face (blog), January 7. http://face2face.si.edu/my_weblog/2009/01/npg-acquires-shepard-faireys- portrait-of-barack-obama.html.

"Obama: In Big Pharma's Pocket." 2009. *First In* (blog), August 14. http://firstin.wordpress .com/?s=big+pharma.

"Obama Inspires Art, Again." 2008. *Paper Magazine*, April 25. http://www.papermag. com/2008/04/obama_inspires_art_again.php.

NYC General Assembly. 2011. "Statement of Autonomy." New York General Assembly. #Occ- upy Wall Street. http://www.nycga.net/resources/documents/statement-of-autonomy/.

Okong'o, Edwin. 2008. "Obama: The Kenya Connection." *Frontline/World*, January 25. http://www.pbs.org/frontlineworld/blog/2008/01/the_kenya_conne.html.

Olson, Lester C. 2004. *Benjamin Franklin's Vision of American Community: A Study in Rhetorical Iconology.* Columbia: University of South Carolina Press.

Overbeck, Wayne, and Genelle Belmas. 2012. *Major Principles of Media Law.* Boston: Cen- gage Learning.

Packham, Catherine. 2012. *Eighteenth-Century Vitalism: Bodies, Culture, and Politics.* New York: Palgrave. http://dx.doi.org/10.1057/9780230368392.

Pariser, Eli. 2011. *The Filter Bubble: What the Internet Is Hiding from You.* New York: Penguin.

Pescovitz, David. 2008. "Shepard Fairey's Obama Poster." *Boingboing* (blog), January 31. http://boingboing.net/2008/01/31/shepard-faireys-obam.html.

Pickering, Andrew. 1995. *The Mangle of Practice: Time, Agency, and Science.* Chicago: University of Chicago Press. http://dx.doi.org/10.7208/chicago/9780226668253.001.0001.

Phelps, Louise Wetherbee. 1985. "Rhythm and Pattern in a Composing Life." In Vol. 1 of *Writers on Writing*, edited by T. Waldrep, 241–57. New York: Random House.

Phelps, Louise Wetherbee. 1988. *Composition as a Human Science: Contributions to the Self- Understanding of a Discipline.* Oxford: Oxford University Press.

Phelps, Louise Wetherbee. 2003. "How We Take Responsibility for Inquiry: An Account of Accountability." Paper presented at the Conference on College Composition and Communication, March, New York City.

Phelps, Louise Wetherbee. 2011. "The Method in Theory: Reconstructing a Tradition of Theoretical/Philosophical Inquiry for International Writing Studies." Paper presented at the Writing Research Across Borders II Conference, February, Fairfax, VA.

Phillips, Whitney. 2012. "What an Academic Who Wrote Her Dissertation on Trolls Thinks of Violentacrez." *Atlantic*, October 15. http://www.theatlantic.com/technology /archive/2012/10/what-an-academic-who-wrote-her-dissertation-on-trolls-thinks-of -violentacrez/263631/.

Pinney, Christopher. 2005. "Things Happen: Or, From Which Moment Does That Object Come?" In *Materiality*, edited by Daniel Miller, 256–72. Durham, NC: Duke University Press. http://dx.doi.org/10.1215/9780822386711-011.

Porter, James. 2009. "Recovering Delivery for Digital Rhetoric." *Computers and Composition* 26 (4): 207–24. http://dx.doi.org/10.1016/j.compcom.2009.09.004.

Porter, Kevin J. 2006. *Meaning, Language, and Time: Toward a Consequentialist Philosophy of Discourse.* West Fayette, IN: Parlor.

"Power of Art." 2011. *Toward a Moral Life* (blog), December 13. http://givesgoodemail.com /2011/12/13/the-power-of-art/.

Prior, Paul, Janine Solberg, Patrick Berry, Hannah Bellwoar, Bill Chewning, Karen J. Lunsford, Liz Rohan, Kevin Roozen, Mary P. Sheridan-Rabideau, Jody Shipka, et al.

2007. "Re-situating and Re-mediating the Canons: A Cultural-Historical Remapping of Rhetorical Activity: A Collaborative Webtext." *Kairos: A Journal of Rhetoric, Technology, and Pedagogy* 11 (3). http://kairos.technorhetoric.net/11.3/topoi/prior-et-al/.

Prior, Paul, and Jody Shipka. 2003. "Chronotopic Lamination: Tracing the Contours of Literate Activity." In *Writing Selves/Writing Societies*, edited by Charles Bazerman and David R. Russell, 180–238. Fort Collins, CO: WAC Clearinghouse.

Propen, Amy. 2012. *Locating Visual-Material Rhetorics: The Map, the Mill, and the GPS.* Anderson, SC: Parlor.

Queen, Mary. 2008. "Transnational Feminist Rhetorics in a Digital World." *College English* 70 (5): 471–89.

Reid, Alex. 2012. "What is Object-Oriented Rhetoric?" *Intineration.*

Reynolds, Nedra. 1993. "'Ethos' as Location: New Sites for Understanding Discursive Authority." *Rhetoric Review* 11 (2): 325–38. http://dx.doi.org/10.1080/07350199309389009.

Rice, Jeff. 2011. "Noetic Writing: Plato Comes to Missouri." *Composition Studies* 39 (2): 9–28.

Ridolfo, Jim, and Dànielle Nicole DeVoss. 2009. "Composing for Recomposition: Rhetorical Velocity and Delivery." *Kairos: A Journal of Rhetoric, Technology, and Pedagogy* 13 (2). http://kairos.technorhetoric.net/13.2/topoi/ridolfo_devoss/intro.html.

Ritchie, Abraham. 2011. "Art and the Revolutions in the Middle East." *Chicago Art Blog*, February 23. http://www.chicagonow.com/chicago-art-blog/2011/02/art-and-the-revolutions-in-the-middle-east/#image/1.

Rivers, Nathaniel. 2014. "Tracing the Missing Masses: Vibrancy, Symmetry and Public Rhetoric Pedagogy." *Enculturation* (17).

Rod, Magda. 2010. "Obamarama." *Magda Rod's Photos.* Facebook, May 28. http://www.facebook.com/album.php?aid=7812&id=1311327192 (site discontinued).

Rodrigue, Tanya K. 2013. "An Interview with Louise Wetherbee Phelps." *Composition Forum*, 27 (Spring).

Rose, Frank. 2009. "Hope and Theft." *Deep Media* (blog), February 28. http://www.deepmediaonline.com/deepmedia/copyright/.

Rosenfeld, Shelly. 2011. "A Photo Finish? Copyright and Shepard Fairey's Use of a News Photo Image of the President." *Vermont Law Review* 36: 355–372.

Ruffin, Casanova. 2010. "For the Record: Tayyib Smith." *The Steel Closet* (blog), February 12. http://steelcloset.com/2010/02/12/for-the-record-tayyib-smith/.

"Rush Limbaugh says Obama is Arab, 'not Black.'" 2008. *Undercover Black Man* (blog), September 23. http://undercoverblackman.blogspot.ca/2008/09/rush-limbaugh-says-obama-is-arab-not.html.

Rushkoff, Douglas. 1996. *Media Virus: Hidden Agendas in Popular Culture.* New York: Ballantine Books.

Sampson, Tony D. 2012. *Virality: Contagion Theory in the Age of Networks.* Minneapolis: University of Minnesota Press.

Sanchez, Raul. 2006. *The Function of Theory in Composition Studies.* Albany: SUNY Press.

Sanchez, Raul. 2012. "Outside the Text: Retheorizing Empiricism and Identity." *College English* 74 (3): 234–46.

Sassoon, Donald. 2001. *Becoming Mona Lisa: The Making of a Global Icon.* Boston: Houghton Mifflin Harcourt.

Schell, Eileen. 2012. "Materializing the Material as a Progressive Research Method and Methodology." In *Practicing Research in Writing Studies: Reflexive and Ethically Responsible Research*, edited by Katrina M. Powell and Pamela Takayoshi, 123–42. Cresskill, NJ: Hampton.

Schjeldahl, Peter. 2009. "Hope and Glory: A Shepard Fairey Moment." *New Yorker.com*, February 23. http://www.newyorker.com/magazine/2009/02/23/hope-and-glory.

Schuessler, Jennifer. 2009. "Steal This Blog Post!" *ArtsBeats* (blog), February 27. http://artsbeat.blogs.nytimes.com//2009/02/27/steal-this-blog-post/.

Scollon, Ronald, and Suzanne B. K. Scollon. 2003. *Discourses in Place: Language in the Material World*. London: Routledge. http://dx.doi.org/10.4324/9780203422724.

Seas, Kristen. 2012. "Writing Ecologies, Rhetorical Epidemics." In *Ecology, Writing Theory, and New Media: Writing Ecology*, edited by Sidney Dobrin, 51–66. New York: Routledge.

Seemel, Gwenn. 2009. "Shepherding in a New Era." *Face Making* (blog), January 18. http://www.gwennseemel.com/index.php/blog/comments/shepherding_in_a_new _era/.

Shapiro, Ari. 2010. "Brand Obama: A Hit Abroad, But What about Loyalty?" *National Public Radio*, April 6. http://www.npr.org/templates/story/story.php?storyId=125627650.

Shaviro, Steven. 2009. *Without Criteria*. Cambridge: MIT Press.

Shaviro, Steven. "Kant, Deleuze, and the Virtual." 2007. *The Pinnochio Theory* (blog). May 9. http://www.shaviro.com/Blog/?p=577.

Sheller, Mimi. 2011. "Mobility." In *Socialpedia*. http://www.sagepub.net/isa/resources /pdf/Mobility.pdf

Sheperd, Michael, and Carolyn Watters. 1998. "The Evolution of Cybergenres" in *Proceedings of the Thirty-First Annual Hawaii International Conference on System Sciences*, 97–109. http://dx.doi.org/10.1109/HICSS.1998.651688.

Sherwin, Brian. 2009. "Was Shepard Fairey's Obama Posters Officially Endorsed by the Obama Campaign or Not?" *My Art Space* (blog), May 5. http://myartspace-blog.blog spot.com/2009/02/was-shepard-faireys-obama-posters.html.

Skordili, Beatrice. 2001. "Peregrination." In *Encyclopedia of Postmodernism*, edited by Victor E. Taylor and Charles E. Vinquist, 277–78. London: Routledge.

Sloane, Thomas, ed. 2001. "Constitutive Rhetoric." In *Encyclopedia of Rhetoric*. New York: Oxford University Press.

"Smears 2.0." 2007. *Los Angeles Times*, December 3. http://articles.latimes.com/2007/dec /03/opinion/ed-obama3.

Spinuzzi, Clay. 2003. *Tracing Genres through Organizations: A Sociocultural Approach to Information Design*. Cambridge: MIT Press.

Spinuzzi, Clay. 2011. "Losing by Expanding: Corralling the Runaway Object." *Journal of Business and Technical Communication* 25 (4): 449–86. http://dx.doi.org/10.1177/1050 651911411040.

Stafford, Barbara Maria. 1998. *Good Looking: Essays on the Virtue of Images*. Cambridge: MIT Press.

Stanford University Libraries and Academic Information Resources. 2010. " Fair Use." Stanford Copyright & Fair Use Center. http://fairuse.stanford.edu/Copyright_and_ Fair_Use_Overview/chapter9/.

Stein, Laura, Tanya Notley, and Stuart Davis. 2012. "Transnational Networking and Capacity Building for Communication Activism." Australian edition, *Global Media Journal* 6 (2). http://www.hca.uws.edu.au/gmjau/archive/v6_2012_2/stein_notley_davis_RA.html.

Stein, Sam, and Arthur Delaney. 2013. "IRS Official: White House Was Not Involved in Targeting of Conservative Groups" *Huffington Post*, June 18. http://www.huffington post.com/2013/06/18/irs-scandal-washington_n_3460904.html.

Stepanek, Marcia. 2009. "Remix Culture." *Stanford Social Innovation* (blog), March 6. http://csi.gsb.stanford.edu/remix-culture.

Stuckey, Mary E. 2012. "On Rhetorical Circulation." *Rhetoric & Public Affairs* 15 (4): 609–12.

Sullivan, Andrew. 2008a. "Face of the Day." *The Dish*, (blog). November 30. http://dish .andrewsullivan.com/2008/11/30/face-of-the-25/.

Sullivan, Maureen. 2008b. "Street Art Got Cred!" *Red Arts Project*, September 2008. http:// www.redartprojects.com/blogs/Shephard%20Fairey.doc.

Sullivan, Patricia, and James E. Porter. 1997. *Opening Spaces: Writing Technologies and Critical Research Practices*. Greenwich, CT: Ablex.

Seemel, Gwenn. 2009. "Shepherding in a New Era." *Face Making* (blog), January 18. http:// www.gwennseemel.com/index.php/blog/comments/shepherding_in_a_new_era/.

Syverson, Margaret A. 1999. *The Wealth of Reality: An Ecology of Composition.* Carbondale: Southern Illinois University Press.

Talbot, David. 2008. "How Obama *Really* Did It: The Social-Networking Strategy that Took an Obscure Senator to the Doors of the White House." *MIT Technology Review,* August 19. http://www.technologyreview.com/featuredstory/410644/how-obama-really-did-it/.

Tampio, Nicholas. 2010. "Multiplicity." In Vol. 2 of *Encyclopedia of Political Theory,* edited by Mark Jevir, 911–12. Thousand Oaks, CA: Sage. http://dx.doi.org/10.4135/97814 12958660.n294.

Terranova, Tiziana. 2004. *Networked Culture: Politics for the Information Age.* Ann Arbor, MI: Pluto.

Thomas, Scott. 2010. "Design and Politics: A Conversation with Scott Thomas." A Live Conversation Hosted by VizThink, July 27. http://graphicfacilitation.blogs.com/pages/2010/07/vizthink-conversation-with-scott-thomas.htm.

Tianen, Milla, and Jussi Parikka. 2010. "What is New Materialism?" Opening Words to New Materialisms and Digital Culture Symposium, Cambridge, UK, June. http://jussi parikka.net/2010/06/23/what-is-new-materialism-opening-words-from-the-event/.

Tinnell, John. 2014. "Computing en Plein Air: Augmented Reality and Impressionist Aesthetics." *Convergence: The Journal of Research into New Media Technologies* 20 (1): 69-84. http://dx.doi.org/10.1177/1354856513514338.

Thrift, Nigel. 2008. *Non-Representational Theory: Space, Politics, Affect.* New York: Routledge.

Totz, Sigrid. 2009. "Greenpeace Protest at NATO Summit: "Angie You Can." *Greenpeace* (blog), April 4. http://www.greenpeace.de/presse/presseerkl%C3%A4rungen/green peace-protest-auf-nato-gipfel-angie-you-can.

Trimbur, John. 2000. "Composition and the Circulation of Writing." *College Composition and Communication* 52 (2): 188–219. http://dx.doi.org/10.2307/358493.

Tumulty, Karen. 2007. "Obama's Viral Marketing Campaign." *Time,* July 5. http://content. time.com/time/magazine/article/0,9171,1640402,00.html.

Ulmer, Gregory L. 1997. "I Untied the Camera of Tastes (Who Am I?): The Riddle of Chool (A Reply and Alternative to A. Sahay)." *New Literary History* 28 (3): 569–94. http://dx.doi.org/10.1353/nlh.1997.0044.

Ulmer, Gregory L. 2003. *Internet Invention: From Literacy to Electracy.* New York: Longman.

Urban, Greg. 2001. *Metaculture: How Culture Moves through the World.* Minneapolis: University of Minnesota Press.

Urban, Jason. 2009. "Merkel!" *Printeresting* (blog), May 8. http://www.printeresting.org/2009/05/08/merkel/.

Vallen, Mark. 2007. "Obey Plagiarist Shepard Fairey." *Art for Change* (blog), December. http://www.art-for-a-change.com/Obey/index.htm.

Vanderleun. 2008. "Obamaganda: Change and Obey. Your Choice?" *American Digest: Dispatches from the New America,* March 12. http://americandigest.org/mt-archives/blather_spew /obama_change_an.php.

Vanhorn, K. B. 2008. "Bottle Caps for Barack." *A Patchwork World* (blog), October 3. http://apatchworkworld.blogspot.com/2008/10/bottle-caps-for-barack.html.

Veiledsongbird. 2008. Comment on Jeff Beer's "Shepard Fairey: Obey Obama." *Creativity,* January 30. http://adage.com/article/behind-the-work/shepard-fairey-obey-obama /124743.

Virilio, Paul. 1993. "The Third Interval: A Critical Transition." In *Re-thinking Technologies,* edited by Verana Andermatt Conley, 3–12. Minneapolis: University of Minnesota Press.

Vivian, Bradford. 2007. "In the Regard of the Image." *JAC* 27:471–504.

Ware, Colin. 2000. *Information Visualization: Perception for Design.* San Francisco: Morgan Kaufman.

Warner, Michael. 2002. *Publics and Counterpublics.* New York: Zone Books.

Wert, Hal Elliott. 2009. *Hope: a Collection of Obama Posters and Prints.* Minneapolis: Zenith.

White, Richard. 2010. "What Is Spatial History?" Stanford University. Spatial History Project. http://web.stanford.edu/group/spatialhistory/cgi-bin/site/pub.php?id=29.

Wilson, Jess. 2008. "SarkObama." *Greenpeace International* (blog), December 3. http://www.greenpeace.org/international/en/news/Blogs/climate/sarkobama/blog/8915/.

Wong, Brad. 2008 "Tagger Defaces Obama Portrait." *Seattle 911—A Police and Crime Blog*, November 12. http://blog.seattlepi.com/seattle911/2008/11/12/tagger-defaces-obama-portrait/.

Yates, Joanne, Wanda J. Orlikowski, and Julie Rennecker. 1992. "Genres of Organizational Communication: A Structure of Studying Communication and Media." *Academy of Management Review* 17 (2): 299–326.

Yates, Joanne, Wanda J. Orlikowski, and Julie Rennecker. 1997. "Collaborative Genres for Collaboration: Genre Systems in Digital Media." In *Proceedings of the 30th Hawaii International Conference on System Science*, 50–59. Hawaii: IEEE Press. http://dx.doi.org/10.1109/HICSS.1997.665484.

Zonker, Brett. 2008. "Obama's 'Hope' Portrait Headed to Smithsonian." *Huffington Post*, January 7. http://www.huffingtonpost.com/2009/01/07/obamas-hope-portrait-head_n_156046.html.

ABOUT THE AUTHOR

Laurie E. Gries is assistant professor in the Department of English at the University of Florida, where she teaches courses in writing, rhetoric, theory, and new media. Her scholarship works to forge connections between rhetoric, new materialism, and actor-network theory. She has published in journals such as *Computers and Composition, JAC, Composition Studies,* and *Rhetoric Review.*

INDEX

Page numbers in italics indicate illustrations. See also illustrations list on page ix.